The physical landscape of Burning Man is a fascination — but of greater interest to culture watchers is the social landscape that forms there each year. What does this gathering mean to our modern times? Steven T. Jones is both a fearless explorer and the definitive guide in this astonishing terrain.

— Ethan Watters,
author of *Urban Tribes: A Generation Redefines Friendship, Family, and Commitment*

From hardcore charity to counterculture politics, from indie circus acts to professional electronic dance music, from sweet community to family backbiting, from massive fire art to tiny gestures of kindness, Steve Jones surveys and captures from an insiders perspective — without oversimplifying or trying to jam it all into an inappropriate pigeonhole — the bizarre wondrous effects as the world's strangest art party morphed in the past decade to a rambling, multifaceted social movement whose effects on our culture are profound and growing.

— Brian Doherty,
author of *This is Burning Man: The Rise of a New American Underground*

A razor-sharp, adoringly told insider's account of the feral inventions, grand intentions and even grander egos that make up the world's wildest neo-pagan desert bacchanal. *Tribes* is packed with journalistic zeal, inimitable characters and the spirit of radical adventure. And fire. Lots and lots of fire.

— Mark Morford, columnist, *San Francisco Chronicle,*
author of *The Daring Spectacle: Adventures in Deviant Journalism*

I'm not a burner; never been to the event, will probably never go. But I was fascinated by the way Steven T. Jones explains how Burning Man is relevant — perhaps critical — to the larger progressive, artistic and alternative culture in America. *The Tribes of Burning Man* is an in-depth look at how one countercultural event is changing American society.

— Tim Redmond, executive editor of *The San Francisco Bay Guardian* and author
of *Not in Our Backyard: The People and Events that Shaped America's Modern Environmental Movement*

As Burning Man's culture vulture, Steven T. Jones has had his dusty and playafied fingers on the pulse of nearly every Black Rock City zeitgeist moment from the past few years. With his "insider" Burner perspective, coupled with a sharp journalistic eye, Jones delves deep into the unique temporal society that rises up out of nowhere every year in the middle of the hot Nevada desert.

— Adrian Roberts,
editor of *Burning Man Live: 13 Years of Piss Clear, Black Rock City's Alternative Newspaper*

Burning Man is a remarkable artistic, social and political achievement cultivating life within and inciting the world beyond "the trash fence". This is the story illuminated by Steven "Scribe" Jones in this page-turner on the "tribes" of Black Rock City, the greatest (temporary) city in the world. Like an embedded freak reporting from the front lines of experience, offering candid insights, his own, and that of the multitude of visionaries, dissidents and flaming aesthetes he's met, Jones negotiates with considerable finesse controversies, campaigns and collaborations that have come to define Burning Man. Navigating life on and off "the playa", and offering deep insights on the art, the politics and the cultural movement of Burning Man, this book is mandatory reading for Burners, and should be of great interest to many others besides.

— Graham St John,
author of *Technomad: Global Raving Countercultures*

The Tribes of Burning Man
How an Experimental City in the Desert is Shaping the New American Counterculture

First Edition

Library of Congress Cataloging-in-Publication Data:
Jones, Steven T.
The Tribes of Burning Man: How an Experimental City in the Desert is Shaping the New American Counterculture / Steven T. Jones
Includes index (Pbk.)
ISBN-13: 978-1-888729-29-0
1. History—Modern, Burning Man. 2. Counterculture—Art, Society. I. Title
Library of Congress Catalog Card Number: 2010934696
Printed in the United States of America.
10 9 8 7 6 5 4 3 2 1

Cover design, page layout and illustrations by Scott Borchardt

Cover photo information: "Garage Mahal Artcar" by Tami Rowan, "Michael Emery's Who Are You Now?" by Dave Le (aka Splat), "Flaming Lotus Girls' Soma" by MVGals.net, "Opulent Temple" by MVGals.net, "How Weird Street Faire" by Brad Olsen, "Burning Man" by Dave Le, "Burners Without Borders in Pearlington, Mississippi" by KK Pandya.

THE

TRIBES

OF

BURNING MAN

How an Experimental City
in the Desert is Shaping
the New American
Counterculture

by Steven T. Jones

aka Scribe

Consortium of Collective Consciousness

www.cccpublishing.com   www.steventjones.com

Table of Contents

In the wake of President Bush's reelection, Burning Man's artists stage a rebellion against the event's leadership, sparking a grand existential debate over its direction as I help create the Opulent Temple sound camp, launch a series of newspaper articles on Burning Man, and become embedded with the Flaming Lotus Girls as they create their masterpiece: Angel of the Apocalypse.

The "Borg2" artist rebellion is a colorful and amusing flop, but Burning Man's renaissance begins anyway, triggered by serendipitous circumstances. As the big sound camps evolve and the party hits its prime, Hurricane Katrina gives burners a new mission, summoning them to the Gulf Coast with a sendoff by NYC's Reverend Billy and the Church of Stop Shopping. And in San Francisco, Burning Man and its artists make a triumphant homecoming, finally embraced by the city of its birth.

Burners Without Borders, launched by a disaster, becomes a vehicle for good works around the world, standing alongside the Black Rock Arts Foundation's success finding new homes for Burning Man artworks and initiatives. Opulent Temple brings the world's best DJs to the playa, blowing their minds and putting Black Rock City on the musical map. Green Man is launched and burners run for public office in the default world. But the event is revisited by ghosts from its past, including a lawsuit-wielding founder and a rebel-turned-arsonist who torches the Man early.

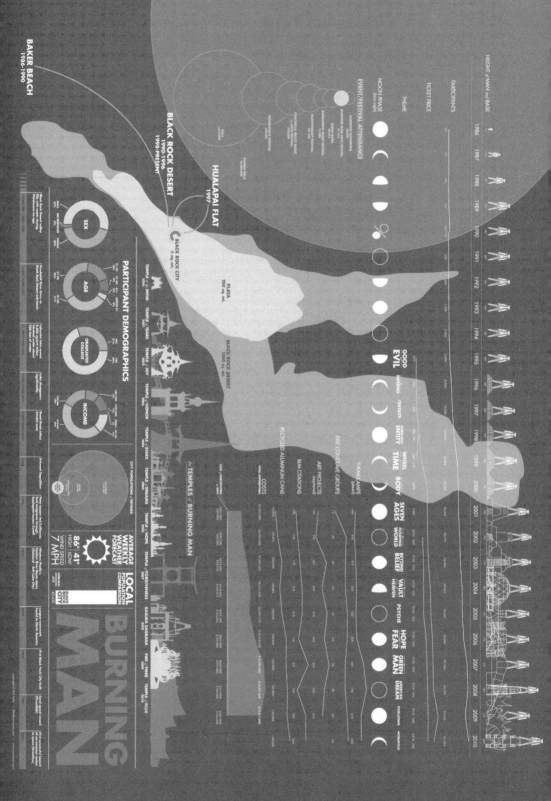

Illustration by Flint Hahn

Prologue: Setting Our Intention

We sat in a circle in Infinite Kaos, an art and party warehouse in San Francisco's gritty Tenderloin district, a group of a couple dozen mostly 30-something strangers who would come to feel like family. It was the summer of 2004 and we were planning to build the Opulent Temple, a sound-based theme camp at Burning Man. But first, we needed to get to know each other and make a plan.

Syd Gris — who was both an aspiring child psychologist and San Francisco DJ and party promoter — led the meeting, asking us all to go around the room, introduce ourselves and maybe say how we came to be here, state an intention for this year's Burning Man, and present our playa name if we had one. We were just waiting for a few more people to arrive, he said, we'll start in a few minutes.

My intention? My playa name? Hell, I barely knew what a theme camp was, except to know that they seemed to be the basic social building blocks of Black Rock City, the place where Burning Man is staged every August. And this time, in my newly adopted city of San Francisco — the city where Burning Man was born in 1986 — I knew that I wanted to be in a theme camp. I wanted to be a part of a tribe.

During my only previous trip to Burning Man in 2001, my then-girlfriend Jennesa and I just tent-camped by ourselves, really not sure what we were getting ourselves into. We knew it was some big crazy party in Nevada's Black Rock Desert, way off in the middle of nowhere. And as a journalist for big city alternative newsweeklies in California, I understood that it was an art festival popular with the counterculture, one that several people told me had changed their lives.

Some of our friends in Sacramento worked for months in one of their backyards building a three-story scaffolding and wood structure they called the Castle of the Red Queen, my first exposure to a theme camp, something that provides a basic infrastructure for its members and artsy, interactive components for everyone else.

But Jennesa and I decided to attend more or less on a whim, spending a couple hundred bucks each on tickets, and skimming the Burning Man Survival Guide to learn the basics: this was a participatory community ("no spectators") with no commerce (a "gift economy") that we build from scratch ("radical self-reliance"), animate while it exists ("radical self-expression"), and break down at the end ("leave no trace"), whatever that all really meant.

So we gathered up some camping gear, costumes, drugs, food and water, and other essentials — forgetting many items that I would later consider essential, such as bikes and headlamps — loaded up her car, and headed toward Reno on a Wednesday night. Two hours past the last sign of city life, we saw Black Rock City shining off in the distance, across a long stretch of flatness they call "the playa."

As we drove slowly along the bumpy surface, past a series of signs with quotes and phrases that touched on that year's "The Seven Ages of Man" art theme, we were awestruck by the alien landscape that we'd entered, a feeling that grew as we pulled up to the exotically beautiful strangers at the Greeter's Station who told us "Welcome home," made us roll around in the dust, hugged us deeply, and answered our question about where to find the walk-in camping area on the edge of this massive, temporal frontier town.

This exotically alluring introduction to Burning Man replayed in my head as I watched my new Opulent Temple campmates mill around this weird warehouse, talking in small groups or seated alone, perhaps also pondering their intentions. I looked around the room and saw rigging hanging from the ceiling, pads set up to one side for yoga or something, several pairs of stilts leaning in a corner, and a lean guy with wild hair who seemed like he lived here cooking in a makeshift kitchen. But my mind again drifted back to the playa.

Jennesa and I selected a camping spot far from anyone, quickly set up our tent and bed, then left on foot to explore and visit the Castle of the Red Queen, using the address we'd written down — on 2 o'clock, between The Child and The Lover — and the city map that the greeters had bestowed on us.

As we walked, sober and wide-eyed as children, a pair of colorful cartoon bunnies hopped along the desert floor, looking over at us occasionally and munching on a bright orange carrot, some kind of light trick that I just couldn't get my head around at the time, filling me with a sort of giddy, surreal wonderment that stayed with me all week.

The surroundings began to get more densely populated when we saw a long zip-line hurling people down from a tower into a massive pad with a loud thunk, which a smiling guy in a top hat and waist-coat encouraged us to try, overcoming our initial reluctance and giving us our first of many thrills. And when we finally arrived at the Castle of the Red Queen, my lovely Jennesa was strapped to a whipping pole as the price for our admittance and given a bare-assed paddling by her good friend Vaughn Solo, before we were sent in to navigate the castle's inner maze.

What was this place and why had it taken me so long to come? Infinite Kaos's testimonial circle — the people who would be my Castle, my tribe, Opulent Temple — began and people started offering their intentions, which seemed genuine and heartfelt, cutting through any lingering cynicism I might have felt about something that initially sounded a little silly and New Agey.

They were coming to find their creativity, to let go of their egos, to dance and enjoy life; they had names like Dash, Sierra, Blue, and Captain Bastard; and it was almost my turn. I tried to listen and be present, to learn what was driving this warm group of people, but I had a hard time focusing, my mind replaying memories as it searched for my intention, and my new identity.

My memories turned darker as I recalled getting up in the middle of the night to try to keep the strong winds from flattening our tent and flimsy shade structure; moments of frustration with the dust that permeated everything; the long, silent walks back to our remote, lonely campsite after a wild night; the emotional intensity that eventually proved too much for our still unstable relationship, breaking us up by the end. I hadn't yet learned to embrace the chaos.

And then my return to the real world, to a job I liked but a boss that I didn't, followed a week later by 9/11 and those planes hitting the Pentagon and World Trade Center, changing everything. Suddenly, my role as a rabble-rousing progressive journalist became more pressing and intense and the world itself became scary and surreal, President George W. Bush elevated from harmless idiot to dangerous holy warrior.

Then, suddenly back in the present, everyone was looking at me, patiently waiting for my introduction and intention, and I began to speak. I told them that I was Steven T. Jones, the city editor for the San Francisco Bay Guardian, and that this would be my second Burning Man but the first with a theme camp.

I'm excited to be a part of creating Opulent Temple and getting to know all of you, and to take a little break from trying to save the world from our country's imperialist leaders. God, that's been so exhausting and disheartening, and can you believe Bush might actually get reelected?

But anyway, my intention isn't just to escape that world and my role as a writer, but to merge it with all the beautiful purposefulness and creativity that I've seen in San Francisco over the last year. I want to use that energy and let it inform my writing, to be a vessel for conveying what we're trying to do here. So, for a playa name, well, I guess you can call me Scribe.

Introduction: Welcome Home

The essential history goes like this: After a few years of this weird little summer solstice beach party called Burning Man, the San Francisco police cracked down, so its stagers and supporters moved the event out to the Black Rock Desert in rural Nevada, a desiccated ancient lakebed now affectionately known as The Playa. And there, it grew and grew, every year, eventually morphing from scattershot frontier filled with freedom-loving freaks into a dynamic city of about 50,000 colorful souls — Black Rock City — that burns brightly for a week in late August and then disappears into dust after Labor Day.

Well, it doesn't really disappear — it sort of decamps. The theme camps and art collectives that make Black Rock City so dynamic — making its art, creating its soundtrack, offering its amenities, building its culture — have come to transcend the event and form year-round bonds back in their communities. After a quarter-century of annual events, these tribes have become the essence of Burning Man, perhaps more significant than the San Francisco-based company that stages the event, Black Rock City LLC, dubbed The Borg by some.

The Man for which the event is named, the effigy that burns as the week reaches its climax, has no meaning, deliberately so, even as it has spawned a vast network of disparate, deliberate tribes, imbuing the central void with layers of meaning and purpose and helping to define the largest American counterculture of the new century — and maybe the most enduring one in history.

I have been fortunate to enjoy a unique perspective on Burning Man just as it was entering its renaissance — which I and many others consider to be the years 2005-2010 — when the frontier town finally became a real city, with a vibrant, well-developed urban culture and a basic ethos that is embraced by a greater percentage of Black Rock City's population than anywhere on earth. As that unfolded, I was in regular communication with everyone from event founder Larry Harvey, who was trying to nudge Burning Man toward greater sociopolitical relevance and impact, to countervailing forces like showman Chicken John and mad creator Jim Mason, the pair who led an artists' rebellion in late 2004 that triggered my deep journalistic engagement with the event. I was taken into the bosom of the Flaming Lotus Girls to learn the fire arts and I helped build the party camps that hosted world-class DJs and seas of undulating dancers.

I remember when I realized that Burning Man was having a profound effect on American culture, particularly in the countercultural realm that it draws from and feeds, those who feel they can create a better society than the one they've inherited. It was a moment that came in two parts, months apart from each other starting after the event in 2005, in telephone conversations from my office at the San Francisco Bay Guardian.

"I've been to 20 Burning Mans and I've never seen a better one," Larry Harvey told me after the event in 2005, during a conversation that later proved to be the first half of my revelation. But it wasn't just the mind-blowing art, the great weather that year, the mushrooming crowd, the joyous party, or any of Burning Man's physical features. "The group that came this year was a bit more noble in their intentions than any I've ever seen in a city this size," Larry explained. "They've really absorbed the idea of participation."

Participation, that central tenet of the burner ethos: No Spectators. This city is created almost entirely by those who buy tickets and spend hundreds of dollars each for the privilege of building a city from scratch, so it is a reflection of their effort and intention. And the intentions of many who attended Burning Man 2005 were channeled in an unforeseeable and strangely fortuitous way when Hurricane Katrina slammed into Mississippi and Louisiana on the first day of the event.

This natural disaster, compounded by the inept and uncaring response of President Bush and the federal government, resonated with the citizens of Black Rock City, a place filled with people who had turned themselves into experts in creative construction and destruction. After all, as Larry told me, the very skills, tools, and motivation needed to stage Burning Man each year were exactly what the Gulf Coast needed.

So when a crew of committed, resourceful, and capable burners established an encampment down there, hundreds of burners followed, pitching in their time, sweat, and money to a nine-month project that became known as Burners Without Borders. "If that isn't applying our ethos, I don't know what is," Larry told me then. "The very skills needed to survive at Burning Man are the skills needed to respond to a disaster."

It was indeed an impressive and empowering project, as I saw firsthand during a reporting trip down there, the details of which are in this book. But what was even more notable is what the experience spawned within the larger Burning Man experiment, changing it into something new and more purposeful. After Hurricane Katrina, BWB organized cleanup and rebuilding projects following massive earthquakes in Peru in 2008 and Haiti in 2010, each time doing countless hours of free work over many months for people in desperate need. But even those high-profile and headline-grabbing disaster response efforts were only a small part of what

BWB was becoming, and BWB was only a small part of what Burning Man was becoming.

"What we found in the wreckage of Katrina was anyone can make an enormous difference if they just choose to. Burning Man is such a key part of that experience," said Tom Price, a BWB founder who called me in early 2006 to say, "Dude, we're still here. It's happening just like you wrote. We're doing it," luring me to the Gulf Coast to see what Larry had explained to me a few months earlier, which I wrote about in a series-capping article entitled, "Epilogue as Prologue." It was those two conversations that awakened me to the larger potential of this community that I'd been enjoying and chronicling.

"Going to Burning Man and learning how to interact with people the way that we do there is an incredible education in how to be effective in the world. Because you get to create your entire world. Everything you experience is created by you and the people around you," Tom told me later.

The value and potential of that can-do spirit that Burning Man cultivates was echoed in San Francisco that same fall, when it manifested in the art of Black Rock City finally returning home to the city where the event was born, thanks to another new burner offshoot known as the nonprofit Black Rock Arts Foundation.

"It felt like there was a lot of serendipity at that point in time, and for BRAF it was a launching venture," Leslie Pritchett, BRAF's first executive director, said of the rapid series of events that saw three high-profile burner sculptures — David Best's Temple at Hayes Green, Michael Christian's Flock, and Passage by Karen Cusolito and Dan Das Mann — placed in separate showcase spots around San Francisco within a six-month period.

By doing temporary art placements using fundraising and volunteer labor from within the Burning Man world, BRAF was able to break through the slow and bureaucratic process of placing public art in San Francisco, convincing city officials that they were easily able to tap into something real cool, in the process elevating the stature of what some had started calling the "Burning Man School of Art."

"The biggest issue was cost, but we were able to handle it because of the Burning Man networks. A lot of people came together to make this happen," Leslie later told me. "It demonstrated to me and a lot of people that art projects can bring a lot of energy to a city."

That energy could even be applied to the emerging field of clean energy. Tom went on to become Burning Man's first environmental director, then founding a burner-staffed organization called Black Rock Solar that figured out how to build renewable energy projects for public agencies and nonprofits at little or no cost. Meanwhile, BWB co-founder Carmen Mauk continued to guide that group and expand its reach into a wide variety of micro-projects around the world, from an anti-poverty project in Kenya to a sustainable commerce network in New York City to artist-created fire circles on the Ocean Beach in San Francisco.

"This is what Tom Price and I were talking about in the very beginning, when we were standing on a mountain of rubble after Katrina, that if we do this right and seed this idea right and we seed this creativity, then it's possible to make a difference and solve problems on *this side of the trash fence*," Carmen told me, using a phrase referring to outside the borders of Black Rock City that has become increasingly common among burners, a way to start talking about the impacts of the event on the rest of the world. "It's going to start to change the event and it's going to start to change this community in ways that are totally unexpected."

After more than a quarter-century of Burning Man events, more than 300,000 people from around the world have attended and taken the experience back into their communities. People have developed a larger view of themselves and what is possible, forming into tribes to pursue huge art projects, pool their resources and expand their social circles, or to create entirely new lifestyles and ways of relating to each other and the world. From San Francisco to New York City to Denver to Oakland to New Orleans to Los Angeles to Austin, Texas — places you'll visit in this book — Burning Man is helping to shape the new American counterculture in interesting and promising ways.

Black Rock City and its citizens have evolved over the years, growing from a strange and indefinable gathering into something that is now best understood as a city, one of the world's great cities during the week it exists, and as a culture that continues year-round in other great cities around the world, affecting them in ways large and small. And it is a story that is still continuing to unfold.

Foreword: Defining My Terms

Before I tell the story, let me define a couple of key terms and their relevance to this book, particularly my use of "tribe" and "counterculture," both imprecise words that largely depend on their context. But they also seem like the best words to describe what I think is important about Burning Man post-2004.

A definite tribal aesthetic crept its way into the fashions and costumes of Burning Man in the early 2000s, with the "feather and leather" look popularized by camps such as El Circo and designers like the late Tiffa Nova becoming a popular burner look by 2006. And there's certainly something inherently tribal about this particular pow-wow, where groups from across the land come to dance around big fires.

But neither meaning was what I had in mind when I chose the title for this book. I meant to convey the most basic definition of a tribe, that of a division of society whose members share certain customs, beliefs, and leadership, even if that leadership is disbursed among members in a non-hierarchical fashion.

Rather than the ethnic tribes of Native Americans or Afghanis, I was thinking more about the extended social groups from big cities across the country that developed a family-like cohesiveness, as writer Ethan Watters discussed in his acclaimed 2003 book, *Urban Tribes: A generation redefines friendship, family, and commitment.* (the paperback version even had a new and more intriguing subhead: *Are friends the new family?*)

In fact, Watters is also a San Franciscan who attends Burning Man, a fact that greatly informs his work and his coining of the term "Urban Tribe." The year-round planning and preparation for Burning Man — and the deep interpersonal connections that are forged or strengthened on the playa — was some of the strongest glue that bound his tribe and others together.

"'Whatever happened to getting married?' I asked a carful of friends. This was half a dozen years ago while we were on our way to Burning Man. The U-Haul trailer we were pulling carried two dozen eight-foot lengths of two-by-fours, thirty bedsheets, a couple hundred yards of rope, thirty cases of beer, and all the other makings of our homegrown art project," was how Watters began his first chapter.

He then explored the social dynamics of these tribes, which had become like surrogate families for many big city denizens, and profiled and discussed a wide variety of tribes from big cities across the U.S. It was a fairly new phenomenon that was related to the fact that many young urban residents were delaying marriage until their 30s and 40s. Watters saw important social significance in how these tribes formed and behaved.

"That the meaning and momentum of an urban tribe might exist outside the combined strength of the individual friendships — that the tribe might have a life of its own — was one distinction these groups had from groups of friends one might have at other points in life," Watters wrote.

Urban tribes can exist in many forms, but as Burning Man endured and became an annual pilgrimage for a growing number of people — particularly in the Bay Area, its most fertile breeding ground — I realized that the event had spawned a fascinating and interconnected network of these urban tribes, many of which had a life and longevity that was beyond the control of any of the individual members who cycled through them over the years. And Burning Man was a touchstone for these groups, in cities through the world.

"You can go all over the country and meet people connected to the Burning Man culture, and you feel a real and instant kinship with them," Watters told me in 2010 as we discussed the intersection of his book and mine. Since he explored the question in 2003, Burning Man had both fed and been fed by the social dynamics that Watters discovered.

Could Burning Man really have achieved the longevity and continuing dynamism that it did if there weren't these urban tribes to create it anew every year? And could these urban tribes have continued for so long without an event like Burning Man and its projects to rally around? The energy of the two sides certainly kept the coin spinning.

And what began to interest me even more was this question: Is Black Rock City best understood as a well-developed urban culture, a city comprised of myriad urban tribes from around the world that pull together for one week out of the year, but continue to shape their surroundings year-round?

"It is a book-worthy question," Watters told me, giving me a few things to think about as I explored the question, from the role the playa's challenging environment plays in shaping tribes to the importance of women in triggering this new generation's "ambient energy" to the fact that "these groups can produce as much human capital as you put into them."

These tribes became incredibly important in the lives of many of their members, altering their conception of themselves and the world in which they lived. The culture that Burning Man helped create began to have a real and tangible impact on San Francisco and other cities. These tribes, and their values and rituals, were altering the culture in their cities.

Eric Meyers, a longtime burner who is one of the editors who generously donated his time to improving this book, took issue with my "counterculture" label, arguing that it was the American culture itself that Burning Man was helping to shape, not simply those who actively resist the larger culture.

"I also feel that BRC is the farthest thing from counterculture out there — cuz it's not anti-anything. It's more of a parallel culture or a benign shadow culture or an alternative culture," he wrote to me, a point that you'll hear event founder Larry Harvey echo later in this book.

And it was a good point, but one that I don't quite agree with, mostly because I think people are drawn to Burning Man precisely because of its countercultural attributes, and they are what have the most powerful and transformative impact on those who attend. Black Rock City stands apart from the larger world — indeed, that's what makes it so special to people and so enduring.

Within a capitalist world, our personas and social standing are often derived from the job we hold or career we have chosen (which itself is often limited by our class and family connections), our environments are usually regulated by corporate or government entities, and many of our daily social interactions are actually economic transactions. We aren't exactly who we really are, so most burners refer to this as the Default World.

The central tenets of Burning Man stand starkly opposed to such paradigms — indeed, deliberately challenging them. Participants are encouraged to build the city of their dreams with almost no regulations or limitations, most economic transactions are prohibited in favor of a gift economy, and the encouragement of "radical self-expression" allows participants to pick any persona they choose (right down to picking a new "playa name" if they'd like), while the twin ethos of self-reliance and participation create the expectation of a far more engaged citizenry than the real world asks of us.

In 2004, writers Ken Goffman (aka R.U. Sirius) and Dan Joy weighed in on defining the term with their book *Counterculture Through the Ages: From Abraham to Acid House*, seeing the same distinction that I'm trying to make: that there are aspects to countercultures that define them by more than just distance from the dominant culture.

As they write, "…we reject the definition of counterculture as simply any lifestyle that differs from the prevailing culture. Clearly, the definition of counterculture is up for grabs, but we contend that, whatever their differences, there is a singular mutual intention motivating nearly all who defined themselves in countercultural terms up until the last few years. They were all anti-authoritarian or nonauthoritarian. Our defining vision asserts that the essence of counterculture as a perennial historical phenomenon is characterized by the affirmation of the individual's power to create his own life rather than accepting the dictates of surrounding social authorities and conventions, be they mainstream or subcultural. We further assert that freedom of communication is an essential characteristic of counterculture, since affirmative contact holds the key to liberating each individual's creative power."

That last notion is at the very core of Burning Man. When someone decides to make fire art with the Flaming Lotus Girls or build a dance camp with Opulent Temple or build the outlines of Black Rock City with the Department of Public Works or create a camp and weird art project from scratch with a bunch of their friends, they choose what kind of person they want to be in this strange new world. They choose how to express whatever creative energy they feel welling up inside of them.

Goffman and Joy overtly place Burning Man on their list of modern countercultures: "Punks, avant-garde artists, the hip-hop underground, anti-globalization activists and Black Bloc anarchists, Wired-reading technoculturalists and hacks, club culture trendoids, conscious rappers, educated psychedelicists, Burning Man, modern primitives with steel implants and piercings dangling from every organ, denizens of the sexual underground, pagans, postmodern academics, funkateer, New Agers, riot grrls, slackers, ravers, natty dreadsters, Zen Buddhists, Gnostics, lonely iconoclasts, Deadheads, poetry slammers, Goths, tree huggers, libertines, and libertarians — all are sometimes defined (and self-defined) as countercultural."

Yet it doesn't feel quite right to place Burning Man on a list that is actually comprised of many of Black Rock City's component groups of citizens. Indeed, many of the thousands of theme camps at the event overtly define themselves with many of the labels above, from the dance camp ravers to Death Guild denizens to the polyamorous players of Space Virgins.

In a society that generally restricts the activities and reach of countercultures, Burning Man courts and magnifies smaller subcultures, giving them a home and base of operations. Perhaps that's why Burning Man has endured for so much longer than most countercultures, because it isn't a counterculture as much as a space that reflects and helps shape a wide variety of distinct subcultures, ultimately giving these disparate groups a bit of shared culture, uniting them into a new American counterculture.

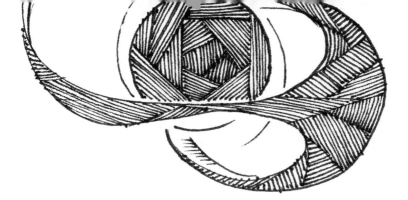

Part I — Rebirth (2004-05)

Monday, August 29, 2004

A light breeze rustles our tent, beckoning me from sleep. There's that waking moment when you're sometimes not sure where you are, particularly after a night of partying, when the morning haze is thickest. But between the floating feel of the air mattress that Rosie and I are warmly nestled into and the powdery smell of alkaline dust in the air, I know exactly where I am. I'm at Burning Man, a thought that makes me giddy with anticipation about the day to come.

"Sweetie," I coo to my still slumbering girlfriend. "Wanna get up?"

She grumbles at me to go back to sleep, turning her back to me and pulling me in to spoon up behind her. That's how we sleep, cuddled up, flipping the spoon back and forth throughout the night. Rosie feels warm and good, but I'm buzzing, unable to sleep, like a kid on Christmas morning.

Mmm, her body feels sumptuous, arousing me, and I think about the hot sex that we had yesterday afternoon, our first day at Burning Man 2004, madly making love and then giggling intimately, freshly but deeply in love, as a sound system in a neighboring camp blasted an extended version of the Peaches song "Fuck the Pain Away."

I kiss her neck and begin to caress her thighs, pressing myself against her, but she clearly isn't ready to be awake yet, so I whisper into her ear, "I'm getting up." Rosie sags to the floor as I climb out of our bed and I make a mental note to pump the air mattress up later.

Fishing through my bag for the sarong, I suddenly have to take a piss, so I just grab my dusty Utili-kilt off the floor and hurry out of the tent, naked. Our porch — with Astro-turf for a floor, a large steel carport for a roof, and sun- and wind-shielding walls made of canvas dropcloths decorated with acrylic paint — is cluttered from last night. It's a good thing the wind never picked up or the cans, cigarette and clove packs, ash tins, and other detritus would have been scattered all over the playa, shamefully transformed into MOOP, or Matter Out Of Place, the burner colloquial term for litter.

I toss my kilt onto a chair, creating a small dust cloud, briefly consider going all the way to the Porta-Potties, and opt for a patch of open playa about 15 feet from the tent. After a few steps, I crunch into a perfect little patch of playa, cracked and corn-flaked, a lunar-landscape that was probably untouched by humans since the last Burning Man. Crunch, crunch, a few more steps, and I'm peeing, relieved, utterly content.

Time to make some art. I draw a big circle with my urine, give him a head, try make an eye with a quick flip of my wrist, and then do a zig-zag down his back, and fill in the body until I'm empty. There, a dinosaur. A Playasaurus Rex. Rowrrrrrrr!

Scanning the landscape, I see that lots of people have arrived overnight, filling in the city. The event officially began at midnight and we saw and heard them streaming in all night, yipping and hollering and laughing, honking to their camps as they arrive, both sides greeting the other warmly, the arrivals saying how happy they are to be here and their campmates telling them, "Welcome home."

It's great to have an early arrival pass for setting up our big sound camp, Opulent Temple of Venus. We only had about 20 passes and they were claimed by the informally named OT A-team, the core group that had done most of the work planning the camp, throwing the fundraisers, and loading all our shit into the huge rental truck that we partially unloaded yesterday. The other 60 or so people in our camp would be rolling in all week.

I breathe in the thick, warm air, filling my lungs as far as they'll go, exhaling, enjoying the feel of sun and a gentle breeze on my exposed body. A beautiful young woman, tan and nude, emerges from a tent in the next camp, maybe 100 feet away, shakes her long braided hair, stretches her arms to the sky, sees me looking at her, and gives me a sly smile and little flutter-finger wave.

And for that moment, we connect, two naked strangers, neighbors in a weird and wonderful city in the process of being born. She disappears behind a dome, I glance at my fading Playasaurus, smiling to myself as I head over to finally put my kilt on and get this day underway.

My large pockets are still filled from yesterday: work gloves, pocketknife, several zip-ties, goggles. I grab my green plastic bottle, empty the last of a

2.5-gallon water jug into it, and head back to the tent to get another one. Rosie seems to be stirring a little so I cuddle up next to her.

"It's a beautiful day out there," I tell her, almost singing it.

She smiles and pulls out her earplugs. "Okay, I'm up," she says, feigning grumpiness but still smiling.

"Great. I'll make us breakfast. Oatmeal?" I offer.

She nods, we kiss, I grab one of 15 rectangular water containers stacked in the corner of our six-person nylon tent and head out to make breakfast. In the tent next ours along the very back of the camp's property line, Syd and Kelly seemed to be sleeping still.

There also doesn't seem to be any activity around "The Lawn," the shaded common area for Dash, Blue, and Geeno, who each had their own tents on the edge of the green turf. And in front of me are scattered dome tents belonging to people that I'm not sure if I know, several that went up overnight. I really only know about half the people I've met, and of those, I only know about half of their names.

As I boil water on our camp stove and putter around the porch, signs of life begin to emerge. Rosie steps out of the tent wearing a shiny silver outfit that she bought a couple weeks ago at Piedmont Boutique on Haight Street, a ridiculously expensive store that caters to strippers and burners and where Rosie spent hundreds of dollars.

"Mimosas?" She offers brightly.

"Hmm," I ponder. "Is that a good idea? We have a big work day in front of us."

It's Rosie's first Burning Man and I feel a need to watch out for her. In 2001, I watched people go down hard from drinking and I know how important it is to drink a lot of water, limit the booze, and stay hydrated out here in this moisture-sucking environment.

"We're on vacation," she says with a smile and I really can't argue with that.

"Absolutely," I say. "I'll open the bottle."

"I'll get the cups and OJ."

After we finish our oatmeal, Rosie offers to do the dishes, but our plastic wash basin has some nasty water in it from last night, so I take it over the big evaporation pond next to the shower stalls that I helped build yesterday. The pond is simply a black plastic tarp, maybe 10 by 20 feet, with the edges wrapped around two-by-fours and stapled on.

I survey the camp. The kitchen next to the shower stalls seems mostly up, a walled carport with tables for food preparation and a sink setup for doing dishes. Mmm, camp dinners start tonight. Two more large carports create the nearby shade structure and chill area, filled with old carpet, couches, and cushions.

Next to that is a large, white geodesic chill dome, and behind that is the nascent dance area, the focus of today's work, and beyond that is the open playa, spreading across the horizon as far as I can see. I can't wait for tomorrow night when we turn on the sound, bringing the dance parties that we've been throwing as fundraisers in San Francisco to this exotic location.

What really sealed the deal for Rosie and me to join Opulent Temple was the party Syd threw early that summer out at Kelly's Mission Rock. Four rooms, two indoor and two out, just thumping infectious beats all night long on the edge of the San Francisco Bay, everyone looking scrumptious in their burner finery — shiny skimpy tops, short skirts topped by elaborate utility belts, shirts embroidered with tribal touches, fake fur shoulder shrugs, frills and feathers inserted here and there, stomper boots still with traces of playa dust — smiling, high, grooving.

And now, here we are, weeks of work about to give way to the greatest party on the planet. Walking back to my camp, I notice that Syd is up and puttering around his porch, so I give him a little smile-nod and go to drop off the wash basin with Rosie.

"Bacon?" offers a young woman walking through camp with a tray of piggy goodness.

"Yes, thanks," I say, taking a piece, giving her a warm hug, and letting her proceed to serve others.

I hand Rosie the tub, she freshens my mimosa, and I tell her that I'm going to go chat with Syd. "Oh, I'll come with you," she replies, "but first, sunscreen." And we slather ourselves with lotion from face to toe, doing each other's backs, filling our waters, completing our morning ritual before walking over to Syd's camp, hand in hand.

"Good morning," Syd says, with his understated gusto. "It's a beautiful day here in Black Rock City."

"Indeed it is, my friend," I say, suddenly filled with joy at the declaration. Rosie heads into the tent to chat with Kelly, and Syd and I discuss the work ahead of us today: place the DJ booth and stabilize the decks, set up the four shadow boxes and eight glowing columns that will form the edges of the dance area, finish the flaming archway and get our fire permit to operate it, decorate the chill areas with the bags full of fabric and frills, and help Temple of Venus raise their temple and tower.

"And then tonight," Syd says, "A-team prowls the playa."

~ Editor's Note: This day continues, in the next year, in the next Part ~

Bush Pushes as the Playa Pulls

It was a gloomy day in San Francisco, like the whole town was hung over. Most of us probably were. What else could you really do but drink as the Fall 2004 election returns rolled in? We woke up achingly aware that Americans had actually validated this naked emperor, George W. Bush, as our president, and rewarded him with a second term.

After washing the stink of several dour campaign parties off of me, I headed into work at the Bay Guardian. This was an independent, progressive newspaper that openly scorned Bush and we had fought hard before the election, pushing on the boundary between journalism and activism with our cover story "Ten things you can do to help defeat Bush and save the country."

We didn't feel bad for so aggressively singling out one politician, or even the de facto backing of a Democrat we didn't much like. Our assessments were backed by years of solid reporting on how Bush had plundered the country and made the world hate us. After giving the rich a huge tax break and placing capitalists in charge of regulating their industries, the Bush Administration used 9/11 as a pretext for extrajudicial killings and kidnappings, torture and other gross human rights violations, and two disastrous wars sold with calculated lies.

With a record like that, I didn't understand how he might actually be reelected, a possibility we labored mightily to prevent. But now, it was over.

I thought about "Ten things…," a project that I had conceived and executed with help from others on staff. It ran in early August, even before the traditional political season began, a clarion call to oust Bush on the grounds that he was a war criminal, a pawn for powerful oligarchs, and a proven liar and incompetent.

Yet personally, I was feeling a little guilty at the time as I prepared for my second trip to Burning Man, that annual festival of countercultural creativity and glee. There were good arguments being made all year that we ought to be putting the time, energy, and resources that we were using on this weeklong art party in the Black Rock Desert into defeating Bush.

The most poignant call came from John Perry Barlow, the former Grateful Dead lyricist and founder of the Electronic Frontier Foundation, who circulated an essay calling for people not to go to Burning Man: "If someone like Karl Rove had wanted to neutralize the most creative, intelligent, and passionate members of the opposition, he'd have a hard time coming up with a better tool than Burning Man. Exile them to the wilderness, give them a culture in which alpha status requires months of focus and resource-consumptive preparation, provide them with metric tons of psychotropic confusants, and then…ignore them. It's a pretty safe bet that they won't be out registering voters, or doing anything that might actually threaten electoral change, when they have an art car to build."

In the case of my camp, Opulent Temple, instead of an art car it was a huge steel DJ booth, along with several big fundraiser dance parties in San Francisco to generate the $20,000 we needed to rock the desert with a wall of sound. But the point was the same and it was a good one that also bothered our camp founder, DJ/promoter Syd Gris.

Syd and I bonded over progressive politics probably even more than we did the great parties that he threw in San Francisco. Just about everyone we knew hated Bush, but Syd was the only DJ I knew who so directly infused politics into his nightlife schtick, opening his gig-plugging e-mails with socialist rants and often doing consciousness-raising midnight rituals at his parties. It actually really bothers some of our fellow partiers and DJs, but I'm a radicalized political junkie, so I've always admired and connected with it.

"Bush was in office, the country was at war, things were fucked up and our community of smart, awesome people were putting their resources into Burning Man rather than social action," Syd told me later, recalling that pivotal, poignant year. He had also read Barlow's essay and addressed it directly in his missives at the time.

"That was sobering and it definitely got me thinking. And where I came through, in that little thing I wrote, is we do this because this one event feeds the human spirit in ways, well, I don't know any other way to be that. It fuels you up to get through the rest of the year and have a little hope in mankind. And that was certainly one of my first reactions to Burning Man is it renewed my faith in people."

It's the reaction that many people have to the event. We are awed by the seemingly limitless creativity and goodwill that Burning Man puts on display every August, which is such a marked contrast to the real world, particularly under the criminally overreaching Bush Administration. Yes, we should fight them, but we did fight them in great numbers during his march to the ill-fated Iraq War, and it didn't matter. So, for many people, it was tough to devote our lives to helping Democratic presidential nominee John Kerry report for duty.

We knew Barlow was presenting a false choice. If we could trade Burning Man for Bush's downfall, most of us would have done so willingly. But would that have happened if we'd gone to New York City to protest the Republican National Convention instead of spending that week on the playa? Doubtful.

Still, maybe that's why I pushed this cover story so hard. Was I trying to assuage my own guilt or maybe urging our readers to pick up my slack while I was partying on the playa? All I know is that I desperately wanted Bush gone and I was aghast it was even a close contest. All fall, the Guardian unloaded at his regime with both barrels — and I probably wrote more words in that quest than anyone.

And still Bush won. Sitting in my messy office, ignoring the periodically ringing telephone, looking over the detritus of a busy few months — desk piled with press releases and stories marked up with my edits, manila folders labeled "the case for impeachment" or "corporate crimes" filled with documents, long checked-off-to-do lists — the words rang in my head: and still Bush won. Never had an incumbent president presented such an easy target, never had so many millions of Americans mobilized so passionately to push for electoral change, and still Bush won. It was depressing, maddening, dispiriting, unbelievable.

But there was one thing I was thankful for: that I'd gone to Burning Man anyway. At least I had that, those beautiful memories and intimate connections with good, interesting, life-affirming people. Lost in a moment of blissful reverie, I studied the Opulent Temple photo montage that was the screen saver on my computer: Rosie and I in front of The Man, Syd spinning records in the DJ booth, people feeling their musical bliss, smiling faces, crazy costumes, inspired artworks, fire. Ah. Then I snapped back to the present reality. Bush. Us against the world. A rainy day. Of course it was raining, but I still needed to attend the late afternoon anti-war rally.

My arrival in San Francisco had been tightly intertwined with peace marches. I first saw the Guardian ad for a city editor on a packed Muni train en route to the massive march in January 2003, when about 100,000 people filled Market Street for miles. Two months later, during my second week on the job, Bush invaded Iraq and mine was one of 2,000 arrests on a massive day of protest. I fell instantly in love with my new city and its creative expressions of people power. But this was still Bush's country, even if we voted for Kerry and protested the war.

It was probably good that the anti-war movement wasn't giving up, but I felt only dread about covering the event. It was going to be a joyless march, a real antithesis to all the beauty and wonder that San Francisco and Burning Man had inspired in me and others. Things seemed bleak, dismal, hopeless — but even though I couldn't see it at the time, the conditions were right for a transformation.

Planting Seeds

The seeds of change were already planted in the playa in 2004, but they were just beginning to sprout, so it was easy to miss them.

The transformation of Black Rock City from a frontier into a city may have begun in 1997, when the civic infrastructure and rules were first instituted, but it took some time for that change and others to really affect the culture.

"Between 1999 and 2004 is when a lot of this stuff hit maturity, and then in 2004 it really took off," says Marian Goodell, an LLC board member since 1996, when she was dating Larry Harvey and he brought her onto the management team.

Another member of the six-person board, city manager Harley Dubois, said they created "enough structure so people could thrive and grow" and then sought to just protect Burning Man and let people develop it organically: "We saw something that was beautiful and we nurtured it and protected it and didn't let it get corrupted."

Marian was most enthused with the network of Burning Man's regional contacts and events that had been growing in cities around the world since 1998, a loose confederation that encouraged Black Rock City LLC to more overtly define the burner ethos, something they it later did by adopting the 10 Principles, an official statement of the community's values.

Whenever would-be burner leaders popped up in communities from Austin, Texas and Vancouver, British Columbia, Marian gave them burningman.com email aliases and advice on how to create networks and events. But the various communities differed in their organizational abilities and ethos, and when Marian and Larry had to keep fielding questions about Burning Man's values, Larry decided in 2004 to develop the 10 Principles while on vacation in Mexico.

"The 10 Principles were written to give a statement of values to the regionals," Marian recalls. "It was 100 percent for the regionals."

But the explanations of the 10 Principles — Radical Inclusion, Gifting, Decommodification, Radical Self-Reliance, Radical Self-Expression, Communal Effort, Civic Responsibility, Leaving No Trace, Participation, and Immediacy — also helped define what Burning Man was about, dispelling some of the myths and misconceptions about the culture and forming a common understanding that its participants could then build on.

"That's not an ideology. It's a description of a value system," Larry later told me. "They are descriptive of a phenomenon that had already occurred, rather than prescriptive."

For Larry, that phenomenon of Burning Man was born in San Francisco's Bohemian underground, with its artists, thinkers, weirdos, builders, and other free spirits.

"I think we've preserved all the good things about Bohemian culture," Larry said, comparing burner culture to the French impressionists of the 19th century and their artistic apprenticeships, while also noting how the ethos and technological advances of San Francisco and the Silicon Valley fed Burning Man, causing new ideas and understandings of the event to be rapidly spread through the Internet.

"When they were looking for those principles," Marian said of the regional contacts, "they were looking for that vocabulary."

For example, a ban on commerce at Burning Man had been in place since the 1990s, but it wasn't clear to everyone what that meant. As late at 2002, most of the bars on the playa were set up on the barter system, in which drinkers would be expected to make an offering of some kind to the bartender.

"The barter bar stuff bugged the fuck out of Larry," Marian said, noting that he addressed the issue in a Burning Man newsletter in 2002, spelling out more fully the concept of gifting. Similarly, the "no spectators" notion was still evolving, from condemnation of those not wearing silly costumes to a more expansive notion of "participation," which included devotion of time, energy, and creativity to the event.

Yet many burners didn't even become aware of the 10 principles for years after they were unveiled. Many of the newly emerging tribes — particularly those in the up-and-coming sound camp world that had almost no working relationship with Larry and the Borg, which had a barely concealed hostility toward "the ravers" — were evolving on their own.

San Francisco-based Lush Camp rocked the key corner of 2 o'clock and Esplanade in 2004, going big and then collapsing, never to return. Neighboring El Circo was also developing a storied reputation for great music, circus-style performances, and a pioneering feather-and-leather tribal fashion aesthetic. Across the playa, Illuminaughty was one of the biggest draws.

The hottest and most venerable mobile sound party was SF-based Space Cowboys, a camp formed in 1996 whose Unimog vehicle and big stable of top DJs could create dance parties at the coolest art pieces, the concept behind their signature Friday night Hoedown event.

"For the Hoedown, we'd find the biggest, baddest art project that was also near porta-potties," said Chip Corwin, aka DJ Mancub, a Space Cowboy since 1999 and native of Baton Rouge, Louisiana. "Back then, nobody had DJs on their art cars."

But by 2004, the Unimog, Garage Mahal, and other sound-pumping art cars were like rolling dance parties. And by using FM transmitters that were first introduced to the playa by the Space Cowboys, the art cars could circle their wagons anywhere on the playa, sync up their sound systems, and get everyone dancing to world-class DJs, who were just starting to flock to Burning Man in those years.

And then there was The Deep End, which came to develop a singular slot in Black Rock City's sound pantheon: the afternoon dance party. Sure, there was sound to be found all day, and huge dance parties along the radial streets of 10 and 2 all night long. But there was just something decadent about a popular day party.

"The whole day party thing somewhat came by accident. We just got out there, decided we liked serving drinks and playing music by day — then going out and exploring at night," says camp founder Clark Hamon, a DJ who goes by Clarkie.

The Deep End started in 2002 as a merger of three camps that had been located near each other along 9 o'clock the previous year, playing off the Floating World theme by creating a pool, tiki bar, and lifeguard stand. But by 2004, which Clarkie considers "a breakout year for us," The Deep End had solidified its status as the best day party on the playa.

Yet it wasn't just great music, which started to include big name DJs. And it wasn't the overhead water lines that misted the big crowd of beautiful, writhing, smiling dancers glistening in the afternoon sun. There was also a bar, a free bar. All you needed was a cup and a friendly bartender would fill it.

"The Deep End changed the way people looked at the gifting economy — especially where it comes to bars. Before we came along, it was much more like barter. What did we do? We gifted an entire bar all day long with smiles on our faces," Clarkie later wrote in an email to his camp members.

That was an important aspect to many Deep Enders, who repeatedly emphasized this aspect of the camp.

"We all very much enjoyed daytime fun in the sun. We also didn't like the prominent idea at the time of Burning Man as a barter and sometimes agro culture. We wanted to fill what we felt was a bit of a void on the playa at the time — an upbeat, friendly, daytime party that we gift to others without expectations of anything in return but a smile and a good attitude," longtime Deep Ender Christian Galindo told me.

"Then 2005 to 2008," Clarkie told me, "we just saw our crowds explode and I would say The Deep End somewhat became an institution at Burning Man."

The artists and Borg insiders had long given much of themselves to the event, but then the dance partiers also started to get into the act, a move that wasn't initially appreciated by many elements of the larger Burning Man culture. But it was part of the transformation that was beginning to unfold.

Building Connections

If nothing else, Burning Man is about collaboration. Nobody can realize their vision alone, so they team up with others to make it happen. The newbies often just latch onto the coolest and most capable people they know, and the ones who really want to create something special on the playa pay close attention and then find the partners they need to pursue their visions.

That was how an aspiring child psychologist named Adam really became Syd Gris, the San Francisco-based DJ and party promoter who fathered Opulent Temple, which became the biggest dance club on the playa from 2005 to 2010. But first, Syd needed to learn a few things and grow his community.

In 2002, he camped with Garage Mahal — a camp I would join years later — helping build an art car in Captain Ken's Mill Valley workshop. Ken could build anything and had made his living engineering television commercials, discovering Burning Man later in life than many, but taking to it with youthful gusto. He had an awesome set of tools, a compound of a property on which to create, and a nurturing yet no-nonsense manner.

"That was a good introduction to how to work on a Burning Man project," Syd later told me. He had just gotten laid off from his job, had time to kill, and poured himself into the project. Like so many thousands of other theme camp minions, Syd listened to his elders and learned: "He was the captain and I followed orders."

The result was a double-decker art car dance floor, with a bar, DJ booth, crow's nest, and the Indian elephant god Ganesh under a disco ball in front. Rosie and I quickly became enthralled with this rolling dance party in 2004. When we saw its elevated red triangles moving across the playa, we would race to catch it, even dropping our bikes if need be. It was a trigger for such wonderful and crazy memories, a gift to the community that brought people together.

"I bought in — hook, line, and sinker — to the ethos of the event and that's this community-generated vehicle for artistic expression and this one week of alternative lifestyle," Syd said of his early years. "Freaks being allowed to be freaks for a week and having a place where you can explore different parts of yourself."

But it wasn't Syd's project. He just helped, just as he would do with the first incarnation of Opulent Temple in 2003: Opulent Temple of Kaos. Syd was DJing and hosting dance parties in clubs and underground warehouses around San Francisco under his Opel Productions banner when he met Rich Martin, a builder and techie who brought Syd into the project.

Rich had come from the Midwest for the San Francisco lifestyle, which he embraced with his two queer life partners. He was good-looking, often gruff and enigmatic, but an incredibly capable welder and designer, if sometimes a little overly ambitious. Rich worked out of The Shipyard in Berkeley, the burner-populated machine shop founded by Jim Mason and Charlie Gadeken, where the Opulent Temple of Kaos crew helped him that year, as well as working in the Infinite Kaos art space in the gritty heart of San Francisco's Tenderloin.

"Rich was working with them and he approached me to help because he knew I threw parties and could fundraise and that I was interested, somehow," Syd said. "But they drove that year. In the same way that I was an apprentice to Ken, I was in the passenger's seat on the first Opulent Temple with Infinite Kaos. Now, they lived up to their name and it was a very chaotic process and it drove me nuts, so in 2004, Rich and I said, well, we can do this."

As Rich put it to me one day when we were working together, he picked Syd because he "wasn't full of shit." They became sort of co-leaders of Opulent Temple — Rich would build a project every year, tapping the camp for money and manpower; Syd handled overall camp logistics, fundraising, and creating the dance camp that he always wanted to see at Burning Man.

"For Rich, it meant, Syd, you can raise money and I can build something. For me it meant, now I need to organize this crew of people and sell them on a vision," Syd said. "So those first meetings, when I was gathering people who I hoped would help me, I had to sell them on what we were doing and hope they bought into it to help me do it, otherwise there was no fucking way it was going to happen. And it worked."

We were in that group when Syd convinced us to join him and create something from scratch, a vision in which we would be deeply invested, and which would morph and change along the way as we all made the vision our own. Some of the Infinite Kaos kids were still involved, but Rich had switched work spaces, renting a shipping container and workspace at the Box Shop on San Francisco's Hunters Point, a poor, mostly African-American neighborhood near a decommissioned Navy base.

So that's where we worked, building the first O-pod, an enclosed DJ booth made of steel that was roughly the shape of a barrel. We cut, bent, and welded steel — this was cool! This was my first real exposure to the never-ending burner culture that spends all year building the craziest shit for no other apparent reason than to watch it on the playa, belching fire, pumping beats, or whatever it was built to do.

It was also the first time that I saw the Flaming Lotus Girls in action and I was fascinated. We were busy with our own project and they were just wildly into theirs, throwing off sparks with their grinders and light with their welders, their gruff countercultural charm a bit daunting for a newbie like me; so filled with passion and style, so hard to fathom, so totally hot. I wanted to understand what made them tick, and by the end of that year, I would get my chance.

A Burning Man Rebellion

It was hard to get excited by the news after the 2004 election. That made work tough because as journalists, we couldn't escape it. We at the Guardian tried to be morbidly upbeat, running a cover photo of American flag draped coffins with the headline, "How to survive four more years," and we covered the growing list of Bush's misdeeds and his devolving war in Iraq.

On the local level, Mayor Gavin Newsom became the overly ambitious capitalist shill we feared he would be, and I would regularly write about his attacks on renters, progressives, and the poor. But my heart really wasn't in it. It was all I could do to pedal my bike to work every morning and try to summon the will to speak truth to a power that was only growing more powerful.

Then I saw the ad: "BURNING MAN PETITION," on page 80 of the Guardian. "We, the artists, feel that this event which we made great has gotten away from us and we would like it back."

It swaggered like a dust-covered artist, cigarette dangling from its lips, adjusting some connection on an impossibly cool flaming sculpture under a bright desert sun. The proclamation made a bold claim, but tried to back it up with signatures that covered more than half the page. The first two were Chicken John and Jim Mason.

The ad continued, "We want the art to be spectacular again and we are willing to step forward to do the work to make it so."

Even I knew they were going to do this work anyway. I'd seen less than a year of the San Francisco burners at work, but I knew they were addicted to it. They'd get these artistic visions and do whatever it took to bring them to life — begging, borrowing or stealing. It was just what they were now, burners, whether they liked it or not. Even most of those who had pointedly stopped coming to the event were still enmeshed in the culture, unable to really escape it. And they were willing to keep lighting up the desert with art? Yes, they were more than willing — they lived for this.

"But for this to happen, we think the 'art curation' should be put in the hands of rotating 'Guest Curators' and all funding decisions should be made by 'Direct Vote' of the full community. The art should also be well funded (10% of the gate) and not subject to creativity squashing litmus tests for 'theme compliance' and 'mandatory interactivity.'"

I found all the peppering of quotes irritating, but understood them as some kind of code I didn't yet fully understand. And the idea of guest curators and democratically selected art seemed like a contradiction to me. Yet I was intrigued by the idea of a rebellion by the Burning Man artists.

My camp was focused on thumping dance music until dawn, the event's nightlife and DJ showcase, blasting the sometimes surreal soundtrack out into the open playa. But the artists were the real rock stars of Burning Man. They knew it and so did the music makers.

The signatories to the We Have a Dream Petition, "require action on these very reasonable proposals or we commit to STOP CONTRIBUTING our art to Burning Man. Repeated discussions over many years have failed to result in meaningful change, so now we are resorting to more extreme measures. TOGETHER we can change things."

Wow. A rebellion in Burning Man. I'd been a full-time newspaper journalist for 14 years and instinctively sized everything up by its story potential. Conflict. Boom, right there. Characters, from Chicken John to Zoe Vaughn with maybe 1,000 between them. Some names — Dr. Megavolt, Jim Mason, Danger Ranger, and Chicken — I immediately recognized as characters in the book that I was reading, *This is Burning Man* by Brian Doherty.

Doherty had an engaging writing style and a distinctly libertarian point of view — consistent with his role as a senior editor at Reason magazine. One of his four opening epigraphs was even an Ayn Rand quote, "Don't work for my happiness, my brothers — show me yours — show me that it is possible — show me your achievement — and the knowledge will give me courage for mine."

But the combination of his Randian emphasis on individual liberty and his 10-year history at the event — as well as then-unprecedented access to and insights from the most central and colorful characters in the events history — made the book a comprehensive and indispensable history of Burning Man. That's what I liked about it, the deep and varied roots it gave to the event. And it helped me appreciate how Burning Man grew directly from the unique attributes of the San Francisco counterculture.

I learned about the "Temple of Three Guys" — founder Larry Harvey and the Cacophony Society's Michael Mikel and John Law — that ran the event for its first 10 years, combining Larry's weird little Baker Beach art festival with the Cacophony Society's anarchic culture-jamming and its "zone trip" getaways to far flung locales like the Black Rock Desert.

Larry was, of course, still the central figure in Burning Man, whether or not his detractors liked it. Michael — aka M2 or Danger Ranger — was an eccentric Cacaphonist who had founded Black Rock Rangers, which polices the event and its borders, and was still a member of Black Rock City LLC's six-member board, although he signed the Petition.

But Law left Burning Man in 1996 and hadn't looked back. For many years, he steadfastly refused to even talk about Burning Man, except in Doherty's book, up to then his final word on a subject he was trying to forget.

Chicken was in Law's camp and sort of carried his banner forward after Law left, a perpetual thorn in the side of the Burning Man organization and a loud voice for staying true to its roots as a crazed art party for the cool kids — although he'd never characterize it that way. But his perspective was clear to those who visited the Odeon Bar, which Chicken opened on Mission Street and which many artists and burner old schoolers considered their clubhouse of sorts. I'd been there a couple times for his regular Wednesday night set piece, the Ask Dr. Hal Show, a quirky and offbeat Q&A show that grew out of a 1998 Burning Man piece called Wizard of Ass that featured a huge butt that shot flame as game contestants were eliminated. He was quite a character.

"Chicken John has a lot of stories. He's a Burning Man prodigal. He's one of many who were attracted to this party for its absurd freedom," is how Doherty began the book's epilogue. Chicken and Jim Mason, who had pulled off some of the event's biggest artistic achievements and also its most spectacular failures, get more ink in Doherty's book than anyone who wasn't there in the beginning or who didn't play a central role in the organization.

Two stories about Mason in the book served to illustrate key dynamics of Burning Man and his relationship to it. One was his ambitious overreaching with the G7 Stock Puppets in 2000, which got a huge art grant from Burning Man but never worked that year, prompting Doherty to capture this scene:

> "How you feeling, Jimmy?" someone asked.
> "I feel good. I failed big. I failed the biggest I've ever failed. I think I failed bigger than anyone has ever failed out here. Over twenty thousand dollars and five months of failure."
> "How's Larry feel?"
> "Larry understands. I think. He's not yelling or threatening to cut my head off or screaming for his money back at any rate. What can he say? He saw me out there crawling in the dust and throwing wrenches and crying."

Three years earlier, Mason had also started the storied clash between the artists and the ravers when he led a mob in his Vegematic of the Apocalypse — a pedal-powered vehicle with a fearsome flame thrower — out to confront renowned trance DJ Goa Gil and those he was grooving out in the electronic music dance party, implicitly threatening to set him on fire unless he switched the dance music to Led Zeppelin. The clash played out a schism in the attitudes of those who attend this all-accepting event.

"Burning Man's vibe, though, is not all love and encouragement. It tiptoes on a knife-edge between two dominant alternative outlooks in American underground culture. They can be roughly characterized by punk and hippie," Doherty wrote, later adding, "Burning Man is full of people openly embracing either possibility — and also many, like me, torn between an attraction to the aggressive wit and piquant tomfoolery of the punk mentality and the warm sincerity and endearing openness of the hippie one."

And here was this petition, onto which Chicken and Jim had signed in John Hancock style, throwing down in a way that made it clear to Larry and the Borg that they were leading this rebellious challenge to their authority. I didn't know whether this was a serious threat or some kind of performance art piece, but it was fascinating to me, raising questions about what Burning Man had become and where it was headed.

Claiming the Story

I knew that we'd have to write a story on this thing. Even though I was the news editor and this was basically an arts and culture story, I decided to just write it myself. Beyond my usual attraction to an interesting news story, I was excited to see the characters in the book come to life in front of me, a much more engaging project than sorting through the ugly remains of the presidential election.

Scanning through the names on the petition, I found two people that I actually personally knew well: Syd Gris and Dona Williams.

Dona was the San Franciscan that I'd known longer than any other, going back to 1995 in San Luis Obispo. We met while I was working on a cover story for New Times about a local group that performed to "The Rocky Horror Picture Show," a piece on a subculture more than anything. She was Columbia and I was at the tail end of an unhappy marriage. And when I went alone to the midnight performance and saw Dona and Leila do the sexiest opening intro that I'd ever seen at a Rocky Horror…well, let's just say I was smitten.

She was just pure sex — beautiful, free, open, what I would later understand as modern and sex-positive. It was innocent enough when I interviewed Dona in her apartment near campus — only cheated in my imagination after almost seven years of marriage — but I was excited by her countercultural energy.

She told me all about Burning Man, which she attended every year with a group that straddled SLO and San Francisco, many of them tech geeks and Cacophony

Society stalwarts like Dave Gross, who I knew from both his leftist politics and his elaborate media hoaxes and other culture jamming exploits — such as the time he was arrested in front of San Luis Obispo High School for passing out literature that, among other behests, urged students to burn their school down.

I wouldn't attend Burning Man for another six years, but not because I didn't basically identify with it. On some level I already did. I got it. I just didn't need to actually go way out to a far-flung desert to get it, or so I thought at the time. Dona and I eventually became friends, and lovers of a few occasions, part of a group we dubbed the SLOhemians.

Although Dona lived in San Francisco in 2004, I had grown even closer to Syd, who was just coming off a big year at Burning Man, but big only to those who follow electronic dance music. After all, we weren't on the high-profile Esplanade yet, but tucked a few blocks back where there was less traffic, dancing in the dust.

But we attracted some great DJs, including The Scumfrog (aka Jesse Houk), a DJ and producer from Amsterdam who had been touring the world playing music for the previous two years and had released two albums and cofounded the music label Effin Records. Syd had promoted some of his San Francisco appearances.

"I had heard about Burning Man for many years from my friends in New York, so when Opulent Temple's Syd Gris approached me in 2004 to come out and play, I didn't need a whole lot of arm-twisting. My agent thought I was insane since the last week of August is generally one of the most lucrative weeks for DJ gigs in Europe, but I knew I had to try the desert-craziness at least once," he told me. "I went with my best friend from New York. We flew into Reno and rented a car at night, and just when we thought we had taken a wrong turn somewhere, the lights and fires of Black Rock City appeared on the horizon. We were instantly hooked and both knew that this phenomenon would become a permanent part of our lives before we even drove through the main gate."

The Scumfrog. This guy had a playa name long before the playa. It's no wonder he took to it so hard and fast. Like a string of big-name DJs who would follow him to the decks of Opulent Temple, he just loved the otherworldliness of Burning Man and all its many facets.

After that first year, Scumfrog said his connection to Burning Man "had only grown stronger. I had come for one performance at the O.T. but soon discovered that this was just one of the many elements that make Burning Man incomparable to any other event or festival in the world."

For those who knew electronic music — and neither I nor most burners were really steeped in that culture — this was becoming a premier event that was still ascendant in the music world. Syd was definitely a hippie to Chicken's punk, but still, they shared an overweening desire to make Burning Man better, whether or not the two men could agree on what "better" actually was.

Chasing Chicken

After I read the petition and decided to write about it, my first call was to Chicken. From the beginning, he was enigmatic, challenging, speaking in parables. The conversation felt like verbal jousting — difficult to get what I needed, but different from my normal interviews with earnest or reluctant sources. It was like a game and I was having fun talking to him, even as I tried to resist his charms and efforts to dictate the story.

Chicken professed to hate and distrust the press — something I understood, alienated as I've long felt from my colleagues in this cursed profession — but he clearly was media-savvy and knew how to get the attention he desired. I sensed early on that the two of us would develop a symbiotic relationship: he would give me interesting stories and I'd help propel and publicize his rebellion, one that I saw as raising the kinds of interesting existential questions that were missing for the vapid national political discussion.

"I think I have talked enough," was one of the first things Chicken told me, explaining why he wouldn't talk to me for the article. Instead, he insisted that I talk to some regular people who had been drawn to his petition, people like Nat the Bat, a young Colorado woman who I later learned had been to Burning Man once but spoke like a jaded authority on it, ending all her e-mails with "and fuck you."

I could see why Chicken liked her, but I was reluctant to let him choose my Burning Man poster children for me. Chicken was determined to define the parameters of this story. He even seemed to be trying to hypnotize me when he explained, "You're going to get what I give you out of Burning Man."

He alternated between claims of knowing nothing about Burning Man to being the one person who knows what it is. Such see-sawing conversations were the hallmarks of talking with Chicken, as he bounced from one provocative pole to the other. Chicken said he wasn't even an artist, but merely an art facilitator, defining art as "intentional and pointless."

In the end, he agreed to talk with me in person, at the Odeon before his next Ask Dr. Hal Show. I arranged to meet Mason at what he called a "yuppie taqueria" in the Marina, near where he worked in the Presidio at the Long Now Foundation on such academic projects as Rosetta Disc, a database of all the world's languages. I definitely wanted to converse with the two dissidents in person, to sense their spirit and get some life into my story.

But I figured that I could simply do a phone interview with Larry Harvey. He was a familiar counterculture figure in town who I'd seen speak a few times. He always wore a tan Stetson hat, chain smoked, and spoke with a mild stutter that made his thoughtful and curious speaking style seem all the more well-considered.

In his book, Doherty described his interviews with Larry as one-sided, more like a rolling monologue punctuated occasionally by outsider questions or comments. I could see what he meant, but I was more struck by something else during that first interview and many subsequent ones: there's no such thing as a short conversation with Larry Harvey. We talked for almost two hours, and the only reason it ended then was because it was getting late in the evening and I had to go to the bathroom.

The first surprising thing Larry told me was that he and Chicken had long been friends, talking on the phone almost everyday, even as Chicken was publicly calling Larry out. "Throughout this thing, I was in contact with him. We're friends," Larry said. "The rumors of this struggle to the death were hooey." We talked through the whole conflict and the issues that it illustrated, Larry sounding bemused by the conflict and contemplative of Burning Man — like he was a detached observer rather than a central player.

I got what I needed for my story and way more. I got a sense that Larry had a vision for where Burning Man was headed, even if he was reluctant to fully spell it out, lest he fuel the chorus of criticism that his ambitions were killing what everyone loved about Burning Man: its blank canvas, onto which you could place almost anything, and those random anythings would add up to a big something that would define the event differently every year.

Chicken and Jim wanted Larry to proclaim that Burning Man was really about what they wanted it to be about: art, or even more narrowly, the sort of explosive or surreal forms of art they preferred. But Larry knew that it had become something bigger than that. He may be a leader, but he's a leader of people unwilling to follow or be told what to do.

Part of his reluctance to spell out his fondest hopes was tactical. Larry knew better than anyone how the current revolt glorified the good old days, even though he remembers that there didn't used to be much art back then and the most exciting thing you could do was blow something up, shoot guns at stuffed animals, or get someone to pull you on a carpet behind a car. Wheeee!

As for the present, he defined the problems not in terms of how much art there was, but one of acculturation. If people weren't bringing in enough great art — as he grudgingly acknowledged was the case in 2004 — it was because they hadn't come to understand the culture of Burning Man before they arrived on the playa, with its focus on participation and creative self-expression, the license to cultivate your inner artist or freak.

Still, I could just hear in Larry's voice where his excitement lay. It wasn't in the past or the present, but in the future. He talked most excitedly about offshoots of the main event like the Black Rock Arts Foundation, which was bringing interactive art projects to San Francisco and other cities, and the network of regional Burning Man events popping up all over the world.

"The regional thing is growing very fast. It's the same exponential growth rate we had with the main event," Larry said. "We're wise enough to know that half of the good ideas are going to come from the communities themselves." The real story, he said, wasn't with the event, but rather "the movement story." It was a theme we would return to again and again over the next year, until I started to actually see it spill out onto the streets and plazas of San Francisco, and I began to share his hope that this thing might actually begin to influence the larger culture.

Burner Central

So I had Larry, Jim and Chicken all lined up. I planned to call Doherty to get his perspective, do some basic research into the organization and the validity of the rebels' points about the art grant process, talk to LadyBee, the organization's art curator, and to even interview my favorite DJ from the scene, Lorin Ashton, aka Bassnectar, to temper the artist's view with that of another burner tribe.

But what I really still needed was some burner artists other than Chicken and Jim, an independent view, preferably from some setting where art was being made. Immediately, I thought of the Box Shop, that hive of the burner culture, where I worked on Opulent Temple's DJ booth and saw the Flaming Lotus Girls in action.

The Box Shop is an industrial arts warehouse and outdoor work space out on Hunter's Point, where artists had been moving because the rent for big spaces was cheap. It's a compound walled by boxcar-sized storage containers between the Hunter's Point Power Plant and a gritty neighborhood with far too many black-on-black homicides.

This was an island of industrial artists dominated by the Flaming Lotus Girls when I was there. These were intimidating women — serious workers, wielding tools that burn, cut or grind — but undeniably sexy, with their tattoos and dreadlocks or with little girly touches that sometimes peeked out from under their grungy overalls, indicating that under their gruff facades they were really fun-loving burner chicks.

And the guys there were tough and knowledgeable, real wrenches who could not only fix their own cars, they could probably build their own cars, maybe even from the metal scraps found lying around the shop. Rich Martin — Opulent Temple's builder — was the only one I got to know who had his own box and tons of tools at the shop and the whole DJ booth was his baby.

Rich occupied a rare intersection between the industrial arts and the rave communities — but could savage either with his biting cynicism. He grew up on a farm, where he learned hard work, mechanics, and a creative resourcefulness — traits he later adapted to his adopted San Francisco.

During our push to the playa back in August, Syd shepherded workers out to the Box Shop and Rich told us what to do when we were out there, ordering us around in a way that I wasn't yet accustomed to, but which I probably needed more than anyone considering how little I knew about working with metal, or any kind of shop work, for that matter. It was new and made me want to learn more. And now, I had an excuse.

So I just showed up at the Box Shop one afternoon with my reporter's notebook in hand to get a perspective and a few quotes for my story. I met Gaspo, someone who I immediately sensed would be involved in many burner dramas, and he told me that the Box Shop was indeed a hotbed of Petitioners.

"The people who are doing (the Petition) come here and talk about it all the time," Gaspo said dismissively. "I can see where they're coming from, but I think they're wasting their time. The Borg doesn't need to listen." The Borg had become a sort of derisive label for Black Rock City LLC, particularly its six-member board. It was a reference from Star Trek to the overbearing governing council of a fantastical new land, a testament to the tendency of burner tinkerers to be huge sci-fi geeks, as well as a handy label for the Burning Man org.

Gaspo and I chatted in the yard next to his camper van as he moved around computer parts and other gear. I didn't know it at the time, but he had designed and built the "hypnotron" that Opulent Temple used at Burning Man on top of our DJ booth, a spinning wand of lights that make weird circular light patterns, just as the Flaming Lotus Girls had lent us a flaming steel archway.

Gaspo said he'd been to the event "six or seven" times and struck an "I'm over it" pose with regards to Burning Man, an event that had clearly been important to his social and artistic development. "I think there are certain types of art that will only go out there," he said.

But the culture had changed, with the artists and anarchists that started it diluted by the sheer number of attendees out there now. I baited him with a question about whether the dance camps had sullied the original vibe of the anarchists and artists, but he modified it: "It's not so much artists versus ravers as much as partiers versus participants."

He thought it was wrong for the artists who helped make Burning Man great to resort to power struggles over its probably immovable direction: "A real artist would just paint a new painting rather than trying to change it." I asked about Chicken, and yeah, Gaspo knew Chicken and where Chicken is coming from: "He still wants Burning Man to be freaky because that's where he came from."

Only at the very end does Gaspo tell me his real name: Scott Gasparian. Soon, Chicken pulled up in his car, noticed the new guy with the notebook, put it together and told me "not to believe anything Scott Gasparian says because he's a liar."

Chicken had come to the Box Shop to get help with some mechanical problem he was having, and since we'd already made plans to talk later that evening at the Odeon, I continued looking for interview subjects, but the shop was fairly empty. Gaspo told me the Flaming Lotus Girls were having a meeting that night and I decided to stop by later. Mmm, the Flaming Lotus Girls.

But before I could really delve into them, I had to write my story.

Conjuring the Spirit of Smiley

Chicken John knew how to push Larry Harvey's button.

Chicken and I were sitting at a table in his Odeon Bar in San Francisco on December 1, 2004, talking about the great Burning Man art controversy before his quirky weekly showman's gig, "The Ask Dr. Hal Show," when he gave me a chance too. "Wanna push Larry Harvey's button?"

I thought Chicken had already been pushing the button of Burning Man's founder pretty well, with the We Have a Dream Petition he'd started a couple weeks earlier with Jim Mason, the mad genius behind some of the event's most ambitious artistic creations.

But then Chicken got up from the table and walked over to a button on the wall. He told me to look up, and there, on the ceiling of Chicken's bar, was the huge triangular head of a Burning Man, that central symbol of the then-19-year-old desert celebration of free expression.

Chicken pushed the button, and a neon smiley face appeared. "That's the whole story right there," he said, as if revealing some great cosmic truth. "It's about Smiley."

Having just read Brian Doherty's book *This Is Burning Man*, I already knew the Smiley story. In 1996, a tempestuous turning-point year for Burning Man, the last anarchic year before the exponentially growing event would begin to develop rules and a civic structure, pranksters secretly placed a smiley face on the man, which they flashed occasionally for just seconds at a time.

"It was a defacing of the icon," Chicken said, a challenge to the control that Larry — who had taken Burning Man from a tiny gathering at Baker Beach to a massive annual extravaganza of 35,000 people at that point — has always exercised over an event he conceived. Smiley was symbolic of the split between those serious about creating a new kind of community open to all and those who are wary of such high-minded goals and who just want to make art, the kind of mind-blowing, fire-spewing art you can only display in the Black Rock Desert.

Event co-founder John Law, who allegedly created Smiley and hasn't returned to Burning Man since 1996, leaned on the bar nearby, paying us no heed. He no longer wanted anything to do with the institution he helped create, an event he refused to talk about, to me or anyone, at least for a couple more years, until he decided to sue his former partners.

Also circulating in Chicken's orbit at that time, and frequenting his bar, was a character named Paul Addis, who would eventually escalate the rhetoric into an actual arson attack on The Man in 2007, one that landed him in federal prison for almost two years. But I'm getting ahead of the story.

At the end of 2004, Chicken and a group of artists were threatening to follow Law out the door, sparking a spirited debate over what Burning Man was, and what the beloved and bemoaned event was to become.

It was a standoff that would presage the renaissance of Burning Man — but not in the way that Chicken and Jim could have intended or imagined.

The "C" Word

Like the best art, Burning Man looks different from each perspective. From a detached distance, you might just see a big art party in the desert. Step up to it and study the details and you'll notice dusty artists toiling over impossible creations, ravers feeling their musical bliss, humans making a gift economy work, and disparate tribes building unique camps into a cohesive — and fairly substantial — temporary city.

But at its most basic level, Burning Man was a business, Black Rock City LLC, a limited liability corporation with an annual budget of about $7.5 million in 2004, derived from selling tickets that at that time cost between $175 and $250, depending on when you bought them (a level that rose to $210-$300 in 2010).

The budget pays for permits and other direct costs and for the salaries of dozens of employees. Beyond creating the event and maintaining the Borg, the budget also paid for art, both on and off the playa. Each of the previous three years, the Borg dispensed about $270,000 to Burner artists who applied. Decisions about who got the money and how much, where the art was placed, and whether it conformed to standards of safety, theme, and interactivity, were made by a committee of three: Larry, curator LadyBee (a.k.a. Christine Kristen), and longtime fire artist Crimson Rose.

There are forms to fill out, hoops to jump through, and authority figures to answer to — none of which sat well with the counterculture artists who were drawn to the infinite possibilities of desert as canvas. Grumbling about Burning Man has always been a favorite pastime among burners.

"It's funny," Jim Mason told me. "We all sit around and bitch and complain about Burning Man, but we all continue to pour tremendous amounts of time, energy, and money into it nonetheless."

But the problems came to a head in 2004 because so many people said the art just wasn't very good. There wasn't enough of it, and only a few pieces really wowed people. At the very least, between artist no-shows and static art-funding levels, it was certainly true that the art wasn't keeping pace with the population growth.

"Everyone noticed, as I did, that there was less work. There not only appeared to be less work, there was," Larry told me. "We had already planned to increase the art funding next year."

Yet for the Bay Area artists who had spent years trying to alert the Borg to their concerns that art had lost its position of primacy, Harvey's realization was too little, too late. They demanded more than just tinkering with the current model. In the wake of that frustrating presidential election, they were looking for a little revolution.

The demands were delivered in a letter, an online petition, and a full-page ad in the Bay Guardian. "Give us our event back or we leave," read the statement signed by hundreds of Bay Area artists. The "We Have a Dream Petition" sought a renewal of the event's art scene by increasing the funding to 10 percent of the total take, democratizing the art selection process, rotating guest curators drawn from the Burning Man art community, facilitating big ideas, and generally emphasizing art over the competing foci of the party and the community.

"The fix must address many issues, but the core issue for the fix is the art. Art, art, art: that is what this is all about. Fix the art and make the process for doing it fair and fun again, and the rest will likely fall into place," the petition read.

Ah, but what about "the rest?" That's more complicated, opening up all the core conflicts among the desert denizens: artists versus ravers, punks versus hippies, old-timers versus newcomers, participants versus partiers, anarchy versus order, and temporary autonomy versus a new way of living. And as the event swelled to more than 35,000 participants, they all got rolled up in the inertia of the collective.

"What they're really afraid of is that the event will become inauthentic," Larry said as we talked about the petition. "And if you think further: can you maintain a sense of community at that magnitude?"

That might be a fair translation, if he hadn't used the C word. It was Larry's focus on the creation of "community" that really rankled many of the artists, particularly Chicken and Jim.

"People go for the art festival, not for the community festival," Chicken said, dripping disdain on the last two words. "If it is to survive, it's going to be for one reason, and that's because of its artists, not because we're a community."

Both Chicken and Mason do appreciate the community that's created every August in Nevada's Black Rock Desert, and the year-round community that Burning Man spawned back in the Bay Area and other regions. Yet they say the community flows entirely from the collaborative, creative process of working with others — friends and strangers alike — to create kick-ass art and watch the wide-open playa steadily be filled with wonders beyond imagination.

"The biggest contribution of Burning Man is that it has convinced a large number of people that it is not just an interesting thing but a critical thing for their humanity, maybe a responsibility of being human, to make a creative comment, and that everyone has the ability to do it," Jim told me. "The community aspect of the event is the easiest thing."

Maybe that was true for Jim, who had proven adept at the creation of art-centered communities in the Bay Area, cofounding the burner-populated metal shops The Shipyard in Berkeley and The Box Shop in San Francisco. But thousands of others were still in the process of developing their tribes around the country's biggest and freakiest powwow.

The Showdown

Being the birthplace and headquarters of Burning Man, San Francisco has more burners per capita than any place on earth, with the exception of Black Rock City in late August. So the rebellion got coverage in the San Francisco Chronicle, SF Weekly, local television stations, and, of course, the Bay Guardian, where I worked.

In the dark period after President George W. Bush's reelection, I relished writing about this existential conflict at the heart of an event I loved, devoting thousands of words to the conflict over several months and helping to elevate it into the grand, high-profile showdown that Chicken and Jim wanted.

Larry told me he was at first bemused by the petition, then perplexed. "It was not only bad policy but unworkable," explained Larry, who said he prefers the consensus process (at least, among the Borg and Burning Man staff) to cruder democratic methods that would also involve the larger group.

So he wrote a response that began, "I've read the We Have a Dream petition with interest. I think it will spur discussion and provoke some new ideas. I think real good can come of this. In writing this response, however, I feel called on to examine the very specific proposals that the petition advocates."

He then went on to tear apart the concept and logistics of democratizing the art selection process, the idea of funneling 10 percent of ticket sales to fund the new approach, and the accusation that the decline in the quality and quantity of art this year signaled an institutional shortcoming rather than just an off year.

Even the artists who travel in the same orbit as Chicken and Jim had varying views on the debate. Stella Ru, one of the Flaming Lotus Girls and an eight-year burner, fully supported the petition. "I think discussion and rejuvenation is always good."

Other key players in the community didn't sign it. "I think the petition itself is childish and annoying, but I support the ideals of it," said Charlie Gadeken, an artist who co-founded the Box Shop and was a member of the Flaming Lotus Girls. "It's the art-versus-community question that is at its core."

The spectrum of opinions got broader when you scanned the voluminous online discussions the petition spawned on Web sites like Tribe.net and E-Playa. "Jim and Chicken stumbled on this whole continent of activity that I don't think they knew was out there," Larry said. "(Jim) was encountering people who thought it was about community. And the art? That's okay too."

Burning Man and the Bay Area's underground art community essentially grew up together during the '80s and '90s, feeding off one another. "We were funding the underground here when nobody else was," Larry told me. "We were funding this little community that we grew up with."

The event and those who attended it have left an indelible mark on the Bay Area's counterculture, affecting everything from its focus to its fashions.

"San Francisco is unique in that it has all these little subtribes that you can often trace back to projects or camps of people at Burning Man," Jim said. And they keep coming back to the playa because, as Chicken said, "This is the vehicle we've found that has the highest-percentage chance of blowing people's minds."

That symbiotic relationship understandably led many artists to feel that their contributions created the event and that their departures can kill it. But it may have been too late for that by 2004. The contributions — artistic, cultural, metaphysical, or just social and entertaining — were just too diverse.

"It's given (Chicken and Jim) a broader view of who our community is," Larry said. "They thought they were the core community, but really, it's been a long time since there was a core community."

Jim admitted that since the conflict began, his eyes have been opened up to a world of burners who see the event as more than an art festival. Some see it as simply a great party, others as a quasi-spiritual endeavor, and others as an amalgam that's uniquely Burning Man.

Yet Chicken and Mason insist the party isn't enough. It's got to be about the art. Chicken derisively refers to the other side of Burning Man as "Operation Desert Snuggle." With a punk rock soul, Chicken doesn't have much use for huggers, ravers, and hippies. But he can accept all of the event's other facets, if they're secondary to the art.

"What has incensed me most, as I have wandered these online forums and talked to people about this, is that I've realized that the leadership has stopped focusing on art as our main vehicle toward community. Instead, we now have a vague affirmation of community, in whatever form it is assembled," Jim said. "I think the experiment has lost much of its power because of this vagueness of purpose."

Burning Man has always been deliberately vague, from the meaning of the Man himself to the reasons an exponentially growing number of people gather each year in such an inhospitable place. Artists focus on the art, but Larry said, "I'm used to thinking of it in a much larger context."

Even with hundreds of burners swept up in the debate over the petition, tens of thousands didn't know about the big standoff and may never know. That included notable figures from the Bay Area's music scene like Berkeley's DJ Lorin Ashton, aka Bassnectar, a decade-long Burning Man veteran whose performances on the playa have created countless peak experiences for those who love dance music.

"It's the ultimate orgy of expression," Lorin told me. "My favorite time of year," a gathering of "counterculture artists and people who are inventing other ways of living."

He tried to keep a balanced view of the event and was critical of its hedonistic waste of human energy and resources. But Lorin wants to change the world, and he would like to see the Burning Man community help — voicing a perspective Harvey sometimes sounds but which Chicken hates.

"Art-shmart," Lorin said. "I would love to see Burning Man as an organization and mobilization front." Perhaps there were some who shared that dream, given what was going on in the country at the time, but it was civic values that were starting to guide the Burning Man culture more than revolutionary values.

"We actually have become a kind of municipality, and that rubs some people wrong," Larry said. "We're the first scene that went civic. Instead of falling apart, we instituted civic ethics. We said it's a city and anyone can come."

That focus on building an inclusive community, rather than an exclusive party for the cool kids, is part of the divide that emerged in 2004. Many artists accused Larry of trying to turn Burning Man into some kind of religion, a characterization he always resists. But he was starting to talk more freely about how Burning Man and the regional gatherings it spawned are a "movement" with the potential to affect the mainstream culture.

That, Larry told me, "is the long-term plan." And it was a plan for which many of the artists of San Francisco weren't yet onboard. "If we want to affect the larger culture," Chicken said bluntly, "it's over."

But it wasn't over, not even close. In fact, the Burning Man Renaissance was about to begin.

The Petition Becomes The Bet

With Larry appearing to reject the petition's demands, Chicken tried one last tactic — The Bet — which he fired off in a December 1st e-mail titled "more woo woo for Larry's hoo ha." It was his proposal for a grand compromise, or as he conspiratorially described it to me, "the endgame."

"I humbly propose we test drive these ideas through a somewhat unique 'event within the event.' The idea is that you do everything that you normally do and we do our own thing. And you simply let us. We want to experiment with the MASSIVELY COLLABORATIVE and RADICALLY DEMOCRATIC methods laid out in the We Have a Dream Petition," Chicken wrote.

So he and his supporters formed their own Borg, Borg2. Chicken asked for "some good real estate" at the event, access to the list of event attendees to ask them for donations toward a goal of raising $250,000, and the autonomy to implement their vision without unnecessary interference from the Borg.

And to top it off, Chicken threw down a challenge, or an "art duel." If Borg2 can create better art than the original Borg, then "I only ask that you consider changing the current Burning Man art system to better reflect the ideas and methods they used to achieve their success. If I am wrong and the petitioners are unsuccessful, I hereby commit to sit in a dunk booth at next year's Burning Man Decompression Party (a massive street fair that is San Francisco's Burning Man after-party) and let everyone soak my ass, all day long."

Art isn't simply what started Burning Man, it's what has sustained it, Chicken insisted. It's why people will travel to the desert year after year. And it's why both the government authorities who police and permit it and the private-sector facilitators who rent the generators, trucks, and sound systems have been willing to cut the event so many breaks over the years. They're willing to facilitate an art festival, not just a raucous party in the desert or burgeoning quasi-political movement.

" 'Art festival' is the 'get out of jail free' card," Chicken said, noting that Larry and his clan have long been able to hide behind that banner when outsiders thought this was some kind of cult or revolutionary training camp.

"He married the art festival," Chicken told me, "but he didn't divorce the art festival."

Larry officially accepted Chicken's challenge a few days later. "On behalf of Borg1, I accept your bet. What is more is truly more. Let a hundred flowers bloom!... The art that you produce will then be matched against our own poor efforts at supporting and creating art. Should your woo woo trump our hoo ha on the playa, I pledge to reconsider my opposition to your radically democratic curatorial methods. Should our hoo ha make your woo woo look ho hum, you commit to sit all day in a dunking booth at next year's Decompression. Let Chaos Provide!"

Larry was calling Chicken's bluff, leaving Chicken and company to figure out how exactly to go about fundraising and setting up the structure and space for filling the playa with art.

"It seems to be a way to regenerate chaos and change in the experience, which I think the event needs," Doherty told me. "But it's premature to say that an agreement means they won. Now they have to raise the money."

Harvey was also skeptical that they get anywhere close to their $250,000 goal. "If they can raise $50,000, I'll be impressed."

Yet everyone I interviewed at the time had big expectations for the coming year. Beyond the likely improvements to the art, the reelection of President George W. Bush had many people feeling more motivated than ever to create an alternative reality, whereas the year before many argued for focusing on electoral politics rather than on Burning Man.

Even artists who resisted signing the petition said they'd contribute to the next year's experiment. "This year they had 1,000 people behind them. Next year we'll have 10,000 people behind us," said Charlie Gadeken, who decided to run for the Borg2 board, moving beyond the "childish and annoying" Petition into something he hoped would be a catalyst for great art. "And we are going to make mind-boggling art in a concentrated space."

The process of getting there may have been rough. "The sad thing is, we've been forced to do this in this ugly manner and look like complete assholes while doing it," Jim Mason told me. But both of the instigators say it was worth it. "This will turn into what saves Burning Man," Chicken predicted.

THE TRIBES OF BURNING MAN

"It needs to have a new grand experiment within the grand experiment of Burning Man," Mason said. "It could fail grandly, but in its failure, something interesting will surely happen."

Just Getting Started

My article in the Bay Guardian was well-received, particularly in the Burning Man community that circulated it around the world via their Internet message boards like Tribe.net, which was the main hub for Bay Area-based burners, and thus, the Borg2 rebels. In fact, the Internet was integral to the evolution and longevity of Burning Man.

But even my long article seemed to just scratch the surface of a culture and conflict that I felt boundlessly fascinated by. I just wasn't ready to let it go. My main political beat seemed downright dismal next to this parallel universe, where colorful characters were speaking their own words about things they deeply cared about.

Where was this event really headed? Could it impact the larger political culture? If so, how, and what would Larry's desire to change the world do to the event? What about all these wonderfully creative and resourceful people that were all around me? What made them tick, what focused them on Burning Man, and could their energies be redirected?

I needed to better understand this world, and help people engage with it, before I could even begin to answer these questions. I wanted to keep digging deeper, and present a perspective on this unique phenomenon that was broader than what I had. And personally, I was more excited than ever to attend Burning Man. My girlfriend Rosie had a transformative experience at her first Burning Man that year, truly moved to look at the world differently, and that epiphany was followed a few months later by the crash of what she believed was a self-correcting political system, one that would never reelect a scoundrel like Bush.

On the day after the article came out, Black Rock City LLC happened to be throwing its holiday party, which I attended. I quickly found myself in a conversation with Larry and party promoter Joegh Bullock, who filled me in about his connection to Burning Man and the long, difficult path that brought music out to the playa. Despite camping with Opulent Temple, few of us knew much about our predecessors, a history that none of the Burning Man books or films had covered.

Even though the sonic landscape was an integral part of the modern Burning Man experience, Doherty's book had given short shrift to the stuff Joegh was telling me, the veracity of which Larry and others confirmed. The tensions between the artists and ravers ran deeper than I knew.

I told them both that I was thinking about doing a series of articles on Burning Man, an idea they encouraged, and I told Joegh that I'd like to speak with him in more detail later. Over the next few days, I couldn't get Burning Man out of my head as I made notes on aspects of the scene that I'd like to cover, including a deep immersion journalism piece, embedding myself with, oh, say, the Flaming Lotus Girls in the same way other journalists embedded themselves in Iraq with the U.S. military. I wanted to get deeper into this event and its significance than the Guardian or any publication had gone.

I finally pitched my series to Executive Editor Tim Redmond. He sensed my enthusiasm and gave me the green light, although he gently suggested that I scale back my plan for nine parts into maybe four or five. Although both Tim and Editor/Publisher Bruce Brugmann liked my first story and commented that our readers always enjoy stories about Burning Man, I knew that this was a project that they were simply allowing me to do to keep me happy. None of the other editors at the paper — the arts and culture types who should have been the ones guiding this series — particularly liked Burning Man, and a few actively resented it.

After all, if something ceases to be cool once it's discovered by the masses, then Burning Man wasn't cool, particularly in such a hip city as San Francisco. The Guardian had covered it as something interesting in the mid-'90s — its sympathetic coverage peaking in 1996 when the mainstream media discovered Burning Man and Wired magazine wrote a widely disseminated cover story on it — but then succumbed to the hater vibe that was almost as strong in San Francisco as that of people devoted to the event.

People who had never been to the event concluded that it was lame or commercial or elitist or past its prime or some kind of faddish cult or whatever other ill motives they could ascribe. They just couldn't stand how so many of their friends devoted so much of their lives to this thing, and they got sick of hearing the cult-like mantras that it would change their lives.

In the Guardian, supportive articles about Burning Man as intriguing cultural happening started to give way to snarky, "over it" articles like the 2001 piece entitled "Fuck Burning Man," which quotes one former burner calling the event, "a giant leech sucking all the creative energy out of every town in this country."

It was an attitude that some of the Guardian editors seemed to share, if they would even give the event that much credit. They were tired of hearing about Burning Man, let alone writing about it. But I wasn't. And as long as I had Tim's okay and the basic responsibility to choose how to fill our News & Culture section, I was going to follow this story.

Borg2 is Born

Chicken's Odeon Bar was decked out like a political convention hall for the first official meeting of Borg2 in mid-December. Red, white and blue bunting was strung among the weird burner paraphernalia that hung on the walls. Patriotic music played as the crowd of freaks, malcontents, and the merely curious filled the seats around the room.

Chicken kicked off the session like a cross between a politician and a shyster pitching some kind of pyramid scheme. This was the core group, he explained, the people who would evangelize the message to the masses and build the organization. With tongue firmly in cheek, he asked for $299 each, giving them the chance to "get in on the ground floor."

But this was just the warm-up act, starting things on a light note before turning the mic over to Jim Mason, who actually seemed sincere when he talked about his desire for Borg2 to be like a "well-lubed penetration" of Burning Man. The idea was to become the future and wait for the Borg to get on board.

"We are asking to be exploited for our creativity and innovation," he told the crowd, as if the path to victory was clear and preordained. "We want to make it work and we want to make it work in a form they can steal from us."

With his Stanford University education, Jim was clearly the more earnest of the pair and I could see his influence on the meeting agenda that was passed out. The eight discussion items included an art council, guest curators, voting on the projects, election details, basic brainstorming, and "goals of the Borg2 and this meeting."

But on the flip side of the agenda, that goal was already spelled out: "The goal of the Borg2 is to orchestrate an experiment in radically collaborative and democratic art facilitation as a demonstration project for how the Borg1 might do this better than the current system. If it works, Larry has promised to consider incorporating our success into the Borg1 art process going forward.

"Therefore our goal is to create models and methods that if successful, can be transferred wholesale to the Borg1 and easily ingested without rethinking and reinterpretation. We want to create models, principles, and processes that if successful, are readymade solutions available for easy take up by the Borg1 for future years."

It was as if they really believed that the Burning Man revolution had begun and that they were leading the charge.

What is Counterculture?

The next week, on December 14, the venerable speakers bureau Commonwealth Club of California just happened to be holding a panel discussion entitled "Impact of

Counterculture" featuring Larry Harvey, punk poet Jello Biafra, Wired magazine publisher Louis Rossetto, and Mondo 2000 founder Ken Goffman, aka R.U. Sirius, who had just written a book entitled *Counterculture Through the Ages: From Abraham to Acid House.*"

The serendipitous event seemed to confirm that I was onto something interesting, a thought that was like a comforting balm as Bush talked on television about how well the Iraq War was going and Democrats were blaming San Francisco Mayor Gavin Newsom's decision to issue marriage licenses to same-sex couples for the presidential election defeat. It felt great to be pedaling through San Francisco on my burner bicycle — fake fur basket on the back illuminated with electroluminescent wire, drawing smiles of connection from like-minded pedestrians — at a time like this.

Inside, there was a distinctly burner vibe to the usually staid auditorium, with hip little fashion tells indicating who the burners were. In the lobby, Michael Mikel, aka M2 or Danger Ranger, had set up a table and was selling Burning Man calendars. More serendipity, because just a day or two earlier I learned that he had announced his candidacy for the Borg2 Art Council. He might actually serve on both the hated Borg and its rival Borg2, a strange development that I wasn't sure quite what to make of.

I introduced myself, pulled out my notebook and we started to chat. "I think I can do something to address the issues brought up by Borg2," he told me, adding that he thinks, "there is potential for large scale reinvigoration."

Now, M2 is widely known as a bit of an eccentric. He was one of the originals, part of the "Temple of Three Guys," torn between loyalties to Law and Larry and essentially choosing the latter. But still, he is on the six-member board of the Borg. Why couldn't he address the problems from within? This was a big topic that I decided to get into later with him if he won, but for now, I decided to just keep it light and let him offer a couple thoughts on his bid to help lead the rebels against his own Borg. "It's worth testing, it's worth trying, and I'm willing to put my energy behind that," he told me. Good enough.

Inside the lecture, Goffman ran through the basic premise of his book, defining the elements of the counterculture: anti-authoritarian, nonconformist, free-thinking, changeable, and often marked by irreverent personalities, pranksters. "The prankster aspect is the special sauce of countercultureness," he said, conjuring up an image of Chicken in my mind.

The moderator, journalist Laura Fraser, asked Larry whether Burning Man was a counterculture. He acknowledged that it probably was, but "now we're back toward the mainstream." He was indeed going there, just as I hoped he would. "We're headed back toward it with an eye toward changing things." Law and Chicken would be aghast, but I was starting to believe in this quasi-political mission. Larry explained that Burning Man was becoming an authentic culture, not just a reaction to the larger culture. "And if you're the possessor of real culture, there are great prospects if you're organized."

Yes, that's it, keep going. But instead, it was Rossetto's turn to weigh in and he threw a bucket of cold water on the discussion, saying that the notion of counterculture is dead if it ever existed in the first place, that we're all plugged in and empowered now, so why rebel? What a spoiler! Why the hell did they invite the publisher of a national magazine to this kind of discussion anyway? He's a power broker, not an outsider hungering for authentic culture. Typical Commonwealth Club, had to stick a shill in.

Luckily, Jello Biafra steered the discussion back where it belonged, recounting his transformation from a hippie kid into the punk rocker who would found the legendary Dead Kennedys, in the process illustrating the hippie-punk divide that I was watching play itself out in the Battle of the Borgs.

Punks had the energy that the hippies lacked, Biafra said, "but it took 10 years for punks to want to save the whales." Plus, even when the people can manage to create a real culture that would help the world, it gets coopted by the capitalists who "sell it back to the originators at twice the price."

He had hit on an important theme, the very thing that Burning Man haters say must have happened once the event became stable and expensive, and which the Borg2 rebels feared might happen if the Borg wasn't held accountable. "I think co-option by the mainstream is something that happens in every chapter of the book," Goffman confirmed.

Ah, but there wasn't a chapter on Burning Man. And it's certainly true that Burning Man has been vigilant about fighting off co-option from the very beginning, taking an aggressive and controversial stance on owning all photography shot at the event, banning commerce, and suing corporations that sought to exploit the growing event for commercial reasons.

"The way you prevent that sort of co-option is get good lawyers who work for free," Larry said, arguing hopefully that co-option isn't inevitable. Burning Man had indeed been aggressive in this realm, successfully suing the producers of the "Girls Gone Wild" nudie videos to prevent distribution of footage they had illegally shot at the event. If we're vigilant, Larry said, we can learn from the past and avoid the fates of those who have gone before.

Then he returned to the notion that Burning Man might not be simply a counterculture anymore, arguing "to simply define yourself as counter to the mainstream is juvenile…It's not enough to be counter. You have to come up with a way to generate culture."

And once that happens, as Larry thinks it already has with his event, then there is potential to become an important sociopolitical force. It doesn't just have to be a way of blowing off steam once a year and then you return to the patriarchy. There is the potential, he said, for the "transcendent idea" that will just keep growing.

At one point, Fraser took the group of four men to task for giving short shrift to the role women have played in rebellious cultural movements. After Goffman fumbled to explain why so few women appear in his new book, Larry took a stab at the topic.

It's true, he said, that men have often led counterculture movements like his through their early transgressive phases, when they argue loudly over the vision, rail against the status quo, and blow things up. But by the time Burning Man moved from Baker Beach to the inhospitable Black Rock Desert a few years into its existence, it was the female energy that ensured its survival and sustainability.

"Once we got into the desert," Harvey told the crowd, "the women took over."

Jam for the Ladies

Such feminist concerns were what LadyBee — the Borg's art curator for the last 10 years — wanted to talk to me about, and why she said my Borg2 article wasn't fair to her or to Burning Man. She'd taken time to talk with me and I hadn't used a single quote from her in the article, focusing instead on the very male power struggles.

"Jim and Chicken are really invested in it being a battle, and frankly, we don't see it that way," LadyBee told me. She accused them of sexism in their approach and me of sexism in my presentation, a charge that cut deep into my pro-feminist self-conception, although I held my ground and contested her characterization.

She may very well have been right that her gender was a factor in the animosities that many artists directed at her, but the bigger factor seemed to me to be the fact that she was in charge of administering all the rules — those set up for reasons of safety, protection of the playa from burn scars, and compliance with theme and trademark issues — and with helping choose who gets funded. So she was a natural lightning rod for artists with strong anti-authoritarian streaks.

Charlie, Chicken, and Jim had certainly all slammed her pretty good. Jim told me, "A large cross section of the major artists contributing to this event has a problem with LadyBee's leadership of the art program," while Chicken told me, "There was less art with the same budget. If this were a corporation, the art curator would have been fired on the spot."

LadyBee reluctantly acknowledged their point about the diminished art, but denied that it was a structural problem: "This year, there were less big, ambitious, large scale projects. Frankly, every now and then, you have an off-year."

But she also counter-attacked pretty strongly, accusing them of ignorance — "I come from the art world and can tell you our grant process is easy. There's no other grant program that doesn't ask for slides, for letters of reference, and for receipts." — and of ingratitude: "We give away a quarter-million bucks a year and they still aren't happy."

And most of all, she said they had an enormous sense of entitlement and chips on their shoulders about having to answer to a woman: "I think the fact that I'm the curator and a woman doesn't help in gaining their respect," she said. "They need me to exist in a way. They have to have someone to rebel against because they're a rebellion-based community."

LadyBee was definitely someone who gave as good as she got and seemed to enjoy being able to say "no" to the temperamental artists. Whereas Larry tried to finesse the rebellion and didn't seem to take it personally, LadyBee pushed back in hard and sometimes condescending ways. Right or wrong, the image of her in a golf cart driving around the playa telling artists what they could and couldn't do was a catalyst for the revolt. And after Larry had consented to the Borg2 experiment, LadyBee remained steadfast in her approach.

"Chicken has agreed to go through all the safety rules, which means they have to answer to us," LadyBee told me. "He makes the statement that they won't have to deal with anyone in golf carts. Well, he'll still have to."

When I related that comment to Chicken, he replied, "We will mine it for golf carts."

It was good stuff, but as I struggled to keep my article within its space constraints, it had to go. I wanted to focus on a conflict that raised big existential questions about the nature of Burning Man, not the technical details of administrating art on the playa or on the personality clash between LadyBee and the artists.

Still, she had shamed me. And when she noted how many women were running for the Borg2 Art Council, I agreed that it was interesting and would make a good follow-up article. Besides, it would present another side of the event that countered the big male egos and allow me to use Larry's comments at the Commonwealth Club. So I called many of the women involved in the conflict and for an article I'd called, "Burning Women."

Following Chicken's earlier suggestion, I called Nat the Bat, aka Natalie Schumacher, who had been among the most prolific on the online discussion boards that gave birth to Borg2. She was a 24-year-old sculptor for an erotic bakery in Denver who was planning to fly into San Francisco for the January 5 candidate's forum at the Odeon.

"It's something I feel like I need to do because I've been so vocal," said Nat, who attended Burning Man for the first time in 2004. "I'm not exactly sure how to make it all happen, but I want to help."

Candidate Angela Knowles, a 23-year-old art student, also had just attended the event for the first time after moving to San Francisco in April. "I really want to be a part of making Burning Man a better event for the artists," she told me.

Both women had only vague ideas of how they intended to accomplish their goals, but they shared an idealistic passion for using the forum to pump up the event's artistic offerings. Angela said, "Because this is fresh and new, there is a refurbishing of people's minds to create new and fresh ideas." Within a few months, Angela would decide to pursue those fresh ideas by joining the Flaming Lotus Girls.

"We have the opportunity to vote and participate," Nat told me, "whereas before it was just Larry Harvey's thing."

Statements like this — which imply that Burning Man limits the artistic expressions of attendees — are what Stephanie Selig, aka Serious, had been spending lots of time online trying to correct. "I've just been trying to get the basic information out and to clear up some of these misconceptions," said Serious, a volunteer with the Artery, which facilitates placement of art on behalf of the Borg.

She said the Borg2 rhetoric had masked the fact that anyone can bring art to Burning Man, and that the Borg was simply enforcing rules for reasons of safety (lighting art at night so nobody runs into it), environmental stewardship (preventing fire art from creating burn scars), logistics (scheduling common use of cranes and backhoes), and acclimation to harsh surroundings: "We just try to get people to think about what will happen to their sculptures in 80-mile-per-hour winds."

Such voices of reason and my follow-up article's focus on the women who wanted to ratchet down this conflict irritated Chicken and his Borg2 cohorts, who were still trying to stoke this fire. But the most biting blow came when I related some information that LadyBee had given me about the Flaming Lotus Girls: they were sticking by Larry and the Borg.

Joining the FLG Mafia

Many members of the Flaming Lotus Girls — a high-profile group of mostly female industrial artists — signed the petition that led to the creation of Borg2. The group was talked about as a potential guest curator for Borg2 and featured prominently on its list of artists.

Yet after a lively internal debate, the Flaming Lotus Girls decided to apply for an art grant from the original Borg. "We talked about it and decided that the only thing that mattered was getting more art at Burning Man. It wasn't that tricky of a decision in the end," longtime member Pouneh Mortazavi told me after LadyBee gave me her phone number. "We are planning to apply to both people, even though we know we can't be funded by both people."

And with the Borg awarding its art grants by March 1 — and Borg2 not even closing its application process until April — the Flaming Lotus Girls were likely to remain where they've always been. Yet Pouneh said they may try to do a second project for Borg2 or participate with it in some way.

Like many of the women involved in Burning Man, she said she rejected the notion that the desire to shake things up and rejuvenate the art meant having to choose sides in the grand debate over what Burning Man should be about and how it should be led. "Change is always good, but the Borg is not the evil that Jim and

Chicken portray it to be," Pouneh said, a comment that I published at the time.

It's this sort of nuanced, community-based dialogue that many feel has been overshadowed by the bravado that has been at the heart of the recent conflict and most of the highest-profile battles during Burning Man's 20-year history.

In my interview with Pouneh, we talked about the FLG project: Angel of the Apocalypse, a massive bird with fire-spewing wings, a burning head, and a driftwood sculpture for a project designed by artist Rebecca Anders. It would be the most ambitious project in their five-year history, a fiery gathering place befitting a year with a renewed emphasis on the art, maybe even a phoenix heralding Burning Man's rebirth.

It sounded exciting and I was eager to spend more time with them out at the Box Shop for my series. So I mentioned the idea to her of working with them on it, following it from conception to completion and learning about both them and the creative process along the way.

She was intrigued, but said she'd have to first discuss it with the group and get back to me. Soon, she called me back and told me it was on and that I should come to their next meeting on January 18. After the meeting, there was going to be an election night party for Pouneh's boyfriend, Charlie Gadeken — a Flaming Lotus Girl who owned the Box Shop and had decided to run for the Borg2 board.

I was still pretty ignorant about the Flaming Lotus Girls and fire arts when I showed up at my first meeting. The fire arts can include fire dancing using flaming poi or other fiery toys, but when I use the term, I'm talking about industrial arts using flame effects, something pioneered in the Bay Area, for Burning Man more than any other single catalyst. I knew it involved steel sculptures and propane lines and tanks, but that's about all I knew — and that feeling only got worse as that first meeting progressed. I didn't know what I was doing and would need to just make it up as I went along — taking notes, staying engaged, remaining hopeful that something interesting would emerge in the end.

And I came to find that's basically how Burning Man camps work anyway. Sure, there are always some very capable people. Charlie and Pouneh were super knowledgeable pioneers in the fire arts (although Pouneh had physical limitations: plagued by severe carpal tunnel syndrome, she used a machine that administered electric shocks to her hands during the meeting), and Rebecca's day job was as a professional welder for an exhibit company in town.

All three were experienced artists, as anyone could tell from scanning their warehouse-like home, its walls and corners filled with groovy art pieces that they and their friends had created. And there was lots of other expertise among the dozen Flaming Lotus Girls at the table, from Hazmatt's materials engineering expertise to Kezia's art school background to Colinne's organizational abilities to Tamara Li's, well…she was like the walking embodiment of the beautiful countercultural artist.

Still, they were still just making shit up from scratch, hoping it would work, trying to expand their connections and web of associates along the way, filling their pool of knowledge and resourcefulness. People need a purpose, even San Franciscans leery of paths cut by nationalist, professional, or theological concerns. So we pursue projects — political, social, or artistic — sometimes just to see them done, so our time and passions have an outlet of our choosing, so we can be part of something bigger than ourselves.

This project was their purpose that year. They had the basic idea, and a name from Rebecca's unsuccessful art grant application a few years earlier, but everything was still on the table. They brainstormed a new name for the project: Psycho Chicken (laughs all around), Ascension, Hot Wings, Hellbird, Ornith. No consensus yet, so they'd just start with Angel of the Apocalypse on the Burning Man art grant application that was due February 15th.

Nicola at the meeting challenged whether the beak should be straight as planned. She thought it should be raptor-like, with curved ends for tearing. Both Charlie and Rebecca argued that the straight lines worked better on the artistic level. "It's important that we maintain a focus on the abstract shape," Rebecca said, noting that she didn't want it to be too literal. They wanted that same ambiguity as to whether the bird was crashing into the playa or rising from it.

A small-scale sculpture of the project that Rebecca made when she conceived it years ago was on the wall of the apartment and we all checked it out. But the ideas for what to do with it, and what scale to use, have blossomed.

"Just in the last couple weeks, the project has doubled in complexity," Rebecca said.

At that point, they talked about seeking a grant for $18,000, which would grow to $24,440 by the time it was turned in. As the time for the election party neared, the meeting began to break up, but not before Rebecca and Pouneh welcomed me to the group and informed me of the Mafia clause: "Once we have you, we don't let you go."

Art, Danger, and Democracy

Charlie was irritated with Chicken. The face-off between the two friends occurred shortly after Chicken arrived for the election party. Halfway through two days of voting for the new Borg2 art council, Charlie was the leading vote getter.

Chicken and Jim had guided Borg2 through the birthing process, and facilitated meetings at the Odeon Bar about what to do next, but then they essentially walked away from any official role. Chicken in particular was far more interested in the provocation than the follow-through, leaving Charlie and others to make it all work, win the bet, and conquer the Borg.

Beyond the logistics, which were tough enough, Charlie and company would need to deal with this experiment's many conflicts and paradoxes: anarchist artists engaged in representative democracy, how to participate in an event whose framework they were rejecting, art simultaneously selected by elected guest curators and a popular vote, serious organizational and fundraising issues facing people who were only serious about art.

Charlie's frustration with Chicken seemed to epitomize the problem. He was mad about Chicken's "dancing and whooping with shit in his pants" story. A day earlier, in one of his last official acts before turning his Borg2 baby over to democratic control, Chicken was allowed access to the 33,000 people on Burning Man's Jack Rabbit Speaks e-mail list.

Borg2 needed money if it was going to get anywhere close to its $250,000 fundraising goal. It needed volunteers and the participation of top-tier artists. And it needed to speak eloquently to a larger audience that hadn't heard about any of this through San Francisco newspapers or the Tribe and E-Playa online discussion boards.

Instead, Chicken chose to tell a strange tale from Burning Man's past about an artist whose project was such a miserable failure that he went fetal in his tent and shit himself during the night, only to have others turn his parts and pieces into a beautiful blinking windmill. When the guy arose to discover what happened, he started "dancing and whooping with shit in his pants," an unsettling image that Chicken tried to turn into a Borg2 mantra of sorts, like his earlier promise to bring more "woo woo for Larry's hoo ha."

Chicken let the story stand as a sort of enigmatic parable, not really bringing it back to anything tangible or helpful to Borg2's plight. It was pure Chicken — offbeat, punk rock, a strange but engaging piece of art. It was memorably unknowable, like much of what Chicken creates.

But to Charlie, it was just a blown opportunity, a squandered chance to rally support. After all, Charlie and company had just months to raise the money and build from scratch a structure for getting great art out to the remote and inhospitable Black Rock Desert, something Larry is still honing 20 years later, even with his built-in funding supply.

To accomplish that task, Charlie had to rely on an often-combative crew of counterculture freaks, temperamental artists, grungy welders and wrenches, mad geniuses, gutter punks, wannabe Warhols, young dreamers, and other too-proud individualists — who all feel entitled to help guide the process and vote on the results.

Charlie — a resourceful leader who ran the Box Shop and was a key FLG member — embodied the best hopes of Borg2, but its continuum ran roughly from the super-organized Network Girl to the downright dangerous New York City-based Madagascar Institute — which was elected to the guest curator position — with Michael Mikel sort of circling the group in his own orbit.

As more than one person has told me, Charlie could probably handle this all by himself, rather than being one of "the Nine." He has the artistic eye, the facilities, and the connections, a quietly capable, no-nonsense guy, although a bit curmudgeonly.

Since the election, he's worked closely with Network Girl, a.k.a. Jeanavive Janssen, in pushing things forward. She's the founder of www.thenetworkgirl.com, which helps artists network, share resources, and do their thing, a similar role to the one she's playing on the art council.

"It's just another avenue for me to express myself and help artists," she told me. But she quickly learned that the many paradoxes and contradictions of Borg2 would make their difficult task nearly impossible. After all, many took Chicken's "radically participatory democracy" rhetoric seriously. And they come from an anarchic DIY philosophical tradition in which there is little use for hierarchy.

Borg2 tweaked this sensibility just a bit by placing people in positions of responsibility, and Network Girl felt that weight probably more acutely than most of her colleagues on the council. She knows that all the many tasks must be completed immediately because projects are already underway, and Burning Man was just six months away, telling me, "There are going to be artists waiting for the money."

Then there's Michael, a legendary figure in Burning Man history, founder of the Black Rock Rangers and now a board member of both the Borg and Borg2. It was a strange role for this eccentric but engaging character. "Michael is like a helium balloon," Larry told me after expressing mild irritation at Michael's new role with Borg2. "If someone forgets to hold his string, he soars up into the stratosphere."

Michael sees it differently. "One of the things I do is push the envelope," he told me, and that's what he was doing. "If the experiment fails, it will just be another Black Rock City theme camp," Michael told me. "But if it succeeds, Borg2 will be the Burning Man renaissance."

Bringing Back the Fear

Much of what motivated the Borg2 rebellion was a longing for an idealized Burning Man past that was less structured and more chaotic, where there were explosions and gunfire and utter madness in the air and the whole experience made you a little scared, and maybe even left you scarred, figuratively or literally. That's what the Madagascar Institute represented to many Borg2 backers.

Madagascar is a New York-based art collective whose motto is "fear is never boring." Whether doing guerrilla performance art on big-city streets or building crazed carnival rides and exploding installation pieces at festivals around the world, Madagascar had cultivated a reputation as street artists on the edge.

In fact, Madagascar Institute had broken ties with Burning Man a few years earlier, with Madagascar founder Hackett coming to hate the event. Larry recalls actually fearing for his safety during a confrontation with Hackett in 2002. But many of the Borg2 folks were still tight with Madagascar, which lent artists Dirty Doyle and

Rosanna Scimeca to the cause of helping them.

"We're trying to make it a little more dangerous and a little more chaotic, scaring people back to life" was how Doyle described their goal for Burning Man. "Try to help people push their own boundaries."

Even though they were elected as guest curators, there are constraints on the ability of Doyle and Scimeca to implement their artistic vision, the main one being the fact that a central tenet of Borg 2's creation was how all its participants would theoretically be able to vote on what art projects the group funds.

"There are ways around democracy. Just ask Karl Rove," Doyle told me. His goal was to package the choices for what should be funded in ways that allow voters to just validate much of what Scimeca and Doyle bring in — like more outside artists and performance pieces.

Most of all, they want to walk the edge. They love the image of the mad artist. "Drive yourself crazy, and your crazy personality becomes an art piece," Scimeca told me. Doyle smiled and added, "Let the monster out of the box."

Borg2 itself was as much a work of art as it was a political movement by artists who had some gripes. It was the creative plaything of these same artists, as became clear at its first fundraiser party, held at The Shipyard. And because Larry had apparently told someone that Borg2 would only be a success when pigs fly, soaring swine became a kind of theme.

The February 5, 2005 party was filled with cool burner art: a remote-controlled, rapidly spinning electronic ball that shot long flames in two diagonal directions, a flying pink pig built on an electric wheelchair base that shot fireballs into the air, a calliope constructed on a washing machine, and other random pieces by Shipyard artists.

But this was a scene built around a centerpiece: two flying, fucking, burning pigs. Their bodies were built of bent rebar, chicken wire, and propane gas lines. They were stuffed with newspaper wrapped around bundles of donated coins, soaked in lard, with some bacon and fireworks thrown in for good measure. The heads were actual pig heads mounted on metal bars, and the top pig had hinged hips and a huge drill for a cock.

As midnight approached, a wild-haired Jim Mason drove the forklift and suspended the pigs from their beams, while Mateo, an Extra Action Marching Band member who was the unofficial jester of the Borg2 court, hung off the back of the forklift jabbering creative gibberish into a megaphone.

It was quite a scene in this grungy, outdoor work space. The fireball whirled, people drank beer and bacon Bloody Marys, the Tanglers taught square dancing lessons, and a guy wearing an Army helmet kept encouraging people to smash him over the head with a two-by-four, harder, harder.

The pigs were finally put into place, and the crowd of hundreds gathered around them, tossing spare change into the pigs, at each other, and especially hard at Mateo. Large barrels were placed below the pigs, then sheet metal was laid over those, with microphones placed underneath to amplify the melodious falling of coins from the burning pigs.

As the excitement built, the pigs started passionately drilling each other as they were doused with more fuel squirted from a fertilizer can. A half-dozen people used their lighters to help Mason get his long torch going, and the pigs were set ablaze.

The various gas lines on the pigs started shooting flames out of several key spots, including the tip of the top pig's cock. Fireworks exploded. When most of the combustibles were spent and the charred innards began to settle, Mason grabbed a shovel and started beating the pigs and the sheet metal, with others joining in to poke and beat the pigs into fully consuming their insides and freeing all the change. The ritual seemed dutiful at first, then percussively joyful, a venting of the buildup, a launch into something new and exciting.

Or as Mason put it to me, "We're having fun with Burning Man again."

Manifesting Back Home

I was also starting to have fun with Burning Man. Every Wednesday night, I went to the Box Shop to record the Flaming Lotus Girls' progress and learn the fire arts, and then I'd use my free time to dive into and learn about other aspects of this fascinating, multi-pronged burner culture.

While Jim and Chicken saw the artists in their orbit as the main attraction of Burning Man — and they decried the influx of the "ravers" as ruining their event — the music scene was reflecting Burning Man's style back in San Francisco more than anything. And Larry, who was no fan of the dance camps, poo-pooed the grand division proffered by the Borg2 crowd.

"In any case, the perception that the ravers have taken over was a myth to begin with. It's bosh," Larry told me in early 2005. "They are attracting people who love the event and like to dance to that music. That's okay. It's a big playa."

At the Get Freaky event in mid-January, the line outside 1015 Folsom stretched around the block, though most of the Burning Man types were already inside, decked out in playa-inspired getups, grooving solo or with their tribes to drippy breakbeats, ass-shaking electronic bass lines, and soaring crescendos.

The lineup included Freq Nasty, Krafty Kuts and A Skills, Lorin, Smoove, Adam Ohana (who puts on the Get Freaky events), Dimitri, Ooah the Turntablist, and other DJs; live Indian music; fire spinners in Mad Max finery; acrobats and circus freaks from Xeno, El Circo, and other local artists' collectives; and performance artists of all stripes.

It was a scene transplanted to San Francisco clubland directly from Burning Man, where all the featured DJs had made names for themselves among tens of thousands of Bay Area residents, as well as far-flung burner tribes like the Freak Factory from New

York and Clan Destino in Santa Barbara — represented that night among the crowd at Get Freaky.

Tribe.net and other electronic burner gathering places had been buzzing for weeks over the DJ lineup. Freq Nasty, a dreadlocked breaks DJ from the UK, had spun at some of the earliest Burning Man dance camps. Berkeley-based Bassnectar's epic performances on burn night (when the eponymous icon gets torched) had elevated him to a DJ god with an international following, while up-and-comer Ooah — mixing his breakbeat grooves with well-placed samples from other big names on hand — rocked the front room at 1015 to a bouncing frenzy rarely seen outside the main room.

During the Burning Man theme-camp fundraiser season that runs from around May through August, there are parties like this almost every weekend, from illegal ones in warehouses to legit functions in the biggest clubs in town — sometimes several a night. Among the San Francisco-based camps lighting up the scene then were El Circo, Opulent Temple, Sound of Mind, Space Cowboys, The Deep End, and House of Lotus.

The draw and energy of the Get Freaky party stood as a testament to the growing year-round influence Burning Man and its participants have on San Francisco nightlife. The vibe was felt everywhere from venues like 1015, Mighty, Nickie's BBQ, and Sublounge to street fairs like How Weird and Decompression, from art spaces like SomArts Cultural Center and CELLspace to random warehouses around SoMa and Potrero Hill.

It wasn't always like this. The rave scene that was the forerunner to the burner-influenced dance scene was slow to be accepted in Black Rock City, as I came to learn in my interviews, while the culture that has developed around the event was separate and distinct from urban clubland.

But as Burning Man grew from a few thousand souls back in the mid-'90s to more than 35,000 in 2004 — with by far the most participants coming from the Bay Area — the scenes have merged and morphed, symbiotically feeding off one another to create something entirely new under the sun.

Even though the entire Burning Man culture hadn't fully embraced this world of sound, it was becoming an increasingly important component of the event, particularly as the artists became more ambitious. The Borg has promised to bump up their art funding, but whenever someone needed to raise real money or throw a great party, they still turned to the DJs and sound camps.

And sound camps were becoming solid tribes with real staying power and the ability to use their communities for new ventures, such as opening cool businesses in San Francisco and other cities, as the Deep Enders did in 2005.

"The Deep End spirit is still very much alive in many of us," DJ Clarkie said, noting how he and others pitched in both time and money to help the three Hosley brothers and Chef Ben — all original Deep Enders — open the restaurant Sauce and then the club Shine in San Francisco in 2005.

"We got lots of help for Sauce from our friends, who are our camp members, then Shine was 100 percent financed through people with Deep End connections," Trip Hosley told me, saying the effort was a great real world manifestation of the Burning Man ethos and community.

Just before leaving for Burning Man in 2005, Trip said that he and his brothers were finally given the opportunity to lease a great club space on San Francisco's Mission Street that they'd been pursuing for months, agreeing to the lease before they even knew how they'd come up with the required money. And while on the playa that year, Clarkie and several other Deep Enders with a bit of savings agreed to contribute their money and time to the project.

"A bunch of people helped build out the place — some for many weeks, some just dropped by to help paint a little. Everyone was supportive and wanted to be part of it," Deep Ender John Garner said of the opening of Sauce. "There is a similar story for Shine. In this case, the Sauce boys invited their friends to be investors. About 10 different people invested $10,000 each in the club. All of the investors had credits to use for food and drinks at both Sauce and Shine. Shine was a big hit and the Sauce guys repaid all the investors in full. There is still a plaque on the wall at Shine with all of their names on it."

It was a great manifestation of the can-do energy that was swirling through the Burning Man world, where people were using the connections and know-how developed on the playa back in the default world. "We definitely always want to bring that feeling of brotherly love giving back here in the city to these places of business but also the many parties/events we co-hosted or were a part of," Clarkie said later. "We are also applying for our non-profit 501c3 status so that The Deep End can continue to have events, but that our proceeds can go more for truly giving back to this amazing community we are all a part of — be it Burning Man, San Francisco or the world."

Deep Ender Christian Galindo said the businesses and nonprofit were natural extensions for a community that had grown strong and deep during their annual treks to Black Rock City: "This idea would be a natural evolution of The Deep End, from 'gifting' exclusively at Burning Man, to 'gifting' in the broader sense throughout the year."

In the Beginning...

The Flaming Lotus Girls' Wednesday night meetings started slowly, just a couple hours to discuss their grant proposals to Burning Man, Robodoc, and the Fire Arts Festival staged by The Crucible in Oakland; plans to buy a new welder and get some company to donate a couple plasma cutters (which use a beam of energy to cut even the thickest steel) to this "women's educational organization"; schedule fundraisers like their March 18th photo show and party at Dogpatch Studios; and to get the shop ready for work that would become a chaotic daily endeavor.

They taught me how to be one of their minions, a term they used affectionately, as I came to learn. One evening as we watched a video from a previous project, there was footage of a guy steadily pounding a large stake into the ground during a blinding dust storm, as Pouneh had instructed, prompting her to fondly recall, "he was a good minion." She was always looking for good minions.

"Everyone spend 10 minutes sorting nuts and bolts tonight," Pouneh Mortazavi told the group one evening, looking first at me and waiting for me to nod my ascent before turning her gaze to the next minion. "If we can sort all our nuts and bolts, we can save hundreds of dollars," reinforced Charlie Gadeken.

They took stock of their tools and other equipment, which the Flaming Lotus Girls mark with pink paint or tape. Charlie showed me how it works one day, borrowing my lighter and walking me over to a shop cabinet as we talked about the group's powers of "Obtainium," that element important to cash-poor Burning Man artists, the ability to procure stuff for free. He found a role of pink tape and applied a strip to my lighter, thus appropriating it for the Flaming Lotus Girls. "That's how we got a third of our tools," he told me with a smile.

The routine changed by the March 9th meeting, which was charged with a new excitement because the Flaming Lotus Girls had just learned that they were getting one of the biggest-ever (at least at that point) Burning Man grants: $23,000, funding everything they asked for except stickers and fireworks, which they would find a way to pay for themselves (a month later, the Hand of God would also be accepted at the Robodoc Festival, meaning they would have to simultaneously refurbish it for an event taking place in Europe just two weeks after Burning Man).

Rebecca Anders led the discussion, dividing the Angel of the Apocalypse project up into four main areas: head ("a cool fire-spitting furnace"), body ("this awesome, bizarre, unknown thing"), wings (which will envelope a project that "is a place as much as a thing, maybe more of a place than a thing"), and systems ("its veins and nerves"). And to coordinate the groups and make sure the project is moving forward, Rebecca and Charlie would be, as she said, "in charge of the logic."

Although we would be free to float among the groups, we all volunteered for one of the body parts — each of us subtly encouraged into one group or another by Rebecca, Pouneh, or Charlie, who worked the room so deftly that it didn't seem coordinated, like I had freely chosen to be on the head team.

At this early stage, it was just a core group of a dozen that would steadily grow over the coming months with new additions and visits by old veterans until the Flaming Lotus Girls became bigger than it's ever been, with many minions available to enhance their reputation for being on the very cutting edge of the fire arts scene.

"It has evolved into this ridiculously huge thing from just a bunch of girls at CELLspace," Tamara said.

The story of the Flaming Lotus Girls really starts in 1992 when Charlie attended his first Burning Man with his best friend, Dave X, who later became the fire safety director of Burning Man, in charge of making sure all the seemingly dangerous fire contraptions on the playa are soundly built.

Charlie was a painter back then, doing massive artworks out on the playa — over 500,000 square feet of printed imagery by his estimate — that he would burn at the end of Burning Man. He called it the Illumination Project, part of the camp he founded where he, most of the Flaming Lotus Girls, and many other artists still camp: Illumination Village. Dave got into the fire arts, an insular community that grew mostly out of the Survival Research Laboratories, with its disciples going off to form groups like The Crucible and Lightning on Demand.

In the late '90s, Dave and artist Jim Mason started building flame-throwers for Burning Man as part of what they called the Impotence Compensation Project. Back in San Francisco, most of the group was working out of CELLspace, where Charlie was living and being taught metal fabrication skills by three of his friends: welder Steve Monahan, shop manager Kevin "Tony" Fifield, and Rebecca, a CELLspace board member and artist in residence.

In 2000, Dave X had the idea of creating a female-dominated fire arts group with many of the women he knew that were becoming interested in the fire arts, including Pouneh, B'anna, Lynn, and Tamara (Tasha Berg also joined at the last minute, as I'll explain shortly), along with Charlie. Dave wanted to call the group "Professor X and the Flaming Vixens," but the girls rejected the idea, instead taking their name from their first project, the fire-spewing flower they called Flaming Lotus.

Charlie moved out of CELLspace and into The Shipyard in Berkeley, an industrial art space he formed with Mason in 2001. The next year, with help from burner artist Dan Das Mann, Charlie and Tony opened the Box Shop in an industrial space on Hunter's Point that was first built back in the '60s by the Hells Angels.

As the Flaming Lotus Girls moved with Charlie, Dave X has mostly moved on to other projects, although he still visits and helps out the Flaming Lotus Girls as needed. Steve and Tamara, who have worked on every Flaming Lotus Girls project, had become these sort of elder statespersons, not as directly involved with Angel of the Apocalypse as the top trinity or even many of the newbies, but still making important contributions, often by parachuting in to solve problems or play the voice of reason and experience.

"I've been cutting with a torch for 27 years. My daddy was a welder," Steve told me one day, explaining how his grandfather started American Welding in Ventura in 1928 and showing me pictures of their welding trucks parked at Port Hueneme, where they would sometimes fix the huge ships. But he also had the eye of an artist, as he showed time and again, from teaching the Flaming Lotus Girls to make steel roses to sell at a fundraiser to crafting beautifully detailed birds of paradise from steel and copper.

"So he's good at helping us no matter what the problem," Rebecca said of Steve, while Tamara told me, "Steve is the Flaming Lotus Girls MVP."

Yet he also had some other traits that would prove problematic, such as an impatience with women doing things slowly or the wrong way and a tendency to push back when Charlie or Tony pushed him to clean up his work area or rein in the many projects he would take on, which sometimes dominated the busy shop nearly as much as the Flaming Lotus Girls.

In other words, as central a figure as Steve was at the Box Shop, there was also a tension in the relationship that would come to a head later that summer. But it wasn't the only point of conflict that was developing in the mostly close and harmonious relationships among the Flaming Lotus Girls.

Birds of a Feather

There are a few paradoxes on which the Flaming Lotus Girls are built. They're an exclusive group that is open to all. Most members are amateurs, but the group is regarded as envelope-pushing experts in the fire arts community. All decisions are made by consensus of the group, except those made unilaterally by small groups for reasons of time, money, expertise, or art.

Perhaps the most interesting is the fact that a third or more of the Flaming Lotus Girls are men. And yet, despite the very macho nature of the industrial arts, the Flaming Lotus Girls retain a distinctly female energy. It is a safe, nurturing environment that encourages people to try new things and work through problems no matter what time pressures may be bearing down on the group.

"It's always ladies first in the shop," Tasha told me one evening. "If a girl is taking a long time to cut something with a torch, that's okay. It's not about just getting it done. It doesn't matter if they're taking a long time."

Her words would ring in my ears a few weeks later when a small subgroup of us was cutting out steel sections of the head. I had recently learned to use the plasma cutter, an awesome tool that slices through steel like butter, and I was anxious to use it on the thick pieces of steel for the base of the head so I blurted out a "me, me, me" when Rebecca asked who wanted to cut first.

Another male newbie and I cut the steel while the women did some grinding and other tasks. Very tactfully, Rebecca approached me after a little while to ask about giving the girls a chance to cut and I immediately realized what I'd done and felt like the pushy man that I was, quickly turning over the cutter and apologizing to all for my transgression. I could picture Tasha, with her dreadlocked hair, tattooed arms, and pierced nostrils and labret, telling me "ladies first."

Tasha is a strong woman — physically and in spirit — but not a forceful one.

She smiles more than most people and loves to pop off funny, saucy one-liners, like when the first feather fired up and she said, "Oh, it made my nipple hard," or when the head group added two days to its schedule and she quipped, "Yay, head three times a week!"

She's grounded in the way that massage therapists often are. That's what she does for a living and it's what she was doing at a resort in Hawaii when she first met Charlie, Pouneh, and Dave X, who were there on vacation.

Tasha was excited to hear Charlie talk about Burning Man, which she'd heard about and was dying to attend. "I said, 'I wanna go to Burning Man! And he said, 'honey, we are Burning Man.'" And thus, Tasha became a Flaming Lotus Girl, flying out to spend a few days at CELLspace working on the first project and then going with them to the playa. She moved to San Francisco six months later.

Tasha was new to the art world, but took to metal work like a natural and decided that she wanted to help design the faces of the Angel's feathers, something that Kezia Zichichi also wanted to work on. The two women had different styles: Tasha was the gregarious and carefree riot grrl while Kezia was more the deliberate and cerebral artist.

Kezia attended art school and started going to Burning Man in the late '90s, and then became the house manager and events coordinator at CELLspace. "The most incredible events and arts came through there," she told me, "everything you could imagine." She liked what Dave X was trying to do, noting "he created a lot of the culture."

At the April 6th meeting, Kezia unveiled her feather designs, which she made with a series of stencils that she said she'd fashioned from studying real feathers. She explained how the positioning and negative space formed abstract images of birds and angels, which the group tried to see but hung up on the fact that they weren't very symmetrical or feather-like.

"First of all, they can't cross over like that because a feather has a fucking spine up the middle," Charlie said as Rebecca, Tamara, and Tasha tried to put a softer, more diplomatic edge of the critique.

"I think we should take this input, work on it some more, and come back," Tamara suggested.

The next week, both Tasha and Kezia showed up with feather designs: Tasha's were simple, symmetrical designs done on a computer and printed on letter-sized paper; Kezia's were more detailed, ornate, full-sized hand drawings done on long lengths of brown paper that she unfurled in the shop.

"Should we vote on it or something?" Kezia suggested, seeming confident in her designs.

But others had some issues with her designs. Steve said both designs were cutting away too much of the steel, which was wasteful, while Tamara offered to help Kezia widen the margins on the edge for easier welding and better structural integrity.

"Let's just call it a work in progress," Tamara said, but Kezia was looking for a mandate from the group. Rebecca suggested that Kezia, Tamara, and Tasha collaborate on the design, but Kezia replied, "No, I'd rather just have a bunch of stuff and vote on them, like we do the stickers."

"I think we should still talk about it and not know right now," Tamara said, reflecting the consensus of the group.

"At some point," Rebecca said of the conflict that was just beginning, "y'all need to come up with a design."

The Melding of Metals

Rebecca offered everybody welding lessons in the spring, encouraging rookies to attend at least two of the three consecutive weekend sessions she offered with Steve's help. But my first lesson was a private session with her March 12th.

Her love of steel was infectious. I had never worked with metal, not even in a shop class growing up, but her descriptions resonated with me. Hook a negative charge to the objects you want to join or the steel table on which they rest. Hold the MIG welder close but not touching. Pull the trigger to activate the positive charge, creating a powerful arc of energy that melts the edges of your surfaces and the steel wire being fed by the welder, creating a puddle of molten steel protected from dust and other contamination by a heavy gas that the welder exhales as the steel cools back into solid form.

"It's an organic experience," Rebecca said, one in which you move slowly and patiently to create the perfect bead of new metal.

Rebecca confirmed my observation that the hardest part is trying to keep my hand and the welding wand poised in the right position as I nod my welding hood into position, plunging me into darkness until I pull the trigger and let the energy illuminate my work, which that day included making steel roses that we'd sell at the next week's fundraiser.

My mom used to solder stained glass pieces together when I was a kid, but Rebecca explained that welding is different from soldering in one important respect. The seam created by soldering is like glue, the weak spot desperately trying to hold different objects together. Welding melds the two surfaces, swirling their different properties together into an amalgam that is entirely new, making them stronger than what came before.

It struck me as the ideal metaphor for the Flaming Lotus Girls.

Fire and Steel

All the planning and preparation by the FLGs turned into actual work with fire, steel and wood just as Daylight Savings Time began, giving the shop a cleaner and brighter feel during the evening gatherings. The people and the place were being transformed. New heads began to emerge.

When the first small-scale models of Angel's head appeared in the shop in April — three versions, built of cardboard and aluminum by Rebecca and Hazmatt — all had the curved beak of a raptor, rather than the straight beak Rebecca originally advocated for. "Yeah," she confessed, "I got talked into it."

Soon, a huge section of the yard was cleared for longtime Burning Man artist Pepe Ozan to build Dreamer, a massive human head sunk down to its nose that Larry Harvey had commissioned for prominent placement between the Man and the Temple, planning to surround it with Angel of the Apocalypse and other fire sculptures. The Dreamer's expressive eyes would grow more detailed each week, watching over the scene at the Box Shop.

From April through June, the project seemed to move forward quickly. Inside the shop, the small Angel's head was turned into a full-scale cardboard model, with its individual sections becoming the patterns that would be used to cut the steel. When most of the Flaming Lotus Girls first saw the massive head at the May 18th meeting, 10 feet tall from neck to the tip of the beak, its beak was drooping in half. "The only bad part," Rebecca said, "is our beak went limp."

The group batted around some impotence jokes, but Rebecca was showing a few signs of wilting herself. She got a cell phone for the first time specifically for this project and it kept interrupting her day job of steel and aluminum fabrication. She'd found herself working on the project everyday handling its various details, from mediating the feather design dispute and other personality issues to materials decisions to coordinating the delivery of steel and how it would be cut (she had wanted the wings to be cut by a computer-driven system at a special shop but later bowed to fiscal realities and group dynamics to cut it by hand using the new plasma cutter that Pouneh had gotten donated).

Back in March, Rebecca was feeling phat. "We have an obscene sized grant to make this thing," she said then. "It's just a huge amount and I don't think we're going to have any problems." But now, the budget was getting tighter after steel prices shot up by 40 percent in just a couple months. And that situation was made all the worse by the group's decision to buy stainless steel for the wings, which is more expensive and heavier than the mild steel they usually work with, but which doesn't turn into the rusty mess that some of the past projects have become. It was partly a decision that they want the Angel's wings to endure and be available for future shows, just like the Hand of God.

"Once you start welding stainless," Steve told a skeptical Tamara one evening, trying to sound sexy, "you'll never go back."

One other stressor on Rebecca was also a blessing: there were a huge number of new Flaming Lotus Girls, drawn to the group through friends, last year's Fire Arts Festival, the fundraiser the group held in March, and just by the Flaming Lotus Girls' growing fame within the Burning Man world. It was more of a management challenge, but they also had enough people to work on the project just about every day as the various subgroups started convening on different days.

They were discovering what I already had, something that I thought rookie Jordana Joseph put very well one evening: "You get sucked in. You give them your money, your time, anything they ask. They're the Flaming Lotus Girls."

Best of all for the group, several of the rookies knew what they were doing. Sarah had a woodworking background that she seemed to easily translate into cutting and welding the feather frames with Michael and they were already cranking them out at a rapid clip by mid-May.

"Two to three people can do one in an hour," she told the group during the May 18 meeting, adding a piece of counterintuitive truth that all the Flaming Lotus Girls veterans recognized. "If you have more, it takes longer."

Rosa Anna De Filippis and Caroline Miller (aka Mills), British friends new to both Burning Man and the Flaming Lotus Girls, seemed to fit in so naturally, had shop experience, and were such quick studies at learning to build the plumbing for the fire effects (learning from Tamara, Lynn, and Pouneh) that the Flaming Lotus Girls were testing the inner feather fire effects ahead of schedule.

"It's different every year. One thing about this year is the rookies have skills," Tamara told me. "Rosa Anna and Mills are the rookies of the year."

The meeting of May 18th was kept fairly short so everyone could get working (including the iron-on Flaming Lotus Girls T-shirt logos that veteran Nicola was making for people), but most dropped what they were doing as it got dark and Mills and the fire effects crew prepared for their first big test.

Charlie and Pouneh had gotten all dressed up and left for an evening wedding, but everyone else was excited to poof a big fireball up into the air above the Box Shop. Steve cautioned that neither Charlie nor the shop neighbors were going to like it but the ball was already in motion. Nothing could get between the girls and their fire.

The feather's long ambient flame was working fine, but something was wrong with the poofer, the term given to propane accumulation chambers that pressurize the flammable gas and then quickly release it to create a fireball. They tinkered with it as about 15 of us stood around, talking, sipping our beers, the anticipation building. Finally, they got it; Tamara did the countdown, pushed the button and then, "POOOOFFFFFF!!!," a massive fireball mushrooming maybe 30 feet into the air.

"That's a pretty impressive poof," said John, a veteran of the group, as Charlie walked out of the darkness of the yard's entrance, all clean shaven (a rare occurrence) in his white linen jacket and black dress pants, a well-dressed Pouneh on his arm. In a voice mixing irritation with amusement, he declared, "Half that poof would have been fine."

Birth of an Angel

Crews of Flaming Lotus Girls started making beach treks in May and filling corners of the yard with driftwood that would form the angel's body. The head design was done and its steel was being cut. The shop rafters were being filled with feather frames. And the feathers were beginning to poof. But they still didn't have skins yet because of the lingering dispute over design.

Much of the problem was legitimate creative differences that illustrated the difficulties of large groups trying to create art. But some of it was personality driven because, as Kezia told me in late April, "I'm really intimidated by Tasha."

So others in the group — Rebecca, Lynn, Tamara, Colinne — tried to mediate the conflict while delicately tip-toeing around the sensibilities on both sides and assuring the rest of the group that this was a healthy and normal process. But frustrations were starting to bubble up, like when Kezia bristled at input from Tamara and said to others, "I don't know why she's picking on me."

By late May, the group began to conclude that a division of design labor was the answer: Tasha would design the inner feathers and Kezia would do the outer, both in consultation with the group. Tasha's designs had been embraced for the most part, causing Kezia to tell the group, "My designs aren't incorporated, how can we be at that point? We haven't even worked collaboratively yet."

Rebecca tried to be diplomatic. "Well," she said sheepishly, searching for what to say, "we will work collaboratively."

But when Kezia — fuming cross-armed in her camo pants — kept pushing, Rebecca departed slightly from the uber-patient approach that was her hallmark, a hint of frustration sneaking into her voice for the first time I'd heard it as she said, "I don't want to talk about it in the group right now because we already have a breakout group."

Later in the evening, Tamara was itchy to get more involved in the project, at which Rebecca asked her, "Where do you want more input?"

"Well, I don't want to input more drama," she replied.

But the feather design drama was winding down, at least in the group setting. At the June 15th meeting, Tasha announced that the patterns (which were being hand cut into long plastic banners to use as guides) were almost done and the cutting of the steel faces for the inner feathers would begin the next day.

Kezia soon stopped coming to the Wednesday meetings and didn't return until early August, although she was still as active as any of the Flaming Lotus Girls, working closely with Charlie to refurbish the Hand of God for Robodoc and the Fire Arts Festival and honing her design of the outer feathers.

Meanwhile, Angel's body was starting to take shape in the yard as summer set in, the team led largely by an unlikely Flaming Lotus Girl, a then-62-year-old rookie named James Stauffer. He had been a literature graduate student back in the '60s before going back to land to work in collectives in the forests of Oregon and Washington. Building a huge structure out of nothing but driftwood and bolts was "a chance to use the skills I had developed out in the forests."

When I first climbed onto the body, I was amazed at how strong it was, but to James and another experienced rookie named Phil Spitler, who was working on the body, it was simple geometry. "It's a triangle," Phil deadpanned. "Triangles are strong."

James moved to San Francisco in 1986, selling newspaper ads and running in literary circles before switching gears and being drawn to Burning Man events, struck hardest by the Flaming Lotus Girls at 2004's Fire Arts Festival, where he made contacts and decided to join them in 2005. As hip and sexy as this female-dominated group is, James' energies fit right in and all have embraced him as one of their own.

For his part, James only grew more impressed by the group as the months wore on: "The most interesting thing about the Flaming Lotus Girls is how they manage conflict." While they smooth over interpersonal conflicts, the Flaming Lotus Girls like to create artistic and mechanical conflicts for themselves. That's part of the fun. For example, Rebecca didn't know exactly how we would be placing a gentle curve in the 3/16-inch steel to form a bird's head, but together we began the process of figuring it out on June 22nd, with occasional oversight from Steve.

"Where's your tangent?" he asked the two of us as we started to slip a long skinny piece of steel into the hydraulic press. "Tangent?" Rebecca replied, launching Steve off into a lecture on geometry and physics and advising us to "count our clicks" so we knew how much each bend bent. Using the unwieldy machine, Rebecca and I spent over two hours and considerable energy to put a jerky curve in the smallest piece. Clearly, we would need to find a better way.

The next week, a half-dozen of us puzzled through the problem. The bigger pieces of steel wouldn't even fit into this press. Could we use weight? Heat? Finally, Steve mentioned that he had a more portable hydraulic press. "Would it move that piece of steel if we put a proper die on the end?" Rebecca asked. Steve nodded quietly and said a simple, "Yes."

So we searched the shop to find the pieces and parts we'd need: a chain, a long pipe, metal pieces to weld and cut into clamps. The idea was to bend the steel like an arrow-shooting bow, using the torch as needed to soften the steel at the bend point. Rebecca had Epona and I work on the clamps one way, but Steve shortly directed us to do it differently, telling us, "There's always shortcuts."

Steve definitely knew what he was doing and Rebecca seemed okay with his approach, but I couldn't help think back to Tasha's philosophy on how the Flaming Lotus Girls work. There are always shortcuts, but it's not just about getting something done, a warning that was illustrated a few weeks later.

Rebecca, Matthew, and I were working on the head, adding greater bends here, lessening them there by jumping up and down on the curved, heated sections. The head was forming up within a pattern that Rebecca had painted on the shop floor, using tape to label it "head space." Some slots had been cut into the metal, forming tabs that we were going to bend in toward one another.

Rebecca used the torch to soften the base of one tab and had me pull it down by a chain, but even after I'd gotten fully inverted in a mountain climber position, pulling with all my might, it was barely budging. Steve saw what was happening, walked over with a big crescent wrench jammed into a pipe, waved me off, and easily used the tool to bend the tab into place.

A few minutes later, Rebecca was working on removing a pull point that had been welded onto another head section when Steve approached, mumbling how she didn't learn her lessons and brusquely using his tool with one hand to wrench the metal piece back and forth as she tried to steady the head section.

Finally, the piece snapped off and the pipe crushed one of Rebecca's fingers against the steel. Steve apologized and tried to help, but Rebecca calmly waved him off, tended by others as she ran her hand under cold water. The injury wasn't too serious, but it seemed to illustrate some issues we'd discussed earlier about when male energies charged into the Flaming Lotus Girls' world.

But she wasn't biting on this larger theme as I tried to draw her out, twice saying only, "He was just going too fast." Later, when I tried to draw out a more feminist critique of the episode, Rebecca said she was content with more incremental progress, saying of male members of the crews, "It's enough that they're here and calling themselves girls."

The Grand Diversion

Tamara had been traveling for a few weeks and returned to the Box Shop on July 6th to find the Flaming Lotus Girls frantically preparing for the Fire Arts Festival at the Crucible, a fire and industrial arts training facility in Oakland, a hub for lots of local tribes whose members were seeking skills and a broader community of artists.

The Fire Arts Festival had become the premier Bay Area event for showcasing the work of various Burning Man tribes to a larger audience and the Flaming Lotus Girls planned to show some of its past projects: Hand of God, Alcyone, Mini-Mega Junior, and some yet-to-be completed feathers from Angel.

"How many are we planning to bring to the festival?" Tamara asked at the Flaming Lotus Girls weekly Wednesday meeting.

"At least two," Rebecca answered.

"And they need to be ready by Tuesday," added Pouneh.

"So," Rebecca said, turning to the rest of the group, "none of you are leaving."

"We have to do a feather binge every night and through the weekend," Pouneh said.

"I think it's too much," Tamara said.

Pouneh explained that the deal had already been cut and the contract signed with the Crucible, which was paying the Flaming Lotus Girls' costs.

"I'm sorry to be a bitch about it, but I haven't been around as much and I'm a little horrified," Tamara said. "Personally, I don't want to work that hard at the fire festival. That's a lot of fucking work."

"But it's a good chance to get things ready," Pouneh offered.

Indeed, the Fire Arts Festival proved to be both a major motivator and a huge distraction. Kezia and Charlie had almost completely checked out from the Angel project to pound and shape the Hand's copper skin until it appeared lifelike. And everyone had to interrupt their work schedules to set up, tend, and break down their festival exhibit.

But they were the hit of the festival. The Hand of God had grown long golden fingernails just before the show, which seemed appropriate. And the complete group got their first taste of what it would be like to work together on the playa, getting everything working just right, each fire-poofer connected to pink control box buttons that passersby could press, creating the interactivity that was a feature of all the Flaming Lotus Girls art.

"This has become the staple warmup for Burning Man," Tasha said as we worked together. "I'm starting to get really excited."

Pouneh had me and another rookie minion, Chris, screw together some propane fittings called pig-noses, which would connect to the propane tanks and fuel the feathers. They twisted in the vice grips we used, but we did our best to make them as tight as possible.

An Oakland fire marshal had inspected the whole setup in the afternoon and everything looked okay to her. But the real test came in the evening when Dave X came by with a sensor that detected any flammable gases, a machine that let out a low buzz as it ran past our connections.

"The things you made are not tight enough," Pouneh told me in an instructional tone. I felt utterly incompetent, a feeling that had periodically plagued me throughout my work at the Box Shop.

"Every one of those pig tails has to be tightened," Rebecca told us frantically, as stressed out as I'd seen her.

"Pig noses," Dave corrected her gently. He didn't seem too concerned, overseeing the work as he played with the sensor, letting Tasha exhale on it to see how it groaned from the small amounts of methane contained in the air humans breathe out.

Cathy, who joined the Flaming Lotus Girls the previous year, saw that I seemed down and consoled me. She also felt like an idiot through much of her first year, and after getting carpal tunnel syndrome from drilling hundreds of holes in Alcyone, she wondered just what the hell she was doing.

But the feeling passed as she saw their creations lighting up the playa, and passed even more once she got home and realized that she'd learned how to change out all the plugs in her house and take on other previously unthinkable tasks. She summed up her Flaming Lotus Girls experience with, "You make art, make fire, hang out with people who are cool, and get skills."

And when darkness finally fell and the pair of complete feathers were fired up, I began to understand what she meant. It was thrilling to see them come alive, moreso than I expected. The whole thing glowed in evocative patterns, flames licking out of the corner of the cutouts to form new feathers of fire that danced against the night sky.

We just sat together on the asphalt parking lot and watched our creations and those around us — the tornado of fire, the huge pendulum with four-way fire jets, the flaming tree organ, Dance Dance Immolation — waiting for the $75 per head gala crowd to emerge from dinner at the Crucible for their fire tour, gleefully poofing the feathers and smiling every time.

"We're going to have 20 of them dueling," Tasha told me as a feather spit a fireball into the sky. "You gotta think of it in context."

Fun as it was, the festival also came in the context of the push to Burning Man, which was starting to slide behind schedule. And just a couple weeks after the festival, the tensions between Charlie and Steve would explode as they openly taunted each other during the July 27th meeting.

"He asked me to leave the shop for good," Steve told me, attributing the decision to a minor dispute over money from a fence project they were welding for the Bayview Boat Club and the fact that, "Charlie power trips things and I just don't buy it."

Later, I would hear from others that some incidents over the summer involving Steve and violence — once when he got tasered in the yard by some guys who showed up, another time involving a pushing and shoving incident — had something to do with it. Or that some of the shop's live-in caretakers objected to Steve's omnipresence.

Whatever it was, both men had calmed down after a few days and both agreed that Steve just needed some time away from the shop, making his home base at one of the many other shops where such an experienced welder was welcome, although he would stay involved with the Flaming Lotus Girls.

"Steve Monahan is a great friend of mine, he can stay at my house if he ever needs to, but he needed to take a break from the shop. It's hard to run a shop," Charlie told me. "He's a piledriver, a seriously great welder, but there's a bunch of women around here. It's hard to balance things, but there have to be rules around here."

After a few months, Steve might be welcomed back. But for now, Charlie was taking what he considered a principled stand that was best for the Box Shop, although he also admitted, "I'm not going to make it to heaven as a landlord."

Push to the Playa

Rebecca looked a bit anguished when I arrived on Sunday, July 31, to work on the head. She was huddled with a small group debating what kind of burn platform to build under the body, which would be set ablaze amid a glorious fireworks display after the Man burned. Sheet rock was cheaper, but it might crack under the intense heat, and they knew more about working with steel.

"We're short on money, period, and we're looking at expensive purchases coming up, particularly if we have to buy more stainless," Rebecca said, noting that they still need more steel for the beak and crest sections of the head.

The first frames for the longest feathers had just come out of the jig that week and Mills and Rosa Anna were using water to pressure-test the long lines that would carry the kerosene — which burns hotter and more erratically than propane — Pouneh insisting that they be able to withstand 100 psi in pressure even though they'll only run at 10 psi.

By evening, they were fire testing the first long feathers and the shop was a whirl with activity as burners raced to finish their various projects. But the test didn't go very well. The fuel wasn't moving steadily up the line. It could have been vapor lock or some design problem…they just didn't know.

During their August 4th meeting — 19 days before the Flaming Lotus Girls needed to leave for Burning Man — Mills and Rosanna briefed the group on the status of the feathers. The smaller feathers are all done. "Yay!" said the group. "Unfortunately," Rosa Anna said, "the outer feathers are not going as well."

The kerosene-fueled fire wasn't even staying lit, let alone achieving the fabulous drip effect they were hoping for. Rosanna called around to several fire arts groups around the country but none knew what to do — although they were impressed that the Flaming Lotus Girls had the audacity to even try a 20-foot-long kerosene drip line.

"The problem is nobody has ever done this," Rosa Anna learned from her inquiries. "They said, 'You guys are the cutting edge and once you figure it out, we'll copy it.'…But we're working on it really, really hard and we will overcome."

Rebecca got the group's attention and said she had something important to say. Everyone listened. She praised how well they were doing, but warned of problems being caused by that success. She referred to some of the minor accidents that have occurred recently, including her own smashed finger, cited the lesson her welding teacher once instilled in her about not "getting greedy" in the shop.

"We cannot let our speed and our progress get in the way of our safety," Rebecca told the Flaming Lotus Girls. "This is why I like working with a female-dominated group because we all have a little bit of mom in us and we take care of each other… Let's just check each other because it's all about love and about safety."

She also announced that at long last, the designs for the outside feathers were done and ready to be cut, the work taking place on Tuesday and Wednesday afternoons. "Kezia made a fabulous design for the outer feather," Rebecca said.

In a conversation with me, Kezia bounced some of the praise right back at Rebecca saying the two of them worked on a computer to transform the designs into something that meshed with the inner feathers and was going to be easier to plasma-cut. "A lot of the essence of what was there is still there, but we just refined and simplified it."

Reflecting on her conflicts with Tasha, Kezia said, "We both had strong work and we needed a way to display it." But she said that the relationship was still strained, although they did have a civil phone conversation that week to discuss some logistical matters. "That's one of the things that happens where you work collaboratively. These things happen," Kezia said. "I'm just happy that both of our work is being honored and utilized."

It was a big week. KQED television would be at the Box Shop the next day filming for a story about Burning Man and the following day, Friday night, the Flaming Lotus Girls were holding a final open house to display the eight inner feathers and a couple of the big ones. Burning Man seemed closer than ever and they started talking about what it will be like.

On the day of the burn, they'll all need to lift the body and build the burn platform underneath. For that and all the other work, Rebecca shared the time-honored trip for recruiting new minions on the playa.

"Dress up in a really cute outfit then stand with a heavy thing and go, 'ugh, uh, oh,'" Rebecca said, playing the damsel in distress. "And then, big guys will come by and say, 'Can I help you?' And then you say," she continues, switching into her assertive, minion-commanding voice, "Yes, move that over here and this over there…"

Everyone laughed. Despite all the work still to be done, the mood was lightening and the excitement was building. The open house was a low-key but first-rate party, drawing old friends, new admirers, and a range of other supporters, including Larry Harvey. In anticipation of group photos for my Guardian article, they broke out their cute outfits, swigged beer, and celebrated their pending accomplishment, which they continued to tinker with during the party.

At one point while I was talking with Charlie, Mills came up to us, a giddy grin on her face. They had figured out how to overcome the vapor lock problem on the large feathers, which had been burning for more than a half-hour now, leaving the Flaming Lotus Girls what would seem to be a clear path to the playa.

"It's working, man, it's working," she said and we all came over to see.

The more I learned and the more time I spent with them, the more I wanted to learn and the more time I wanted to spend time with them, helping the Flaming Lotus Girls transform fire and steel into art, even as I started doing work for own camp, Opulent Temple, which was putting a fire poofer on top of the DJ booth.

I started off in January as just a journalist working on a story. Then I became a minion. And now, as all these beautiful characters have told me over and over, I was one of them, in for life, a Flaming Lotus Girl. But even more importantly, I was starting to understand what was driving this culture at the moment when it was about to explode in unexpected ways.

Burning Man founder Larry Harvey runs Black Rock City LLC, aka The Borg. ~ Photo by John Curley

Arts impresario Chicken John launched the Borg2 rebellion at his old bar, The Odeon. ~ Photo by Alita Edgar

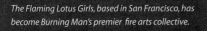

The Flaming Lotus Girls, based in San Francisco, has become Burning Man's premier fire arts collective.

The Flaming Lotus Girls' Hand of God lit up the Fire Arts Festival in 2005. ~ Photo by Karl Seifert

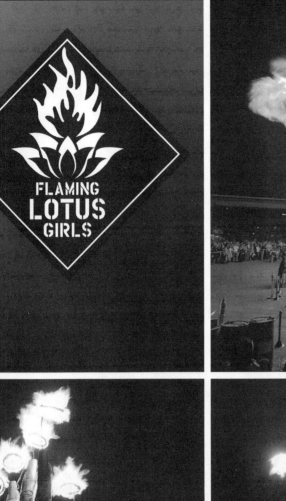

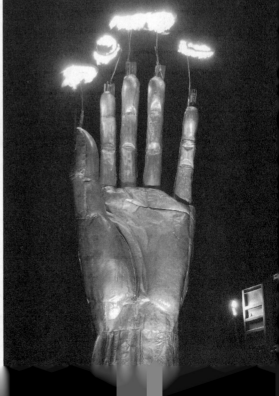

Bassnectar built a successful musical career on the reputation he developed spinning epic sets at Burning Man. ~ Photo by Gina Grandi

Paul Oakenfold with DJ/promoter Syd Gris (right), who has drawn other top DJs to play at his Opulent Temple theme camp. ~ Photo by MV Galleries

Sound camps rock the Burning Man nightlife and have helped fuel the event's growing popularity. ~ Photo by MV Galleries

The Flaming Lotus Girls have created some of Burning Man's most ambitious and evocative fire sculptures. ~ Photo by Gary Wilson

The Flaming Lotus Girls' 2005 piece, Angel of the Apocalypse, was a gathering place surrounded by fire-spewing feathers. ~ Photo by Caroline Miller (mills)

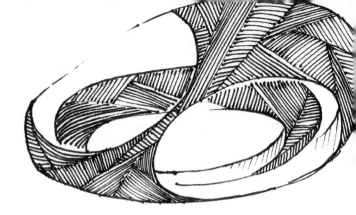

Part II — Baptism (2005-06)

Tuesday, August 30, 2005

At this time yesterday, the mid-morning, we were embarking on a big workday. But today, there's nothing but play in my future, at least until tonight when we debut the Opulent Temple dance party at the corner of 2 o'clock and Esplanade, one of the most high-profile locations on the playa.

Ah, life feels wondrous as I sit on a dusty couch in OT's fabric-decorated shade structure, on the edge of civilization, just gazing at the vast, panoramic open playa. How decadent to be sitting right along the Esplanade, Black Rock City's main avenue, greeting beautiful strangers with a smile or a few connecting words as they stroll past, the horizon dotted with art.

In the distance, I can see the tall steel wings of Angel of the Apocalypse reaching up into the clear blue sky, and the curved beak of its bird head that I helped build. Wow, there it is, and here I am, just kicking it in my camp, my home for the week, the destination of my long journey. And of course, the weather is perfect, still air now warming to hot as the sun begins to cook the city.

I can feel an enormous sense of accomplishment welling up inside of me, a sort of giddy pride mixed with the waning pangs of physical and emotional fatigue. Working on Angel with the Flaming Lotus Girls for the last nine months, documenting it for a Bay Guardian cover story that came out a couple weeks ago, then switching gears to help my own camp with its biggest year ever

— wow, I can barely believe we did it.

Despite the heat, I feel a slight, momentary tremble as a light breeze crosses my exposed torso, but it passes quickly and my inner strength returns. Several of my campmates share this space, a few on couches and the foam pad, sleeping off last night, two doing yoga stretches, a few more, like me, just gazing speechlessly out onto the playa.

Near the Angel, I see the purple head of Dreamer, which had been the centerpiece of the Box Shop's yard as I toiled on my trio of projects, watching it form up as it watched us work. And to its right is The Temple, its red pagodas built by a new team this year, headed by a guy named Mark Grieve.

Scanning the horizon toward my left, I see Passage, steel sculptures of a mother and daughter, six times larger than life, walking plaintively away from The Man, palms upturned. And to their left, The Man stands tall over a funhouse pavilion, its head standing 75 feet in the air but seeming even higher in this sprawling flatness.

It is the center of this entire beautiful city, the golden spike from which the streets and everything else radiates outward, but this year, The Man is little disorienting. I study The Man as it slowly rotates, its triangular head turning to face me. The Man is usually like a compass, telling you where you are — profile shot means you're at 3 or 9 o'clock, looking at you means you're at 6 — but this year it's hard to tell where you are.

But I have my own Man this year, right on my chest, and it's always looking forward. My first two years, I shaved my chest hair into a heart, a simple daytime costume that got a great response, so this year I decided to shave it into The Man, with a triangular head and sideways Vs for arms and legs. And to top it off, I brought several tubes of body paint, brushes, and a small palette, all of which are in a little pocketed apron that I sewed from flame-printed fabric, which I'm wearing right now, waiting for my artists.

And there they are, Gina and Sierra, walking right toward me, changed into shiny, skimpy costumes for the day ahead, smiles on their faces, returning to the spot where I asked if they wanted to be today's artists, part of a series of women that I'm recruiting each morning to decorate me and my hairy man.

"Ladies, have you come to paint The Man?" I call out to them.

"Let us at him!" Sierra answered, and they titter together as I rise to greet them warmly with big hugs. They lead me over to one of the large blanket-covered foam pads, kneeling beside me, fishing the paints out of my apron, and studying my chest like a canvas, looking for inspiration.

"Mmm, you have a nice chest," Sierra flirts, rubbing a hand over my chest and leaving me uncharacteristically speechless for a moment. This was a great idea, I mentally congratulate myself. Yes, it's little dorky, perhaps even a tad creepy for some people, but as these lovely young women start finger-painting the cool colors onto my stomach and chest, I feel nothing but bliss.

They seem to be enjoying it as well, with Gina using red and yellow to create flames around the man's base on my stomach while Sierra outlines the Man in black and then borrows the red to brighten my nipples, giggling at the indulgence of it all. As the girls finish, Rosie walks up, gives me one of those "Omigod, you're so ridiculous" smiles, and compliments her girlfriends on their artistry.

"Yeah, thanks, I like how it's turning out," Gina says seriously, filling in a few blank spots. "Thanks for letting us paint you."

"No, thank you," I respond.

"You almost ready?" Rosie asks.

"Yeah, I think so."

"Great, I'll go make us some sandwiches before our bike ride. Turkey or PB&J?" Rosie asks. "Oh and Donnie and Lucky are coming with us."

"Lucky's here? Great, that'll be fun. Turkey."

"You drinking enough water?"

"I think so," I answer, reaching for my water bottle and taking the last swallow as Sierra admonishes me, "Hey, be still, we're almost done."

After a quick lunch, we mount our wildly decorated bikes — mine with a fake fur basket and bobbing plastic rose on the back and high handlebars that I custom-welded at the Box Shop a couple months earlier — and set off across the open playa, pedaling easily across the hard-packed earth, a world at play wafting past us.

We see some people playing a huge game of croquet, swinging long mallets into 10-foot balls, and then do fly-bys at The Man, vowing to return to its funhouse maze, and The Machine, where visitors worked the wheel to raise its massive arms. "Wanna check out the Dicky Box?" Lucky asks, and I respond with more ferocity than I intended, "Fuck Dicky!"

For some reason, the Dicky Box — a supposedly shy guy named Dicky living in a plexiglass box for the week, forced to interact with whoever stops by — is a concept that really gets on my nerves. Larry told me he loved it, but it seems like a big ego trip to me and I vow to myself to go fuck with Dicky at some point this week, the only dark thought that has entered my head since I arrived.

"Okay, let's check out Center Camp," Lucky offers, and we pedal in that direction, entering the keyhole past Colossus, with its three suspended boulders slowly spinning around, two women pulling on ropes to put it in motion while some guy hangs upside down off the third one.

The bike racks around Center Camp are packed, so we decide to just peek in for a few minutes and continue our tour into the neighborhoods, slowly riding a few blocks, tempted to stop at a zip-line and maybe a dozen other expressions of theme camp creativity before Rosie finally says, "Omigod, Jenga!" She loves Jenga.

Indeed, it's a giant Jenga game, the tower of blocks just taller than I am and an equally large box with the familiar blue packaging, but upon closer inspection, we see it's actually Junga, with each block that you remove from the tower and place on top imprinted with sayings and prompts from the noted Swiss psychologist Carl Jung.

It's a small theme camp, maybe a dozen or so people, with a simple concept that's clearly derived from this year's art theme, "Psyche: The Conscious, the Subconscious, and the Unconscious," fusing an amusing game with concepts from the father of the Collective Unconscious.

The neighboring camp offers us tea, which we graciously accept into cups we brought for a tour that we know will end at The Deep End for some afternoon ass-shaking, and play a game of Junga, probing ancient archetypes and strange synchronicities as we try to keep the tower from succumbing to the wind that has just started to pick up.

The Evolution of Sound

At the end of my long article about the Flaming Lotus Girls, I declared, "I am a Flaming Lotus Girl." But it wasn't true, not really. Honestly, I was more of a bumbling poseur. I'll always feel a connection to them and answer their calls to action when I can, but even as I wrote my story, I was still closer to the party-hardy ravers than a serious metal worker, let alone an artist.

Yet there were intriguing new dimensions being added to my experience as a member of Opulent Temple, making it far richer experience than it seemed in 2004. We did a series of fundraisers to meet our $30,000 budget, helping create the social scene that was heavily influencing San Francisco's nightlife, while I worked on my Burning Man series for the Guardian by researching the storied history of big sound camps at Burning Man.

Promoter Joegh Bullock — who threw Anon Salon's underground parties and was an early advocate within the Burning Man organization for allowing amplified music — explained that the term "burner" had become shorthand for a certain style of party, a sort of code for the freaks who like to dress outrageously, dance madly, and be embraced for doing so.

Discovering that this community exists, Bullock says, could be an epiphanic experience for those who had tasted the fruits of this subculture: "Suddenly you knew that you weren't alone now. You know that you can go anywhere and recognize a burner."

While use of the term "ravers" is sort of derogatory shorthand that many artists use to describe dance camp denizens, it's certainly true that the dance camps grew out of the underground rave scenes in San Francisco and other urban centers around the world, as I learned.

"Rave" had such strong connotations of drugs, reckless behavior, and illegal parties that Burning Man organizers (who need official permits to stage the event) avoided becoming associated with electronic dance music for as long as they could. Longtime board member Harley Dubois, who handles theme camp placement, told me, "The cops told us that if they hear the word rave, 'We're shutting you down.'"

But by 1995 raves were getting huge across the country, especially in urban areas. That was the year that Brad Olsen (aka Santosh) and a group of American travelers who had ended up in Goa, India — going to huge parties with trance music — decided to settle in San Francisco. They rented a commercial warehouse on Howard Street, pitched in for a sound system, and started throwing underground psychedelic trance parties they dubbed the Consortium of Collective Consciousness (known as the CCC warehouse parties) that developed a big following. It is in this warehouse where Santosh started his publishing business, CCC Publishing, the publisher of this book.

"So when we heard about Burning Man, we said, 'Hell yeah, let's bring our sound system out there,'" Santosh, a travel book author under his real name of Brad Olsen and the CCC Publishing label, told me back in 2005, well before this book was conceived.

When Santosh and the CCC crowd showed up in 1995, they joined up with another group of ravers from Wicked Sound System and set up camp about two miles from the main Burning Man camp. They were only loosely connected to Burning Man, which had a few thousand people and few restrictions or signs of civic organization. They loved it and planned to make it a regular ritual.

The next year, a member of the music community named Terbo Ted made contacts with the Burning Man organization, and what was dubbed the "techno ghetto" became more of an officially recognized camp, albeit still placed a few miles away from the main camp.

"He was the one who came to Larry and said we want to do electronic music," Bullock says of Terbo Ted, an active musician in the East Bay Area.

"Ninety-six is still my favorite year. It was awesome," Santosh said. "We had our complete autonomy, which basically went away in the coming years."

But it was also a tragic year. Early Monday morning, three people sleeping in a tent got run over by someone driving back from the techno ghetto.

"That made everyone realize that the rave camp had to be a part of things," Bullock said. One of the resulting changes was restrictions on driving, which meant the dance camps needed to be brought into the camp.

"Larry Harvey didn't want anything to do with electronic music," Santosh said. "Larry and the top dogs just weren't into it. They wanted to create a counterculture that they thought was the counterculture, so they kept neglecting us until they couldn't anymore, so they let us have just one night."

Bullock and fellow Burning Man staffer Michael Gosney fashioned the compromise: the Community Dance, one night only, after the burn, for just eight hours. Everyone agreed that the name was a little dorky. It was wholesome-sounding enough so police wouldn't think it was a rave, but the growing legions of electronic music lovers would get their night.

"I was the one who said let's do a big dance party after the burn," Gosney, who also goes by DJ Goz, told me. "That's what turned it."

But that first dance in 1997 was pretty ho-hum by most accounts, largely because it was an especially cold night, although it was a night when the tension between established artists and this new medium would spill over into the storied standoff between Jim Mason and the metalheads versus DJ Goa Gil and the ravers. Mason led his mob in the Vegematic of the Apocalypse, a pedal-powered boring vehicle with a massive flame-thrower.

Mason came to stop the electronic music, but Gil stood his ground and refused to back down. Some say the mob started chanting "all ravers must die" and "Led Zeppelin," their demand for the music they wanted, but Gil just turned up the electronic beats. The incident solidified the division between the punk-rock artists and the hippie ravers.

"It was very mean-spirited and intimidating," Santosh says, but Mason still maintains it was "a joke" and piece of performance art, although he admits that his animosity toward the dance camps has only grown since then. "We were pretty pissed off and disenchanted at that point," Santosh said. "For us, it was the straw that broke the camel's back…We went to a lot of effort to integrate and got only one night to play, and then we were met with an angry mob with a menacing flame thrower who threatened to kill our friend and who happens to be one of the most famous DJs in the world."

But 1998 was the year that many say Burning Man and dance music permanently fused. Bullock actually got Santosh and the Community Dance crowd some money for lasers and an art project — a huge UFO designed to replicate the one that some say crashed in Roswell, New Mexico in the '40s — the only time Burning Man has given money to a dance camp.

"So as soon as the Man burned, the UFO started shooting off the lasers and the

Community Dance was on. Everybody came over, and it was a big hit. People were just dancing and grooving," Santosh said.

Electronic dance music became a part of Black Rock City forever, although the Community Dance was replaced by Harley's idea of placing large sound camps along the 10 o'clock and 2 o'clock radials, aimed out at the open playa to minimize their disruption of other camps. "We solved the problem by zoning," Larry said of the noise conflicts.

After burning out on building dance camps at Burning Man, Santosh and his crew turned their focus toward re-creating that vibe on the streets of San Francisco, creating the How Weird Street Faire, which in 2005 drew more than 10,000 people to Howard Street in San Francisco, an event thrown by burners that has a distinctly burner vibe, with heavily costumed creatures grooving at more than a half-dozen stages, most hosted by Burning Man veterans.

"We want groups that are hot on the scene and have a following. And Burning Man is sort of a test of what's hot," Santosh told me then, noting that How Weird is held at the start of the burner fundraiser season each May, and many of the stages serve as previews for upcoming Black Rock City Projects, such as Brass Tax's massive Boombox.

The How Weird stages that year were hosted by CCC, El Circo, Get Freaky, Space Cowboys, Low-Pro Lounge, Joegh's Anon Salon and Syd's Opel Productions, Tantra, and Sunset. Among the DJs were Michelle Bass, Goldilox, Nathan Vain, Goa Gil, el Papachango, and Random Rab. The event has drawn talent from a variety of Burning Man dance camps, including Sol System, Lush, Illuminaughty, Oacious, and Space Lounge.

But the How Weird Street Faire was about more than just the music. There was a craft area and a stage featuring a range of creative expression — as well as a certain sense of style prevalent throughout, something emanating perhaps most strongly from the stage of El Circo, which had fused a musical style and a fashion sense that are major departures from the old rave scene.

Before moving its base of operations to San Francisco in 2003 and hooking up with Get Freaky's Adam Ohana, Bassnectar, and other Bay Area locals, El Circo began as an annual party up on Mt. Ashland, in Oregon, thrown by a bunch of young hippies, circus freaks, and music lovers who lived in Ashland. Electronic musician Random Rab recalls the group's decision to go to Burning Man in 1999.

"We really had our feelers out and realized what the whole thing was about," he said. They absorbed it and metastasized it, returning in 2000 with their iconic tear-drop dome and huge sound system to stage a fashion show, perform fire dancing and metal work, and become a music-centered artists' collective.

"What we do is an echo of what we first learned at Burning Man," Rab told me. "We became what we adored and admired about it."

Much of what El Circo has done since arriving in town has been to try to re-create in San Francisco what they developed on the playa. Matty Dowlen, who managed El Circo's operations, said they're always wrestling with this question: "How can the flow be maintained and re-created in the city?"

Bassnectar and his El Circo buddies contemplated that as they strived to be about more than just music, cultivating a new kind of culture and communal ethos.

"Some of the deepest and most magical moments of my life have been involved in the dance floors and freakish movement ceremonies that occur on the playa," Bassnectar told me. "I feel like, collectively, we are channeling forces of nature that don't exist anywhere else in the world. That's why the sound system aspect of the festival is so sacred."

Lost in Space

Burning Man draws like-minded people into tribes, as well as people who are just groups of friends. When Peter "PK" Kimelman moved from the East Coast to San Francisco in 1996, he knew some old friends who had gone to Cornell University with him, including Rebecca Anders, long before she was a Flaming Lotus Girl.

PK had never been to Burning Man, but she had been going for years and convinced him to go for the first time in 1999. Together, they built an elaborate tiki hut shade structure together for their informal camp of friends, and he was hooked and wanted to get more involved.

"So after that, I wanted to be a part of a camp, so I joined Space Lounge and quickly became a leader of it," PK said of the "retro-future" sound camp his friends were in that had a super collaborative style that was new to this hard-driving over-achiever who was on his way to getting a master's degree in architecture. "It taught me a very different way of leading or running an organization, or working with an organization, where it's really about collective organization."

Back in San Francisco, they would do big elaborate fundraisers, with themes like Cult Lounge or Pimp Lounge, underground happening in warehouses that they would prepare for weeks. "It could never be over-the-top enough," he said. "It was the dot.com days and everyone had money."

Former Space Lounger Manny Alferez, a DJ who goes by M3, said the camp pioneered the notion of the free bar at Burning Man in the late '90s, beating The Deep End by several years. "People were like, oh, you're giving drinks away for free? Wow," Manny recalls. "We were the first people giving away drinks."

But Manny had left Space Lounge in 1998, breaking off to form his own sound camp out of a record label and sound collective named Green Gorilla Lounge he started in the early '90s, spawning it into a Burning Man camp that became known for a distinct sound that was funkier than most.

During PK's next year at Burning Man, 2000, as Space Lounge was setting up its sound system, it somehow shorted out and blew up, totally fried. But they still had their art car named Martha, which was sort of a rolling lounge, and they cruised around and eventually started talking to some of the Space Cowboys, another sound camp that had sort of mirrored them for a couple years and drank their booze.

PK said the two San Francisco-based groups barely knew each other, but the Space Cowboys loved hanging out in Space Lounge's bar, "so they offered their entire sound system to us out of the generosity of their hearts," PK said. "So we all became good friends within a week, and now there are people who are married out of that meeting. So we merged, essentially, we started coexisting."

But the Space Lounge members who joined the Space Cowboys helped elevate it into a musical institution on the playa and back in San Francisco, where they play regular parties and fundraisers from a mobile sound vehicle known as the Unimog that they decided to build after the merger.

Among the Space Cowboys biggest and most notorious events are Breakfast of Champions on New Year's Day, SnowFest at Squaw Valley a couple months later, and Ghost Ship, a massive Halloween party on Treasure Island, all of which support and are supported by the larger Burning Man community.

"We have one of the longest running Burning Man theme camps doing proper parties in the Bay Area," longtime Space Cowboy DJ Mancub told me.

Smoove, a burner since 1994 and longtime Space Cowboy DJ before he left the group in 2005, said there's a wonderful synergy that occurs among the tribes: "There is a nexus of people who all draw from each other and they create the connective tissue of the city that gets built year after year."

While Mancub really misses Burning Man's wild days, he sheepishly admits "I'm more into the community-ish part now. I can't be so balls to the wall all the time anymore." And he gives PK credit for helping the Space Cowboys support the development of the larger Burning Man community: "He's a networking genius. He's always about connecting with people."

"Burning Man has become a part of the fabric of life in the city," PK said proudly. "We're able to raise a lot of money and funnel it back to the community."

But PK's ascent within the Burning Man, architectural, and artistic worlds hit a major snag at the event in 2001. "I took a nap in the shade structure and I woke up in the back of a pickup truck with all this mayhem going on around me and my best friend was lying on top of me," PK said.

People asked him what drugs he was on and he hadn't taken any. "It turns out I had a seizure and they flew me in a helicopter to Reno. I felt completely fine but they did a CAT scan and an MRI and came back with a picture of a giant egg in my head. And they said, 'You have a brain tumor.' So I said, 'What do I do?' And they said, 'Go home.' They basically said take two of these anti-convulsants and call a neurosurgeon in the morning."

But he was living in Los Angeles at the time going to grad school, all his closest friends were at Burning Man, and his family was on the East Coast. "So I went back to Burning Man."

He felt okay and was tending bar at Space Lounge, visiting with strangers and friends alike, including Rebecca, when "I started feeling funky again."

So Rebecca left the playa with him and helped him get home safe. A week later, at UCLA Medical Center, "they took the thing out of my head, which left me paralyzed on the my left-hand side. So any function I have on my left side is relearned. But unfortunately, it put a crashing dash on my aspiring career as an architect and artist. I can't really draw or draft anymore. I can't even type anymore and building things is extremely difficult."

Yet he kept going to Burning Man, even after two rounds of brain surgery, radiation treatments, and chemotherapy, even though the recurring tumors are likely to kill him someday. Throughout it all, he remained relentlessly positive and productive, and eventually, PK and Rebecca would aspire to one of Burning Man's most exalted artistic positions.

"The minute you give up the lust for life," PK told me in 2010, as he prepared for the biggest artistic challenge of his life, "is the minute your life is over."

Transformation Begins

It's safe to say 2005 was one of the most eagerly anticipated of any of the Burning Man events, with the Borg2 rebel artist movement raising questions about whether the event was in decline and a bunch of restless energy within the country as a whole, and this counterculture in particular.

There had been a subtle shift in the Burning Man world that began even before The Petition and Borg2, maybe even before that dismal presidential election, when the country validated its bumbling would-be emperor. Larry Harvey told me he saw it begin two years before and the public generally takes three years to comprehend new realities.

But by the end of Burning Man 2005, it was clear to everyone that Burning Man was back — and that there had been a palpable shift in this universe. The frontier had finally become a real city, and its culture was starting to grow in interesting ways. Larry told me it was the best Burning Man he'd ever see, both with the art and the culture of people who have "really absorbed the idea of participation."

Call it the event's renaissance, the perfection of the experiment, its return from the desert. The longstanding question of whether Burning Man can survive had been answered, and now the question became whether it can project outward onto this troubled country.

"We've come through," Larry told me. "This is the revolution I'd hoped for all along."

He wasn't talking about a political revolution, but a social one. He saw it in the Flaming Lotus Girls' enlightened approach to gender roles and creative collaboration as they turned Angel of the Apocalypse into the warmest, most inspiring gathering place on the playa. And Larry saw it in the gracious spirit that characterized the Critical Tits topless bike ride's after-party, where even the excluded male gawkers outside were served chilled mango slices.

"Here I was, amid 500 tits, and I was principally paying attention to the social aspects of the event," Larry said. "It was neither puritanical nor prurient."

He even saw the new reality in the acrimony that swirled around Borg2. The group threatened and taunted the Burning Man organization, but ultimately pumped new energy into an event they all loved. In other words, even when some members tried to pick a fight, when they mutinied and tried to force an internal schism, it brought the whole community closer. There aren't many groups of 35,000 people that function this way. There may not be any others.

Even though this was a banner year for Burning Man art and culture, the Borg2 rebellion pretty much flopped. It raised a fraction of the funding it had promised, its elected art curators eventually walked away in frustration, and even some of its funded artists publicly admitted failure.

It withered and faced a well-earned death. A few die-hards tried to keep it moving, but Jim, Chicken, Charlie, M2 — anyone with a say in the matter — said it was over. Even Nesdon Booth — whose Borg2-funded Cognitive Firewall project was a huge failure — frankly admitted in the online forums afterward that the movement was a bust, objecting to contrary descriptions by noting that you could see the tumbleweeds blowing by their camping space. It wasn't even a good theme camp, let alone the promised revolution.

Even in defeat, Jim, Chicken, and Charlie — who split his time between the FLGs, running the Box Shop, and serving as president of the Borg2 Art Council president — claimed victory for providing the "art spark" that made that year so outstanding, which even those curmudgeons acknowledged it was. Larry disputed their impact on his art funding decisions — something even Borg member Maid Marian disputes, telling me Borg2 was what prompted a substantial increase in the art budget and "if Larry tells you it wasn't then he's full of shit." But Larry did acknowledge Borg2's social impact.

"What they can take credit for is the increased local interest in Burning Man," Larry said. "If people care about Burning Man as much as Borg2 indicates, they might turn their attention away from the small, embattled group that created it."

And where might they turn their attention? Larry had some ideas, but there was no way for him or anyone to foresee the real opportunity that came during the 2005 event, the perfect storm of serendipitous timing, an act of God, inaction by a deteriorating president, and burners stepping up to use their skills and fill a void.

Flooding our Bubble

I'll never forget when I heard about how Hurricane Katrina had destroyed much of New Orleans and the Gulf Coast. For four days during the week of the 2005 event, I'd been in a bubble of ignorant bliss at Burning Man, working to build Opulent Temple with other early arrivers and then savoring the fruits of our labors.

With no cell phone service or Internet access, Burning Man is almost totally separated from the rest of the world, a welcomed state for a bleeding heart political journalist like myself. When I left for Burning Man that year on Saturday, August 27th, Hurricane Katrina was still gathering power as it approached the Gulf Coast, news that I barely noted amid my frantic preparations.

Katrina first made landfall as a powerful Category 5 hurricane just as Burning Man officially opened at midnight on Sunday. It would make landfall three times along the coast of Louisiana and Mississippi throughout Monday morning, with the eye of the hurricane passing over the border town of Pearlington, Mississippi at 10 a.m.

By early afternoon, the levees around New Orleans had broken in several places and much of the city was flooded, with the world watching televised footage of poor people stranded on rooftops and trees or packed into the Superdome. But it would still be a couple more days before President Bush would end his vacation in Texas to fly over New Orleans, which was 85 percent underwater by August 31st.

So many of the new arrivals at Burning Man knew about the Katrina tragedy, but I still spent a couple more days in lovely ignorance, traipsing around the playa without a care in the world. Then I decided to finally visit the Temple, which is sort of the spiritual center of Black Rock City and a place where people write messages on its wooden walls.

That year, the Temple of Dreams project was led by Mark Grieve, who had taken the torch from longtime Temple builder David Best, who created his own mobile Temple of Memories that year. But the temple was the temple, and I marveled at its overall beauty before I even started to read the writing on the walls.

Most of the messages were about New Orleans and the Gulf Coast: general statements of support, concern for individuals there, outrage over federal govern-ment inaction. It was clear something terrible had happened, but I still didn't know what, so I just said, to anyone who was listening, "What the hell happened in New Orleans?"

Strangers looked at me incredulously. "You...," one guy said me, studying my face to see if I was playing a tasteless joke. "You...don't know? Dude, it's gone. New Orleans is gone."

Many of us found out about this disaster in a similar way: belatedly, but with the full impact of a slowly unfolding tragedy happening in one shocking moment. For those with lives or loved ones there, it was even worse. But by the end of the week, everyone knew what had happened and they began to come together as a community to figure out how to respond.

Redemption and Projection

By burn day at the end of the week, Burning Man's leaders — those with Black Rock City LLC and just the leaders among the random burner tribes — had developed a strategy for responding to the disaster on the Gulf Coast and it was publicized by word of mouth and through Black Rock Information Radio (BMIR, 94.5 FM).

Food, money, and supplies that could be used on the Gulf Coast were collected from departing burners, and some even blazed a trail for a more direct response. Matt Lindsay, a Temple Crew member from Seattle, helped spearhead an effort to drive supplies and equipment from Burning Man to the Gulf Coast, and was joined by his father, Phillip Lindsay, whose Seattle construction company he worked with.

The encampment they and others created would become an inspiring nine-month cleanup and rebuilding effort. It began mostly with the builders who had already focused on creating and breaking down Burning Man, including the Department of Public Works and the Temple crew, but would eventually draw more than 100 volunteers and spawn the group Burners Without Borders.

But first, burners came together on the playa in a special event on Sunday afternoon, promoted heavily by BMIR and led by folk singer Joan Baez (who had attended Burning Man several times) and the anti-consumerist collective Reverend Billy and the Church of Stop Shopping.

Billy Talen is a performance artist and political progressive who had adopted his alter ego of Reverend Billy, the charismatic, Jimmy Swaggert-like leader of a church devoted to critiquing hyper-capitalism. He had been doing some street-level political satire and small theater in San Francisco in the early '90s when he found his calling.

"My mentor and teacher, the person who talked me into this was himself a priest, not a preacher, and his name was Reverend Sidney Lanier," Billy told me when I visited him in New York City. "He took me out to lunch and he told me, 'I'm not too sure about your play, but you have a prophetic note in your voice.' And he said, 'We now need a new kind of American preacher.'"

Lanier convinced Billy to use his theatrical skills to sound the alarm that there was something deeply wrong with the country — something at the intersection of political, economic, and religious power — and so he talked to Billy about his vision for Reverend Billy and led him to Times Square.

"He brought me to New York and he placed me in front of that Disney store and he left," said Billy, who began to preach, "Mickey Mouse is the anti-Christ! I want you to take that little tourist family and go back to Iowa! These are sweatshops products on these shelves, children. This Disney-fication of neighborhoods, it's the devil monoculture!' So, my theme hasn't changed much in these 10 or 12 years."

But there have been some key events in the development of Reverend Billy and his group that turned it from a performance piece to something like a real church. The first was the 9/11 attacks, when they counseled and consoled affected New Yorkers, and the next was their decision to come to Burning Man in 2003, where Larry Harvey and others wanted them to be a part of the Beyond Belief theme that year.

"I got a call from Larry. He carved a Broadway-sized stage in the Man. And I started to get phone calls from burner friends saying, 'You don't know what this is. Say yes!" Billy said, noting how reluctant he had been to attend. "All my friends went, but I was like contrary Woodrow, and I'd say, 'Fuck all of you,' and I was going to the Aleutians or something. I was always a contrary guy, and I'd say, 'You're all just a bunch of lemmings going to the desert, I'm going over here.' And I'd go to some other place. But we got talked into it and it changed our lives."

Most newbies are profoundly affected by their first trip to Burning Man, but for Billy and his crew, the event went right to the core of what they were about, transforming them as they dealt with the usual playa adversity ("In the choir, everyday someone would faint and everyone else would save that person and take them to the medical tent.") and forging permanent ties to the event.

"We became a church at that point. We became a community about collective conscious and radical self-reliance. We became much closer," Billy told me. Why, I asked him, how? "It's the weather, it's the beauty, it's somebody running toward you in a fluorescent bikini and combat boots. Everything is extreme but it becomes ordinary after awhile and then you're in the dream state," he said. "We were transformed by our week on the playa. There were 43 of us that came out together."

Most of that group has been together ever since, working together on new and ever more creative ways of bringing the ethos of the playa back into the world, something that Billy says has always been at the center of his connection to Burning Man (whose Black Rock Arts Foundation has helped fund some of the church's tours, performances, and the 2007 film about them, "What Would Jesus Buy?").

"That was the message that I worked out with Larry Harvey back in 2003: What about the other 51 weeks of the year? Something very strong and honest and magical happens here and we have an obligation, don't we, to see how it can manifest in our communities. When Katrina happened in the middle of the week, that was supposed to be our year off, but the Bests gave us their bus and said you can come out to the Temple on Sunday night, so before the Temple burn, and Joan Baez magically showed up and got on the bus with us."

They spoke of love and connection and redemption and transformation, and they sang — together with a large crowd of burners — "Swing Low Sweet Chariot" and "Amazing Grace." And the Temple burned that night and soon everyone went home. Well, not everyone.

Using our Skills

Burning Man's images and culture had been seeping out of Black Rock City for years, but after Katrina, its people and skills found a very practical use in a country where the federal government essentially abandoned a major U.S. city after a devastating hurricane. It was like the Third World, but burners stepped up to help fill the void.

Afterward, Larry told me the burners were well suited to the task, given how they create and then dismantle a big, beautiful city every year under the most adverse conditions. "The irony is we went way out of the world and had to learn worldly skills to survive out there," Larry said. "What people who understand us discover is we have experts in every field of human endeavor."

Those skills came in handy that fall when burners set up camp in Biloxi, Mississippi, where they did hurricane relief, followed by cleanup and rebuilding. They were supported by a Burning Man fundraising drive that quickly gathered about $35,000, and eventually $80,000, and various supplies for the relief effort.

"If that isn't applying our ethos, I don't know what is," Larry said. "The very skills needed to survive at Burning Man are the skills needed to respond to a disaster."

And what about those who see our current political system as a disaster? "Everyone seems to be feeling that great change is in the offing, but nobody knows what it's going to be," Larry said. "And that raises questions about the creative class."

Could the creative class from the Bay Area and beyond — which extends from the underground artisans who propel Burning Man to the more mainstream art, technological, and political communities — influence the country's worldview and political dialogue in a substantial way?

On a more immediate level, would the ethos of Burning Man maintain its basic integrity as the event continued to grow? Could Burning Man's social revolution evolve into a political one? What would that even look like? And can what works for 35,000 people really work for 5 or 10 or 100 times that many?

Nobody knew the answer to that question, but Larry started to nudge his baby in that direction, announcing that the 2006 art theme was going to be "The Future: Hope or Fear." It was the first art theme that had an overtly sociopolitical character to it, the first of three consecutive themes that Larry hoped would more directly engage the event with the larger world.

"You can't predict what people will do," Larry told me, "but some people will do things that will resonate." That's where he said Borg2 went wrong, in assuming Larry could control what the culture was becoming. Only the larger group can now do that.

Despite continuing squabbles over where to focus its resources, energies, and speakers, there was a new cohesion developing in the Burning Man culture, an excited sense of possibility. It had flipped from reaction to action, from negation to affirmation, or as Larry casts it, from the countercultural to the cultural.

And therein lies the larger hopes of Burning Man, which at that time were in the process of blossoming in new and unexpected ways down on the bayou. It was an exciting time, particularly for me, a political journalist and burner who wanted the event to impact the world. And if Larry was willing to promote that kind of engagement, so was I.

OT Rocks the Esplanade

I had been Scribe for almost a year, covering the culture, getting to know many of its top people, and writing about 10 articles for the Guardian. I had even spent an intensive nine months with the Flaming Lotus Girls — the biggest immersion journalism project of my 15-year newspaper career — and considered myself one of them by the end.

But my personal connection to Burning Man was through Opulent Temple and the sound camps, which were also trending upward and outward by 2005, although perhaps not in the dramatic fashion that Hurricane Katrina or even the Borg2 rebellion had triggered.

All of us in Opulent Temple — about 80 in all, but a core "A-team" of more like 20 of us did most of the work — wanted to go big and earn our prominent new location on the playa. So we spent countless hours at the Infinite Kaos warehouse drilling and screwing holes for glowing string-art walls designed by artist Andres Amador, and out at the Box Shop modifying the DJ booth and giving it flaming, poofing wings of fire that the DJ controlled with a fireball button.

The work we did was only for half of a camp whose full name was Opulent Temple of Venus. We were Opulent Temple, a self-contained unit, and we shared space with Temple of Venus, a camp devoted to providing sensual services to women (I'll get into the sex tribes on the playa a little later). They had their own schtick, delivering sensual services that sometimes seemed a little sleazy, and our formal interactions with them were minimal. We each had our own infrastructure and meals, but shared the space in a cooperative and symbiotic way.

Syd was the one who maintained that relationship, worked hard for OT, and lined up the DJs: "It was Bassnectar on Wednesday and it was a madhouse. Thursday was Scumfrog, Friday was Paul Oakenfold, Saturday was Tiesto and Lee Coombs."

Lee is a successful London-based DJ who attended his first Burning Man in 2005, but he had been plugged into San Francisco's burner scene since 2000, when he played a Space Cowboys fundraiser and became good friends with up-and-coming burner artist Peter Hudson, aka Hudzo, who created mind-blowing stroboscopic zoetropes that when set in motion and combined with strobe lights looked like swimmers paddling through the playa or monkeys swinging through the trees.

Hudzo was so anxious for his friend to experience Burning Man that he fetched him from the Reno airport and brought Lee back to playa, where he became instantly hooked on the event. "We traveled into the playa just as it got dark and I thought I'd landed on the moon," Lee recalls. "It's really quite something to come across Burning Man for the first time at night. All the different camps with all the music clashing everywhere, nothing looks or sounds like it anywhere else — a totally Mad Max style."

Paul Oakenfold was a legendary DJ from rave's heyday and one of the first star DJs to play Burning Man, but he had camped with us in 2004 and did the rock star thing in the tour bus, staying just a couple days and interacting little with any of us. I wasn't impressed by him or his music. But Tiesto was an even bigger star that turned out to be a nice, accessible guy who was super involved with the camp.

"Part of that was he was the victim of circumstance and he couldn't get an RV, which would have allowed him to be sheltered for a lot of it, so he shared an RV with Annette and I and his girlfriend. So rather than being sheltered, he was on the front lines with the guys running the camp. He heard everyone knock on the RV door, 'Syd, this is happening, Syd, that is happening,' and that gave him a good sense of what it took to do what we were doing," Syd said.

Before we even went to the playa, Syd was excited and secretive about a big DJ that he had lined up. Part of that was because Syd wasn't even sure that he was going to spin at the camp — Tiesto had a big gig in August and just wanted a cool vacation. He had heard about Burning Man from a friend in Whistler and someone with the promoter Spundae told him to contact Syd.

"At the time, and the argument could be made still, he was literally the biggest DJ in the world, the most successful, the number one voted (in music magazines), however you want to measure it, and to have the biggest DJ in the world play your camp and stay in your RV, it was cool," Syd told me. "It really is something special. It's a gig like nothing else in the world and everyone who has come and played for us has got that sense."

For Tiesto, another twist of fate made his visit all the bigger. While he was out there, he found out that his mother had been diagnosed with cancer. "So he almost skipped out and left but decided to stay and play, and it was an extra meaningful personal experience for him. He dedicated the set to his mom and there was more of an emotional connection to the event than there might have been for someone who just came and played."

But even by that first of five years that Opulent Temple would spend on the Esplanade — the longest that any sound camp has ever rocked such a prominent position — other big name DJs were already like family to us at Opulent Temple, such as Scumfrog, who would come into San Francisco to play our fundraisers that year.

After his first year in 2004, Scumfrog knew that "we had merely experienced the tip of the iceberg during our initiation trip, so, like most other first-time burn-ers, we started plotting and planning for the following year almost immediately." And when he returned, he felt an even deeper connection to Burning Man that went well beyond the sound scene. He just loved the otherworldliness of Burning Man, which he couldn't compare to other events he played.

"The biggest difference is that all other festivals are on planet Earth. This really sums up both the positive and negative. It's quite the journey to get there and quite the ordeal to stay afloat once inside. But on the other hand, for one week a year, you are truly removed from any forces that propel our everyday society," Scumfrog told me. "Other festivals may last up to a few days, but Burning Man, to most attendees, becomes a year-round lifestyle."

Burners Go Everywhere

Everything just seemed to expand outward when the Burning Man tribes returned from Black Rock City in 2005. That was particularly true in San Francisco, which Larry Harvey told me was the "beachhead" for their triumphant return from the wilderness and occupation of the "default world."

Down on the Gulf Coast, Burners Without Borders was becoming a new tribe based around good deeds. The Flaming Lotus Girls went international, taking Hand of God to the Robodoc Festival in Amsterdam, Europe's premier industrial arts extravaganza. They had ascended to superstar status on the playa and rode that wave to the other side of the planet, where they would influence and be influenced by the metalworking artists of the old world.

The DJs and dance community from camps like Opulent Temple staged a rocking Love Parade in San Francisco, with a huge international crowd that called it the best ever outside the original parade in Berlin. Bass-pumping floats rolled up Market Street and into a full-blown rave in and around City Hall. Even Ross Mirkarimi, a Green Party progressive who was newly elected to the San Francisco Board of Supervisors, attended with a giddy grin, telling me, "I can't believe there's a rave in City Hall. I love this town."

And it was the burners who were making it happen, including Love Parade board members Syd Gris and Dave Cutler, the contracts attorney for Black Rock City LLC. It wasn't just music, but the Burning Man style and ethos, with a playa-inspired fashion show in City Hall and fire art at some of the satellite parties around town.

The mainstream culture was also beginning to take note of Burning Man and its growing influence. The popular television sitcom "Malcolm in the Middle" did a Burning Man episode that September, in which the whole family decided to attend the event. Some in the burner community saw it as one more sign that the end was nigh, with corporate co-option finally gaining a foothold. But then it actually aired and the general consensus was that it celebrated the event more than it mocked it. It even had a Larry Harvey character, portrayed sympathetically, and Malcolm got laid by a sexy veteran burner portrayed by Rosanna Arquette. Talk about gaining credibility.

Even the massive artworks that seemed to only be possible on the huge expanse of the playa started to make their way back to San Francisco, where they were displayed prominently and feted by top city leaders, thanks to the help of Black Rock Arts Foundation, which provided the facilitation, fundraising, and labor that made it easy for city leaders to just say "yes."

"At Burning Man, it's all about the project team. And without them, these projects wouldn't have happened," said BRAF's first executive director Leslie Pritchett who, with just one other staff person but volunteers from many disciplines, paved the way for burner art to be displayed in San Francisco, a city that had long resisted it. "There is an attraction and a resistance within the art bureaucracies of the Bay Area. They are proud of being associated with Burning Man, but at the same time, they struggle with their desire to be connected with the A-list mainstream art."

But to Larry and others, it seemed inevitable that Burning Man would eventually come to be embraced by the leaders of the city where it was born, a city whose creative energies helped make the event what it is.

"San Francisco has always been a place apart, and a center of eccentric and independent thinkers. And what we started here, I don't think could have grown up anywhere else," Larry told me that fall. "You can create a social context in which culture can be created, but you can't directly create the culture."

Harvey told me he saw this Burning Man renaissance as a return to the avant garde approach to social progress that was replaced in the 1950s by countercultural movements: the beats, the hippies, the punkers, and others who "didn't want to reform society, they simply wanted to be apart from it."

Burners, by contrast, were deciding that they wanted to engage the world and start shaping it in ways that were more to their liking.

"Bringing Burning Man to the People"

In the summer before that transitional 2005 Burning Man, a key symbol of the culture came home to San Francisco, where none other than the mainstream Mayor Gavin Newsom decided to put it on display in the heart of the city's newest showcase strip and main city entrance, Octavia Boulevard. The Temple at Hayes Green, built by Burning Man artist David Best specifically for placement in the default world, was both a hit and a learning experience for the city.

"It is the first time in my 22-year career in public art that a piece has pleased everyone," said Jill Manton, the San Francisco Art Commission's director of public art who helped Newsom bring The Temple to SF. "Everyone was excited about bringing Burning Man to the people."

The writing on The Temple — words such as participate, kindness, tolerance, equality, and compassion; messages like "May our hearts be enflamed with love and passion" — spoke to an ethos burners hold dear, but their form said more than their content.

City officials initially freaked out when people started writing on the art they had placed, at least until burners explained that it's just part of the project. We've been writing on our temples since David first started building them. And now that city officials got it, they were excitedly talking about more such interactive art projects, as well as regular fall displays of Burning Man art.

The next big event was on November 17th when Mayor Newsom joined the leaders of Burning Man, both official and artistic, to bring artist Michael Christian's Flock sculpture into Civic Center Plaza, right outside City Hall and just down the street from the Temple, which proved so popular that city officials kept extending the removal date for this temporary artwork.

Michael, who had steadily become one of the most innovative and ambitious large-scale artists in the Burning Man orbit, seemed a bit haggard when I talked him as he was finishing his setup.

"Did you get any sleep?" I asked.

"I got a couple hours sleep," he replied.

In typical Burning Man fashion, he had recruited a large crew of volunteers to help him assemble this beautiful monstrosity on the lawn outside City Hall. After many years of getting ready for the event, it wasn't hard for someone like Michael to summon a large group of volunteers to weld and stay up all night with him for something like this. "I was having a blast, right here in the middle of the city," he told me.

I asked what his impressions were now that Flock was up. "It doesn't look very tall," Michael said, sizing up his work against the City Hall, the Asian Art Museum, and the Bill Graham Civic Auditorium. It was true. Flock is four stories tall, its long legs shooting its abstract body high up into the desert sky above the people. Here, he noted, it looks small.

When one of the mayor's people came over to get Burning Man board member Michael Mikel so they could start the ceremony, burner and political activist Mera Granberg told me, "I love that there's an event involving Burning Man and they just said 'the mayor's here, they need you.'"

Longtime iconoclast burner Flash Hopkins was frolicking impishly around the gathering. Larry was there in his usual tan Stetson hat. Leslie Pritchett, executive director of Black Rock Arts Foundation, which helped fund and facilitate the project, started the procession by talking about the burners' new relationship with city officials: "We want to cause conversations and I can say with some confidence that it's happening."

Arts Commission member Richard Newirth spoke next, sucking up to the mayor a bit, "our mayor is an arts mayor." But then he called the David Best's Temple in Hayes Green "an enormous success."

Mayor Newsom took the mike like a daytime talk show host, a crowd of middle school children behind him that his people had evidently invited out for the occasion. Rather than addressing the crowd in front of him, he turned back toward Flock and the kids and said, "What the heck is that thing?"

He went around to the kids, asking each what they thought it looked like: "It's a recreation from Burning Man." "You could imagine it as a lot of different things every time you come here." "It's art and it's cool." Then Newsom spoke.

"We have some of the best and the brightest people who are doing incredible things," Newsom said. "Trust me, we've got a lot more in line."

It was true. Soon, a key waterfront spot near the Ferry Building would host a succession of Burning Man artworks, starting with the striking Passage sculpture that Karen Cusolito and Dan Das Mann created for the event in 2004. And Pepe Ozan's Burning Man sculpture Monicacos y Monicacas was then displayed in a new shore-line park on Hunter's Point near the Box Shop, the worksite where Pepe built his big purple Dreamer head, which went to Burning Man in 2005 and ended up back on a meadow in Golden Gate Park for the summer.

The problem with public art, Newsom said, is that it's impossible for art to please everyone, making it necessarily controversial. So they take a long time deliberating over it before it goes in. Yet with the Temple, which was scheduled to be dismantled the next month (a date that was repeatedly pushed back), "We've discovered if you do temporary public art, you can just do it in a way that gets things done," he said.

"I love this piece," Newsom said, turning to Flock, which he could see from his City Hall office window. "It's exceeded my own expectations."

Then Michael took the mike, doing the same sheepish and speechless routine he did at a fundraising party that Rosie — my live-in girlfriend at the time — had hosted a few weeks earlier. "This is a great city," Michael said. "When we first built this on Hunters Point, we couldn't have imagined it would be up in Civic Center."

He spoke lovingly of his community. Describing all of the burners who helped him with his many projects, and those who had stayed up late helping him weld this thing together, it seemed clear to me he meant the Burning Man art community when he said, "I feel blessed to be part of this community," but he could just as easily have been talking about San Francisco, a city filled with his people.

"This is a great start and I'm really excited by the possibilities of this," he concluded.

Larry spoke next, talking about seeing Flock on the playa in 2001 and how "we were simply stunned by the scale of it." But here, it doesn't look that big. "It's a trick of scale," he said. "Tricks of scale conspire with our imagination."

Larry was speaking in code, but it was clear enough to me and others. Burning Man has gotten huge in the desert, but back in the real world, where its ethos and attributes are needed most, it still looks small, like there's no way it can make a dent. But there are ways of achieving transcendence.

Watching Flock in Civic Center Plaza, it didn't look as massive as it did by itself in the open desert, but here it may resonate even more, transporting people from their workaday lives to another place. Just as each of the kids saw something different in it, so too will everyone see what that want in it. A horse. A monster. A welded work of human creativity. A little piece of Burning Man placed in San Francisco. Transcendence.

"This sculpture is a harbinger of things to come," Larry told the crowd.

But it wasn't Burning Man that was coming, or the Black Rock Arts Foundation, or either of the Borgs. It was the burners, people who have gone to the desert to get their freak on and who in the process discovered their inner artist, builder, spiritual being, or engaged member of a community, finally part of something bigger than themselves. They were transformed, rejuvenated, restored.

"Every one of you here is at least as large as Burning Man," Larry concluded. "Hell, I've known that for years."

At a nearby reception after the Flock event, Michael told me the 2005 event and its aftermath were indeed a triumph: "In 1990, we were thrown out of the city and now we've returned."

David Best didn't quite agree with that sentiment: "We've just grown up. We're getting more mature and more responsible." In that maturity, David said burners are starting to use the gifts that the event has given them. "Burning Man has fed a lot of us. Are we just going to get fat or are we going to run with this nourishment?"

Chicken in the Tank

The one tribe that never really returned from the desert was Borg2, which didn't develop into a tribe at all. The year had begun with a high-profile conflict, and that's also how it ended. Jim Mason and Chicken John started The Petition, which turned into The Bet, which spawned Borg2, a group dedicated to bringing more and better art onto the playa.

It was the young turks against the establishment, a clash of the monster egos, well-intentioned ridiculousness, or a battle over the soul of Burning Man, depending on your perspective. But in the end, there was no denying that Burning Man had found a way to restore itself, and that Borg2's contribution to that was minimal. Or less generously: it flopped.

"So I'm going to go in the dunk tank, and people are going to talk about me," Chicken told me after that Burning Man, complying with the terms of The Bet by planning to sit in a dunk tank during Decompression, Burning Man's annual post-event street fair, which took place that October.

But of course Chicken, the prankster and showman, still had a few cards up his sleeve. When he told Larry Harvey that he intended to charge attendees money to try their hand at dunking him — something Chicken argues is a standard feature of the traditional dunk tank, gathering money he intends to place into an art fund that he'll control — he was told that was out of the question. After all, the prohibition on commerce is a central tenet of the Burning Man world.

"So I'm just going to do what I want to do, and if they try to stop me, I'm just going to start punching people," Chicken told me, a comment intended as a joke that he later regretted uttering after I published it in the Guardian. "If they don't let me charge money, they will have to do so physically."

Of course, it was all bluster. Chicken did indeed try to charge people, which inspired few donors but many observers just ran up to push the button, several times, despite the best defensive efforts of Chicken loyalists. But he showed up at Civic Center for the Flock event the next month with an oversized check for $1200 that he said was the proceeds from his Decompression dunk tank.

Neither Larry nor I believed he had raised that much, but you never know. It's hard to tell with Chicken. He is the ultimate byproduct of Burning Man, or perhaps its prototype, a creative creature with a stunning knack for reinvention, which he employed two years later to run for mayor of San Francisco. But we'll get to that later.

At Decompression, which I consider San Francisco's best street fair (How Weird is a close second), Chicken was just one spectacle of many. Everyone comes in costumes and other playa finery (which is encouraged by charging twice the admission price for those in street wear), and much of the playa art is on display.

But first and foremost, this is just a rocking great party, with Opulent Temple, the Deep End, and other sound camps bringing out their sound systems and their DJs and dropping the beats for a solid 10 straight hours, well into Sunday night. Many of us plan to take Monday off work if possible. It's that kind of party, a bit of Burning Man plopped into San Francisco for one glorious day.

The Rise of Bassnectar

The success of Opulent Temple helped elevate Syd's status as a DJ and promoter in San Francisco, where he threw regular parties under the name Opel Productions. "I'm certainly happy that what I've done with Opulent Temple increases my profile and increases the level of respect I get from the community, because that feels good," he said.

Yet for his personal finances, it was sort of a mixed blessing for Syd. His opportunities to throw Opel parties, where the profits or losses from each party were his, would rise and fall with OT's financial fortunes: "Every party I throw for Opulent Temple is a party that I can't throw for Opel and make money on. I can't do both."

That balance was still pretty good back in 2005, before Opulent Temple would really go big. And Syd was becoming a better and more popular DJ in town, partly because he had mostly dropped his affinity for trance and switched to breakbeats, the style of San Francisco's reigning superstar DJ at that point: Berkeley's Lorin Ashton, who had just changed his DJ name to Bassnectar and spent most of the year touring to burner-inspired gigs around the world.

Santosh recalls when the long-haired raver kid known as DJ Lorin got his start in the mid-'90s with the Santa Cruz collective called Koinonia, which sometimes collaborated with CCC. Established San Francisco DJ Adam Ohana (aka An-Ten-Ae) was playing the main room at one of the CCC warehouse parties when Lorin, an eager newcomer, asked him "What was that last track you played?" And according to a story that became local lore, Ohana replied "Hush up kid and roll another spliff."

But the two DJs would end up closely collaborating and camping together at the El Circo camp at Burning Man, our neighbors on the playa in 2004. By then, Lorin was already becoming a legendary DJ in the Burning Man world, absorbing the strange environment and energy of the happy bouncing multitudes and reflecting the vibe right back. One might even say Bassnectar was born on the playa.

"He got his panache playing sets at Burning Man, and that carried over into San Francisco and other places," Syd said. "He told me he would play places and see posters saying, 'DJ Lorin, the biggest DJ at Burning Man.' And that was how they were selling him to the public. It made him cringe, but it was an undeniable marketing tool that kinda speaks for itself."

I had also gotten to know Lorin and quoted him in my first Guardian article about Burning Man, when he dismissed the artist rebellion by saying "Art-shmart. I would love to see Burning Man as an organization and mobilization front," a comment he later regretted. But I interviewed him a few more times and loved to dance to his energetic sets and absorb the scene that was growing up around him.

At the Scorpio Party that November, DNA Lounge was transformed into a Candyland game. The downstairs dance floor was ringed in giant lollipops and neon orange slices, harking back to the candy raver days of old. Bassnectar was the headliner and the place was packed.

The DJ before Bassnectar on the main stage was rocking hard breaks, which seemed a little premature for a pre-midnight crowd that was still trying to settle into a party that would go until 10 a.m. So I headed upstairs, past Hard Candy Cavern and up Licorice Lane to the Gingerbread House — which indeed looked like a gingerbread house, candy trim covering the brown paper walls that went all the way up to the high ceiling. But it sounded more like the second dance floor that it was. DJ Brother was nicely rocking a beautiful crowd with downtempo dub beats that seemed much more appropriate to the mood, or at least my mood.

As midnight passed, Brother began to slowly pick up the tempo and get the crowd warmed up and moving. It sounded great and I was beginning to find my groove, but pretty soon the dance floor started to thin out a little, which could only mean one thing.

I walked back into the main room, and sure enough, Lorin had taken to the tables, his long dark hair flipping through the air, arms clad in black leather wristbands twisting and punctuating the beats and changes of the music he knew all too well. After all, in addition to working on his music everyday, he was touring almost non-stop, doing almost 150 shows per year.

His energy is always infectious and his bass heavy breakbeats filled the dance floor, as well as a big stage behind the DJ booth, which had been empty when he started and full of dancers by the end of his first song. Behind the dancers, the video screen alternated short clips of Wizard of Oz with an old school Hansel and Gretel, sometimes psychedelically morphing images in and out, a nice touch by VJ CaroLuna. At most burner parties, the VJs, or video jockeys, are almost as honored as the DJs. Almost.

Lorin was dancing as hard as anyone of the dance floor, spinning knobs and pushing buttons with a flourish. He's strictly an electronic music DJ, leaving the two turntables on the decks he was using sitting idle. But the crowd — particularly the women clad in sexy corsets, lacy negligees, or strategically torn shirts with hints of nipples peaking through — didn't seem to require vinyl purity. They had clearly come to dance and party until well into the next day.

The neon candy décor definitely said rave, but that was tempered by the DNA Lounge's clubber-cum-burner aesthetic and by some fun touches like a cotton candy machine and a chocolate waterfall for dipping strawberries, pretzels or whatever. And yes, I saw a couple whatevers being dipped.

I loved Bassnectar's music and considered him my favorite local DJ in those years, during which my nightlife consisted mostly of hitting the best dance parties that came onto my radar — and Lorin would always top that list. He had recently played some epic sets on the Thump Radio float outside City Hall during Love Parade (despite a couple technical difficulties), at the Opel Halloween party, and on Wednesday night at Burning Man during the White Party at Opulent Temple.

Ever since his breakthrough set at Arena during the 2000 Burning Man, Lorin has been the king of burner breakbeats just as that electronic music style was ascendant in the San Francisco nightlife. And I consistently hear people talking about how his albums Diverse Systems of the Throb and Motions of Mutation are among their favorites, music that will always make their hearts soar and asses bob not matter what their mood.

But Lorin doesn't want to be just a DJ. In fact, he doesn't even want to be Lorin anymore, officially switching over completely to his alternative pseudonym, Bassnectar, with his album Mesmerizing the Ultra. "I don't want to identify as a DJ anymore," he told me in his house in Berkeley a few days before his DNA gig. "I don't just want to identify as a category of dance music."

What Lorin wanted to be is a serious musician, someone known for transforming what's inside him — melodies that go from his head to humming to his computer. Rather than a DJ, spinning the music of others to entertain a party, he wants to be something closer to a band like Radiohead or Coldplay, creating an emotional musical ride that goes up and down, twisting this way and that — rather than just the consistent thump-thump-thump that moves bodies on a dance floor.

"I want to ignite an experience," he told me. But to be honest, the experience that I was having was only so-so for much of Lorin's set. It was probably mostly me, because other people seemed to be digging it and because I had been pulling back socially as the days had gotten shorter and I'd changed gears from the rockin' days of summer.

"I don't think I'm as groundbreaking as people say," he told me as he shared a few techniques for how he creates music on his computer. "It's not so much that I have a different sound as a different intention."

With Lorin and the people who love him, intention is everything. He truly wants to speak from his soul, to find those moments of resonance with his audience, and — in his fondest hopes — to enlighten people about the political and social problems that he internalizes more than most.

That's why you'll hear clips of revolutionary rhetoric — from Noam Chomsky, Mumia Abu-Mamal, Mario Savio, and other progressive thinkers — on each of his albums. Particularly after the 2004 presidential election, Lorin didn't believe his music would really change anything, but he still wants to use it to connect with people, to help create community.

And in the end, he finally got me. He was nearing the end of a set that was almost two hours long, the dance floor was full but not packed, and Lorin was layering a few tracks over one another, beat-matching them in a way that is one of his great strengths as a DJ. My body slipped into the groove and my mind drifted into a place where there was just this music, tracks moving toward and away from each other, colliding in crescendos of body rockin' bass, bouncing the crowd in unison as big dumb grins grabbed my face and others. Uh-huh, yeah, that's why I came: that moment of connection, of musical resonance, of bliss, when nothing else matters.

And for dessert, a sexy redhead — Catherine D:Lish — followed Lorin's set with a burlesque strip tease and feather dance that ended with her nude in an oversized martini glass on the stage, squeezing sponges full of bubble bathwater over her beautiful body. This was a fun scene and an undeniable part of the larger Burning Man culture.

But I would soon be pulled into a very different aspect of the culture, one that had quietly been building since we left the playa.

News from the Front

Tom Price called me from the hurricane-ravaged Gulf Coast. We didn't know each other, but he'd read some of my articles about Burning Man, including "Epilogue as Prologue" from 2005, which culminated my seven-part Guardian series by looking at how burners were projecting their culture, skills, and ethos into the outside world.

The most striking example I used was the group that went straight from Burning Man 2005 to Mississippi to help clean up after Hurricane Katrina. "If that isn't applying our ethos, I don't know what is," Burning Man founder Larry Harvey said in my article. "The very skills needed to survive at Burning Man are the skills needed to respond to a disaster."

Price had been a little busy mucking out flood-damaged homes and rebuilding a Buddhist temple in Biloxi, Mississippi, but the camp he'd called home for the past five months had finally gotten an Internet connection in early 2006, and he'd just found my article. "Dude, we're still here," he told me excitedly by phone. "It's happening just like you wrote. We're doing it."

As I started to learn, Price was an accomplished idealist for whom "doing it" means working to save the world. During college in Utah he spent a year living in a shanty he erected in the main college square urging the university to disinvest in apartheid South Africa, and his forcible removal led to a court case that expanded free speech rights.

He later worked as a journalist chronicling threats to the indigenous Kalahari tribes in Botswana and then as an environmental activist and lobbyist in Washington DC, where he eventually became the main contract lobbyist for Black Rock City LLC, advocating for an event he loves. Larry told me that he considered Tom to be one of the most dedicated and effective people that he'd ever met.

In Mississippi, Tom turned an encampment of do-gooder burners into an organization he dubbed Burners Without Borders. He spoke so passionately and eloquently about what they were doing — with such an infectious energy and with a journalist's intuition for conveying a good story — that I just had to go.

By that time, the encampment had moved to Pearlington, Mississippi, a small town on the Louisiana border that the eye of Katrina had passed directly over. Finances were always tight at the Guardian, so I contributed an airline travel voucher to the project, got the approval of my editor, and booked my flight.

My approach was going to be the same as the one I had developed working with the Flaming Lotus Girls: experiential journalism. I would do the work, learn, and be a part of what was going on. I would have my reporter's notebook, do my interviews, then put it away, put my work gloves on, and contribute to the cleanup and rebuilding effort.

When I arrived at the airport in Biloxi, Tom was there to great me along with someone who was more familiar to me, Andie Grace, the Borg's media liaison, who had been sent to make sure I got what I needed. Actually, I think she was just taking advantage of a chance to see Burners Without Borders in action — and to see Tom, an old friend of hers who would soon become much more.

Spreading the Word

I was truly touched by what I saw and did that week, in between spending cold nights camping in a cot in one of the shelters that they had constructed on the pad of what used to be a new Post Office. My outrage at my government stirred, my belief in the burner ethos confirmed, I returned and wrote the following cover story for the Guardian, which ran on February 22, 2006:

From Here to Katrina

Hit hard by the storm and abandoned by their government, some Gulf Coast residents have found themselves relying on a few unlikely saviors — Bay Area burners.

Pearlington, Mississippi — It's hard to imagine the devastation until you see it. It's even harder to fathom why so much wreckage remains almost six months after Hurricane Katrina slammed into the richest and most powerful country on Earth, laying to waste hundreds of thousands of homes between Biloxi, Mississippi, and New Orleans, Louisiana.

In the path of Katrina's eye, buildings were ripped apart or crushed by trees, boats, or other houses. The homes that still stand are now freckled with black mold and awaiting demolition. The southern Mississippi coastline was wiped clean by the 30-foot storm surge, except for the ghostly, darkened hull of a pirate ship built as a casino. The New Orleans levee breaches knocked out almost all of the small homes in the Lower Ninth Ward.

The failures of the government to prevent this disaster or respond effectively — both during the storm and since then — are a national shame. The corruption and incompetence — some would even say greed and racism — that have hampered efforts to plan for the return of residents to poor urban neighborhoods is a tragedy that is still unfolding.

But there's another story here on the Gulf Coast, a more hopeful story. It's a story of people from around the country — including many from the San Francisco Bay Area — who have descended on the region, placing their lives on hold so they can help their fellow humans dig out of the muck and rebuild.

In New Orleans, community organizers and social justice advocates with roots in the Bay Area came together to form Common Ground, which operates a soup kitchen, a medical clinic, and a political and legal advocacy network. Emergency Communities forms a similar structure in St. Bernard Parish, serving 1,400 meals a day from its Made with Love Café domes.

Throughout the Gulf Coast, religious groups from around the country — from Salvation Army to Islamic Relief to Presbyterian Disaster Assistance — have settled into communities big and small, setting up in tent cities to rebuild church halls, distribute relief items, or lend a hand with the work. Other residents turn to the Red Cross, which distributes food and supplies, or to the subcontractors of the subcontractors actually doing work on behalf of the Army Corps of Engineers, workers who will haul away their rubble if residents can get it to the street.

Many of these groups have a presence in Pearlington, a small community along the Pearl River, which divides Louisiana from Mississippi, a town the eye of Katrina passed over on August 29th, leaving only five of its roughly 2,000 buildings repairable.

But there's another organization in town, one that's a lot less conventional — and in many ways, a lot more effective.

Burners Without Borders

Burning Man, the giant art festival in the Nevada desert, has a reputation in some quarters as a self-indulgent freak fest. And for a lot of the people who make the trip, it's mostly a party. But behind the scenes, the event is a serious operation: Someone has to build from scratch and then take down what amounts to a medium-size city every year.

So Burning Man has spawned a large network of resourceful people with all manner of survival, construction, and cleanup skills — and when Katrina hit, during last year's festival, some people decided to put their well-honed community-building skills to work on the Gulf Coast.

Thus Theme Camp Katrina, also known as Burners Without Borders, was born, an informal disaster relief crew that has been working out of encampments on the Gulf Coast since the first week of September, consisting of up to a couple dozen people at any one time and cycling more than 100 people through since it started.

Many took vacation time to come. Among those who have stayed for longer stints, most were at transition periods in their lives — between jobs or just getting out of romantic relationships — or the work caused them to create a transition. It seems easy to linger here. There's no rent or other real living costs, and the three square meals a day from a well-stocked kitchen, made by a fantastic cook known as Spoon, are better than most people eat at home.

After spending four months in Biloxi — distributing supplies, doing home demolition and cleanup, and rebuilding a Buddhist temple — the group moved to

Pearlington in early January, setting up camp where the post office had been before it was destroyed by Katrina, its pieces strewn among the trees and other debris in an adjacent bayou forest.

"We're the only heavy-equipment operator out here," said Richard Scott, 50, who works for Burning Man using cranes and other equipment in support of artists. He's been on the Gulf Coast since right after the hurricane, and managed to get Daewoo to donate an excavator — a massive, dinosaurlike piece of equipment capable of ripping apart a house — and a large front-loader tractor, each vehicle weighing 28,000 pounds.

The donations joined the large trailer and smaller Kubota front-loader that Matt Lindsay (who spearheaded the effort), his father, Phil Lindsay, and other family members drove down from their construction business in Eugene, Oregon, the first week in September. That was what started the influx of burners to the Gulf Coast, people ranging from low-skilled grunts to experienced carpenters, like Philip Zeitgold, a former San Francisco resident, and Mark Grieve, the San Rafael, California resident who oversees the construction of the temple at Burning Man.

"It became a Burning Man thing, but it didn't really start out that way," Scott said. "People came down here because they had a connection."

And once they came, many simply stayed. Zeitgold planned to be here for a week but found the work so fulfilling that he has stayed for two months and intends to remain until the group breaks camp April 1st. Many share that story, including San Francisco resident Carmen Mauk, who came in late December and just can't leave. "This hurricane could have rolled right through here yesterday," Mauk said as she surveyed the debris around Pearlington. "That's where they're at."

They work all day, usually every day except Sunday, in white neighborhoods and black, on soggy little shacks and a once exquisite Frank Lloyd Wright house, picking up debris by hand or doing skilled specialty work, and never taking money from the locals for their efforts. And all the while, they add a lively splash of color to this devastated community, with their tattoos and piercings, brightly colored cruiser bikes, and art projects they burn in a campfire that never seems to go out.

To say they've been welcomed here is an understatement, particularly given what Pearlington residents have been through.

Storm Stories

Every project the crew has taken on comes with a story, and many of those stories involve the stately, gnarled oak trees that fill the region, perches that saved most of those who stayed to ride out the storm.

One photo from a surveillance camera conveyed the power of what hit Pearlington: It showed a surging wave of seawater as high as the 40-foot oak trees, a massive shrimp boat just a speck in the wave, the sea in the background just as high. Once it washed through town, the entire region was under more than 10 feet of water most of the day.

Samuel Burton and his 28-year-old granddaughter, Freda, came into the camp my first day there to ask for help removing two large pecan trees that had fallen in their yard. A couple of us went to check it out, driving into an African American neighborhood with a massive oak tree at its center.

"I was in that house there, and I ended up in that tree," Freda Burton told me.

I hadn't yet grown accustomed to the stories of people escaping from floodwater in the trees, so her story seemed almost unbelievable. The floodwaters came in the morning, when she was lounging around the house with her aunt and pregnant sister wearing just a T-shirt and boxer shorts. They all ran outside to try to get to high ground, but the water was rising too fast. Burton couldn't swim, so she desperately clung to a car, then some vines that hung from the oak tree. Eventually, the rising water allowed the three of them to make it up into the tree's branches, where they sat shivering for the next 12 hours. Samuel Burton, holding his dog, and a nephew were in a smaller tree nearby.

"I sat in the tree and watched my house go underwater," she said.

The next job was over at Santa Looter's, a nickname we'd given to a house owned by a guy named Buzzy, who'd placed a sign next to the Santa Claus figure in his front yard that read, "Keep out or all you'll get for Christmas is SHOT!"

The two houses on the property were tear-downs, the floors full of dried mud cracked into jigsaw puzzle pieces, the walls pocked with black mold. To enter the house and hope to avoid the dreaded "Katrina cough," one had to wear a respirator or a mold mask. The cracked mud in the houses sometimes bore an eerie resemblance to the playa floor at Burning Man.

Buzzy and his wife had evacuated before the storm, but his son and daughter-in-law had stayed behind and ended up in an oak tree. Within a couple of hours, our crew of a half dozen had transferred a yard full of smelly debris into a pile by the street, and Buzzy dropped his good-ole-boy demeanor and fumbled for the words to properly express his gratitude, still seeming to not understand why all these strangers had helped him for free.

Across the street, the excavator was parked in front of Matthew Abel's large, white house, his demolition permit number and "Tear Me Down" written in red on the walls. Richard Scott would attack his house in the morning, but that night Abel came by the campfire to have a few beers and share his story.

"I was sitting in my front room getting drunk, watching WLOX on TV," Abel said. He grew up in New Orleans before coming to Pearlington, and he'd heard many hurricane warnings, none of which ever amounted to much. "But this time, it happened, man."

He watched the rising water through a window and thought about making a break for it in his car until an oak tree fell across his driveway and blocked him in. Then the water started to rise through his floorboards, and he dove to save his cat: "I just wanted to make sure Nunu was all right."

Abel put Nunu in a cat box and set it on his mattress, which was now floating. "It's weird to see everything you own floating," he told me. The water level continued to rise, so Abel bailed out of the house and climbed an oak tree. That night, once the water level had fallen, he retrieved Nunu and saw that the waterline had come within a couple feet of his ceiling.

Wright House Tour

After dealing with Buzzy's mucky mess, the group pedaled its bicycles over to a slightly more upscale part of town, Belle Isles, where many of the houses had private fishing boat docks along a man-made canal that paralleled the Pearl River, the bridge to Louisiana looming on the horizon.

It was a field trip to investigate the Frank Lloyd Wright house that had partially collapsed and been buried under a pile of debris. The owners, Billy and Sharon Graham, had contacted Scott in tears and asked him to tear it down. It had been their dream house, and they couldn't even bear to deal with its wrecked remains. Upon inspection, it seemed a treasure trove to Burners Without Borders.

Built almost entirely of cedar and brick, with Wright's signature double-cantilever design roof extending to the ground, it had clearly been a magnificent house. Indeed, much of it was still solid, except for the fact that the waterside columns had given way and collapsed half the roof onto the living room. That, and the water damage.

The more striking impact of Katrina here was the deep pile of wood and debris between the house and the water, the remains of destroyed homes, piers, and other structures from who knows where. Here was a massive pile of boards, many of them solid, usable wood — everything from 2-by-4s to 2-by-10 planks — from which the carpenters in the group could help other Katrina victims rebuild. After all, the burners were working for free, the camp surviving almost entirely on donations from other burners and outside groups. Plus, there was enough scrap wood to keep the campfire burning for weeks.

In the morning, Scott used the excavator to single-handedly tear down Abel's house — and his oak tree perch — before lunchtime. Before that, he made an announcement. After demolishing dozens of homes — sometimes two a day, unleashing their mold spores in the process — and spending a solid five months on this devastated coastline, he needed a change.

"I'm getting really tired of wrecking houses. I want to build something. I need to leave something other than empty lots," he told the group during the Friday morning meeting, proposing that the group focus much of its energy on rebuilding the house of Tony Vegeletta, a 71-year-old man who'd lost everything in the storm and had been one of the first Pearlington locals to befriend the group.

Some resisted. "If we were only building, I'd feel like we weren't contributing as much," said Lisa Benham, a volunteer from the South Bay Area who had arrived January 7th.

"Every day, we have three or four people ask for help," Scott said, noting that the workload was endless and it was beginning to take its toll on his health, mental and physical, a statement his look and tone seemed to validate.

"I want to make my last month here as enjoyable as possible. I've done my commitment," he said. "We all put our own expectations on ourselves."

Beads, Deeds and Seeds

It had been a big workweek, so on Saturday, February 11th, Mauk, Benham, and Jim Jordan from Seattle decided to join me for a tour of New Orleans, visiting the major aid groups and seeing the devastation before watching the very first of the season's Mardi Gras parades, Krewe du Vieux, in the French Quarter.

At the Emergency Communities site, I met Luke Taylor, a student from a Sebastopol high school whose senior trip had been moved from Mexico to New Orleans so the students could help with the relief effort. He said it had been an eye-opening experience.

"Nobody expected to arrive here and have it look like a third world country," Taylor said. "We really feel good being here, and we wish we could stay."

It was a common sentiment among volunteers on the Gulf Coast. It's hard work in a sometimes emotionally jarring setting, but intensely satisfying. The volunteers at Common Ground — which operates out of the only restored and repainted house in the Lower Ninth Ward, among other locations in the city — said the same thing.

"Common Ground has been the great leap forward for the global justice movement," Bay Area activist James Tracy, an early volunteer for the group, told me. "You had all these different factions of the US left actually working well together for a change."

Former Black Panthers (including Common Ground founder Malik Rahim), labor leaders, community organizers, tenants rights activists, doctors from the Bay Area Radical Health Collective, antiwar protestors — they came together to do physical work on behalf of the displaced poor of New Orleans.

"It was on the ground, gutting houses. Every morning, Common Ground would marshal volunteers to help residents try to salvage their houses," Tracy said. "We literally saved people thousands of dollars just by helping them out for a day."

Over at the Parkway Partners' Sun Don Organic Community Garden, we ran into noted San Francisco writer and activist Starhawk on her way to teach a class on bio-remediation, which involves introducing red wiggler worms into the soil as a way of breaking down the toxins left by the floodwaters.

"It's the kind of work that the EPA should be doing but isn't," Starhawk told us, noting that New Orleans is a good place to test this approach to cleansing the soil. "Then we want to go home and bioremediate San Francisco."

Most of the city was abandoned; much of it was destroyed or mildewing, the most active signs of life being the new signs stuck to posts or displayed in yards: "We buy damaged houses," "for sale by owner," and advertisements for house-gutting and mold-removal services.

But the worst was the Lower Ninth Ward, a poor, predominantly African American neighborhood that had taken the most direct hit from the levee break — from the water, the debris, and a block-long steel barge that crushed houses and people and was still sitting right where it came to rest. And if the devastation wasn't bad enough, a steady stream of tourists poured through taking pictures, the most life we'd seen in New Orleans all day.

I almost couldn't bear to return to this neighborhood in the late afternoon, when local residents would be getting out of a community meeting Common Ground had called. But then I met Deborah Harris. She had lived there half her life, 26 years, and when I asked if her house was still standing, she replied with a sassy, "That's about all it's doing."

Although people in Pearlington all seem to want their damaged houses torn down, in New Orleans there's a different sentiment. Many seem to feel that once their dwellings are gone, the residents will be displaced.

Not Harris. "I'm going to rebuild," she said. "I'm going to start small and build up."

It won't be easy. Her property and those of her neighbors had just been assessed at a ridiculously low $750. And even though she'd applied for both demolition permits and a FEMA trailer in early October, her applications were still pending. She believed New Orleans officials were trying to keep poor residents out so the prime riverside real estate of the Lower Ninth Ward could be turned into casinos and a golf course. Her reasoning rang true after my stay in southern Mississippi, where just about every standing house had its demolition permit number written on the side and a trailer in the yard.

"Everyone wants to make this a black or white issue, but it's a human issue," Harris said. "I'm 51 years old, how the hell am I going to start over again?"

The answer: She's not. Harris said she's going to stay in her community, on her property, no matter what designs corrupt New Orleans officials have on her neighborhood. "If I have the only tent that's in the yard, I'm going to be here, and I dare them to try to get me out."

This same resilient, defiant spirit was on display during the Krewe du Vieux parade that evening in the French Quarter — a part of New Orleans that didn't flood and seemed completely intact. Floats and paraders mocked FEMA and the whole range of government entities, dressed in the blue tarps that are ubiquitous on Gulf Coast rooftops, and appealed for a reversal of the Louisiana Purchase with the slogan "Buy us back, Chirac."

Along with the beads and other traditional throws to the large crowd, Krewe du Vieux handed out little life preservers with the slogan "C'est Levee." Yet there was one parader who subtly offered the grim reminder not to let the grand distraction of Mardi Gras interfere with the work at hand.

"Seeds and deeds, not beads," he said solemnly as he walked the route. "Seeds and deeds, not beads."

Biloxi's Buddhists

No single deed performed by Burners Without Borders was more striking than its reconstruction of the Chau Van Duc Buddhist Temple in Biloxi. The Vietnamese American residents of this fishing village had spent more than 10 years raising money for the temple and four years on its construction — holding its grand-opening ceremony August 28th, the day before Katrina, which severely damaged the temple and surrounding village.

When the Lindsay family, the construction workers from Oregon, arrived with their equipment, they set up camp in the temple's parking lots, helping to run what became an important disaster relief center for Biloxi. Many of the burners who followed came from the Temple Crew, a perfect match for the temple reconstruction efforts that began almost immediately and was completed by Christmas.

Other groups helped. In fact, at one point Islamic Relief asked for supplies from the Mormon Church in Utah, which were delivered through the Salvation Army to the burners, who used them to help the Buddhists. But when we had tea in the temple — now a stunningly beautiful sanctuary — with a monk named Ti, he credited the burners with the temple's restoration.

There was stunning workmanship on display at the beautifully restored temple, along with a subtle signature that the burners left behind: in the woodwork on the back of a door leading to the main temple room, I could see the subtle image of the Burning Man, his arms raised as they are just before he is set on fire.

I was taken on a tour of the group's former stomping grounds, and much of the Gulf Coast, by Tom Price, who more than anyone else was responsible for the transformation of Camp Lindsay into Burners Without Borders, using the Burning Man networks and resources to increase the effort's longevity, volunteer base, and impact.

Price, a former Washington, DC, lobbyist for environmental groups, is a contract employee for Burning Man, serving as the group's liaison to political and law enforcement officials.

Price pointed out the Imperial Palace casino where FEMA workers stayed in Biloxi. "They were incredibly thoughtless, arrogant people living just blocks away from people who had lost everything," he said.

The casinos figured prominently in the camp's decision to leave. They were among the first businesses to reopen in Biloxi, creating a steady stream of traffic through devastated communities — an unsettling situation compounded by the fact that many poor renters were being served with eviction notices, the landlords preferring to sell their now-cleared land to build even more casinos.

"Yeah," Price said, momentarily lost in memories of those days, "it was time to go."

So they toured the devastated region, talked to other relief groups, sized up where they could do the most good, and finally settled on Pearlington, where local government didn't exist and federal agencies and their contractors hadn't even yet arrived to deal with the mess.

Rebuilding

As we chain-sawed and hauled away the Burtons' fallen pecan trees, parishioners from the adjacent First Baptist Church were gathering for lunch in a new hall that had been built for them by a visiting church group from Florida. It was one of the first new buildings in Pearlington, having hosted its first service just days earlier, and they invited us in for lunch.

Jacqueline Bradley and Johnnie Robinson, who rode out the hurricane in nearby Stennis Space Center, talked about how the storm aftermath has been hard to cope with, although they take hope from the outsiders who have come to help.

"It's the best and the worst. My house went underwater, and it's as tall as this," Bradley, 51, told me, gesturing to her new church hall. Robinson, 60, added, "We're just thankful for all that's been done for us."

It's understandable why Scott wanted to leave behind something other than empty lots, something he was still off to create more of on Monday morning. "I got a house I have to demo today for a tugboat captain, and it's a wet, stinky mess," he said.

As the only one who could operate the excavator, he was having a hard time disengaging from the destruction. But he'd sown his seeds: Mark Grieve arrived on Sunday with a truck full of carpentry tools and others were on the way. "I throw fishing lines out there with a little bit of bait, and they come," Scott said with a sly grin.

"My friends have come and told me about it," Grieve told me, explaining his intention to work on Tony Vegeletta's house during his planned week-long visit. "I'm going to get his house started, give him a little hope."

While Scott tore down the tugboat captain's stinky house, some of us pulled four large trailers full of good boards out of the Wright house, others used crowbars to rid the boards of nails, and others assisted Grieve as the frame of the new house started to take shape.

My week there was drawing to an end, and I had that same impulse to just stay, to keep plugging away at this unending task, that has grabbed so many.

In my last 24 hours, I'd met Bill Schierholz, 67, alone and disabled and reluctant to appeal for assistance; I'd listened to the Vietnamese owner of the only gas station and store in town ask for the help he needed to reopen; I'd watched Scott replace a crypt that had floated away from the cemetery.

And as I watched the sun drop into the Pearl River for my last time, on our way back from picking up debris in Schierholz's yard, Price took me to the marshy banks of the river on the southernmost section. There, we saw more than a football field's worth of wood and debris, who knows how deep, who knows how many houses worth, who knows how many people-hours it would take to deal with.

He surveyed the scene and smiled. "Where do you even begin?"

Building from Disaster

Burners Without Borders opened many doors for Tom Price, someone who had been searching for a way to marry his passion for social justice with his simple love for Burning Man: "What we found in the wreckage of Katrina was anyone can make an enormous difference if they just choose to," he told me. "Burning Man is such a key part of that experience."

The encampment they created in Pearlington had a sense of play and whimsy that the other do-gooders there lacked. On the front of the encampment was a ubiquitous sign from Burning Man: "This area reserved for theme camps." And like a theme camp, they played as hard as they worked, a spirit that Pearlington residents found infectious.

"It is incredibly toxic to be in an environment like that," Tom said. So they would gather around the campfire at night to commune, drink and smoke, tell stories, burn weird creations, and occasionally create explosions. And the locals joined in, bonding with the burners.

"By the time we left, there were 600 people in that town, and on the night before we left, 150 of them came and they brought crawfish and moonshine and we played techno and we made art, we looked at it, enjoyed it, and let it go. And they got it. Still to this day, we get letters from them. At the entrance to their town, their pride and joy on their website, was a sign we made entirely of garbage and debris, a testament to the ability to create art and beauty out of literally garbage," Tom said.

He, Carmen, and others carried that feeling and those lessons forward, keeping Burners Without Borders going with a proposal to collect the spare wood from next year's Burning Man for Habitat For Humanity and pursuing other social justice projects.

"Going to Burning Man and learning how to interact with people the way that we do there is an incredible education in how to be effective in the world, because you get to create your entire world. Everything you experience is created by you and the people around you," Tom told me later. "It's one thing to know something intellectually, and it's another thing entirely to put it into practice. In Mississippi, we learned, for example, that a group of completely unorganized people with no central support at all could do a tremendous amount of work. We did a million dollars in free demolition and debris removal in six months with virtually no support at all."

That was an incredibly empowering thing for Tom and the others to experience while there. But Tom also got a little something else from the experience. While we were there, on that week of cold nights, where Tom's trailer was sometimes a very welcome refuge, Tom Price and Andie Grace finally hooked up.

Tom moved to San Francisco to be with Andie, working on a film about Katrina and the birth of Burners Without Borders as they built a life together. And a year later, when they had a baby together, they named her Juniper Pearlington Grace.

Meanwhile, Carmen tried to find new missions for Burners Without Borders, and to help Burning Man realize the potential that she had long seen in it, continuing a quest she began before she had ever heard of Burning Man. She left college in the mid-'90s to work for the Fourth World Movement, a nonprofit organization in France that worked on anti-poverty and other grassroots projects.

"I got my burner experience when I was 25, before I even knew that Burning Man existed at all. I was working with people who just had this yes mentality," Carmen said, referring to the group as "very small but it got a lot done. It was a very long project that worked."

In 1999, shortly after moving to California, Carmen attended her first Burning Man. She had a good time, but not a great one, mostly because she went with new friends that she didn't really jive with. But she saw the enormous potential of the event and its participants. She moved to San Francisco that year, starting volunteering with the organization, then became its first volunteer coordinator.

"I thought there was a tremendous amount of creativity that I had never seen anywhere before. I felt like there was so much potential and I couldn't understand why it wasn't being carried over. That's why I started the radio station for Burning Man," she said, referring to Burning Man Information Radio, FM 94.5, which still operates during the event. "There was not a Burning Man community when I started in 1999. I have gotten to see and be a part of the growing emergence of the Burning Man community. Even in San Francisco, I've seen it change. Not that people weren't doing things. I think community means when people are finally aware of each other."

There had been communities involved with Burning Man from the beginning, from the Cacophony Society that brought the Man to the playa to artists who brought their creations to the CCC crew that brought sound systems and a party vibe to the event. But it took some time for Burning Man, for burners, to think of themselves as a community, one made up of various tribes.

But the Borg2 rebellion defined itself as the voice of the Burning Man art community, even if some of its agitators weren't fond of the C word. And when Katrina hit during the event, a community that had been making art and music together, and having crazy fun together, discovered that there was all kinds of things they could do.

"Now we're aware of ourselves. Now we know there are others. Now we're starting to do art together. Now we're starting to talk about what we care about and we're starting to take a stand for that, whether it be at City Hall or wherever," Carmen told me. "People are starting to say that's the celebration event, not who we are. People are starting to define themselves around these community events they're creating, and those are starting to become the culture of Burning Man. Burning Man is starting to be more in its proper place, as an event."

A Final Word

Just before I left for Burning Man 2006, a time of great anticipation given President Bush's steep slide in public opinion polls over the previous year since Katrina hit and the Iraq War turned bad, I wrote the following Editor's Note that appeared on the cover of the Bay Guardian:

There's an intriguing confluence of anniversaries coming up that together offer an opportunity for societal awakening.

This week I'll be among thousands of Bay Area residents leaving for Burning Man and the 20th birthday of the most significant countercultural event of our times. Five years ago, right after my first Burning Man, the September 11th attacks ushered in radical changes to US foreign policy and political dialogue. And last year during the festival, Hurricane Katrina hit the Gulf Coast, another event of international significance, which New Orleans writer Jason Berry explores in this week's cover story commissioned by the Association of Alternative Newsweeklies.

Burning Man, 9/11, Hurricane Katrina — aside from the timing of their 20th, 5th, and 1st anniversaries, what's the connection? Before I answer that, let me layer on a more personal anniversary: this summer marks my 15th year working as a reporter and editor for various California newspapers.

I got into the business mainly because I felt like the American people were being duped, at the time about Iraq's invasion of Kuwait, a war used by the first President

Bush as a pretext for establishing permanent US military bases in the oil-rich Middle East.

American bases in Saudi Arabia caused Osama bin Laden to threaten a terrorist war against the United States unless we withdrew — a threat that we seemed to ignore while he carried through with a series of attacks that culminated in 9/11. Rather than reevaluating our relationships with oil and the Islamic world, this Bush administration upped the ante: invading and occupying two more Islamic nations, adopting energy policies that increased our oil dependence, and withdrawing the United States from international accords on global climate change and human rights.

Then Hurricane Katrina hit, opening up a second front of attack on the choices this country is making. I was already at Burning Man, in an isolated bubble of ignorant bliss that was eventually popped by the news. As we left the playa, burners gave significant money, supplies, and people to the relief effort. An eight-month cleanup and rebuilding encampment turned into a movement dubbed Burners Without Borders, which is still developing ambitious goals for good works and greening the event.

I believe Burning Man will be using its 20th birthday as a transition point. We've built our community and allowed it to mature, and now we're talking about where we go from here. Most of those discussions are happening right here in San Francisco, where Burning Man was born and is headquartered. There is tremendous will to use our creation as a force for good.

Progressives will use the anniversaries of 9/11 and Katrina to urge our government to reevaluate its relationships with oil, other countries, and its own cities and poor people. Unfortunately, San Francisco isn't where those decisions will be made.

But if there is a will to change this country's direction, what better place to launch that movement than here? And what better army than Burning Man's attendees, expected to number more than 35,000 — people known for their resourceful ability to build a city from scratch, clean it up, and leave no trace?

We'll be back in a couple weeks, ready for what's next.

The Deep End created a popular playa day party using a free bar and rocking sound system. ~ Photo by MV Galleries

The Temple at Hayes Green by David Best led burner artworks into San Francisco. ~ Photo by Scott Beale / Laughing Squid

Passage by Karen Cusolito and Dan Das Mann (above) on the SF waterfront. ~ Photos by Scott Beale / Laughing Squid

Reverend Billy preaches anti-consumerism with the Church of Stop Shopping. ~ Photo by Gabe Kirshheimer

Flock by Michael Christian in the plaza outside San Francisco City Hall (also below). ~ Photos by Scott Beale / Laughing Squid

Billy and singer Joan Baez led a Hurricane Katrina rally at the Temple. ~ Photo by Gabe Kirshheimer

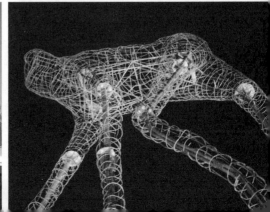

Using heavy equipment and volunteer labor, burners created one of the most effective hurricane cleanup groups on the Gulf Coast. ~ Photo by KK Pandya and Burners Without Borders

Part III — Renewal (2006-07)

Wednesday, August 30, 2006

There's an electricity in the air as we bounce and sway with hundreds, maybe thousands, of dancers at The Deep End. And I don't simply mean that metaphorically; the air feels strangely charged, like there's something brewing with the weather, but nobody seems to care, not when the music is so good on this playful afternoon.

"I've got beats, deep in my soul," sings the song as DJ Clarkie pumps his fist behind the decks, a sea of smiling, scantily-clad souls on the stage and down in the dust just losing their minds. "I've got love, making me whole. Since you opened up your heart and shined on me."

Several of my Ku De Ta campmates are dancing in my orbit, or occasionally walking over to the crowded bar to refill their drinks, and we're all in great spirits, feeling buoyant after some minor conflicts and difficulties in setting up a new theme camp of just 16 people from scratch.

When the chorus starts to come around again, Rosie, Smoove, Splinter, and I exchange knowing smiles and belt out our inside joke modified lyrics: "I've got meat, deep in my hole." Pure silliness and frivolity, but the sky has started to darken with dust as the wind begins to blow from the west, opposite of its usual direction.

The goggles and dust masks start coming out, but the dance floor stays full and the beats keep pumping, even as the wind starts flapping some parachutes and tarps that had been battened down against easterly winds. I love these weird playa moments, when groups of people are transformed into swarms of insects, goggled eyes peering out from faces shrouded in scarves or masks.

Burners learn to just take moments like this in stride, howling with glee as the sudden dust storms hit their peaks and shrink visibility down to their immediate surroundings, empowered by our preparation and knowledge that this will pass and we'll all be okay.

But as the air begins to thicken and bikes and structures can be heard crashing to the ground and into each other, the dance floor starts to empty out as people deal with their shit or seek shelter from what's beginning to feel like an unusually powerful storm. "Let's go back to Blue's bus," I suggest to my nearby friends, referring to a Deep Ender friend's home for the week, where I was hanging out doing Whip-Its and getting high yesterday.

There's a fairly crowded party in the full-sized, camping-modified bus once we finally find it in this disorienting environment, but Blue warmly welcomes our group of a half-dozen and offers us margaritas. I recognize maybe half the crowd, which is chatting in groups, puttering with drinks or supplies, or flopped all over each other in the huge bed in the back of the bus.

That's where I head after getting my drink, greeting friends and strangers on my way back and filling in a freshly vacated spot on the bed between two cute girls that I vaguely recognize but can't really place. "Whip-it?" offers my friend Mack, who is fiddling with the whipped cream cracker and balloons as he chats up the girls.

"Love one," I answer, and he introduces me to the girls, whose names I promptly forget. He hands me a balloon filled with laughing gas and I lay back, breathing in the nitrous oxide, respirating it between the balloon and my lungs until I disassociate from my surroundings and hear the familiar "wah, wah, wah" in my head, mixed with the distant thump of Deep End's bass. The girls stroke my hair and stomach and I feel a moment of perfect bliss before reality returns.

"Mmm, this is nice. Thanks," I say, handing Mack back the empty balloon. And it goes like that for an hour or so — it's hard to be sure, really — just absorbing this warm and tactile environment as the wind outside wreaks havoc on Black Rock City. Finally, Rosie says the wind is dying down, and Dash offers, "Dude, I wonder how our camp is doing."

Good question, good enough for us to leave the party and head back outside, where everything and everyone is coated with a thin layer of fine dust. We head back over to the dance floor, remembering that Syd Gris is supposed to be spinning the set after Clarkie's. Several of our Ku De Ta crew — me, Rosie, Dash, Captain Bastard, Donnie, Carla, and Smoove — were defectors from Opulent Temple, and as much as we couldn't do another year with the massive dance camp, we were still all close to Syd.

The sun reemerges, brightening a dance floor that's starting to fill up again, but as we climb onto the stage and peek into the DJ booth, we learn that Syd hadn't arrived yet, apparently unable to cross the playa from Opulent Temple during the storm, but Clarkie is still rocking strong.

We decide to head back to camp and assess the damage, mounting our bikes for the journey across the playa as the sky turns a brilliant blue and the heat of the day returns. The wind seems to have cleansed the playa, leaving it feeling fresh and restored, but dotted with MOOP that we occasionally stop to pick up. It's a straight shot from The Deep End on 9 o'clock past the Man and over to Ku De Ta, which was assigned some amazing real estate at 3 o'clock and Anxious, just a block back from the open playa on an extra wide avenue.

On the way, we veer to the right to do a fly-by on the Flaming Lotus Girls' amazing Serpent Mother project, a huge flaming snake with animatronic head that we can see clearly from the couches or scaffolding in our camp. After the success of Angel of the Apocalypse, the FLGs went even bigger this year, fueled by lots of new members and an even larger art grant from the Borg.

I don't see any familiar faces, so we ride back toward camp and as we approach the Esplanade, what's left of Ku De Ta comes into focus. The three-story scaffolding that marked the front wall of our camp is mostly bare, the muslin fabric on which we'd painted our camp name in large letters shredded by the reversed winds, the remaining pieces hanging tattered from single points, flapping in the now-gentle breeze.

Scott, Julio, and Mary had arrived back at camp shortly before us, walking out to greet us as we pull up, and we all share a laugh at our fucked up camp's expense. Even before this, we had to scale back our ambitious plans for our revolutionary compound concept, abandoning plans for a maze that had to be overcome to gain entrance and elaborate façade with the heads of Bush Administration war criminals stuck on pikes.

It turns out that small camps are even more work than big ones. A few of us ended up carrying most of the burden, while others weren't fully engaged with the project. Rosie, for example, is in the middle of a difficult political campaign, running for the San Francisco Board of Supervisors as the first candidate to overtly identify herself with the Burning Man world. And Smoove is a prima donna DJ, and we had a bunch of newbies, and our renegade dance party fundraiser was more fun than lucrative, so, well, we fell a bit short of our goals.

We did manage to rent and erect the scaffolding, topped by a pair of fire poofers that Dash and I built at the Box Shop with help from Pouneh and some Flaming Lotus Girls supplies. And we had the requisite shade structure filled with couches and old carpets, and a loosely covered geodesic dome, but it was nothing like the description that we'd promised to rate such a great address.

After we finish laughing at how our ridiculous camp is now in tatters, we fan out to collect the various pieces of our massive muslin sign and pound the dust out of our couches. Pretty soon, the ragtag army of Ku De Ta settles into the chill area to lick our wounds and rest up before dinner and the big night ahead.

But I decide not to be so easily defeated in a camp that I conceived, so I gather some rope, bungee cords, and zip ties into my kilt pockets, grab the pile of sign pieces, climb the scaffolding, and start putting Ku De Ta back together, Frankenstein-style. "Way to go, Scribe," Mary says, as my campmates rise to help.

Going Green

With great weather, solid community intention, a Black Rock City population that reached 40,000, and mind-blowing art — from the FLG's Serpent Mother to a massive, gravity-defying wooden structure on the deep playa named Uchronia (affectionately nicknamed the Belgian Waffle after the nationality of its builders) — 2006 was universally considered another of Burning Man's best years ever.

Without a doubt, Burning Man had become the best party on the planet, in a temporary city with a vibrant, well-developed communal culture. But that wasn't enough for Larry Harvey, who was still trying to elevate the event into something more, an intention that had caused him to pick an art theme for 2006 with a strongly sociopolitical character: "The Future: Hope and Fear."

It was a new direction for Burning Man that Larry continued with the announcement at the 2006 event of the next year's theme, "Green Man," which he intended to have a stronger impact on Black Rock City and its community than his past art themes, which didn't really alter the basic character of an event that had an inertia that was tough to change.

"It's the first theme that has any kind of practical, political character," Larry told me in early 2007, noting that "Green Man" was sparking big changes in how the event would be staged, a campaign to improve burners' environmental practices, and a new way of relating to the outside world.

Larry said he was inspired by the amount of good that Burners Without Borders did in Mississippi and that started him thinking about the green theme and the idea that Burning Man needed to start turning its energies outward at a time when global warming and other environmental problems were growing public concerns.

"We're working our way back into the world. Maybe not the mainstream but certainly onto Main Street," Larry said. "There's a lot out there that needs reform. The time of the reformer is at hand, I believe."

And to propel those reforms, Larry tapped Tom Price, giving him a full-time job as Burning Man's first environmental director and turning him loose on ramping up the organization's sociopolitical relevance and environmental responsibility.

"We're looking at every aspect of the event: solid waste, energy, and materials," Tom told me for an article on the theme that I wrote in January of 2007.

Two years later, with more time to reflect, he put it this way: "Coming back, I got hired to be the environmental manager for the Green Man theme and the idea was, let's create a space where we can share the best practices and ideas about how to interact with the world in a way that is completely decommodified. Let's take these 10 Principles and apply them to a particular topic, the environment. Well, we then took the next step and said let's take that topic, the environment, and let's take these 10 Principles, and then let's take it outside the event. And what we learned is if you are open to the idea of focusing on the social rather than financial bottom line, and you're interested in helping a community and protecting the environment in leaving no trace, you can do tremendous things outside the event as well."

That would eventually lead Tom and his allies to take Burners Without Borders into other countries and to create new enterprises such as Black Rock Solar. But in early 2007, he was focused on Green Man, developing his romantic relationship with Andie Grace, and pursuing projects in his new hometown of San Francisco.

And that meant working with some familiar Burning Man names, like Jim Mason and Chicken John, the main instigators of the Borg2 rebellion. Mason had developed a gasification system that turned waste products like coffee grounds and walnut shells into usable fuel, which would power the art car slug that he was creating, a project he called Mechabolic. And to demonstrate it, he converted Chicken's pickup truck to run on walnut shells.

"So I'm proposing drag racing to a more responsible environmental future. As usual, the ravers are not going to save the world. But at least they can power their indulgent disasters with the fuel the local gearheads turned reluctant environmentalists have made for them," Jim told me, once again getting in a gratuitous dig at the longstanding target of his ire.

Tom said he was excited by the implications of Jim's project, noting that it simultaneously addresses energy issues and waste disposal. At the time, Jim was talking about using the coffee grounds from Center Camp to power his vehicle, although that didn't really materialize.

"If he can do this, he will have solved two problems," Tom said. "Our relationship to nature on the playa is very intimate. Just being at the event, we've learned in a way those in the city haven't what it means to deal with your garbage and to provide your energy."

It was a point that resonates with anyone who had been to Burning Man, where attendees are responsible for dealing with their own trash and providing their own power, giving each burner a practical understanding of the notion of conservation. Larry said he wanted the theme to be a turning point.

"In some ways, we hope this year will be an environmental and alternative energy expo," he said, although he expects it to penetrate to an even deeper level that participants will carry back into their communities. "It's a much broader thing than environmental politics. It's about our relationship to nature."

Tom worked on expanding the already large recycling effort at the event (including the Burners Without Borders lumber recycling camp that debuted in 2006), finding ways to use more solar panels and fewer generators, coordinating theme camps to share power sources, using an anonymous donation of $350,000 worth of solar panels to power the Man, purchasing of emissions credits to partially offset the greenhouse gases created by the event, and creating incentives for art projects to use alternative fuels.

"The whole process is being driven by the community," Tom said.

Ramping up Burning Man's environmental activism and commitment had been the goal of several movements within the larger event, such as Cooling Man and Greening the Burn, as well as being a priority for many Black Rock City LLC employees, such as technology dominatrix Heather Gallagher, a.k.a. Camera Girl, and facilities manager Paul Schreer, a.k.a. Mr. Blue.

"We've been hippie busybodies pushing for this on the inside," Heather told me. "And when (Larry) announced the theme, I was, like, 'Yesss!'"

"What's exciting about the Green Man theme and this year's event is it's a perfect illustration of the power of community," Tom said, noting that networking and experimentation have always been hallmarks of the event. "Going back 10 years, Burning Man has been a place for early adopters who are on the cutting edges of a lot of disciplines."

That makes it a good place to experiment with new technologies and evangelize those that work well. "I've always believed Burning Man would eventually partner in some way with the environmental movement," Larry said. "It's almost a historic inevitability."

A Burning Man Mystery

Even as the Burning Man world was becoming more intriguing, so was the San Francisco political scene and covering it was my main job at the Bay Guardian. Mayor

Gavin Newsom had made international headlines with his unilateral decision to issue marriage licenses to same-sex couples, but had then largely withdrawn from local politics to play the ambitious celebrity.

Progressives on the Board of Supervisors, leftists who were Newsom's main political opponents, had filled the void and taken control of the city agenda, often beating Newsom's downtown allies. But after a sordid sex scandal, when Newsom was revealed to have been sleeping with his campaign manager's wife, and with his reelection approaching, the mayor reengaged and the political battles were fierce.

So there was plenty for me to focus on without Burning Man, particularly as my resources were limited by layoffs and cutbacks at the Guardian. But when I was approached by members of one of the Burning Man world's most storied and fascinating tribes, about a big news event that had a strong air of mystery about it, with great characters in both the Bay Area and Nevada — well, it was just irresistible.

After digging into it with some investigative reporting that I married with Burning Man cultural coverage, I wrote the following cover story for the Bay Guardian that ran on January 7, 2007:

The Mystery of La Contessa

A galleon destroyed by fire. A priceless missing statue. Welcome to one of the great mysteries of the San Francisco underground.

La Contessa was a Spanish galleon, amazingly authentic and true to 16th-century design standards in all but a couple respects. It was half the size of the ships that carried colonizers to this continent and pirates through the Caribbean. And it was built around a school bus, designed to trawl the Burning Man festival and the Black Rock Desert environs, where it became perhaps the most iconic and surreal art piece in the event's history.

The landcraft — perhaps like the sailing ships of yore — wasn't easy to navigate. It was heavy and turned slowly. The person driving the school bus couldn't actually see much, so a navigator sitting on the bow needed to communicate to the driver by radio. Those sitting in the crow's nest felt the vessel gently sway as if it were rocking on waves.

Inside, it was a picture of luxury: opulent, with a fancy bar, gilded frames, velvet trim — a cross between a fancy bordello and a captain's stateroom. And adorning its bow was a priceless work of art, a figure of a woman by San Francisco sculptor Monica Maduro.

The ship and its captains and crew — most of whom are members of San Francisco's wild and popular Extra Action Marching Band — hit more than their share of storms in the desert, developing a storied outlaw reputation that eventually got them banned from Burning Man.

By 2005 much of the galleon's crew was dispirited and unsure if they'd ever return. The ship was no longer welcome at the Ranch staging area run by the event's organizers and unable to legally navigate the highways without being dismantled. So it returned to its berth on Grant Ranch, on the edge of Nevada's Black Rock Desert, where Joan Grant had welcomed La Contessa and two other large artworks since 2003.

Then, late last summer someone looted the ship, stealing Maduro's work, which was stored in a special box and hidden deep within the ship's hold. Maduro and others have kept the theft a secret until now in the hope that they might find it, fearing that publicity and police involvement might drive the piece further underground, particularly after the reported sighting of a photo of the figurehead on Tribe.net, with a caption indicating it was the latest addition to someone's living room.

And in early December, apparently without warning, prominent local landowner Mike Stewart set La Contessa on fire and had her charred remains hauled away.

It was a sad and unceremonious ending for La Contessa, a subject of ongoing legal actions, and an illustration of what an explosion of creativity leaves in its wake — a challenge that Burning Man faces as it seeks to become more environmentally responsible as it grows exponentially.

It was also a sign of the lingering tension between the giant countercultural festival and the residents of Hualapai Valley, who endure the annual onslaught of tens of thousands of visitors to their remote and sparsely populated region, along with the cultural and economic offerings they bring.

Grant had recently sold her 3,000-acre spread (although she retained a life-long lease of her ranch home) to her neighbor, Mike Stewart, a landlord who didn't share Grant's love for the annual Burning Man event and its colorful denizens. In fact, Stewart led a legal and regulatory battle against Burning Man in 2003, trying unsuccessfully to shut down the Ranch and thus kill the event.

"I've been with them since they started out there, when they were just little bitty kids.... I adopted them, and they've always been supergood to me," Grant told me. Although she owned the Black Rock Saloon (which she spelled "like a drunk would say it" and later sold it to the Black Rock City LLC), Grant said she was initially ostracized by many of the locals for supporting the event.

While La Contessa's creator, Simon Cheffins (who also founded Extra Action), fruitlessly looked for land that might permanently house the galleon, it sat at the ranch, battened down against the elements and interlopers. When a grease fire destroyed Grant's ranch house last year, sending her into the nearby town of Gerlach, La Contessa had nobody to watch over her.

A Question of Intent

Stewart is one of the biggest property owners in the region. In addition to possessing land and water rights that would be lucrative in any development project, he owns Orient Farms, Empire Farms, and a four-megawatt geothermal power plant.

He leased Grant Ranch (also known as Lawson Ranch) for five years before buying it in October 2005; in that transaction he gave Grant a lifelong lease of her house, a provision she believed also applied to the art pieces she stored within sight of her home. That was before the fire, which police say Stewart set December 5, 2006, around noon.

"My understanding was it was okay to park it there. But I guess he had it burned down," Grant told me. "As far as I'm concerned, it was arson."

Washoe County sheriff's deputy Tracy Bloom also told me that he considers the fire to be third-degree arson, which is punishable by one to six years in prison under Nevada law. Yet Bloom said he believes Stewart thought he had a right to burn and remove the seemingly abandoned vehicle and therefore lacks the criminal intent needed to have charges brought against him.

"According to him, they had attempted to contact the owner to no avail, so he decided to set it on fire," Bloom told us.

He wrote in his police report, "I asked Stewart if he was the one that set the La Contessa on fire and he said, 'YES, I DID.' I asked him why he decided to burn it. Stewart said, 'Because the property was abandoned and left there and I was forced to clean it up.'"

The report indicates that Bloom, who lives in Gerlach, helped organize a community cleanup at that time, in which a scrap dealer named Stan Leavers was removing old cars and other junk. "Stewart said that was the biggest reason for burning the La Contessa so that it could be removed by Leavers," Bloom wrote. Nonetheless, Bloom confirmed to me that didn't give Stewart the right to burn the artwork.

"I told him, 'You can't just do that, and if I found any intent or malice on this, you're going to jail,' " Bloom told me. "But I don't believe there was any malicious intent. If I felt like there was any malicious intent, I would have arrested him right there. I thought that boat was really cool. It was one of the coolest things out there."

Many burners who live in Gerlach — a town with a population of a few hundred people that happens to be the nearest civilization to Burning Man's site — have a hard time believing Stewart made an innocent mistake. "I think it was a malicious arson," Caleb Schaber, also known as Shooter, told me. "He's the guy who tried to shut down Burning Man, and he associated La Contessa with Burning Man."

Stewart refused to comment for this story, referring questions to his lawyers at the Reno firm of Robison, Belaustegi, Sharp, and Low. Dearmond Sharp, a partner in the firm, belittled the value of the piece and implied Stewart was within his rights as a property owner to burn it.

"What would you do if someone left some junk on your property?" he asked me.

Nevada law calls for property owners to notify vehicle owners "by registered or certified mail that the vehicle has been removed and will be junked or dismantled or otherwise disposed of unless the registered owner or the person having a security interest in the vehicle responds and pays the costs of removal."

"What he should have done is get letters out and make a good-faith effort to find a (vehicle license number) or see who the owner is, little things like that," Bloom told me. Nonetheless, after talking with the prosecutor, Bloom said criminal charges are unlikely. He said, "Chances are this is something they will pursue civilly."

(Three years after this article came out, the crew sued Stewart for $900,000 under the federal Visual Artists Rights Act of 1990, which makes it illegal to destroy artwork even if it is no longer in the artist's possession. That suit was still pending as this book went to press.)

Also destroyed in the fire, according to Schaber, was an International Scout truck with a new motor and a MIG welder inside, owned by Dogg Erickson, which he said he parked alongside La Contessa so it would be partly protected from sandstorms.

"Everything was toast," Erickson said. "I was pretty pissed, both about my truck and La Contessa. It floors me, and I don't know what to do about it."

Cheffins, mechanical design engineer Greg Jones, and others associated with La Contessa and Burning Man all say they never received any message from Stewart asking for La Contessa to be removed. And Cheffins said he believed he had the implied consent of Stewart to store the ship where it was.

Jones and Cheffins said that while they were securing La Contessa for the winter of 2004–5, Stewart drove by and talked to them but said nothing about removing the ship. "We talked to him about all kinds of stuff, and we were impressed by him," Jones said.

La Contessa caretaker Mike Snook also said that he met Stewart in 2005 while he was with the ship and that Stewart didn't express a desire to have the piece off the property. Jones said there were plenty of people in town connected to Burning Man through whom Stewart could have communicated: "It's a visible enough art piece that if he really wanted to get it off his property, someone would have known where we are," Jones said.

Burning Man spokesperson Marian Goodell told me Stewart never contacted the organization and that if he had, it would have facilitated the piece's removal from the property. "We were surprised to hear about the fire, absolutely shocked," she said. "It was a very iconic piece, and a lot of people are going to miss La Contessa."

According to Bloom, Stewart also claims to have contacted Grant about removing La Contessa and other items from the property. "He contacted her and said, 'What are you going to do with it,' and she said, 'Do what you want with it,'" Bloom told us. But Grant (whom Bloom did not interview for his report) told me, "That's not truthful," adding that she hasn't spoken with Stewart in a very long time and wouldn't have given him permission to destroy the artwork.

Sharp did not directly answer my questions about what specific actions Stewart took to contact the galleon's owners, but he did tell me, "He didn't know the owners, and they weren't identified...The vehicle wasn't licensed and had no registration and wasn't legal to drive on the road. It wasn't a vehicle."

Whether or not it was a vehicle is what triggers the notification provisions under Nevada law: the section on abandoned vehicles prohibits leaving them on someone's property "without the express or implied consent of the owner."

"It was dumped there, and there is no written consent or implied consent," Sharp told me, responding to a question about implied consent. "In our eyes, it was a piece of junk."

But Ragi Dindial, an attorney working with the La Contessa crew, said that this "junk" was actually a valuable artwork and that he is working on filing a claim with Stewart's insurance company, alleging the fire was a result of Stewart's negligence. If that doesn't work, he may file a civil lawsuit.

And then there's the lingering question of the sculpture, which survived the fire because of the theft — but still hasn't seen the light of day. "It's one of the greatest mysteries in the San Francisco underground," longtime Burning Man artist Flash Hopkins said. "Where is the figurehead?"

Building a Galleon

La Contessa's massive scale has created problems since the beginning, when Cheffins had the idea in 2002 of rejuvenating Burning Man and his own enthusiasm for it by building a Spanish galleon. The project was a huge undertaking that created logistical nightmares.

"It was such an ambitious and, I think, exciting idea.... I wanted to do something fairly splashy, and the idea of a ship had always been powerful," Cheffins told me. "I was strong on the fantasy-imagination side of things and stupid enough to want to do it. Luckily, my ass was saved by Greg Jones."

Jones, a mechanical design engineer, had been playing trumpet in Extra Action for a few months when Cheffins pitched the La Contessa project at one of the band's rehearsals.

"I said, 'Who's going to design it?'" Jones told me, describing the moment when he took on the project of a lifetime. "That first night I had in my mind a way to do it.... For me, it was a challenge of how do you make it and how do you get it out there."

Hopkins said there should have been another consideration: "You have to build something that you can take apart. Sadly, that was part of its demise."

But that doesn't take away from what he said was one of the best art projects in the event's history: "What those guys did when they built that ship was incredible because of the detail of it. It was an incredible feat."

The idea of a ship fit in beautifully with Burning Man's theme that year, the "Floating World," so Black Rock City LLC awarded Cheffins, Jones, and their crew a $15,000 grant, which would ultimately cover about half the project's costs, even with the hundreds of volunteer person-hours that would be poured into it.

Cheffins researched galleons, learned to do riggings as a volunteer at the San Francisco Maritime Museum, directed the project, and insisted on materials and details that would make La Contessa authentic. Jones translated that vision into reality by creating computer-aided architectural designs for the ship's steel skeleton, a hull that would hang from that skeleton and be supported by an axle and hidden wheels separate from those of the bus, and the decks that would support dozens of passengers and hide the bus and frame — all with modular designs that could be broken down for transport to Nevada on two flatbed trucks.

"In the beginning I thought they were crazy," said Snook, an artist and Burning Man employee who worked on the project and later took control of La Contessa after the Extra Action folks ran afoul of festival organizers in 2003 for repeatedly driving too fast and breaking other rules.

The ship was built mostly at the Monkey Ranch art space in Oakland and a nearby lot the crew leased for three months. "My mom even helped," Jones said; she joined nearly 100 volunteers who pitched in, many of whom brought key skills and expertise that helped bring the project to fruition.

"The idea of the ship is it was a lady that you end up serving, and she took on a life of her own," Cheffins said. "We all came to feel like servants at some point."

Meanwhile, Cheffins commissioned Extra Action dancer, event producer, and sculptor Maduro to build a figurehead that would be the most visible and defining artistic detail on the galleon. Cheffins conveyed his vision — including the need for it to be removable so a live model could sit in her place — and Maduro added her own research and artistic touches.

"We wanted her to be beautiful, sexy, strong, and also unique," Maduro told us.

All the ship figureheads that she researched had open eyes, except one that had one eye closed, purportedly the same eye in which the ship's captain was blind. That gave Maduro the idea of a figurehead with closed eyes.

"The figurehead is supposed to guide you through the night and see you to safety," she said. "We liked the idea that our figurehead would guide us blindly."

Maduro worked for six months in relative isolation from the ship site in Xian, artist Michael Christian's Oakland studio. The face was designed from a mold of their friend: model and actress Jessa Brie Berkner. The armature was wood and metal, covered in carved foam coated in fiberglass veils dipped in marine epoxy, with sculpting epoxy over that, and wearing a real fabric skirt dipped in epoxy. The idea was to make it strong enough to stand being dropped by people and battered by the elements.

"This is one of the most emotional projects I've ever been a part of," said Maduro, who spent six years creating lifelike exhibits for natural history museums across the country, among other projects. "It was a magical mix of all these individuals that made it happen."

Yet there wasn't enough magic to allow the shipbuilders to meet their schedule. They weren't where they'd hoped to be when the trucks arrived to haul La Contessa to the playa, requiring a final push on location under sometimes harsh conditions.

"The intention was to build the whole deck and reassemble it," Jones said. "But we ran out of time."

Instead, the crew spent the final weeks before Burning Man — and most of their time at the event — frantically trying to finish the project, completing it on a Friday night just a couple days before the event ended. Jones recalled, "We stained it Friday afternoon during a sandstorm."

Ah, but once it was finished, it was an amazing thing to behold, made all the more whimsical by the large whale on a school bus that Hopkins built that year. La Contessa's crew loved to "go whaling" that first year.

"The ship and the whale were the right size, and so it was like Moby Dick and the Pequod," Hopkins said.

Those who sailed on La Contessa insist it had a feel that was unique among the many art cars in Burning Man history. People were transported to another place, and many reported feeling like they were actually cutting through the high seas.

"It was about creation. It was about inspiration," Cheffins said. "The whole thing was a gift."

"That's what we heard a lot after the arson," Jones said. "This was the thing that inspired (people) to come out to Burning Man."

Stormy Seas

A lore quickly grew around La Contessa — and the ship and crew developed something of an outlaw reputation. There were the repeated violations of the 5 mph speed limit and what looked to some like reckless driving as they pursued Hopkins's white whale. There were people doing security that Cheffins says "were overzealous and got very rude."

Some thought the La Contessa crew members were elitists for excluding some people from the limited-capacity vessel and for making others remove their blinky lights while onboard.

There were minor violations that first year because, as Jones said, "we didn't have time to read the rules for art cars." And there were stories that La Contessa's crew insists never happened or were blown way out of proportion. But it was enough to convince Burning Man officials to tell the crew at the end of the 2003 event that it wasn't welcome to return.

"They thought we were fucking terrorists," Cheffins said.

Goodell insists that the organization's problems with La Contessa have also been blown out of proportion. "I don't think we consider our relationship to be tumultuous," she said. "They were banned because they broke the rules on driving privileges.... Following driving rules can be a life or death situation out there."

La Contessa remained at Grant Ranch during the 2004 event, which the Extra Action Marching Band skipped to tour Europe. Snook negotiated with Burning Man officials to allow La Contessa to return in 2005 as long as he retained control and did not let Cheffins, Jones, or their cohorts drive.

The fact that there were inexperienced drivers at the wheel was likely a factor in what happened the Tuesday night of Burning Man 2005.

The crew had made arrangements to take a cruise outside the event's perimeter and within 15 minutes crashed into a dune that had formed around some object, tearing a big gash in the hull and bending a wheel. The crew was instructed by Burning Man officials to leave it until the following day, and when its members returned, the sound system, tools, a telescope, and other items had been stolen.

It was a dispiriting blow for Extra Action and the rest of the La Contessa crew, one that played a role in the decision not to try to bring La Contessa back to the event. "Last year (2006) we didn't take her out because of a lack of enthusiasm on our parts," Jones said.

Yet they checked on La Contessa on their way to Burning Man and discovered that it had been looted again and the figurehead was gone.

Insult to Injury

As mad as she was about the theft of the figurehead and as sad as she was about the fire, Maduro said she feels a sort of gratitude toward the thief. "Assuming we get it back and it wasn't the person who burned the ship down, then I actually owe this person a debt of gratitude."

Particularly since the fire, Maduro just wants the figurehead back, no questions asked. At her request the Guardian has agreed to serve as a neutral site where someone can drop it off without fear of prosecution; we will return the figurehead to its owners.

"I was really sad, and it surprised me how sad I was because it doesn't belong to me personally," Maduro said. "I just always thought we would have her."

The mystery surrounding the figurehead grew after Burning Man employee Dave Pedroli, a.k.a. Super Dave, found a photo of it in someone's living room on Tribe.

net — before he knew about the fire and the theft.

"Right after the fire was reported, within a day, I put two and two together and talked with Snook," Pedroli told me, referring to his realization that the photo depicted the stolen figurehead. "Right after that I started to look for it."

But it was gone and hasn't been seen since. "I couldn't imagine someone walked into that space looking at all the time and attention that went into every detail and wanting to defile it," Maduro said.

But in the world of Burning Man, where most art is temporal and eventually consumed by fire, it wasn't the fact that La Contessa burned that bugs its creators and fans. It's the fact that Stewart burned it.

"He still looked at La Contessa as a symbol of Burning Man, and he didn't know it wasn't really wanted at Burning Man anymore," said Hopkins, who has heard around Gerlach that Stewart has been boasting of torching La Contessa.

"If it had burned with all of us around it, as a ceremony, it would have been okay," Hopkins said.

That was a sentiment voiced by many who knew La Contessa. Jones said this was the ultimate insult. "If someone was going to burn it down, I wish it could be us."

Private funeral services for La Contessa were planned for February 2.

P.S. While the figurehead was never returned or found, the crew did get a chance to burn La Contessa, at least in effigy. The artists built a small-scale replica of the ship and then gathered around it for funeral services on February 2, 2007, on an isolated section of bayfront property on Hunter's Point in San Francisco.

Attendees placed their offerings on the ship as we partied around her for a few hours. Then she was carried to the water's edge and secured on a small barge and set on fire, towed by a rowboat as she burned and as the Extra Action Marching Band walked up and down the waterfront, watching and playing a slow funeral dirge.

The Return of John Law

Another ghost from Burning Man past returned to haunt Larry Harvey and Black Rock City LLC at the beginning of 2007, a specter that had been quietly watching from the shadows as the event hit its renaissance period. And he brought with him a credible threat to destroy Larry's big plans.

"Burning Man belongs to everyone. Burning Man is the sum of the efforts of the tens of thousands of people who have contributed to making Burning Man what it is. The name Burning Man and all attendant trademarks, logos, and trade dress do not belong to Larry Harvey alone or to Black Rock City LLC. If they don't belong to anyone, they belong to the public domain," was how John Law began a January 9, 2007 blog post announcing his intentions.

This was more than a rant from a bitter old-timer or the bold bluster of artists who believed they had more power than they really did. Because when John Law said the Burning Man name and logos didn't belong to Larry alone, he was right — they also belonged to John, and now he was back, making public a legal fight that had been simmering in private for much of the previous year.

Larry Harvey started Burning Man on Baker Beach in 1986 (with help from carpenter Jerry James), but it was John Law, Michael Mikel, and their Cacophony Society cohorts who in 1990 brought the countercultural gathering and its iconic central symbol out to Nevada's Black Rock Desert, where it grew into a beloved and unique event attended by 40,000 people in 2006 (a population that grew to 50,000 in coming years).

John hadn't wanted anything to do with Burning Man since he left the event in 1996 — until January 2007, when he filed a lawsuit in San Francisco Superior Court seeking money for his share of the Burning Man brand. Even more troubling to Larry and a corporation that has aggressively protected the event from commercial exploitation, John threatened to move the trademarks into the public domain.

The suit roiled and divided the Bay Area's large community of burners. Some supported John and his declaration that "Burning Man belongs to everyone," hoping to break the tight control that Larry and Black Rock City LLC have exerted over their event and its icons, images, and various trademarks.

"If it's a real fucking movement, they can give up control of the name," John told me in the first newspaper interview he had given about Burning Man in years. "If it's going to be a movement, great. Or if it's going to be a business, then it can be a business. But I own a part of that."

Yet those who control the business, as well as many attendees who support it, fear what will happen if anyone can use the Burning Man name. They envision MTV coverage, a burner clothing line from the Gap, Girls Gone Wild at Burning Man, billboards with Hummers driving past the Man, and other co-optations by corporations looking for a little countercultural cachet.

"We've been fighting attempts by corporations to exploit the Burning Man name since the beginning," BRC communications director Marian Goodell wrote on the Burning Man Web site in response to the lawsuit. "Making Burning Man freely available would go against everything all of us have worked for over the years. We will not let that happen."

Larry, John, and Michael became known as the Temple of Three Guys as they led the transformation of the event from a strange camping trip of less than 100 people in 1990 to a temporary city of burners experimenting with new forms of art and commerce-free community. By 1996 it had grown to about 8,000 people.

"Plaintiff is recognized as the one individual without whose leadership and ability the event would not have been planned or produced," the lawsuit alleged. "Plaintiff alone became recognized as the 'face' of the event to local residents and authorities, and was the event's facilitator, technical director and supervisor."

John's central role in the event was also spelled out in Brian Doherty's 2004 book, *This Is Burning Man*, and in my interviews over the years with many of the original attendees. As John told me, "I put everything I had into it."

Michael, also known as Danger Ranger or M2, played a key role as the event's bookkeeper and the founder of the Black Rock Rangers, who oversee safety and security and serve as the liaison between attendees and outside authorities.

The lawsuit minimized Larry's role in the 1990 event, even drawing on Burning Man's spectator-participant paradigm to call him out: "Harvey, however, did not participate at all other than to arrive at the event as a spectator after it was completely set up.... the 1990 event on the playa motivated Harvey to take a more active role the next year, so he adopted the role of artistic director thereafter." The three men then entered into a legal partnership to run the event.

Yet Larry was always the one with the vision for growing the event into what it has become today — a structured, inclusive gathering based on certain egalitarian and artistic principles — while Law preferred smaller-scale anarchy and tweaks on the central icon.

"That was really the underlying conflict, but it got charged with emotion because 1996 was a harrowing year," Larry told me, one of the few comments he would make on the record at the time because of legal concerns.

That was the year in which Law's close friend Michael Furey was killed in a motorcycle accident on the playa as they were setting up for the event. And on the last night, attendees sleeping in a tent were accidentally run over by a car and seriously injured, prompting the creation of a civic infrastructure and restrictions on driving in future years.

John had a falling-out with Larry and no longer wanted anything to do with the event, while Michael opted to remain; today he and Larry serve on BRC's six-member board of directors. But John didn't want to completely give up his stake in Burning Man, in case it was sold at some point.

So the three men agreed to create Paper Man, a limited liability corporation whose only assets would be the Burning Man name and associated trademarks, which the entity would license for use by the BRC every year for a nominal fee, considering that all proceeds from the event get put right back into it.

Larry has always seen that licensing as a mere formality, particularly since the terms of the agreement dealing with participant noninvolvement have caused John's share to sink to 10 percent. In the meantime, however, tensions have risen in recent years between Larry and Michael, who has been given fewer tasks and even joined the board of the dissident Borg2 burner group.

Larry didn't pay Paper Man's corporate fees in 2003, but the corporation was reconstituted by Michael, who was apparently concerned about losing his stake in Burning Man (Michael wouldn't comment on the dispute at that time, but he stuck with the Borg and resolved his differences with Larry and the Borg). Larry resisted formal written arrangements with Paper Man in subsequent years, but Michael insisted.

Finally, on August 6, 2006, Larry drew up a 10-year licensing agreement and signed for Paper Man, while business manager Harley Dubois signed for the BRC. Michael responded with a lawsuit that he filed in San Francisco Superior Court on August 23rd, seeking to protect his interests in Paper Man. That suit later went into arbitration, which was suspended by both sides when John filed his suit. John said he was prompted by the earlier lawsuit.

"I didn't start this particular battle," John told me. "My options were to sign over all my rights to those guys and let them duke it out or do this."

Most burners have seen Larry as a responsible steward of the Burning Man brand, with criticisms mainly aimed at the BRC's aggressiveness in defending it via threats of litigation. But John still believes Larry intends to cash in at some point, telling me, "I don't trust Larry at all. I don't trust his intentions."

John was skeptical of Larry's claims to altruism and even saw the Green Man theme — which includes a commitment of additional resources to make the event more environmentally friendly — as partly a marketing ploy.

"If they're going to get money for it, then I should get some to do my own public events," John said. "And if they don't want to do that, then it should be in the public domain."

Yet as Burning Man spokesperson Andie Grace wrote in response to online discussions of the conflict, "Our heartfelt belief in the core principles of Burning Man has always compelled us to work earnestly to protect it from commodification. That resolve will never change. We are confident that our culture, our gathering in the desert, and our movement will endure."

And it did, without losing control of the Burning Man trademarks. John eventually dropped the lawsuit after reaching a confidential settlement with the Borg, the terms of which remain secret, but which knowledgeable sources tell me was a monetary payout to John Law.

Stoking the Fire

While the ghosts of its past were coming back to haunt Burning Man, its off-playa future was being charted by the growing number of do-gooders who wanted the culture to be about more than the annual event.

Carmen Mauk really wanted Burners Without Borders to become a hub for facilitating good deeds, not simply an organization for responding to natural disasters. She wanted to help channel all that wondrous burner energy that she'd been observing since 1999.

"We tried to get enough projects going in enough places that we could say, don't look to (Hurricane) Katrina to understand what Burners Without Borders was. That was sort of a space in time thing. Look to what your community is doing and how they are making an impact everyday on things they care about," Carmen said.

And fire was one of those things they cared about. The National Parks Service was proposing banning bonfires on Ocean Beach in San Francisco in 2007, its final solution to a long simmering concern about the debris left on the beach by impromptu bonfires. For Carmen, it seemed like just the kind of problem that burners could solve.

After thousands of people complained — many of them prompted by a notice sent out on the Burning Man online lists — the NPS delayed the announced ban and took groups that included the Surfrider Foundation and BWB up on their offer to help develop an alternative solution limiting where fires could be lit.

The initial proposal called for standard concrete fire rings that Surfrider volunteers would help maintain, but Burners Without Borders got involved and sponsored a design competition, putting out the call to the vast community of Burning Man artists.

"If there's any two things we know about, it's fire and not leaving a mess," Tom Price told me in January of 2007 as I wrote about the resolution of a conflict that I'd been covering for my newspaper since before BWB got involved. "The beach will be safer, cleaner, and more beautiful."

BWB and NPS selected the designs on January 17, 2007 including a beach primrose flower ring by Rebecca Anders and Yasmin Mawaz-Khan of the Flaming Lotus Girls, and a starfish design by Box Shop owner and FLG Charlie Gadeken. They were separate proposals, but both were built at the Box Shop with volunteer help from its many associated minions.

Rebecca later told me that Burning Man inspires people toward art and creativity, but that it is the act — that proactive gesture to do something big or impactful, something that elevates the culture — that was the essence of what burners started to become during those years.

"The fire blooms on the beach was a prime example of that because a creative solution came from outside the Parks Service, which is not in the business of administering public art and all the bureaucracy inherent if you were to do it the way the city does it," Rebecca said.

NPS spokesperson Rudy Evenson told me that he and others in the agency were happy about the compromise: "It has a lot of potential to be a win-win situation." And it was, one that endures to this day, with beachgoers enjoying some low-tech Burning Man fire art on weekend night bonfires that have become more popular than ever. To Tom and Carmen, it was an example of what's possible within the ethos and spirit that Burning Man cultivates.

"Because Burners Without Borders-like things were happening before the name came about, it just became a convenient name and thing for people to point to and for people to be like, wow, this is something I want to be a part of. I want to be a part of something larger than Burning Man because it's only one week a year," Carmen said.

Rebecca also said she that it was during this period that she was starting to see the formation of a renaissance within Burning Man. "It is spreading and the seeds of it are going and becoming new things and different things," Rebecca told me. "Multiple strands of the ethics that have grown out of the Burning Man culture are spreading in really good ways."

For Carmen, it was about extending the wild visions that burners would pursue with art projects and theme camps, and applying it to, well, just about anything: "It might be a stupid, crazy idea, but a good burner will say, 'You know what, that sounds crazy, but there's something there so let's keep talking about it.' Not ever shutting someone down."

Like Burning Man itself, Burners Without Borders was beginning to evolve. And for Tom, who was becoming more deeply involved with both the event and his adopted city of San Francisco, the relationship between the two seemed telling.

"Burning Man is this graduate study program in reinventing yourself. It's an immersion language program in the language of self. And for tens of thousands of people, it has become this annual ritual where they go out there and reinvent themselves, or they manifest a self they can't be the rest of the time," Tom told me later. "I often come back to something Larry Harvey told the Wall Street Journal once. He said, the thing about San Francisco is it tends to attract people who are looking to find themselves, and the ones who do, tend to stay. Well, Burning Man is the same way, a place where people who go looking to find a new self, and they try on this and they try on that, so on and so forth, and the ones who find themselves in that, many come back every year because they need that reboot. Others, on the other hand, go find themselves, and realize they can live in that self all year long and they don't really need to go back. But it has created this culture where people understand they have permission to architect the universe pretty much whichever way they want to. And so San Francisco is this ongoing experiment in mashing people up and seeing what happens."

It is indeed tough to predict the future, or where its events will lead. Andie and Tom had their baby, Juniper Pearlington Grace, on August 5, 2007. Ten days later, a massive earthquake hit Pisco, Peru, and Burners Without Borders responded with its biggest cleanup and rebuilding effort since Hurricane Katrina.

A Threat to Burner Workspaces

Renegade artist Jim Mason heeded Green Man's call in his typically exuberant fashion, developing an innovative gasification system that turns biomass waste products into a usable fuel similar to natural gas. Collaborating with fellow artists and engineers in The Shipyard space that he created in Berkeley, Mason was doing groundbreaking work with interesting environmental implications.

The group converted Chicken John's 1975 pickup truck to run on substances like wood chips and coffee grounds, and Jim and Chicken have been working principally with artists Michael Christian and Dann Davis to develop a fire-spewing, waste-eating, carbon-neutral slug called Mechabolic for Burning Man.

"Chicken's shitty truck is going to be sitting in front of the Silicon Valley's big alternative-energy conference for venture capitalists," Jim told me on May 22 as he headed to the Clean Technology 2007 confab, an illustration of the place little innovators were starting to find amid the big.

The New York Times featured Mechabolic in a technology article it ran earlier in May about the Green Man theme, and the project was a centerpiece of Tom Price's green evangelizing, much of which centered on the big potential of small innovators like Jim Mason.

"It's the Internet versus the big three networks" was how Tom compared the big and small approaches to environmental solutions. "The goal is to show how easy and do-it-yourself profound solutions can be."

Jim would eventually perfect his technology and later push the project to the point of marketing his Gasifier Experimenter Kits to hobbyists, burners, university researchers, and industrial engineers, selling hundreds of the kits for $2,695 each through his "Gek Gasifier" website with the help of his then-girlfriend, Flaming Lotus Girl Jessica Hobbs.

"Through gasification, we can convert nearly any solid dry organic matter into a clean burning, carbon neutral, gaseous fuel. Whether starting with wood chips or walnut shells, construction debris or agricultural waste, the end product is a flexible gaseous fuel you can burn in your internal combustion engine, cooking stove, furnace or flamethrower," advertised his website.

But first, Jim had to fight a battle against the Man on behalf of quasi-legal burner workspaces like The Shipyard throughout the region. Ragtag approaches like Mason's don't fit well into institutional assumptions about art and technology, as he discovered May 11th when Berkeley city officials ordered him to shut down The Shipyard or bring it into immediate compliance with various municipal codes.

"They need to temporarily leave while they seek the permits that ensure it's safe to be there," Berkeley Planning Director Dan Marks told me. He criticized The Shipyard for using massive steel shipping containers as a building material, doing electrical work without permits, and not being responsive to city requests.

The conflict illustrated a larger struggle that Burning Man artists and builders were starting to face at a time when their numbers and ambitions were increasing. They were becoming victims of their own success, unable to keep flying under the radar. The Box Shop suddenly faced inspections from fire and building officials in San

Francisco after my article on the Flaming Lotus Girls came out, and Oakland officials would later threaten both the American Steel and NIMBY warehouses with closure for various code violations, both of which took burner community mobilizations to counter.

Berkeley's move stopped work on gasification and other projects as The Shipyard crew scrambled to satisfy bureaucratic demands — but it also prompted a letter-writing campaign and offers of outside help and collaboration that convinced Mayor Tom Bates and City Council member Darryl Moore to meet with Jim on May 21st and agree to help The Shipyard stay in business.

Berkeley Fire Chief David Orth and other officials fighting The Shipyard said that Bates asked for their cooperation. "A request has been made to see what can be done to keep the facility there but bring it into compliance," Orth told me.

All involved say The Shipyard had a long way to go before it was legal and accepted by the city, but they eventually prevailed. Among other things, Mason had to prove that the old, recycled oceangoing shipping containers (which form the walls that enclose the Shipyard and other Bay Area artists' collectives) are safe.

Stanford-educated Jim Mason thought the whole episode was ridiculous, and the fight left him embittered with how mainstream authorities quash small innovators for what he considered spurious reasons. In 2009, Jim helped lead the fundraising drive to help Mike Snook (La Contessa's former captain) and NIMBY Warehouse make expensive improvements to their isolated Oakland warehouse to satisfy city regulators, personally contributing at least $1,000 to the cause.

"Each of us has been here. Each of us is really still here in some manner. And each of us will most likely continue to be here in some manner or other forever," Jim wrote in a fundraising appeal. "I don't really think these institutions are beatable. I've lost my idealism on this one. The best we can hope for is management of a chronic problem to a state of tolerable pain. And the next project we do, the creatives vs. standards enforcement dance will start again, with blood soon flowing across the dance floor."

Burning Man started as an underground happening, but within just a few years, it needed to negotiate with the cops and other authorities to survive. As it grew, those challenges became all the more difficult and expensive (the Borg paid $1.3 million in fees to various government agencies to stage Burning Man in 2009). Yet burners believed deeply in the do-it-yourself ethos, seeing it as the key to salvation and innovation.

"Places like The Shipyard, which is a cauldron of ideas, don't fit into the traditional model of how a city should work," Tom told me at the time. "The fringes, where the rules are a little fuzzy, is where surprisingly creative things happen."

Corporate Barbarians at the Gates

Rather than small artists and innovators, it was Burning Man's relationship with corporations that had started to become a simmering concern as the 2007 event neared, particularly after a long article about Burning Man appeared in the magazine Business 2.0, "Burning Man Grows Up," about corporations involved with the Green Man theme.

As the article said, "The event is supposed to run on what participants call a 'gift economy.' They have no truck with U.S. currency once inside the event's trash fence. Even bartering is frowned upon. The fact that the organization sells coffee and ice is controversial enough. Imagine the reaction, then, when Burning Man makes the riskiest business move in its history: It's going to allow companies to exhibit products at the 2007 event."

The article talked about Burning Man's close relationship with Google, whose founders are regular attendees and who were creating an application called "Burning Man Earth" that would be on display that year, along with other corporate intrusions.

"A venture capitalist is bringing a vast solar-power array. Four wind-power companies will be placing turbines around the Man. PR maven Melody Haller of the Antenna Group will be bringing a camp full of her clean-tech CEOs. 'We're inviting the Greeks into the heart of Troy,' says Tom Price, Burning Man's new environmental director. 'Burning Man may have to destroy itself to save the planet.' Destroy itself? Well, possibly. Those 40,000 attendees are Burning Man's only tangible asset," read the article.

R.U. Sirius, the author of *Counterculture through the Ages* who appeared with Larry at the Commonwealth Club event at the end of 2004, raised the issue on his popular "10 Zen Monkeys" blog with an article entitled, "Has 'The Man' Infiltrated Burning Man." I also mentioned the controversy on the Guardian blog and Scott Beale did the same on Laughing Squid, a blog popular with burners, highlighting this quote from the article: "America's biggest counterculture jamboree is also a $10 million business. Now it's trying to leverage its brand — and save the planet — by (gasp!) inviting corporate participants."

Online message boards were filled with the comments of burners angry that the event was opening itself to corporate intrusion. Much of the Business 2.0 article seemed to equate growing up with becoming more businesslike, and it raised fears that Burning Man wasn't just going green, it was going mainstream and looking for corporate partnerships and synergies and other MBA lingo. But Larry insisted that just isn't the case, and that the 30 small environmental entrepreneurs that will fill the green pavilion is not the opening of Pandora's Box.

"It all started with the Business 2.0 article. That's what ginned it up. We had announced our plans in detail months before and no one said anything. And with the Business 2.0 article, I believe, people are responding to the writer's attempt to translate what we were saying into business-speak," Larry said in July on the R.U. Sirius radio show. "And then they got the idea that we were opening our gates to big corporations."

Which Larry said wasn't true. Any big corporations that had expressed interest in setting up shop in the green pavilion were driven away by the Burning Man rules, and the principle of "decommodification," which states, "In order to preserve the spirit of giving, our community seeks to create social environments that are unmediated by commercial sponsorships, transactions, or advertising. We stand ready to protect our culture from such exploitation."

With the John Law conflict over Burning Man's trademarks still fresh and unresolved, the process of creating a "green pavilion" around the base of the Man created concerns that corporate America had finally found a wedge into the Burning Man world, sneaking around the edicts against advertising, commodification, or other commercial intrusions by bearing green gizmos.

"In some ways, we hope this year will be an environmental and alternative energy expo," Larry had told me in January, using language more reminiscent of a Las Vegas trade show than the middle-of-nowhere freakfest he fathered.

Larry, Tom, and company are very aware of the dangers of letting the business people ply their wares on the playa, and they made clear that all the rules against logos, advertising materials, or other forms of overt marketing applied in the green pavilion. But it was a tough balancing act that had hit some early rough spots — such as what kinds of donations that could be accepted from questionable companies trying to greenwash their image — and the jury was still out about how it would all play on the playa.

Burners by the Bay

The Burning Man scene was thriving in the San Francisco Bay Area in 2007 as many of the camps prepared to go big, which meant that there were fundraiser dance parties pretty much every weekend. And more than ever, the Burning Man parties took on a certain unmistakable style.

The culture's regular flair for costuming was still there, but it had also spawned burner-inspired fashions by designers such as Tamo, Silver Lucy, Anastasia, and Miranda Caroligne, imbuing the party scene with unique sartorial styles, from the feather and leather tribal look popularized by El Circo to the retro-futurism look of the steampunks from Kinetic Steam Works to an infinite variety of sexy and colorful fashion mash-ups.

Burning Man performance arts, from burlesque to circus acts to unusual dance troupes, were also bringing a creative element into the parties, something I planned to explore more by delving into the indie circus tribes that were collaborating on creating the Red Nose District at Burning Man in 2007.

The most ambitious art installations that Black Rock City LLC funded in 2007 were also being built in the Bay Area by huge volunteer crews. Peter Hudson — an artist whose specialty was stroboscopic zoetropes, which used motion and strobe lights to bring figures to life — had dozens of volunteer workers cycling through his San Francisco workspace to build "Homouroboros," and all were sworn to secrecy about what it actually was.

In Berkeley, Jim Mason and company were working on Mechabolic and Michael Christian and his crew were just down the street building his massive Koilos sculpture — both of them funded projects. But the real action was in nearby West Oakland, where a collective of burner artists had opened and occupied the old American Steel warehouse.

Dan Das Mann and Karen Cusolito, whose Passage sculpture from Burning Man 2005 was still perched outside the San Francisco Ferry Building, occupied a large section of American Steel to work on their most ambitious creation to date: Crude Awakening, which was a series of massive human figures made of steel gathering around a tall wooden oil derrick.

One afternoon, I arrived at massive warehouse on my newly refurbished burner bicycle — furry basket on the back, custom-welded handlebars, covered in a thick red paint that looked like stucco — and pedaled through an indoor neighborhood divided up into streets, each street containing several camps of burner artists at work, maybe 20 camps in all. It was like riding through Burning Man, in miniature and indoors. Dan and Karen's huge human sculptures dominated their section of the shop and guarded the entrance outdoors.

But it was the smaller projects that filled out this workspace, the biggest of its kind in the Bay Area. I had gotten the call from my old camp, Opulent Temple, that they needed some extra minions so I agreed to help out with their impossibly ambitious project: a massive 10-foot tall steel "star" stage (which is actually five stages, all cut and welded from scratch) and a huge open air bamboo dome.

I'd already put in a few recent work days on the stage at the Box Shop and I wanted to see and help with the bamboo dome, Rich's grand dream from the beginning of his relationship with Syd and Opulent Temple. "The culture of Burning Man is to reinvent yourself and do something better than the year before, so inevitably that usually involves getting bigger. And we've gotten caught up in that," Syd told me later, after a bit of reflection.

I found OT's dome crew on the last street, just down from Neverwas, a steam-powered Victorian house on wheels that also got funding that year, and I truly got a sense of how overly ambitious Syd and his crew had become. They were bolting, cinching, and constructing 20 sections of the dome, each one 50-foot long arcs that they had painstakingly engineered over the last couple months.

They were putting in long hours every night in a race against the clock to get it all done — and then just hoping that it would all go up on the playa as planned. "We bit off more than we could chew… If we'd had a couple more cool heads, we might have listened that that was a bad idea," Syd would later tell me. "Rich is a crazy artist, and that should be taken literally. Talented, smart, capable, but you should not follow them down every path they want to go. And we did, and we paid for it."

Sound and Fury

One key difference between ambitious projects like Crude Awakening and the Opulent Temple's effort was that the latter project wasn't qualified to receive any money from Black Rock City LLC because it was a sound camp, and sound camps — no matter how artistic or expensive — weren't considered art projects.

Yet it was the DJs associated with these camps that were the prime draw to the dance party fundraisers that were the main source of revenue to Burning Man camps, and where the DJs would usually spin for free to support their community. "The greatness of the event relies on the ability of these people to creatively fundraise," Syd said. "It's the dance culture that gives them the resources to throw the kind of party they want, as well as the kind of party we want."

Yet Burning Man's leaders hadn't recognized that contribution. Larry had certainly defended the sound camps against the attacks by Borg2. "The perception that the ravers have taken over was a myth to begin with. It's bosh," Larry told me at the time. "They are attracting people who love the event and like to dance to that music. That's okay. It's a big playa."

But Larry also told me and others, including Syd, that he didn't personally like the big sound camps and had never even visited one to see what that scene was like. "It's still a head scratcher that Larry has never been to the Opulent Temple. He's never seen it in action. And in that sense, he has no idea what goes on out there," Syd said of a camp that was the most popular spot on the playa some nights.

To Syd, that showed a real disregard for his contribution to Burning Man, an event whose attendees were rapidly growing at least in part because of nightlife that Opulent Temple helped create. "Even just being honored and respected is motivating to people, and not getting that is discouraging," Syd said.

Syd and Laird Archer, another DJ who had long supported the Burning Man scene, had talked about making an issue of it in 2005, but decided to back off when the Borg2 standoff erupted. But after El Circo left Burning Man in frustration with the lack of support and other camps burned out on the cost and difficulty of staging sound camps, they appealed to Black Rock City LLC for some support, such as free tickets (which many artists received), logistical help on the playa from Art Support

Services, a common generator, something.

Syd and others — including Matty Dowlen with El Circo and Manny Alferez from Green Gorilla Lounge — appealed to Burning Man brass for help. After a meeting and correspondence, the Burning Man board discussed the issue and the Borg's Business Manager Harley Dubois delivered the response to Syd. "In so many words," he said, "they said we can take you or leave you."

"They said, no, we don't really consider music art," Manny told me. "I remember being in the meeting, with them saying, 'We don't care.'...I think they're still in disbelief that people come for the music."

Tom Price and other Borg employees who appreciated the sound camps tried to soften the blow, and there where back channel discussions about allowing the camps to use cranes and other resources available to artists. But officially, the sounds camps were on their own. "Even when we approached it the right way," Syd said, "the response was still no to everything."

Why does he think some burners are resentful of the ravers?

"That's a complicated answer," he told me. "It goes back to the history of conflict between artists and ravers and their perception that what we're doing has nothing to do with what they want the event to be in terms of showcasing art. To them, speakers and a DJ, that's not art. And I get that perspective, in a way, but at the same time, I have to ask whether they've seen what some of the camps do, which is way beyond speakers and a DJ," Syd said, adding, "People like to say what is and is not Burning Man."

"If it wasn't for the people, there wouldn't be Burning Man," Manny said, noting that Black Rock City became an amazing place, "but I don't think it was because of the help of Burning Man Inc. or anything Larry Harvey does. It was just a bunch of people putting in their hard work to create this."

So, like El Circo, Manny decided to stop going to Burning Man, instead putting the time and effort he used to create Green Gorilla Lounge on the playa into opening up Triple Crown, a club on Market Street in San Francisco popular with the Burning Man community. "I said, that's it, I'm done. Music is my life and when they said music isn't art, well," Manny said. "I'm definitely supportive of the people who go build the camps, but I'm not supportive of Burning Man Inc."

Syd was also disillusioned with the conflict and down on the Borg, but he had his hands full with Opulent Temple's ambitious project for 2007: the star stages being built at the Box Shop and bamboo dome they were building at American Steel. The dome proved especially problematic on the playa that year.

After a frustrating first weekend of trying to get the dome up, on the Monday before a much-anticipated lunar eclipse that night, Opulent Temple made one final stab at it after somehow securing the use of the biggest cranes on the playa. In that final effort, one of the sections broke, meaning the dome would never go up, instead stacked in a pile on the playa throughout the event.

"The bamboo project was one of the great failed projects in Burning Man history, just in terms of the money and effort that went into it," Syd later told me, totaling up the costs from that year: about a $80,000 budget, including $20,000 for dome supplies that was "down the toilet," leaving the camp more than $30,000 in debt.

Opulent Temple seemed fucked, but Syd said he didn't lose hope: "I knew we had a community."

The Man is on Fire

The Man is built to burn, but not on a Monday and not by the hand of an outsider. Yet that's how it burned in 2007, lighting up a playa darkened by a full lunar eclipse and illuminating the widening divide between Burning Man's anarchic past and its well-ordered present.

Black Rock City was truly alive that night. Maybe it was people arriving early for the long, slow eclipse of the moon that occurred on the first day of the event, but I'd never seen so many people there on a Monday. There was a palpable energy in the air, an electric anticipation.

But Syd was feeling something closer to real despair by the night of the lunar eclipse, when he had been booked to DJ on the dance floor art car of Garage Mahal — his old camp and my new one — as we threw a party in the deep playa, near the trash fence at the city's edge, where we could get freaky in the dark and watch the eclipse.

With the failure of Opulent Temple's broken dome still so fresh and his fatigue deep, Syd seemed to be barely hanging on, moving between completely blank and close to tears. "I was more exhausted than I've ever been at Burning Man. I was totally tapped out. And the only reason I played was Garage Mahal was my original camp and Tamo asked me to play for this very special occasion, the lunar eclipse. The night was very fuzzy. One of my only memories was Joe West telling me the Man was on fire and I didn't believe him."

I also didn't believe it at first, thinking that someone was messing with us, maybe with some bright lights to simulate a fake burn. But it was enough for us to take the party mobile and check it out, joining a wave of art cars rolling in from the deep playa. I still thought it was a prank or piece of theater until we rolled up next to the darkened Man and sniffed the distinct smell of the recent burn. The area around the man was cordoned off when we rolled up, with Black Rock Rangers and members of the crew that built the man keeping people out.

Nobody knew much about what happened, other than it was an apparent act of sabotage, the early arson that had long been a threat of disgruntled old burners who longed for a return of the chaos, and everyone on the perimeter was somber and dejected. They'd been busting their asses for weeks to get things ready and were looking forward to a little recreation time, but now this.

For all of the writing about Burning Man that I have done for the Guardian, I didn't work as a journalist at the event, which was my vacation. But that changed in 2007. For the first time, I brought my laptop computer with me so I could do a reaction piece to the Green Man theme for the Guardian.

And as we sat silently watching the burned Man, the sky starting to lighten with the approaching dawn, I was struck by a powerful thought: "Shit, now I have to work tomorrow." This was big news, coming at the end of a big night. We boarded Garage Mahal and headed back to camp to sort it out.

As the night moved toward dawn and the moon emerged from the eclipse, bits and pieces of information began to trickle in. Witnesses saw someone scale the man using rope and set off some incendiary device and he was arrested while making his getaway. But it was hard to put stock in playa rumors, which continued to come into our camp as the moon set and the sun rose in perfect synchronicity.

After a few hours sleep, I grabbed my notebook and set to work, first finding a campmate with a satellite phone. I called my editor to see what the outside world knew about what happened and learned that only the basic details had gotten out. Internet connections on the playa are spotty at best.

Next I called the Pershing County Sheriff's Department, who told me the suspect is Paul Addis, 35, of San Francisco, and that he was being held on charges of arson, possession of illegal fireworks, and resisting arrest. Now, the main question was, "Why?" which I hoped to answer by heading into Media Mecca, the press camp next to Center Camp, where I could also pick up an Internet connection to post a report.

"We have the means and the will. The event continues on schedule, and the Man will burn on Saturday night," Burning Man communications director Andie Grace said during a press conference on the playa that day.

Chicken had even more for me when I found him tinkering with his gasifier-fueled truck. He'd known Addis since 1995 when they attended Burning Man together, and he said that he 86ed Addis from his old Odeon Bar maybe a dozen times. They ran in the same social circles, both tied closely to estranged Burning Man founder John Law and the Cacophony Society.

"Paul Addis was a Cacophonist. If there was any one flag he saluted, that's the one," Chicken told me. "He was a contrarian fighting the world."

Chicken, Law, and many of their cohorts who helped run the event in the early days have long talked about burning the man early. In fact, Chicken said founder Larry Harvey clashed with Law in 1995 — the beginning of their falling out — when Law wanted to burn the man early and had to be talked out of the idea by his friends.

"Everybody talks about it every year," Peter Hudson — creator of Homouroboros, perhaps the best interactive art piece on the playa that year — told me on the playa as the Man was still down. "We talk about, 'Let's burn it down on a Monday.'"

Yet arson is still arson, even in Black Rock City. And if Larry and the other leaders of Black Rock City LLC appreciated the art and irony of an old-school burner with a painted face and manic intentions rappelling off of a prematurely burning 40-foot wooden man at 4 a.m. like some kind of demented superhero, they didn't show it.

"He's a hero. He did the thing that we've been talking about doing for a decade," Chicken told me on the playa. "No matter how misguided he was, his intention was to facilitate art." But if there was a teachable moment or opportunity for community building here, the Borg didn't appreciate it.

"I think this was an excellent opportunity to have some democracy," Chicken told me, noting that the burner community should be able to weigh in on whether Black Rock City LLC presses charges or pushes for leniency, or even whether and how the Man should be rebuilt. "The reaction has been very top down."

Years later, then I discussed the criticism with Larry, he denied that the LLC had simply ordered a new Man built, saying the crew just did it themselves without consulting Larry or the Borg: "The builders just did it. That's the culture. There was no order."

Addis on American Dream on Acid

Not everyone took the early burn so lightly. Many online commenters to my Guardian post and others were outraged by the arson and noted that someone could have gotten killed. And many of those who worked for Burning Man, particularly those who needed to frantically rebuild the Man, were outraged.

Years later, longtime Black Rock City Department of Public Works employee Bruiser boiled over with anger when I downplayed Addis's act, showing me an expensive knife that he said Addis had dropped on the playa during his arrest. With menace in his eyes, Bruiser told me, "When he gets out of prison, he can come and get it from me."

I wrote a couple articles about the early burn from the playa, but Chicken warned me on the playa to be careful what I wrote about Addis, because he was potentially dangerous. When I got back to the Guardian office the next week, Addis had left a note and his business card in my mailbox, saying he wanted to talk to me about the things I'd been writing.

In the meantime, Addis had posted a comment on the Guardian website, addressing his critics. "This is the *alleged* arsonist/douchebag/attention whore himself," he began, going on to cast the arson as a well-planned operation by a group he called Black Rock Intelligence. "We could give a fuck less what you all think of us for doing this. Most of you are newbies who have been drawn in by the semi-religious nature of the event, or maybe just the easy drugs and easier sex. You have nothing to offer the event other than your fucking money and obedience."

Despite the tacit support in my Burning Man coverage for Larry's efforts to push the event toward greater sociopolitical relevance, particularly as we approached the end of President Bush's disastrous reign, I was disgusted and dismayed that week when Larry announced the 2008 art theme: "American Dream." So were most of the people I talked to, who were vocal in publicly criticizing it.

Larry may be trying to reclaim America from the red state yahoos, which is a fine goal, but to overtly make this countercultural event about American patriotism seemed to me to be an unforgivable mistake and severe misreading of the sensibilities of his core audience.

Personally, I tend toward Russian writer Leo Tolstoy's view that patriotism is a vice that implies racism and causes warfare, and the sooner we can recognize it for the evil it is, the sooner we evolve. So when I called Addis, I was surprised to learn that he was an unlikely supporter of Larry's new theme.

In a long and rambling telephone conversation, Addis generally reinforced his disgust with the state of Burning Man and American society in general. But when I asked about the theme, he said that he thinks nationalism and patriotism are good things worth celebrating: "People have a right to be proud of where they're from."

Addis told me he considers himself a Scottish nationalist, among other things. Despite his comments in messages to the Guardian, Laughing Squid, and other media outlets (which he didn't deny writing), in which Addis talks about being part of the plot to burn the man early, he told me, "I didn't burn shit."

Asked about the witnesses who say they saw him do it and who subsequently detained him, he told me, "Maybe there were a bunch of dopplegangers out there....It could have been any one of them." But he said he definitely applauds the gesture: "Like so many other people, I thought it was a great prank. Monday is the new Saturday."

Throughout the conversation, Addis seemed to be channeling Hunter S. Thompson, who he played at the time in a one-man show he created, and whose "B. Duke" moniker he adopted. Maybe his erratic diatribes were exacerbated by the fact that he had just dropped acid a few hours earlier, or so he told me. But he wasn't happy when I noted his gonzo schtick, telling me, "Some of us don't have to channel anything, we just happen to have a certain mindset. It's possible that we were both just born this way."

Addis seems to believe that big gestures like torching the man can prompt people to rally for change. "In any situation, it only takes one person to make a difference. I firmly believe that." Beyond just taking back Burning Man, Addis wanted to reclaim the country from the screwheads and war mongers, to end the Iraq War, and help "rehumanize" the returning soldiers.

As he announced grandly, "We're taking it back, that hulking retard known as America."

Burning the Man

Years later, after Addis was released from the two-year prison stint that he got for burning the Man, I finally got a chance to hear how things went down that night from his perspective, when he was allowed to freely discuss it without fear of criminal sanction.

Addis can be very grandiose and self-important, prone to presenting himself in heroic terms or as the innocent victim of other people's conspiracies, such as the police in two West Coast cities who arrested him in a pair of bizarre incidents within weeks of his arrest at Burning Man.

Addis was arrested in Seattle for carrying a bag of guns in public, which he says were props for the one-man play about outlaw journalist Hunter S. Thompson he was doing at the time, following a conflict with a hotel clerk about problems with his credit card. Then, a week later, he got busted for possession of fireworks and an air gun near Grace Cathedral in San Francisco, a high-profile incident that police said at the time was a plot to burn down the church, a widely reported notion that Addis calls preposterous.

"It's a stone building and I've got a fistful of firecrackers," said Addis, who served more than five months in jail for the Grace Cathedral incident, which was magnified in the media and people's minds by his pattern of arrests and bizarre behavior during that period.

Addis has innocent narratives for each incident, blaming others for overreacting, and going so far as to blame police for trying to silence him after he used his Man-burner notoriety to speak against the Iraq War and the docility of consumer culture, saying they saw his as "someone up and coming as a potential leader."

John Law celebrated the attack, writing on the Laughing Squid blog after his sentencing in 2008: "Paul Addis' early burning of the corporate logo of the Burning Man event last year was the single most pure act of 'radical self expression' to occur at this massive hipster tail-gate party in over a decade."

But it was only Addis and a small circle of Burning Man malcontents that really wanted to elevate him and his act. Although he had grabbed the Holy Grail of disgruntled old cacaphonists, burning the man early, most burners and the general public didn't appreciate the meaning of the arson attack.

"The act itself was like the performance art I do: I don't tell people what to think about it," Addis told me when I asked him to relate the message his attack conveyed.

Among the group of Burning Man haters and malcontents that gained a few new members with each passing year, a faction that included both self-imposed exiles like John Law and provocateur attendees like Chicken John, there was always talk about burning the Man early as the ultimate strike against how ordered the event had become.

"Everyone knew it needed to be done for lots of reasons," Addis said of his arson attack.

So, after following from the outside an event he attended from 1996 to 1998, Addis returned to Burning Man in 2007 with the sole purpose of torching the Man in order to "bring back that level of unpredictable excitement, that verve, that 'what's going to happen next?' feeling, because it had gotten orchestrated and scripted."

Addis said members of his group had hatched plans for burning the man early starting in 2004, but nobody actually summoned the will to do it. Finally, Addis said he realized that he was the one person who could safely execute the plan and decided to do it.

"Obviously a gesture like burning down Burning Man is very dangerous and very provocative. From my perspective, the number one concern was safety. No one could get hurt unless it was me," Addis said.

Critics of the arson attack often note how dangerous it was, pointing out that there were a dozen or so people under the Man when it caught fire, included one man who needed to be awakened. But Addis said that he was on site for at least 30 minutes beforehand, encouraging people to move back with mixed results, shirtless and wearing the red, black, and white face paint that would later make for such an iconic mug shot.

As a full lunar eclipse overhead darkened the playa and set the stage for his act, Addis waited for his cue: someone, who Addis won't identify, was going to cut the lights that illuminated the Man and give him at least 15 minutes to do his deed in darkness.

"I didn't do this alone," Addis said. "The lights were cut by someone else…The lights were cut to camouflage my ascent."

Unfortunately for Addis, the operation didn't go as smoothly as he'd hoped. He misestimated the tension in a guide-wire that he planned to climb and the difficulty in using the zip-ties that attached a tent flap to it as steps, slowly pulling himself up the wire, "hand over hand."

Once he reached the platform at the bottom of one leg, "I reached for this bottle of homemade napalm that I made for an igniter and it's gone," dropped during his ascent. And his backup plan of using burlap and lighter fluid took a long time when he couldn't get his Bic lighter to work under the 15-mph wind.

Then, the lights came back on. "And now I know I'm exposed. Because the whole thing was not to get famous for doing this. It was to get away and have it be a mystery. That was the goal," Addis said.

But then, Addis got the fire going and it quickly spread up the Man's leg, and Addis used nylon safety cables to slide down the guide-wire like a zip-line. "I landed perfectly right in front of two Black Rock Rangers who watched me come down," Addis said. "And I turned to them and said, 'Your man is on fire.'"

Addis said he was "furious" to see about nine people still under the burning structure, blaming the rangers and yelling at the people to clear the area before declaring, "This is radical free speech at Burning Man" and taking off running. Addis said he stopped at the Steam Punk Treehouse art exhibit, hoping to get lost in the crowd, but headlights converged on his location.

He ran again, with a ranger close behind, and was finally caught, arrested, and taken to Pershing County Jail. The rest — from a controversial sentencing hearing a year later, in which he blames the Borg for intentionally sending him to prison, to his release back onto the streets and stages of San Francisco — would later become the source of Burning Man controversy and lore.

But at the end of Burning Man 2007, there were other signs of Burning Man's evolution, including Chicken John's strange and quixotic entry into the mainstream politics of San Francisco, his "city of art and innovation."

Chicken for Mayor

When I reentered real life back in San Francisco, I was surprised to discover that the only San Francisco mayoral candidate who was poised to qualify for public matching funds was "Chicken" John Rinaldi, a political neophyte who made his name in the Burning Man world.

Chicken knew he couldn't win against incumbent Mayor Gavin Newsom, who had millions in the bank and high poll numbers, but he wanted to make a statement about life in San Francisco, which he often called the "city of art and innovation."

It was a lark as much as anything. Chicken told me that he'd never even voted before and didn't really believe in electoral politics. So when I washed off the dust and returned to the Guardian offices, it seemed strange that he was the only Newsom challenger organized enough to seek public funds.

So I called him up and set up an interview at his home and performance space on César Chávez Street. Someone else let me in to wait because Chicken was at the Ethics Commission office, trying to become the first and only mayoral candidate to qualify for public matching funds, a goal that requires raising at least $25,000 from among 250 city residents — and having the paperwork to prove it, which was proving the hard part for someone traditionally more focused on big ideas than small details.

Chicken said he'd raised about $32,000 since getting into the race the previous month, including $26,700 from city residents, $12,000 of which came in on the deadline date, August 28th. It was an impressive feat that could transform this marginalized, improbable candidate into one of the leading challengers, despite his enigmatic persona, maddeningly elusive platform, and admission that he can't possibly win.

Chicken wasn't your typical politician, as his history and home demonstrated. The high ceilings held rigging and pulleys for the regular performances he hosts, although his bar and a pair of church pews were pushed back against one wall this day to make more space for campaign activities. Dammit the Wonder Dog, one of many characters Chicken has promoted over the years, slept on a deflated air mattress still dusty from Burning Man.

The red brick walls of his main room looked like an art gallery, with paintings hanging on one wall selling for up to $2,000. On another wall hung the massive sign for the Odeon Bar — which Rinaldi owned from 2000 to 2005 — with Odeon spelled diagonally from right to left.

In the kitchen area, just inside the front door, the walls held framed posters from many of his projects — the Life-Sized Game of Mousetrap, Circus Ridickuless (the poster for which, at its center, has Rinaldi's face and the label "Chicken John, Ringmonster"), the Church of the Subgenius (in which Rinaldi's eponymous partner on The Ask Dr. Hal Show is some kind of high priest), and "The Cacophony Society Presents Klown Krucifixation" — as well as a framed poster of Pippi Longstocking.

Suddenly, Rinaldi blew in the front door, apologized for his tardiness, and declared, "The fucking Ethics Commission. I'm in so much trouble. I've probably already racked up $5,000 in fines."

Chicken's focus and rhetoric from when I first met him in 2004 during his Borg2 rebellion — arguing for a "radical democratization" of the art-grant selection process and the creation of a more inclusive discussion of the direction and future of both Black Rock City and San Francisco — were echoed in his mayoral campaign.

"What I'm talking about now is the same thing I was talking about with Borg2. It's the same thing," Chicken told me.

It's about inspiration and participation, he said, about coming up with some kind of vehicle through which to facilitate a public discussion about what San Francisco is, what it ought to be, and the role that can be played by all the Chickens out there, all the people who help make this an interesting city but aren't usually drawn into political campaigns or other conventional institutions.

"The number one qualification for mayor is you have to be passionate about the city you're running," Chicken said. "The left of San Francisco can't agree on anything except the idea of San Francisco."

And it is Chicken's San Francisco that helped him transform his pickup truck into a "café racer" that runs on coffee grounds and walnut shells, an alt-fuel project inspired partly by the Green Man theme of this year's Burning Man. It is the San Francisco that supports his myriad projects — from wacky trips aboard the bus he owns to offbeat performances at his place — and asks for his support with others.

"This is part of the innovation thing," Chicken said of his candidacy. "Take a mayoral campaign and turn it into an artwork project that raises interesting questions and ideas."

But should that be funded by taxpayers? Mayor Gavin Newsom's campaign manager Eric Jaye said he had concerns about Chicken getting money from that source. "It would be interesting to see public money go to someone's art project," Jaye said. "This is not the intent. The intent was for this to go to a legitimate candidate."

Yet how did Chicken raise $12,000 in one day? "I sent out one e-mail," he said. "At one time there were 12 people outside my door, sliding checks through the slot."

Again: How? Why? Chicken responded by quoting Albert Einstein, "'There is nothing more powerful than an idea whose time has come.'" But when you try to pin down Chicken on what that idea is, why his candidacy seems to have resonated with the underground artists and anarchists and geeks of San Francisco, the answer isn't entirely clear. And he disputes the idea that this is about him or his connections.

"These aren't fans," Chicken said of his contributors. "They are equals in a city of art and innovation. It's just my time.... I asked for something, and they gave it to me.... People don't necessarily support me, my ideas, or my platform."

But in the city of Burning Man's birth, at a time when the culture was expanding and exploding in fascinating and myriad ways, San Francisco was beginning to open up to the idea that the burners were coming home with new ideas and energies that they wanted to put to use in places other than the playa.

In the end, Chicken never did get the public financing that he sought because the Ethics Commission said he was never able to properly document the source and residency status of enough contributors. And despite receiving the Guardian's third place endorsement in this ranked-choice election, he finished in sixth place.

"More than half of what I do is a dismal failure," Chicken admitted. "But failure is how we learn."

San Francisco and Black Rock City were also learning from Chicken's high-profile failures. His campaign garnered more local media attention than any of Newsom's other challengers, raising the profile of San Francisco's well-established Burning Man community, which was beginning to spread its influence and ethos into new realms.

Courtesy of Pershing County Sheriff Dept.

Paul Addis (left, in his memorable mug shot) burned The Man early in 2007 and served two years in prison for it.~ Photo by Pilar Woodman

Homouroboros by Peter Hudson brought a monkey and apple-wielding snake to life. ~ Photo by Dave Le (Splat)

Crude Awakening by Karen Cusolito and Dan Das Mann paid homage to Americans' relationship to oil. ~ Photo by Jake Balakochi

Photo by Waldemar

La Contessa by Simon Cheffins and Greg Jones was an iconic art car destroyed by arson, but its maidenhead sculpture by Monica Maduro remains missing. ~ *Photo by Marcy Mendelson*

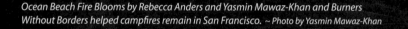

Ocean Beach Fire Blooms by Rebecca Anders and Yasmin Mawaz-Khan and Burners Without Borders helped campfires remain in San Francisco. ~ Photo by Yasmin Mawaz-Khan

Chicken John ran for mayor in 2007.
~ Poster by Kevin Evans

The Man meets Rosie the Riveter in this Burners Without Borders logo. ~ Logo by Scott Borchardt

Part IV — Striving (2007-08)

Thursday, August 30, 2007

As I stand on the rain-dampened playa in the middle of my super-organized new camp, Garage Mahal, staring at a spectacular double rainbow that just appeared in the dark grey late afternoon sky, I'm filled with a sense of the surreal. What a crazy week this has been!

Just a couple hours ago, I watched the newly rebuilt Man — still headless, but with a phoenix image over his heart to mark his rise from the ashes — raised by cranes and placed on the central perch where his predecessor had burned during the lunar eclipse on Monday night.

That night, it seemed as if some sort of cosmic madness had taken hold of Black Rock City, which already was bursting with more people than I'd ever seen there on a Monday, a crowd that has steadily grown since then. The guy on the radio said the population is now over 47,000, a huge jump from last year's official count of 38,989 burners, and I can feel the difference everywhere I go.

The rainbows are gorgeous, breath-taking, drawing out primal howls and cheers from all over our Black Rock City neighborhood. But they're also giving me another one of those moments that I've felt several times this week, a strange mix of excitement and uncertainty, like nothing is going to be the same, ever again, like we've gone as far as we can go without bursting.

But I know that isn't really true. If there's anything that you learn out here, it's that even the biggest moments — when you're out of your mind with ecstasy, fear, wonderment, isolation, connection, enlightenment, or whatever powerful emotion seizes your soul — are followed by other moments that aren't quite as intense. It's going to be okay; we'll be fine, probably better than fine.

"Scribe!" Molly yells, seeing me standing there alone as she wanders into camp, running full speed and leaping into my arms, almost knocking me over as I spin her around and she nuzzles her dusty face and curly, unwashed hair into my neck. We work together at the Guardian but we haven't seen each other all week.

We watch the rainbows, which seem to only be getting brighter, as Cat walks up and we all hug tightly, holding it for a long time, then continue watching the rainbows, each of my arms around beautiful women who I just love. Yes, things are definitely better than fine.

"I love this place," I say, and they each squeeze me harder. I introduced Cat and Molly and now they live together in San Francisco and have even formed a sexy dance troupe together, The Cheesepuffs, which performs at clubs, parties, and events to songs by Richard Cheese, a lounge singer who covers pop hits.

We casually chat about how we're doing and the things we've seen, comparing notes, making recommendations, telling stories, communing. Our consensus favorite art pieces are Homouroboros, the swinging monkeys built by Hudzo and a large San Francisco crew, including lots of Garage Mahalers and other friends of ours; and Crude Awakening, the 100-foot-tall wooden oil derrick surrounded by worshipful steel figures who sometimes drip or spit fire, an over-the-top piece funded by the biggest art grant the Borg has ever awarded.

"I can't wait to see it burn on Saturday night," Cat says of the oil derrick, conveying some intelligence that she's gathered from the Crude Awakening crew about how it's going to shoot a column of fire 1,000 feet into the air — the biggest fire effect in the history of Burning Man — during a burn that's scheduled to follow the burn of the new Man.

"Did you see Dr. Megavolt over there the other night?" Molly asks, telling the story of how his Tesla coil created lightning effects as it interacted with the massive steel sculptures.

"No, I missed that, but last night there were some amazing fire effects coming from the heart of that tall, twisting woman with the long hair," I offer.

Nearby, the Garage Mahal dinner crew is barbecuing and chopping, and my stomach growls as I catch a whiff of what promises to be another exquisite feast. Cat and I convey to Molly how great the dinners have been in our new camp, and Molly says that it's about time for her Cup-O-Noodles and to maybe catch a nap before dark.

"Yeah, I wanna grab a shower before dinner anyway," I say and we kiss Molly goodbye. Cat and I chat a bit more, catching me up on the minor drama with her ex-boyfriend's new girlfriend over at the Steam Punk Treehouse, where he's one of the creators of that whistling, warm, steam-powered contraption. Cat is such a beautiful, wildly sexy creature, someone who takes to playa life with more gusto than anyone, leaving many broken hearts, jealous girlfriends, and a vast network of good friends in her wake.

"I love you, Cat," I say, really meaning it in every sense of the phrase in that moment, even though we're just friends and Cat is close to my girlfriend, Rosie. "Mmm, I love you, too," Cat coos genuinely. We hug, kiss, let go, and I say, "Okay, I'm taking a shower," and we head over to our encampment, where Cat and Donnie have a tent under the shade structure outside the RV that I'm sharing with Rosie and Tamo.

It's luxurious, if expensive, to be in an RV after years of dusty tent camping, protected from the elements; but we don't use its shower, or even its toilet very often, lest we fill its graywater tank too quickly. I spent hours yesterday trying to lure Johnny On the Spot back to pump it out, a task that does require money at the otherwise noncommercial event.

As I gather my shower supplies in the empty RV, Rosie arrives back from a shift volunteering with the Scrap Eden project for Black Rock Arts Foundation, whose advisory board she was invited to join earlier this year, after burners helped her make a solid showing in her run for the San Francisco Board of Supervisors.

"Shower?" I ask.

"Yes!" Rosie says, looking dusty and exhausted.

So we fall into our regular day-end routine, gathering towels, shower supplies, and the solar bag that has been heating our water since morning, walking across camp over to the communal wooden showers, with space for four people at a time, surrounded by curtains. It's starting to get a little cold and breezy, so we and the other couple in the shower briskly move through our bathing routine.

People are already starting to gather their camp chairs in a circle for dinner as we head back to the RV, so we throw on some clothes, grab our plates, utensils, water bottles, and camp chairs and join the rest of Garage Mahal for dinner and a discussion of the night to come.

Turning it Around

I was disappointed with how the Green Man theme ultimately played out on the playa, as I wrote in a story that appeared in the Guardian issue that came out during Burning Man: "The environmental pavilion was only open for a few hours before the Man's premature August 27th burn, and most of those who went in were underwhelmed. It was like a wordy trade show exhibit, too earnest and static to stir much inspiration in the average burner. One exhibit just outside the perimeter displayed an electric car, complete with promotional signage with phrases like 'Electric cars equal freedom.' Ugh."

There, in the center of Black Rock City, which is perhaps the most car-free and bike-friendly city on the planet while it exists, was an advertisement for an automobile. Sure, it was an electric car, but I'm a political progressive who doesn't own an automobile and regularly rails against the pervasiveness and entitlement of car culture, so it really rubbed me wrong.

In my story, I also voiced concern with how Black Rock City LLC handled the Addis incident, noting that the eponymous man's early arson outbreak wasn't treated like the catalyst to community discussion it could have been. But I was truly flabbergasted when Larry picked "American Dream" for the event's 2008 art theme and I lashed out against this nod to patriotism in my Guardian blog post, "Addis on American Dream on acid."

It was a trifecta that burst my bubble of enthusiasm for the event and caused me to rethink my support for Larry's efforts to give the event more sociopolitical relevance. I even used my Addis interview to drive home my point and get a bigger audience for my criticism of the theme. And just to make sure Larry got the message, I also sent him a lengthy e-mail, citing Tolstoy and how patriotism was an evil to be vanquished not a virtue to be celebrated and telling him how he was alienating his core audience. He didn't respond.

Well, at least he didn't respond for a few months, when he sent me a long e-mail with the subject line: "My reprehensible theme." We argued a bit more by e-mail and coincidentally ran into each other that weekend at a fundraiser for the Black Rock Arts Foundation, where my sweetie Rosie was by then serving on the advisory board and had bought me a ticket.

Larry and I locked into a conversation that lasted for almost two hours, pretty much ignoring everyone else as we debated nationalism, art, provocation, conformity, and the impact of a desert full of freaks engaging in the most creative burnings of American flags that the country has ever heard of.

It was a good discussion and I came away with a better understanding of where Larry was coming from, but I still wasn't convinced, didn't like the theme, and didn't think it was a good idea. Even before the 2007 event, I was already thinking about taking a year off of attending Burning Man in 2008 to travel and use my resources and vacation time in other ways. The theme nudged me even further in that direction.

But then I had an inspiration that changed my mind. I had planned to cover the Democratic National Convention in Denver for the Guardian, writing about what I hoped would be Barack Obama's presidential nomination, a historic occasion that would occur simultaneously with Burning Man.

The last few years had been dismal for political journalists like me, with newspapers in decline and the political spinmeisters running amuck, putting out dangerous and divisive lies that were splitting the country, angering the world, and corrupting a political process that I had once believed in, a belief that succumbed to creeping cynicism during the Bush years.

Burning Man was at least a world of more earnest and authentic communications, where people already felt some degree of the "hope" that Obama was trying to reinstill in the American electorate. But Burning Man was also fairly apolitical, despite Larry's efforts to nudge the event toward greater political engagement.

Yet this synchronicity of my two big interests seemed to offer a moment for real inquiry and exploration, to perhaps find the connections that weren't apparent from the outside or confined within Larry's hopes. What form was the connection between the burner counterculture and the mainstream political culture taking, and was there hope that the former was beginning to affect the latter?

Then I had the idea of driving to the DNC from Black Rock City, seeing the Western U.S. as I pondered modern America in some gas guzzling vehicle, a journalistic cross between gonzo journalist Hunter S. Thompson's *Fear and Loathing in Las Vegas* and Jack Kerouac's *On the Road* that I started calling "Fear and Loathing On the Road to the American Dream."

I would watch the birth of Black Rock City's tribute to America, head into the Rockies to see the Democrats pick either the first woman or black man to be a presidential nominee, soak up the partisan weirdness and drink cocktails provided by corporate lobbyists and other purchasers of power, then head back down the hill for the Burning Man blast off, cranking out news stories, blog posts, and photos the entire time.

When I presented the idea to my editor and colleagues at the Guardian, they loved the concept, so it was on and the circle started to seem complete. I planned to explore — literally and figuratively — the connections between this counterculture and the dominant political culture that was emerging from the wreckage of the Bush years.

OT Spawns True Believers

Also trying to emerge from the wreckage was Opulent Temple, whose bamboo dome failure had left its members dispirited and the camp over $30,000 in debt. But Syd wasn't giving up: "Even at the end of that week, I knew we were coming back.

That was not going to be how we left Burning Man. This was fucked, and I don't want this to be my last experience. I wasn't going to limp out. I'd rather go out in a blaze of glory than fade away."

And from a strictly musical perspective, Opulent Temple really had ignited into a blaze of glory. While the carcass of the dome sat idle in a pile on the playa, the camp's dance floor and high stages would often be packed with thousands of people, listening to the world's best DJs, many of whom were getting their minds blown at their very first Burning Man.

Those reactions were confirmed in interviews that I did with the DJs. Christopher Lawrence came to Burning Man for the first time in 2007, overcoming his doubts to find a love for the event as true and deep as I've found. Even though he was from San Francisco, lived in Los Angeles, and had been heavily lobbied to attend Burning Man for years, he had resisted, even though his Australian wife, Sara, had expressed a desire to go.

"It wasn't until we were on holiday with our good friends Ryan and Elisa Kruger from Toronto that they made such a convincing and relentless argument that we made a pact that we would share an RV and go to Burning Man with them. Ryan is a producer of some of the largest Canadian festivals under the Destiny brand including the annual World Electronic Music Festival. When he said it was a life changing experience like nothing I had ever experienced, I trusted him," Lawrence told me.

So Lawrence went, arriving at the gates in 2007 during a blinding dust storm, a "hell on earth" that he says almost made him turn around and drive right back home: "Nothing I had been told, nothing I had seen online, nothing at all could have prepared me for that first time that you encounter the playa. We arrived at the front gate in a dust storm, a complete white out. The gates were closed and we had to sit in the car for four hours while the wind and dust whipped around our car and came in through every vent and chink in the car that I never knew existed. My first experience was utter horror and fear. I had committed to five days at Burning Man and this was only the first four hours."

His bad first impression didn't really improve at the front gate when he was greeted by an old guy with "dust caked balls swinging in the wind who threw dirt all over me," or even when he finally found his camp, located the RV he was sharing with the Krugers and "found six dirt covered strangers in all manner of dress and undress flopped around the RV in various states of consciousness."

But after a few hours decompressing in the RV and getting used to the dust, Christopher started to find his groove and give in to the experience. "As it became dusk I was instructed to take some magic mushrooms, put on my warmest clothing and assemble with the rest of the members of our camp who all mysteriously appeared geared up with their camelback backpacks and their bikes."

As they rode, he began to appreciate the vastness, creativity, and almost universal goodwill of Black Rock City, an appreciation that grew into an epiphany. "Then it happened, a moment I will never forget. We rode out of Center Camp and out onto the playa and my mind exploded with sensory overload like nothing I had experienced before. The music, the noise of explosions, flames shooting into the air, art cars of unimaginable design, neon lights, flares, people in costumes like Disney on acid. There is no way to describe the opening of awareness that accompanies the first impression of the playa. There are no words, no pictures, no videos that do it justice. Now I understood and in that instant I knew I belonged."

Lawrence makes crystal clear that Burning Man had a profound effect on him: "The experience and enlightenment that I encountered on my first visit to Burning Man only increased my desire to return. The sense of belonging was so great that upon my return to Los Angeles I became severely depressed and felt empty. I spoke with other Burners and was told that those feelings were natural and that the only cure was to return 'Home to Burning Man' the following year. That is why I go back."

It wasn't just the party and the art that impressed these jaded old DJs, but also the community that was being created in an egalitarian context that didn't involve any money. That was particularly true with the cadre of England's top DJs that had played with Opulent Temple by 2007, such as Lee Coombs, DJ Dan, Ali B, Paul Oakenfold, and Dylan Rhymes.

Oakenfold, a founding father of the rave scene, had been coming to Burning Man since 1998, but still related to me that his favorite moment ever came in 2007: "I've had many favorite moments at Burning Man, it's tough to pick just one but if I had to, I'd say it was in 2007 when a storm had just come in and immediately after everything settled, these two massive rainbows swept across the perimeter of the playa. I've never seen anything like it."

But many of the others were just making it to Burning Man for the first time. "A lot of these UK guys had never heard of Burning Man until I started talking about it. They played for me in San Francisco with Opel and that established my credibility with them, throwing good parties, and inevitably when they come, they are really taken with it. I've never had a DJ come and not be taken with it, or be just like, yeah, that's cool. No. They're always like this was one of the coolest things I've ever done. That's the unanimous feedback," Syd said.

Dylan Rhymes, whose real name is Marvin Beaver, also fell hard for Burning Man. I met Marvin on the playa in 2007, introduced through our mutual friend, the DJ and fashion designer Tamo. With my sweetie Rosie, we all had some big nights roaming together on the playa, the kind of times that bond you and make you feel like close friends the next time you meet and forever after.

"I popped my Burning Man cherry in 2007," Marvin told me. "My initial impression was of huge excitement as I had heard everyone tell me of their life altering experiences." Like Christopher Lawrence, who also started in 2007, that epic year of the lunar eclipse, the early burn, Green Man, and just fabulous conditions all week, Marvin was hooked hard.

"Burning Man has a sense of welcome that you don't get from other festivals that I have been to. I guess the non-corporate approach and the general kindness that is boosted by the lack of materialism is a huge reason for the relaxed vibe," Marvin said.

It's true. I love that part of it and it's one of the things that I bonded with Marvin and so many others over. Everyone's equal, there's no money, just sharing. Marvin said the music scene he knows has benefited from the burner ethos: "It has put a great amount of reality back into the scene for me. Stripping away money and hierarchy allows me to just do what I love, play music without a care in the world."

And unlike earlier DJ arrivals on the playa like Oakenfold, who pulled up in his tour bus for a few days and didn't really interact much with Opulent Temple members or other burners, Marvin and the new generation of burner DJs absorbed the notion of participation as more than just spinning records.

"The first year I arrived at OT camp on the Sunday morning and began helping out straight away. I knew a lot of the guys anyway from doing events in San Francisco so I just jumped straight in there. The feeling was one of unity and welcome anyway so anybody would have had the same treatment. It is a very rare thing for me to do as usually I turn up for gigs maybe an hour before I am due to play and the venues/ festivals are already set up and running. I felt compelled to help out because straight away you can see that it is a community, a family base, and it is natural to help your family," Marvin told me.

And after 2007, Opulent Temple needed all the help it could get from its extended family of DJs.

Calling All DJs

In deep debt and after having its pleas for some help or support rejected by Larry and the Borg, Syd Gris turned to the DJs to bail out Opulent Temple and determine whether it would return in 2008. None had been paid for playing at Burning Man, but most of the big name DJs still expected to be paid for playing camp fundraisers back in the real world.

"I went to the DJs even before the community, and I said if you want us to come back, then you have to help. And if we're able to come back, then those that do are going to be the ones who get to play for us. And almost everyone answered the call. In a certain light, it was audacious to ask. But I figured the worst they could say is no, and then you're back where you started anyway, so why not ask?" Syd told me.

So he did a mass e-mail to everyone who had ever played on the Opulent Temple decks, basically telling them performance slots of the playa would in the future be reserved for DJs who donated their skills to a camp fundraiser. "And DJ Dan was the first to say, I'm there," Syd said, noting that Dan had professed to him that his life had been changed by Burning Man. "To this day he will say that it renewed his love of DJing and music, it personally changed him, and to this day he'll say to me, you have no idea, Syd, you have no idea. And he's being a little dramatic, but it's true."

And it was true, as DJ Dan later confirmed, telling me, "Honestly, there is a real primal instinct that kicks in when you arrive on the playa. All I can say is that as a DJ, you play with more passion than you have ever played in your entire life."

His fundraiser at San Francisco's Ruby Skye made $12,000 for Opulent Temple. And all the other top DJs — including Lee Coombs, Scumfrog, Dylan Rhymes, Ali B, Christopher Lawrence — all followed with OT fundraisers in cities that included London, New York, Boise, Los Angeles, Denver, Albuquerque, and Salt Lake City.

"I volunteer my DJ services to Opulent Temple willingly, gratefully. Not only do I play for them on the playa, but I perform at OT fundraisers in San Francisco. I am compelled because I want to be a part of the Opulent Temple experience," Lawrence said. "My only hope is that it continues and that after each burn I can take with me a little of the love that I found at home on the playa."

Lee not only helped Opulent Temple, but did fundraising for his burner artists friends like Peter Hudson. They all need money to bring their creations to life, and dance parties have proven the best and most consistent way to raise it. "It's how the Burning Man world goes round," Lee said. "I have had a lot of support from many people over the years who come to my gigs and help me with my music and events in San Francisco. It is only right that I should give back and help them raise funds for their camps and art. I feel like they are all my friends and family so I want to help out."

The electronic music world had also started to take note of Burning Man, and OT in particular. DJ Magazine did a long feature story on the camp in its annual Best DJs issue in 2008, calling it one of the world's best dance parties. Burning Man had been indelibly affected by electronic music, and increasingly, vice versa.

"I can most assuredly say that it is Burning Man that has influenced the DJs that play there and in so doing shaped the electronic music scene, and not the other way around. What I do as a DJ on stage is a minor contribution of my art to the greater good of Burning Man," Lawrence said.

"Burning Man is without doubt one of the best festivals around the world," Oakenfold told me, while Scumfrog just loved the otherworldliness of Burning Man and said he even couldn't compare to other events he played.

"The biggest difference is that all other festivals are on planet Earth," Scumfrog said. "This really sums up both the positive and negative. It's quite the journey to get there and quite the ordeal to stay afloat once inside, but on the other hand, for one week a year, you are truly removed from any forces that propel our everyday society. Other festivals may last up to a few days, but Burning Man, to most attendees, becomes a year-round lifestyle."

So Scumfrog has felt compelled to give back. "I have performed at fundraisers for OT, The Deep End, and Robot Heart," he said. "When you get a glimpse behind the scenes of those camps and how much time, money and effort goes into making them a reality each year, then helping to raise funds by showing up and playing music feels like the very least thing I can do."

And it wasn't just the DJs who came to OT's rescue, but even some of its casual visitors. "We also had an angel that year that came out of nowhere and gave us $10,000," Syd said, referring to some random guy from Vancouver who just had a great time at Opulent Temple and then heard about its plight. "And all the sudden, we got out of $30,000 in debt and raised the money for the following year."

American Dream Analysis

By early in 2008, the annual Burning Man buzz had already reached a high pitch in San Francisco, which is home to most of the event's best artists.

The Borg was about to announce its art grants for the year and many of the artists I'm close to — such as Pete Hudson and the Flaming Lotus Girls — were already starting to hear that their projects had been funded, and now they needed to gather hordes of volunteers to actually build them.

I put in a little volunteer time on Pete's project for the year, helping with the human form molds that would become parts of Tantalus, his latest stroboscopic zoetrope, in which a man would be emerging from the playa to try to grab the golden apple that was just out of his reach. It was fun, hands-on work, but a long and meticulous process.

The workspaces in San Francisco and the East Bay, from the Box Shop to The Shipyard, were being transformed into buzzing hives of colorful and creative activity, sculpting artworks that fit directly or very loosely under the banner of the controversial American Dream art theme.

That spring, I finally sat down with Larry in his art-filled, rent-controlled apartment overlooking Alamo Square to talk about his "reprehensible theme," the state of the country, and the prospects for the fundamental political changes that he, I, and those like us were seeking.

"It struck a chord," Larry said of his theme, for which he'd been widely lambasted, even by those close to him. For example, someone came to the Burning Man holiday party sporting a T-shirt that read, "American Dream? Larry, Larry, what were you thinking?" But he was going for provocation, telling me, "I know why I wanted to do it."

"There was a cascade of denunciation and maybe that wasn't a bad thing. It pricked people where they should be stimulated," Larry said.

At a time when so many people were viewing the United States with such scorn — particularly among the counterculture that is attracted to Burning Man — Larry said it was important to rediscover the country's positive attributes (such as the Bill of

Rights, which he placed on that year's tickets) and find the affirmative path that we'd lost, particularly during these imperial years of Bush II.

"America has lost its way," Larry told me. "But to do this theme, I had to find things that I wanted to be proud of with America."

For Larry, that was how the U.S. behaved in the wake of World War II, when we rebuilt Europe under the Marshall Plan and essentially forgave and helped to restore Germany and Japan, our bitter enemies in that terrible war. He suggested that people needed to find something about this country to believe in if we are to restore ourselves in the eyes of the rest of the world.

"Americans need to find our pride again. We can't face our shame unless we find our pride," he told me.

Personally, I was wary of the word pride as I was of the word patriotism, both of which imply a kind of elitism and egocentrism that have been our worst enemies as a country. But I did understand what Larry is getting at, particularly because he doesn't gloss over the need for Americans to decide whether we want to rejoin the world or play out the endgame of a careening empire in decline, blinded to its fate by hubris.

"Now, the time has come and a real decision has to be made by everyone," he said.

Do we embrace the moment's potential for transformative change, which Barack Obama had made a centerpiece of his campaign, or will we be scared back into the politics of the past that both Hillary Clinton and John McCain seemed to embody? Larry was wary of flying the partisan flag, but it's safe to say he's for the former, something he'd been driving at with his last three themes — Hope and Fear, Green Man, and now American Dream — the only three in the event's long history that have been overtly sociopolitical.

"Next year, I plan to take it another round, but I can't tell you what it is," Harvey told me, hinting only that it "straddles psychology." (The theme ended up being Evolution.)

Larry said that he was done with themes like Floating World that could just as easily be high school prom themes, and he has no use for those who complain that they want politics-free escapism from their Burning Man experience.

"Burning Man doesn't mean anything unless it affects the way we live our lives back home," he said, citing his favorite pair of signs that mark the arrival at Black Rock City: "What happens in Vegas stays in Vegas. What happens in Black Rock City goes everywhere."

Through offshoot groups like Black Rock Arts Foundation, Burners Without Borders, and a new solar power venture that Tom Price was spearheading, Black Rock Solar, Larry said burners were actively applying their social networks and ethos to important projects in the real world. And he said that was happening in countless other ways that would manifest in the coming years.

"That city is connecting to itself faster than anyone knows. And if they can do that, they can connect to the world. That's why for the last three years I've done these sociopolitical themes, so they know they can apply it. Because if it's just a vacation," Larry said, his voice trailing off as his mind moved to his main point. "Well, we've been on vacation long enough."

Black Rock Solar

Tom wasn't happy with me for criticizing the execution of Green Man. He had a good point that I probably should have interviewed him again before penning my Bay Guardian reaction piece from the playa, but I countered that a reaction piece was just that, a reaction, and I and others weren't terribly impressed by what we saw.

Yet it was the stuff that we didn't see that mattered most, he said, like the fact that the Man's lights and pavilion were solar-powered, or that the relationships that he was establishing with solar companies and other green energy entrepreneurs was a valuable step for Burning Man to take.

That experience would end up translating into the next big thing for both Tom and Burning Man, Black Rock Solar, the culture's next do-gooder outreach effort. After basically turning over control of Burners Without Borders (which was still doing rebuilding work in Pisco, Peru after the devastating earthquake there) to Carmen Mauk, Tom launched Black Rock Solar in 2008.

The concept was a simple one: marry Burning Man's volunteerism and can-do spirit of participation with the need to place more clean-burning solar arrays at schools and other public entities, particularly in the rural areas that burners travel through on their way to Black Rock City.

The first project to grow from that endeavor finally came into full bloom on December 18, 2007, when a 90-kilowatt solar array — some of which was used to power the eponymous Man that year — was placed in the town of Gerlach, Nevada, as a donation to the Washoe County School District.

It gave the school free, clean power for the next 25 years, saving the district about $20,000 annually — money that could surely be put to better use than paying for fossil fuels. The project was a collaboration between the venture capital firm MMA Renewable Ventures (which put up the money), Sierra Pacific Power (which offered a substantial rebate for the project), and the burners who donated their labor.

"MMA put up the money, and the rebate from the utility paid back almost all of it, with the difference made up by Burning Man and its volunteers," Tom said.

Tom said 10 volunteers — including Eli Lyon, Matt Deluge, and Richard Scott, who were in Pearlington, Mississippi with us — worked eight hours per day for 51 days to do the work that made the project pencil out. And it was the direct result of Tom's efforts as the environmental director for Green Man.

Matt Cheney, CEO of MMA Renewable Ventures and a resident of Potrero Hill in San Francisco, said he approached people he knew at Burning Man a year earlier, wanting to help the event's new green goals. "One of the simplest ways to do it was to green up the Man with solar," he said.

Tom helped guide the project past the anti-corporate sentiments of burners. "A lot of people were afraid that Green Man would spell the end of Burning Man because there was corporate participation," Tom said.

Instead, this creative partnership has became a model for the future and a job for Tom, who became executive director of the nonprofit Black Rock Solar, which aims to replicate the Gerlach project at schools, hospitals, and other public institutions in Nevada and other states.

"We're taking fiscal capital and social capital and combining them in a way that's really never been done before," Tom said. "Our first project that we did was the largest solar array ever given away, and it was immediately eclipsed by the second one, which was three times larger."

In the first year and a half of the project, Tom said they had completed eight projects in Nevada (from the Paiute-Pyramid Lake Tribal Clinic in Nixon to a church and high school in Lovelock to the Children's Discover Museum in Reno) with 270 kilowatts worth of power, which would save the struggling entities more than $1.5 million over the life of the projects.

John Hargrove, who runs the rebate program for Sierra Pacific Power, agreed that burners have created an entirely new model. "They're able to do installations that wouldn't get done otherwise," Hargrove told me. "Clearly, they are donating a tremendous value to the project. The Burning Man, Black Rock Solar people are very unique. They're not in it to make money."

Yet the model they've created allows capitalists to make money, albeit at lower returns, by tapping into a universal sense of goodwill and a desire to save the planet. "We call this not-for-profit work. We're operating on metrics where we don't have to make our typical returns," Cheney said.

He said the price points for the first project were about 25 percent lower than for a typical big solar project. And he thinks the undeniable public benefits of projects like this will attract more support from powerful players in the public and private sectors.

"It was the right moment in time to do something like this," Cheney said. "It's one of those good ideas that happened at the right time and has taken on a life of its own."

And to Tom, it was a wonderful outgrowth of the overall Burning Man project, which he had worked so hard to inject out into the larger world. It was innovation meeting with intention. As he told me later, "Here in the Bay Area, people talk about creating the next great app, they talk about creating disruptive technology. What we're creating is disruptive culture. We're demonstrating the ability of really anybody to make real substantial concrete change in the world and do it from a values-based place, do it with a focus on the social, rather than financial, bottom line. And that's destabilizing. And it's empowering."

A Clown's Life

There were other Burning Man tribes that I'd long been fascinated by and hoped to capture, particularly after conversations about this book started with my publisher. One of those was Indie Circus, the sexy circus freaks that were becoming a big thing in San Francisco and Los Angeles clubs and who formed the Red Nose District at Burning Man starting in 2007.

I approached Boenobo the Klown, frontman of the rocking clown band Gooferman, about the idea and he suggested that I start on the inside: he offered to turn me into a clown for the May 2008 edition of the Bohemian Carnival event that he organized. That seemed like a fine idea.

As makeup artist Sharon Rose transformed me into a happy clown backstage at DNA Lounge, I asked Boenobo what I should do (besides interview people for my story). We just needed to clown around, keep the drunks from crowding the performers, help clear the stage between acts — whatever needed doing. "We're the scrubs," he told me, clown-to-clown.

As we spoke, the acrobats stretched, a corpse bride goofed off as she prepared for her aria, members of the Extra Action Marching Band started to slink in, clowns applied their makeup, and female performers occasionally came back from the stage and unabashedly whipped off their tops for a costume change.

When Gooferman went on, I still didn't know what I was supposed to be doing, so I stood next to the stage, watched, and awkwardly tried to be a little goofy in my dancing. A tall, beautiful blond woman stood next to me, catching my eye. She was apparently alone, so after a couple songs, during a lull, I asked her, "So, do you like clowns?"

"I am a clown," she said with a grin.

"Really?" I said. "You don't look like a clown."

"But I am," she said. "I even do clown porn."

She turned out to be 27-year-old porn star Hollie Stevens, who told me she "grew up as a clown" in the Midwest before moving to California and getting into porn seven years earlier. She even starred in the film Clown Porn and still sometimes dons the red nose and face paint for her public appearances. "Clowns, you either love them or you hate them," she said, and she loves them.

I asked why she was there and she said that she'd come to see Boenobo. They had talked but never met, and shared a sort of mutual admiration. It was a clown thing. Clowns ... they get all the hot chicks.

While we talked, an acrobat worked the pole on the stage, followed by an aerialist performing above the dance floor, one scene woven seamlessly into the other. The clowns of Gooferman puttered around the stage, removing equipment to get ready for the next act, flirting with the girls, trying to scam more free drink tickets, or simply entertaining others and themselves.

In the old days, people disenchanted with their towns or cultures were said to want to run off with the circus. These days, they still do, particularly those who have been liberated by an event like Burning Man, one that reflects and draws from the ancient circus arts, just as it does many other creative cultures from throughout the ages.

I saw them begin to proliferate in the nightclubs of San Francisco even before they caught my notice on the playa. These sexy and talented dreamers brought a creative energy that transformed the city's nightlife and counterculture. Spinning aerialists and dancing clowns became fixtures on the urban party scene, and their numbers more than doubled from 2004 to 2008.

They came from towns across the country — often via Burning Man, where they discovered their inner performers, dying to burst out, and other kindred spirits — to a city with a rich circus tradition, which they tweak and twist into something new, a hybrid of the arts and punk sideshow weirdness. It's the ever-evolving world of Indie Circus, burner-style.

One of the biggest banners these performers began to dance and play under was Bohemian Carnival, which drew together some of the city's best indie circus acts, including Gooferman, Vau de Vire Society, and Fou Fou Ha, acts that fluidly mix with one another and the audience.

On a Saturday in late November 2008, as families across the country shopped and shared Thanksgiving leftovers, this extended family of performers rehearsed for that night's Bohemian Carnival. Fou Fou Ha was in the Garage, a SoMa performance space, working on a new number celebrating beer with founder/choreographer Maya Culbertson, a.k.a. MamaFou, pushing for eight-count precision.

"Do it again," she told her eight high-energy charges, who look alternatively sexy and zany even without the colorful and slightly grotesque clown costumes they don for shows, adding hilarious improvised shtick as they drill through the number again and again. "That's what we love the most, the improv element to it," MamaFou told me. "We see how far you can take it and not break character."

As Fou Fou Ha wrapped up and headed home to get ready for the show, Gooferman and Vau de Vire were just starting to rehearse and set up over at the party venue, DNA Lounge. Reggie Ballard was up a tall ladder setting the rigging, the dancers stretched, Vau de Vire co-founder Mike Gaines attended to a multitude of details, and Gooferman frontmen Vegas and Boenobo played the fools.

"I feel like I'm on acid," Vegas said evenly, his long Mohawk haircut standing tall.

"Are you?" Boenobo said, perhaps a little jealous.

"No, I wish," Vegas replied. "But that's why it's weird."

"Huh," Boenobo deadpanned. "Weird."

Fucking clowns. I decide to chat up a dancer, Rachel Strickland, the newest member of Vau de Vire, who stretched and changed into her rehearsal clothes as she told me about why she moved here from North Carolina in July 2007.

"I waited a long time for this. I always knew I wanted to come to San Francisco and work on the stage, doing something in the line of Moulin Rouge, with the costumes and that kind of decadence and debauchery," Strickland said, oozing passion for her craft and the life she's chosen, one she said has met her expectations. "I danced as much as I could my whole life and I have an overactive imagination, so it's hard to shock me."

Not that Vau de Vire hasn't tried. Shocking people out of their workaday selves is what the performers try to do, whether through vaudeville acts, dance routines, feats of skill, sideshow freakiness, or just sheer sensual outlandishness. Vau de Vire choreographer Shannon Gaines (Mike's wife of 19 years) also taught at the local indie circus school Acrosports.

Shannon has been a gymnast and dancer all her life, skills that she's honed into circus performances she does through five different agencies, often doing corporate events "that involve wearing a few more clothes" and other more conventional performances. "The other seems like work to me. But this," she said, a wry smile coming to her lips, "is like dessert. This is what excites me."

She's not the only one. With their growing popularity and a steady stream of new recruits from Burning Man, the indie circus freaks were juggling an increasingly busy schedule. As Boenobo told me, "It's a moment in time when there's something big developing in San Francisco."

And the tribes of circus freaks that were gathering momentum in San Francisco, Los Angeles, New York, and other cities often found each other and their motivation in another great city: Black Rock City.

Big Top Burning Man

The circus arts are ancient, but San Francisco's unique role in morphing and perpetuating them — what some call the New Circus movement — trace back to the 1970s and entities such as Make-a-Circus, Pickle Family Circus, and the San Francisco Mime Troupe, a guerilla theater group.

"It really started with the San Francisco Mime Troupe, and it flourishes here because of the rich arts culture that we've always had here," Jeff Raz, a longtime performer with those original SF troupes who started the San Francisco Clown Conservatory and had the title role in Cirque du Soleil's Corteo, told me.

In fact, it was San Francisco's rich history of circus and other performing arts that really fed directly into Burning Man, which borrowed from those theatrical, irreverent traditions to feed the event that started on Baker Beach in 1986. The city's arts scene helped make San Franciscans receptive to Burning Man and willing to help build it into something unique.

"San Francisco felt like a place where things could happen that were socially and politically relevant," Wendy Parkman, longtime performer and San Francisco Circus Center board member, told me. "Circus has always been a people's art form. It's a great way of getting a lot of people involved because it takes a lot of people to put on a show."

"The Pickle Family Circus was a grassroots circus that was part of a real renaissance. Unfortunately, it didn't go very far," Dominique Jando, a noted circus historian who has written five books on the circus and whose wife teaches trapeze at the Circus Center, told me.

American spectacles like Ringling Brothers and Barnum & Bailey Circus commercialized the circus and transformed it into the three-ring form that sacrificed intimacy and the emphasis on artistry and narrative flow. Burners drawn to the circus arts were seeking something very different, something more personal and intimate, something that felt like a real expression of inner creativity more than a well-disciplined craft.

Raz, Jando, and Parkman all pointed to the sterile excesses of the televised, digitized, Twittering, 24/7 world we live in as feeding the resurgence of circus. "It points to a demand by the audience to see something more down to earth and real," Jando said. "There is a need to go back to basics."

Raz said the rise of Indie Circus and its influence on the local arts scene is consistent with his own experiences as an actor and clown, letting one inform the other and opening up new forms of creative expression. "That melding that you're looking at, from the club scene to Burning Man, is seeping into a lot of the world," Raz said. "Circus is very much a living art form."

"Somehow," Jando said, a bit dismissively, "it has become a sort of counterculture on the West Coast."

He hadn't been to Burning Man and seen how it awakens people, so he didn't quite understand the connection. But the burners I talked to understood. It's often just about being someone else.

"The clown thing floats my boat. It is a persona I really dig. And the band kicks ass. We're all just super tight. The Bohemian Carnival is just a bunch of friends, like a family ejected out of different wombs," Boenobo said.

The band does kick ass. Setting aside the clown thing, their tunes are original and fun, evoking Oingo Boingo at its early best. They performed at the Hillbilly Hoedown inside a giant maze made of hay bales in Half Moon Bay in the fall of 2008, with the clowns and circus performers creating a fantastical new world for the partygoers. As Gooferman played, Shannon broke the rules and danced atop a hay bale wall behind the band, conveying pure danger and backwoods sex appeal.

"The Gooferman character is called Bruiser or Shenanigans," Shannon said of her performer alter egos. "She does the things that you'd get kicked out of a party for, but I can get away with it."

Their world not only includes practitioners of circus arts (contortionists, aerialists, trapeze artists, clowns, and the like), but also the fashion scene (including outlandish local designers such as Anastasia), painters, sculptors, dancers, actors, fire artists, and DJs such as Smoove who bring a certain zany flair to the dance parties that follow the circus acts.

Bohemian Carnival and its many offshoots try to break down the wall between the performers and the audience, who often show up in circus or Burning Man styles, further blurring the borders. "When you break down that big third wall, there's no pretense," Mike Gaines said. "It's really about the party and the community."

Clowns circulate in the crowd, interacting with the audience while aerialists suddenly start performing on ropes or rings suspended over the dance floor. It draws the audience in, opens them up, makes them feel like they're part of something. "All of the sudden, people get to realize the dream of running away with the circus, but they get to leave it at the end of the night," Boenobo said with a wink, "which they generally like."

But Burning Man encourages some to run away with circus for real. That was how the talented aerialist and hooper who calls herself Shredder got into this world, which she explored in both the traditional circus and the indie variety, preferring the latter.

"I didn't even know it was possible, but I just love it," said Shredder, who worked as a firefighter, EMT, and environmental educator before getting into performing through Burning Man, where Boenobo set up the Red Nose District in 2006 for all the many offshoots of the indie circus world that attend the event.

Shredder developed hula hoop and aerial routines, training hard to improve her skills and eventually was hired by the Cole Brothers Circus in 2006 to do aerial acrobatics and hooping. Founded in 1882, Cole is a full-blown circus in the Ringling Brothers tradition, with a ringleader, animals, and trained acrobats. Shredder toured 92 cities in 10 months until she felt the creativity and joy being snuffed out by the rote repetition of the performances.

"We did the exact same show everyday. It was like (the film) Groundhog Day but worse; same show, different parking lot," said Shredder, who later that Saturday night did a performance with more than a dozen hula hoops at once. "Then I heard about Vau de Vire through some fellow performers and I just heard they were doing really well and I wanted to be with a group like that ... I was just so happy that they were willing to help me design my vision as an artist."

Calling All Freaks

The Bohemian Carnival name and concept was actually an import from Fort Collins, Colorado, where Mike and Shannon Gaines created the Vau de Vire Society as part of the performance and party space they operated there in a 100-year-old church that they purchased.

Mike's background was in film; Shannon was a dancer; and the world they created for themselves was decidedly countercultural. So was their space, the Rose Window Experimental Theater and Art House, which they operated from 1997 to 2001 and lived in with 20 of their bohemian friends.

"It allowed us to really get to know ourselves. We had all day to just rig up any kind of performance we could imagine," she said. "If you had a crazy idea, you could just come on over at 3 a.m. and do it."

Their signature events were themed parties that would open with performances of about 30 minutes, usually combining music, dance, and performance art, followed by a dance party that was essentially an all-night rave. Initially the performances just drew off of the creativity of their friends, including those Shannon danced with. The themes were often risqué and sometimes included nudity.

The performances evolved over time, bringing in talent such as Angelo Moore of the band Fishbone, who is still a regular part of their crew. They were all attracted to the freaky side of performance art, which drew them toward sideshow, vaudeville, and circus themes and expanding what was technically possible. "We ended up getting a rigger in and just flying around the theater," Mike said.

They did their first Bohemian Carnival event in 2000. "That's when we started dabbling in the circus," Mike said. While the events gained regional acclaim in newspapers and were supported by notable figures, including the town's mayor, there was a backlash among local conservatives, including some who objected to how a traditional church was being used for raves by these bohemian freaks.

In 2001 they decided to search for a new home. "We looked around for the place that would be most accepting of what we were doing," Mike said. San Francisco was known to be accepting of their kind, and there were groups there that were edging toward similar kinds of parties, including Infinite Kaos and Xeno (and its predecessor, Awd), as well as the band Idiot Flesh, not to mention the more serious circus being done at the Circus Center and Teatro Zinzanni.

"San Francisco, in this country, is a real hotbed for circus. So we were like, 'Now we can bring in legitimate circus performers," Mike said. Shannon got a job teaching at Acrosports, allowing her to be immersed full-time in her art and to help grow her community.

Serendipitously, in August 2001, indie rocker Boenobo of the band Chub — a funky ska outfit whose members would wear different costumes to each of their performances — formed Gooferman, which wasn't originally the clown band it is today: "The idea was you had to be in a costume and you had to be stoned."

They morphed into a full-blown clown band, and began collaborating with circus performers. The two entities came together in 2004, the year that reviled President George W. Bush won a second term and when longtime Burning Man artists staged their ill-fated Borg2 revolt against the event.

"When people get too serious, they need this shit even more," Boenobo said of the increasingly irreverent, naughty, and participatory parties he started throwing. Burning Man, which was rapidly growing and starting to have a bigger impact on San Francisco's culture than ever before, fed the rise of indie circus.

"At Burning Man, there's all this peculiar shit that just spontaneously happens. That's why I love it," Boenobo said. "What other festival or big event has taken a very pure thing that happens and taken it out and tried to replicate it?"

Meanwhile Fou Fou Ha was developing its act. Culbertson and Raymond Meyer were waiting tables at Rose Pistola in 2000 and decided to put their big personalities to work for them, bringing in other performers such as Slim Avocado and setting up routines to perform at San Francisco's CELLspace and other venues.

"We're sort of like the children of Cirque du Soleil in a way, but we wanted to give it an edge," Culbertson, who became MamaFou, told me.

Fou Fou Ha's shows play off the dark and surreal kind of performance that is more European than American, a style MamaFou was exposed to while studying choreography during her Fulbright scholarship in Holland in the late 1990s. When she returned to the United States in 2000, "I wanted to form a [dance] company." But she wanted it to be fun. She hung around with the Burning Man artists at CELLspace, ended up doing some dancing with Rosin Coven, and she finally gathered her friends and fellow artists to form the early version of Fou Fou Ha.

"I was influenced a lot by Burning Man," MamaFou said, referring to how the event gives "permission to let certain things come out," that sense of play and silliness. "People really like the idea of serious dance combined with comedy, where you can fall out of your pirouette."

"We're kind of like guerilla circus," Slim, a trained ballerina, said. "It's a whole new movement. It's like '30s cabaret, but edgier."

Even the style of sexuality that it encourages, ranging from risqué to grotesque to just plain dirty, can be liberating for workaday stiffs. "There's something in us that wants to be raunchy," MamaFou said. "It's sort of like Burning Man: you have permission to let certain things come out."

Boenobo started the Red Nose District on the playa at Burning Man in 2006, drawing together his Bohemian Carnival friends, a local group of stilt-walkers known as Enheightned Beings of Leisure, installation artist Michael Christian's crew from the East Bay, the Cirque Berserk folks from Los Angeles, and others from the growing circus world.

"It's a safe environment to be and do what you want," Mike said of Burning Man, noting how those breakthroughs on the playa then come back home to the city. And that ethos carries into Vau de Vire, which is truly a collective of like-minded friends, one that eschews hiring outside performers for their shows. "They're all just part of it."

"Our local family is super comfortable with one another," Boenobo said, something he's never felt before after 25 years as an indie rocker. "It's rare to not have a lot of ego to deal with, and it's super rare with this kind of high-quality performance."

Ah Yes, Hedonism

This book is more than half over and we really haven't talked about sex and drugs yet. How can we talk about the counterculture without getting into sex and drugs? We really can't, although it's not an easy subject to broach.

For one thing, there are very few full-time burners out there. Most of us, even the total freaks in this book, also have day jobs and so talking about drugs is a sensitive subject, one that was either implicitly or explicitly made off the record with many of my interview subjects.

I'm also a father and media professional, so it's even difficult for me. But I do work for an alternative newspaper with a tendency to sometimes glorify drugs, as we did before the 2009 Burning Man. So I'm just going to run the following piece, for which I was the editor, and let it speak for itself:

Packing for the Trip

The art of taking drugs to — and at — Burning Man
By "Anonymous"

San Francisco has always been a big recreational drug town, from its opium dens of yore to the pill-popping beats and acid-eating hippies to business elites doing bumps in bathrooms to ravers on E and cranked-out clubbers, not to mention the tattered street souls scoring fixes of crack or smack.

But in terms of sheer numbers of Bay Area partiers stocking up on the full illegal pharmacopoeia all at once, it's hard to top right now, the month of August, the run-up to Burning Man.

Now I know what they say. This event — which started in San Francisco in 1986 and now occurs in the Nevada boondocks — isn't simply a big drug fest. Many burners don't even do drugs anymore. It's about "radical self-expression" and "radical self-reliance" and all kinds of other radical stuff, like a gift economy, public nudity, and massive fire cannons. Radical, dude.

But let's get real, m'kay? Burning Man may be many things, but among those things is that it may be the best time and place on the planet to ingest mind-altering substances, something recognized even by attendees who don't regularly do drugs — although most burners also do them here.

Why? Because DRUGS ARE FUN!!!

Okay, so you're getting ready to head to the playa. You're part of a mid-sized Burning Man camp that's giving away peach schnapps Sno-Cones from a big peach-shaped art car and you're all calling yourself James. Or whatever. Not important.

You got your goggles and combat boots. Your bike is covered entirely in fake pink fur and wrapped in blue electro-luminescent wire. You've packed enough costumes for a month, from the fire-crotch thong to an elaborate Ming the Merciless getup, complete with death ray. Again, whatever, not important.

What is important are the drugs. You're going to spend a week frolicking through the planet's preeminent adult playground, past all manner of tripper traps and the weirdest, most mind-blowing shit you've ever seen, mixing with a multitude of beautiful souls with Cheshire Cat grins. You'll want one too.

I suppose you could do it sober, and I've heard stories about people who do. But why? This particular party environment is a lifeless desert that sucks the moisture out of you and everything around you, so booze just isn't the best choice of intoxicant. I've known many people who have ended up in the medical tent from drinking, but none from using drugs.

In fact, it's safe to say that drug cocktails are the real cocktails of Burning Man. Everyone has his or her drug combo of choice, but mine is flipping out. Candy-flipping (LSD and ecstasy) or hippie-flipping (shrooms and ecstasy), depending on my mood and agenda. It's the perfect combo: E for the euphoria and psychedelics to amp up the weirdness. It's like a wild, joyful ride into a parallel universe.

On a big night, I'll often re-up several times, taking another dose of one or the other every few hours, balancing my buzz like the pro I am. And then, as dawn approaches after a long night of flipping around the playa, that's the best time to get into the Ketamine. Believe me, Special K is just the right dessert for a meal like that, bringing all the night's adventures into a sort of twisted focus.

Of course, you're going to want to vary your experiences night to night, and for that you're going to need to be well stocked with substances such as K, MDA, MDMA, acid, shrooms, pot, Foxy, nitrous oxide, cocaine, 2CB, 2CT7, mescaline, and, well, I'm sure there are others. At that level, you begin to count sobriety as its own drug.

By the end of the week, once the tolerance has been ratcheted up by daily drug use, some burners start to really pile on the chemicals, trying to regain the high highs from the early part of the week. Burn night, the week's penultimate party, can get downright ugly, walking zombies with glazed expressions and wan, serotonin-depleted smiles.

It can take weeks to fully recover your senses after a run like that. But we do come back. Humans are remarkably resilient creatures.

Serious week-long benders aren't for everyone, but almost everyone dabbles in the desert. Newbies want to maximize their experience and veterans just know, including the fact that (no matter what their intentions going in) they'll want drugs, which can be tough to score out there.

Cops with night-vision goggles and plain-clothed narcs prowl the playa and we've all heard outrageous stories of vile, sneaky busts. As a result, we're so guarded around people we don't know that uninitiated newbies sometimes sadly conclude that nobody does drugs at Burning Man, despite all the giddy grins and oversized pupils. Remember: you aren't paranoid if they really are out to get you.

So we down our drugs carefully and stock up here. But most of us are professionals — more so in the working than party worlds — who don't have dealers on speed dial. So right now, we're all banding together to place ridiculously large orders — hundreds of pills, pounds of fungus, all just for personal use — with the handful of multidrug dealers who can make more money in August than the other 11 months put together.

But drugs busts don't spike in August, and busts at or en route to Burning Man have also been flat in recent years, despite eager law enforcement. That's because we're smart, creative professionals who really don't want to get caught. And we've devised crazy, inventive ways of hiding them — systems I won't reveal. We all have drugs, but bring your dogs and all your cop knowledge, and you still won't find them.

We are determined and we love our drugs. BTW, for great advice on dosage and warnings about various drug combinations, consult www.erowid.org.

Sex, Lies and Playa Dust

Burning Man is sexy, whatever your taste. Hot young women with bare breasts and frilly booty shorts dancing in the afternoon sun. Muscled, stubbley studs sweating through acts of artistic creation. Hip geeks playing someone else's game, giddy grins sneaking through too-cool nonchalance. Your type, whatever that is, in a new context. Everyone pushing their boundaries and feeling their bliss.

Potential partners galore, everyone on vacation in this strange world where normal rules don't seem to apply, the possibility of some random hookups in every strange art car or bouncing party tent. The atmosphere is supercharged. Then add to that the overtly sex-oriented camps and events: Jiffy Lube, Bianca's Smut Shack, Critical Tits, The Great Canadian Beaver-Eating Contest, Porn 'n Eggs, Mystic Temple of Bliss, the Love Sub, Spanky's Wine Bar, and the Temple of Atonement.

Yes, there's lots of sex on the playa, in just about every form imaginable. But talk to some of the playa's sexual superstars, people known as leaders and innovators in the communities of sexual libertines and experimenters in notoriously sex-positive cities such as San Francisco, and they'll offer surprising takes on playa sex.

"Sex on the playa is gross. Everyone's all sweaty and dusty," Polly Superstar tells me as we chat in her sex party space, Kinky Salon's Mission Control. "I'm not going to be sucking some dusty cock when I don't even know that person, who's been in some kind of pleather costume for the last two days and hasn't bathed. That shit is fucking nasty. Or you have the option of going to the sex party, where you get hosed down by the old dude at the entrance."

"Yeah, we kind of stay away from anything like that. There's a sexiness to people and an openness, but things that specifically describe themselves as sex-related or oriented, we've always stayed away from it," adds Polly's partner, Barron Scott Levkoff.

Polly and Scott are far from prudish — this polyamorous couple is closer to the opposite. Sex plays a central role in their lives, and they've tapped the Burning Man community and ethos to create a "safe container" for open sexual expression at their Kinky Salon parties in San Francisco. It's a paradox that others in their orbit share, including Dona Williams, another sexual adventurer who first attended Burning Man in 1996 and has been part of sexually experimental communities in California for even longer.

"Burning Man is not necessarily conducive to getting down," Dona told me. "It's dirty and not very hygienic."

But in her larger world in San Francisco, the people she does get down with and knows from the sex party circuit, Burning Man is still a common denominator. It even crosses over into her profession as a computer geek, such as doing IT work for Kink.com founder Peter Acworth's Porn Palace — a porn set, company office, and party space — at one point. Many of those sets were built by Peter Hudson, the Burning Man artist behind such beloved pieces as Homouroboros and Tantalus.

Acworth has become the godfather of fetish porn in San Francisco, a city that has become the capital of that hardcore genre. He is so successful that he paid millions in cash for the San Francisco Armory in 2007, turning its block-long cavernous, labyrinthine interior into a series of dungeons and other porn sets for his porn flicks. He's also a single man who regularly dates a variety of hot women and even performs in some of Kink's films, but he shared Dona and Polly's take on playa sex.

"I didn't find sex on the playa to be overt. In fact, I have never had sex there, and never even seen it directly! I remember there was an orgy in someone's tent at one point, but the prospect of sweat and dust was not appealing," Acworth told me. "The expression of alternative sexuality that I have been talking about is in the art, or in the open way people talk to you, or the free and open way they dress and act, or in the communities that come together around a specific form of sexuality. For instance, of course you see gay people being openly affectionate, BDSM folk spanking each other, cross-dressers cross-dressed, etc, but there will also be whole camps consisting of people who are into a specific form of sexuality or lifestyle, such as the Temple of Atonement, which is a large BDSM camp."

Spanky's Wine Bar is a camp where visitors can get some bondage play with their chardonnay, or a visit to the groping booth or Orgasmatron, a custom-made vibrating ride for women and their partners in a private booth. Yet beyond such overt expressions of sexuality, Burning Man feeds the sex-positive culture that prevails among its attendees in more diverse and interesting ways.

"I think people's first visit to Burning Man opens them up to all kinds of new ways of thinking, of which alternative forms of sexuality is just one," Acworth said. "When I think of 'Sex Positive Communities' I think, for example, of people who are in favor of gay marriage, who understand gender issues, and are just very accepting and tolerant of people who have made all kinds of choices about how they want to have sex and relationships, such as open marriages, polyamory, BDSM, etc. When you talk to people in these communities here in San Francisco, Burning Man is a fairly regular topic."

Destin Gerek is someone whose inner erotic rockstar was released by Burning Man, and who has in turn taken that rebirth and persona (see www.eroticrockstar. com) and helped feed the conversions of others by holding sensual workshops at Burning Man every year, as well as back at home in San Francisco.

"Much of the Erotic Rockstar was born at Burning Man as sort of a personal exploration, and deciding what being a man means to me," Destin told me. He always had an interest in human sexuality, which he studied at New York University, San Francisco State University, and the Institute for the Advanced Study of Sexuality in San Francisco, as well as boning up his tactile talents and interest in massage school.

Destin is basically bisexual but doesn't like the label, and he was engaged to the indie circus performer Megan Anastasia, the beautiful and colorful woman he credits with helping to expand his horizons, sexually and as a performer, instructor, and costumed freak. His long hair was dyed a bright red when I interviewed him at the Guardian office, and he wore a stylish, sleeveless shirt with large copper bracelets.

"One of the things Burning Man is great for is people get into a ridiculously open state," Destin said. "You have all these people that are going there looking for a transcendent experience and it becomes a self-fulfilling experience."

Destin first attended Burning Man in 2002, and by 2006 he was leading hundreds of people per year in workshops on topics that include orgasmic breathing, tantric massage for couples, and "celebrating our erotic selves." We spoke in 2009 and his goal for Burning Man that year was a "simultaneous group breathgasm experience" with more than 1,000 people.

Burning Man can break old habits and patterns, whether through classes like Destin's, the deep connections people form when working and camping together, just the surreal nature of Burning Man, or use recreational drugs in the pursuit of new consciousness and experiences.

"Yes, psychoactive substances play a big role in this," Destin said. "I do think that substances play a role. They help people drop their inhibitions…There is a deep part of our souls that knows there's something else and Burning Man gives us permission to just throw it off…It gives people an opportunity to try something they weren't comfortable with before."

Dona agrees that the playa can open people up to new experiences and ways for thinking about sexuality. "In our case, it didn't really change us. We brought our sexuality there," she said of the crew she started attending with in 1996. "All the people we went with were already experimenting with different relationship paradigms: bisexuality, communal living, polyamory."

But they brought it there, where others could be exposed to and absorb it, like spreading seeds of possibility among the squares looking for new ways of being. "The rules didn't seem to apply there," she said. "At Burning Man, you want to have a blowout experience. If there's something you want to try, you'll do it."

And if you like it, you may just want to bring it home and play with it there.

Kinky Salon

Polly and Scott like to play off of that theme of making the exotic a reality, as they do when we chat in Mission Control.

"You have a playa name, you have a costume, and it gives you permission to do whatever it is that your creativity wants to do. Normal people are given a permission that they're not normally given in everyday life," Polly said.

"And to discover the mythic component of life. I think a lot of people are really longing for a sense of the mythic in their lives. And Burning Man gives them the chance," Scott said.

"They have names and stories and some people are in character all night. So that kind of permission is a very liberating thing for a lot of people. And as far as sexuality, you're giving yourself permission to do a lot of things you might not do if you didn't have that kind of mythic identity to connect with. So in a way, mythic identity makes you more authentic," Polly said.

Scott described the connection between San Francisco and Burning Man as "a feedback loop," and they use that link as they develop the culture off-playa.

"What is that vibe about Burning Man? What is it that makes people feel more safe to explore themselves, to be creative? How then do we create the space that allows for people to be similarly at home, to be creative, to be a little more sexually liberal than they might not otherwise have been. What are the safety factors that we need to recreate that vibe?" Polly said.

They met in 1999, shortly after Polly arrived in San Francisco from London, where she was a latex fashion designer involved in the fetish scene. They gravitated toward the same sex-positive community here, which they have tapped or morphed for the Kinky Salon parties they throw at a San Francisco space they've dubbed Mission Control.

"I've been involved since 1990 with different costume subcultures in San Francisco," Scott said. "Like the Costumer's Society, like Dark Garden, doing fairy tale masquerade balls, doing the Renaissance Faire, getting involved with Burning Man early on."

Sex has always been central to this open couple's lifestyle, but the sex at their parties is almost secondary to the parties themselves, where costumes and other forms of creative expression dominate. As they like to say, they aren't sex parties, but parties where sex and sexual expression happens, usually in the rooms off the dance floor.

"Me and Scott both come from a history of fetish clubs. That was our original scene. So when we started Kinky Salon, we intended it to be a fetish club, although we were fetish by default, because that was the only way we could really dress up and be sex-positive and really do all the things that we wanted to do," Polly said.

Instead, what they were really after was facilitating a very intentional and involved community, and placing it in the safe container of this great, sprawling party space along Mission Street. And they've become so popular that the monthly parties they've thrown since 2002 went twice-monthly in 2009, always with a different theme for the costumes.

"I think what started to make Kinky Salon really interesting is when things started to go wrong, basically," Polly said. "As event producers, we really wanted to put together something that was for the community, for whatever it was they wanted to make happen. And after about six months or so, we basically threw a public hissy fit and said, 'Okay, people, Kinky Salon is over. We're tired of being your barkeepers if all you want to do is consume and take and be sloppy and make a mess…'"

"Yeah, be sloppy, fuck shit up, destroy the toilets," Scott added.

"Then you can go and do it someplace else. We're not your fucking barkeepers. But if you want to really create something with us, then let's make it happen. And we posted that kind of statement on a bulletin board. And we said, what do you think? How can we stop this from happening again? And everybody just rose up, the whole community," Polly said.

"People really stepped up. We basically facilitated a process by which Kinky Salon came to craft a container for itself that was intentional. Standards. Methods. Hosts. People checking in at the door. We have a lot of ideas about how to do this, but we really opened it up to people," Scott said. "Because we wanted it to be of, by, and for the community."

Rather than the debaucherous, egotistical, exclusive atmosphere that was being created, they shifted it to something more proudly intentional — but where public sex was still happening and people were allowed to get their freaks on, in their own unique ways.

"We wanted to create something that is participatory, where people get involved and where everyone is responsible for maintaining, and creating something that is really a reflection of the community itself," Polly said.

They all felt the polar tugs between keeping it cool and making it inclusive, and they've opted to strive for the latter, the same path Larry Harvey chose for Burning Man when he was confronted with a similar dilemma, with the coolness factor maintained by the creativity and personalities of its regular attendees.

"People have suggested making it members-only and closing the doors, but we've always said that is not what Kinky Salon is about," Polly said. "Kinky Salon is about inclusivity and, really, our doors are open to anybody who can find us. As long as you can find us and you have someone who have vouch for you, as long as you're looking out for each other, you can come to Kinky Salon."

Road Trip

It had been almost a year since Larry Harvey announced the 2008 art theme for Burning Man: "American Dream." I hated it and said so publicly.

But I came to see a bit of method behind Larry's madness as I prepared to take my sixth trip to Black Rock City, this time treating it as an extended checkpoint on my drive to and from an even bigger patriotic pageant, the Democratic National Convention in Denver. It was a trip made possible by synchronous — but probably not coincidental — timing.

My normal Burning Man preparations were far more complicated that year. I had arranged my Democratic National Convention press credentials, a pair of them, deputizing an acquaintance to take the trip with me and help with coverage: Kid Beyond, an amazing beatboxer and performance artist, political progressive, and burner who camped with Acworth at the Department of Animal Control, whose shtick was to collect burners in animal costumes.

And there were lots of logistics involved, from securing Burning Man early arrival passes to figuring out how to do daily blog posts from the road to renting the car and setting up accommodations, interviews, and key invitations for our coverage in Denver.

Beyond simply covering the events, the journey was a big part of how I envisioned the project. I had never driven past western Nevada or anywhere near this far (seven hours to Black Rock City and another 16 hours on to Denver). Hell, I don't even own a car and don't particularly like the things, opting instead to get around mostly by my silly, Burning Man-inspired bicycle, as I would also do in Denver and BRC. So this was sort of a Bizarro version of my last project of this nature: covering the Towards Carfree Cities conference in Portland with daily Guardian blog posts.

The automobile is a huge part of our national mythology and ethos, so much so that the streets of Black Rock City (which are renamed each year according to the art theme) in 2008 were a tribute to American cars: Allanté, Bonneville, Corvair, Dart, Edsel, Fairlane, Gremlin, Hummer, Impala (the very vehicle I had reserved for the trip), Jeep, and K-car.

My alternative transportation advocate compatriots howled over this apparent celebration of fossil fuel consumption (a real U-turn from 2007's Green Man theme), just as they complained when the Democratic National Convention organizers decided to ban bicycles from the convention grounds (although they would still come in incredibly handy in getting around that locked-down town).

For Barack Obama and the Democratic Party, America's stubborn affection for automobiles represents a real challenge. On the final night of the convention, Al Gore was expected to renew his call for drastically rolling back fossil fuel consumption to the massive crowd that drove or flew to Denver for the party. All the experts say dealing seriously with climate change, air pollution, or declining public health means we all have to drive less, but politicians say so at their professional peril.

As for Larry Harvey, he's just trying to be provocative. After announcing the theme, Larry told me, "There was a cascade of denunciations and maybe that wasn't a bad thing. It pricked people where they should be stimulated." He asked critics to read his essay explaining the theme: "It says that America has lost its way."

As a journalist, I never really subscribed to the impossible standard of objectivity, hewing toward the most important standards of truth and fairness. I really wanted both Burning Man and the Democratic Party to succeed in spreading more progressive values through this troubled country. I stated publicly that I wanted a Democrat in the White House in January and considered Republicans at that point to be, well, not evil exactly, but certainly corrupt, dangerous, hypocritical, naive, discredited, untrustworthy, and simply bad for the country.

So if readers were looking for objective, dispassionate analysis, this wasn't that kind of project. I wanted the Democratic Party and Burning Man to change the world, but I was sort of like a disgruntled lover of both, grown bitter and critical of their many shortcomings. In fact, I was sort of hoping that they'd be like cocoons, dying off in their old forms as they spawned something new after their big events in 2008.

Yet I also planned to be a far more credible source of information than many of my supposedly objective colleagues in the mainstream media, simply because of how I work: I call events as I see them, eschew political spin, rarely let powerful people speak off the record (and never let them say contradictory things in public and private), refuse to join any political faction or even sign petitions, and feel no need to curry favor or cultivate friendly sources by pulling punches. It's the only way I knew how to work and it had served me well through two decades of writing for newspapers in California.

Like Hunter S. Thompson wrote in *Fear and Loathing: On the Campaign Trail '72*, my goal was to report and write, "as close to the bone as I could get, and to hell with the consequences." He ignored the clubby, confidential modern conventions of political journalism, and I would as well. Instead, I tried to cut through the bullshit and tell readers what Democratic power brokers are really saying. As the good doctor wrote, "The main trick of political journalism is learning how to translate."

I had been rereading *Fear and Loathing* as I prepared for my trip and planned to draw from its lessons and essence, without descending into cheap mockery. The other voice in my ear in those days was that of Jack Kerouac, whose *On the Road* is the seminal guide for San Francisco to Denver road trips: "Now I could see Denver looming ahead of me like the promised land, way out beneath the stars, across the prairie of Iowa and the plains of Nebraska, and I could see the greater vision of San Francisco beyond, like jewels in the night."

As I wrote in the paper that week, I may have been nuts to take this trip. And I knew full well how crazy many of the characters are that I'd be encountering on the playa and in the convention hall. These were two groups that have watched America slowly and steadily go insane, going a bit bonkers themselves in the process.

Yet I was drawn to the same types of people as Kerouac, who wrote, "the only people for me are the mad ones, the ones who are mad to live, mad to talk, mad to be saved, desirous of everything at the same time, the ones who never yawn or say a commonplace thing, but burn, burn, burn…"

Opulent Temple threw some of the biggest nightly dance parties
throughout Burning Man's renaissance years. ~ Photo by MV Galleries

Gooferman front men Boenobo (left) and Vegas combine
solid musicianship with circus shtick. ~ Photo by Neil Girling

Erin Shredder and Miriam Telles from Vau de Vire Society work the trapeze. ~ Photo by Neil Girling

Garage Mahal brings three levels of rolling dance party to any corner of the playa. ~ Photo by Tami Rowan

Black Rock Solar has used volunteer burner labor to install millions of dollars in solar arrays at almost no cost to schools and nonprofits. ~ Photo by Tom Price

You You Hu is a burner-inspired dance troupe that is zany, sexy, funny, and slightly grotesque. ~ Photo by Neil Girling

Kinky Salon founders Polly Superstar (left) and Barron Scott Levkoff with burlesque performer Sparkly Devil. ~ Photo by Neil Girling

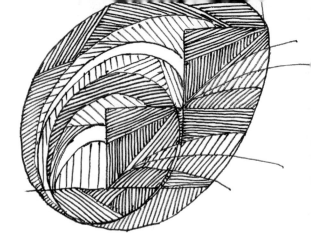

Part V — Evolving (2008-09)

Friday, August 29, 2008

The last few spoonfuls of rice and green chicken curry warm my belly, but I still feel so strange and unsettled, like I'm dreaming. I set my plate down on the playa next to my camp chair, lean back, and take a long, slow gulp out of my mug of wine. I probably just need some sleep, but that can wait for now. A big night is about to begin.

I look around the circle at 60 to 70 Garage Mahal campmates, who are chatting or finishing their meals, and I'm struck by how bedraggled they look. I guess it isn't so surprising. After all, I might have been driving all night and day through four states, but they've been partying at Burning Man since I left them five days ago.

"Well hey there, welcome back," Bill says, grasping my shoulder warmly. "How was it?"

"Awesome," I say, a little absently. "It's still hard to believe that I watched Barack Obama accept the presidential nomination in Mile High Stadium last night, and now I'm here."

"When did you get back?"

"Just a couple hours ago, maybe not even that. We left Denver around 2 a.m. and think we pulled into camp about 5:30 or so."

"Whoa, quite a trip. Well, it's good to have you back," Bill says, patting my back and heading back toward his seat as Captain Ken calls the evening meeting together.

Ken and some of the other camp elders run through a few items of business — how great the art tour was earlier that day, the status of problems with the graywater pump on the showers, the importance of tonight's art car volunteers spotting people and sand drifts for the driver — but I'm having a hard time paying attention.

I'm thinking about Barack Obama and the things he said and didn't say, and about Sarah Palin, who was named as the GOP vice presidential nominee this morning, and the Guardian cover story on this whole saga that I just sent to my editor from the road, and the work that I will still need to do on it when I arrive at the hotel in Reno on Monday.

Fuck that, I tell myself, shake it off, Scribe. You're at Burning Man. The work is done now and it's time to have some fun in this big, beautiful city. "So let's have a great night," Ken concludes and Mahalers yip and howl as they rise and start hauling their chairs and dishes back to their tents and RVs to start getting ready. I'm still disoriented and don't really know where I'm going, so I just survey the camp, trying to make it my home again.

The rough-hewn Shiva statue is ringed in fire and throwing off warmth. The dinner crew is washing dishes in the kitchen area. Rope lights and paper lanterns illuminate the pillows and fabrics in the covered chill area, momentarily tempting me to go lie down before I decide to plow through and get ready.

Digging into the bags in my trunk, I throw on the first costume I find and head into the camp area that Donnie, Heather, Rosie, and Kay are sharing, still in a daze. The place is abuzz with activity as we all dress and pull together the supplies for the evening. Heather applies some eyeliner to me at one point. The passing of time is only a vague concept.

"Rrrrrroooooooowwwwwwwwwrrrrrrrrrrrrrrrr," sounds the air horn on the art car, the first of many warnings that it's almost time to go, sending the women into a more frenzied pace of preparation while Donnie and I fill everyone's water bottles and bags and load a small ice chest with beer and other beverages.

It's nice to have the car as a home base on nights like this, a place where we stash our stuff and the long fur coats that we'll probably need later, once the chill of night sets in. We aren't as mobile as we are on the nights when we decide to prowl the playa on our bikes, so forgetting your goggles or other key supplies can end up being a major regret.

Tick, tick, tick. "Rrrrrrooooooooowwwwwwwwwrrrrrrrrrrrrrrrr."

"Okay, I'm going to stash our stuff on the car and grab a seat," I tell Rosie or whoever is listening.

The car is fairly full, mostly with Garage Mahalers, but also some randoms that I don't know as well. There's already a couple nestled into the crow's nest and our flame is burning a few feet above their heads. Below them, the top floor has 15-20 people standing around, and Jive is on the decks, playing some solid downtempo beats, giving me a nice surge of anticipation about the dance party out at Tantalus, way out in the deep playa, our main planned destination for the evening.

Ten minutes and three sirens later, Rosie, Heather, and the last of the Mahalers who have indicated an intention to join us arrive, the three spotters take their watchful positions around the car, and the "beep, beep, beep" of shifting into reverse indicates that we're off.

Rosie grabs the seat I've saved next to me and we flip around to face out, leaning on the padded bar and letting my legs dangle off the edge. "So, here we are again," I say to Rosie, starting to settle into playa life, as excitement begins to overtake my fatigue.

We just watch this wild world go by, the neighborhood street ending at the open playa, intricate patterns of fire and blinking lights filling the horizon in front of us, creative creatures floating past us on foot or bicycles, art cars ranging from a small neon head to massive whale sailing along at our same 5 mph pace, all making wide arcs around the deep drifts of sand that are the worst I've even seen, catching bicycles like beartraps.

As we look out, outsiders look in, passersby dancing to the bass-heavy breakbeats that we're now cranking at full volume, drawing some passersby to board us in the back as we chug along, some stepping into our lower area, some climbing the ladder to the top.

We pass Big Rig Jig, two semi-tractor-trailers dancing up into air like a double helix. We pass the Man, then the Temple, and continue on into the dark, deep playa, the horizon now far less intense, dotted sporadically with lights of fellow burners. Far in front of me, I can make out Opulent Temple and barely hear its beats even though we're maybe a mile away, but the cacophonous sonic landscape has begun to simplify around the Garage Mahal sound, our music and voices.

And then we stop, and Ken sounds the siren, indicating that we've arrived. But where? The playa in front of me is vast and black on this moonless night as everyone pours out of the art car, and then, as I flip my legs back around to get out, I see where we are and remember: the red, white, and blue spinning top hat, the strobe light flashing through the darkness, putting Tantalus into motion, a naked man emerging from the muck and mire, reaching for the golden apple that is just beyond his grasp, falling back in defeat, over and over again.

This is where my long odyssey began, out here last weekend, chatting with artist Peter Hudson as he and his crew built what I considered the best artwork on the American Dream theme. It was a compelling metaphor that I pondered on my drive to Denver, wondering whether I'd find something like a Golden Apple in my journalistic exploration.

Did I? Right now, my mind a mix of road numbness and sensory overload,

I'm really not sure. It's all such a jumble of heady experiences that I captured in a half-dozen long blog posts and a 5,000-word cover story. But I try to just shake it off and be here now, heading toward Tantulus, hoping to find Hudzo.

Reaching for the Golden Apple

How would the American Dream theme shape Black Rock City during this huge political moment in time? Was Burning Man going to somehow manifest the "hope and change" that Barack Obama was promising a war-weary nation? Were there others like me who wanted to explore the road between this isolated counterculture and a dominant political culture that was seeking new blood and energy?

Those are some of the questions that I pondered as I explored the still-forming Black Rock City for a couple days before I was to set off for the Democratic National Convention. Initially, it was hard to spot any discernible difference in life on the playa in 2008, although there may have been a bit more political provocation than normal or than there had been four years earlier, during that last pivotal presidential election.

Around Center Camp, there were some guerrilla posting of messages urging personal action in fighting the power and saving the planet. And the usual series of signs that greet visitors driving in featured pointed quotes by thinkers such as Thomas Jefferson, William T. Sherman, and Alexis de Tocqueville (but not a single quote by a woman).

But most of the political statements out there were in the artwork, like Bummer, a massive wooden Hummer replica slated to burn, or Tantalus, the only piece that really seemed to resonate with this particular American moment and my exploration of how this counterculture saw the national political culture.

The ancient Greek story of Tantalus was of someone who stole ambrosia and nectar from the gods to share with his people, and for that and other mistakes he was punished for eternity by having the water at his feet and fruit over his head pulled back whenever he reached for them.

Artist Peter Hudson, famous for using stroboscopic lighting to simulate the movement of his sculptures (include the swimmers of Sisyphish and swinging monkeys of Homouroboros), reimagined the legend as a man reaching for a golden apple that was being pulled out of his reach.

Visitors would help power the movement by working the pumps of what looked like on rail cards, but when I saw the static piece on that Sunday morning in the deep playa, it looked like a giant red, white, and blue top hat, the kind I anticipated seeing at the Democratic National Convention, where performance artist Kid Beyond and I would be headed that afternoon.

Tantalus seemed like a telling metaphor for such a big week in American politics, and I was curious how Barack Obama and the other Democratic Party speakers would try to define that Golden Apple and who's keeping it out of reach, and to perhaps explain how they'll help the average American reach it.

The news that Obama had just selected Joe Biden as his running mate slowly trickled out to the playa with the new arrivals, but nobody there really cared much. Everyone was too busy setting up or getting adjusted, and when we did talk politics during rest breaks, Biden seemed to everyone an understandable if boring choice.

There were plenty of political junkies out there, including two friends who let me crash in their RV for the last two nights and who were both headed to Denver in the coming days. Democratic Party consultant Donnie Fowler would be staffing Al Gore, and his sweetie, Heather Stephenson, founded the green tip website Ideal Bite and was headed out Monday to appear on a panel on alternative energy with the mayors of San Francisco and Colorado.

"The American Dream to me is not having barriers to achievement," Heather told me when I asked. It is Tantalus getting some apple if he really reaches for it. Donnie said it's, "the freedom to pursue your own dream without interference by government or social interests."

Burning Man was certainly about pursuing dreams and pushing past barriers, but the conversations didn't really illuminate much for me. Besides, Donnie and Heather worked in politics and came to Burning Man for their vacation, so they didn't seem to really be burner ambassadors interested in bringing this culture into the halls of power.

So I kept looking and asking around and eventually found what I was looking for: The Philadelphia Experiment. Most of their members were busy building a theme camp and performance stages at the corner of Esplanade and 8 o'clock in Black Rock City. But four of their key members would soon be taking a little side trip to the Democratic National Convention.

They were part of the Archedream dance troupe and would be joined in Denver by three other members from their native Philly that couldn't make it out to the playa this year. Burning Man figured prominently into how this highly political performance came together and with the message they were trying to spread.

It was on the playa that the Philly crew linked up with Bay Area artist Eric Oberthaler, who used to choreograph San Francisco artist Pepe Ozan's fire operas on the playa, and the collaboration resulted in "Archedream for Humanity," which went on a national tour after premiering Tuesday at the Democratic National Convention.

To three of the young and idealistic artists behind the show — who I interviewed during a dust storm on the playa on the Sunday that I left for Denver — the connection between these two big events is important. And they say the artistic and collaborative forces that Burning Man is unleashing could play in big roll in creating a transformative political shift in America.

"These are two amazing events that are kind of shaping the world right now," Archedream director Glenn Weikert said of Burning Man and Obama's acceptance of the Democratic Party nomination for president. "A lot of the ideas and views are similar, but people are working in different realms."

As we spoke, a Black Rock Ranger came over to tell us that a cold front was coming in and "it's going to get windier and colder," making me feel a bit better about my impending departure. Greg Lucas said his main reason for getting involved in the performance was to try to somehow make a difference: "I wanted to do something that would have a social and political impact."

The country under President George W. Bush had gone astray, and they wanted to be a part of the correction. Their three-act performance shows the past, present, and future of American life. "Act One ends with the loss of hope," Weikert said. Then the audience overhears a modern dinner table conversion, with people just trying to get by in this hyper-consumerist culture. And the future they envision is one of liberation, awakening, "and the concept of the choice that we have going into our future," Weikert said.

Such messages often aren't well understood by the average American, who has been too scared, selfish, and busy to really step back and contemplate what was happening in the country. They said Burning Man offers a chance to just slow down, think, and reflect, away from the daily rat race.

"Burning Man is a great town for that," Bill Roberts, one of the performers, told me. "It's about engaging with your community and trying to turn off that crazy business."

Yeah, turning off that crazy business and creating an intentional community, although the ridiculously long drive into the heart of mainstream modern politics that we were about to take could certainly qualify as crazy business. But to these guys, one's intention determined the value of the act.

"Just us deciding to spend our labor and capital making a statement is a political act in its own right," Roberts said, and he was right, although I still wondered about how effective it could be. Weikert said they were like burner ambassadors: "Maybe the Burning Man community is trying to reach out.

Traveling Between Dreams

Kid Beyond and I left the playa around 3 p.m., just as the dusty winds were beginning to howl, starting the 16-hour drive from Black Rock City, cruising through Nevada, Utah, Wyoming, and Colorado, states which Barack Obama would need to win at least a couple of in November if he was to take the White House.

There is a certain romance to the road trip, and I imagined the insights that would come to me with so much time to ponder my quest. But it was mostly just a mind-numbing trek punctuated by the minor stresses of trying to stay awake and almost running out of gas as we neared the Utah border, which would have been a major complication to our trip. We needed to pick up our Democratic National Convention press credentials by noon on Monday or they would be reassigned to other journalists.

Kid, aka Andrew Chaikin, wasn't a journalist. He was a beatboxing musician who also did voice-over work (his was the voice of Sprint Communications at the time), designed games, and did consulting work naming companies and products. But it was his roles as a burner and political progressive that brought him on my trip and earned him one of the Guardian's two press passes.

In figuring out the logistics for the trip, I knew that I couldn't do it alone, but having the Guardian pay an accomplice was financially prohibitive. Then, at a party in San Francisco, I mentioned it to Kid and his immediate reaction was, "I'm going with you," a stance he never wavered from. He was a welcome addition whose help and insights I still appreciate.

"Monday morning. Just finished the 18-hour drive from Black Rock to Denver — Steve and I switching shifts throughout the night, fueled by Radiohead, live Floyd, Rage Against the Machine and drive-thru Burger King," Kid wrote in his first blog post for the Guardian. "I'm aching to augment my 2.5 hours of sleep, but there's only enough time to wash the playa dust out of most of my crevices and head downtown to the Circus. And a circus it is: part rock concert, part revival meeting, part infomercial, part telethon."

We headed south toward Denver just as a gorgeous dawn was breaking, arriving with a few hours to spare before our Democratic National Convention press credential would have been reclaimed by other journalists, who reportedly numbered more than 15,000 here. But we were the only ones with silly burner bicycles on the back of an overloaded, dust-covered rental car.

The convention kicked off that night with Michelle Obama, Nancy Pelosi, and Ted Kennedy, among others. But after picking up our credentials at the Sheraton and starting to switch roles and get myself engaged with covering a very different kind of spectacle, we mostly just needed a nap.

That evening, the massive Pepsi Center was less than half full a couple hours after the gavel fell to open the Democratic National Convention, but the city of Denver was bustling and eventually so was the hall. I rode my burner bike along the beautiful and efficient Cherry Creek Bike Trail to get there and it was a smart move because most of the streets around the convention are closed off and patrolled by police in riot gear riding trucks with extended running boards, with military helicopters circling overhead.

Many of the delegates and other attendees that I talked to said it took them a long time to get from their hotels into the hall. Even riding a bike here involved a long walk because of the huge perimeter they've set up around the hall. But the broadcast media had it good, with prime floor space that made it all the more congested for the delegates and others with floor passes. Most journalists were tucked behind the stage or up in the cheap seats.

CNN also has a great looking patio restaurant set up across from the entrance advertising, "CNN Bar: Burgers, Beer, Politics." But by the "must have credentials" sign on the door, they actually meant CNN personnel only, not their media colleagues in general. Jesus, how many of them could there be?

The convention was mostly a big infomercial for the Democratic Party and a way to rally the faithful, but I set out to do some reporting on the San Francisco delegation, catching up with Hillary Clinton supporters Laura Spanjian, Mirian Saez, and Clay Doherty.

Despite the fact that Clinton announced that she was releasing her delegates to vote for Obama, they were still planning to vote for Clinton on Wednesday, although all said they would enthusiastically support Obama thereafter.

"It's important for me to respect all the people who voted for her and to honor the historic nature of her candidacy," Spanjian said. "And most of all, to respect her."

"This morning, Hillary showed up at the Latino caucus and gave a great speech," Saez said. "She said it's not about her or about him, it's about taking back the country."

"It's about the Republicans and we can beat them this time," added Spanjian.

We. They. It seemed so binary, despite how I shared their desire to see Obama in the White House. In many ways, the convention had about as much to do with achieving real change — the kind of bottom-up, grassroots transformation that the country needed — as Burning Man did.

Saez was serving as a delegate for her third presidential convention in a row. I asked her what value she saw in conventions like this, which seem to be mostly about preaching to the choir. Yet she said the string of speakers at the podium are valuable in reaching undecided voters and changing the political language.

"One of those people are going to resonate with someone who's undecided," Saez said. "And for us here, we gain energy so we can get the job done in November."

Speaker of the House Nancy Pelosi tried to rally the faithful for the "historic choice between two paths for our country." The emotional highlight of the evening was the speech by Ted Kennedy, who was battling brain cancer and was reportedly not certain if he was going to speak.

"Barack Obama will close the book on the old politics of race and gender and group against group and straights against gays," Kennedy said, adding, "This November, the torch will be passed again to a new generation of Americans."

Inside the Big Tent

The real action seemed to be in the streets outside the hall, where divided America was on display. There were anti-war protests that sought to "Recreate '68," referring to the disastrous protests outside the 1968 convention in Chicago, which helped elect Richard Nixon and set the country on a more conservative course.

The right-wing culture warriors were on the streets in a smattering of protests, flying their flags and displaying their signs, the most disturbing being a half-dozen anti-abortion activists bearing signs that read, "God hates Obama," "God is your enemy," "The Siege is Here," and one, wielded by a boy who was maybe 12 years old, reading, "God hates fags."

Jesus, who would want to worship such a hateful supreme being? For all the hope that Obama seemed to be ushering in, it was already becoming quite clear what kind of right-wing backlash this uppity black lawyer with the funny name would provoke. But there were also positive signs of life from grassroots America there as well, the same kind of people I could imagine meeting in Black Rock City.

The Big Tent, which was the central hub for bloggers and progressive activists there in Denver, offered free beer, food, massages, smoothies, and Internet access — almost like a theme camp, organized with the same online tools that were essential to the rise and longevity of Burning Man. But the Big Tent offered something even more crucial during this big political year: the amplified voice of grassroots democracy, something finding an audience not just with millions of citizens on the Internet, but among Democratic Party leaders.

New media powerhouses including Daily Kos, Move On, and Digg (a Guardian tenant in San Francisco that sponsored the main stage in the Big Tent) had spent the last year working on the Big Tent project with progressive groups in Denver, many of whom have offices in the Alliance Building, the parking lot of which houses the Big Tent, which was built with a simple wood-framed floor, stairs, and decks above it, covered by a tent.

"This is where we have the people on the ground doing the work on progressive causes," said Katie Fleming with Colorado Common Cause, one Alliance Building tenant. "It's been a year in the planning. The idea was having a place for bloggers to cover the convention…It's a way for us to all come together for the progressive line that we carry."

But it was really more than that. It was a coming together of disparate, ground-level forces of the left into something like an real institution, something with the power to potentially influence the positions and political dialogue of the Democratic Party — a feat that would be the first necessary step toward real change.

"When we started doing this in 2001, there just wasn't this kind of movement," Move On founder Eli Pariser told me as we rode down the Alliance Building elevator together. "The left wing conspiracy is finally vast."

Pariser said that political conventions aren't really his thing, but that "it's an interesting anthropological phenomenon." Indeed it was, and I immediately spotted many similarities to Burning Man. Both were part-party, part-movement; collections of basically like-minded people with myriad agendas and only a vague sense of common purpose. And both had an inertia to them that made change or reform difficult. They simply were what they were, try as we writers and talkers might to inject them with special meaning and significance.

On the Tuesday I was there, populist pundit Arianna Huffington was among the notable visitors to the Big Tent, speaking from the Digg Stage about the obligations and failing of today's journalists. "Our highest responsibility is to the truth," said the founder of the widely read Huffington Post blogger hub. "The truth is not about splitting the difference between one side and the other. Sometimes one side is speaking the truth…The central mission of journalism is the search for truth."

Parties and the Party

Political conventions are scripted affairs, right down to the actual vote that selects the nominee, which is ostensibly the reason for the convention and the only real democratic business to take care of.

"This is the best part of the convention, roll call. It's cool," San Francisco Supervisor Chris Daly, a convention delegate and serious political junkie, told me as I joined him on the convention floor during the nominating speeches and roll call vote. "The speeches are okay, but this is what it's about."

Daly was an early Obama supporter who was anxious to see the party finally dispose of Hillary Clinton and rally around his guy. After the previous night's Clinton speech and the ongoing statements of support for her by many delegates, the room was starting to show its most enthusiastic support for Obama yet. "It feels like it's just switched from being Hillary Clinton's convention to Barack Obama's convention," Daly said. "We're getting close to unity."

Each state reported out their vote totals for each of the candidates, but when it came California's turn, state party chair Art Torres said, "California passes."

"What!?!?" exclaimed many delegates, and there was bedlam among the delegation. What the hell was going on? Immediately, Daly and others speculated that Hillary had gotten too many votes and the state party was passing in the name of party unity. "It's probably because of Hillary," Daly said.

Ultimately, it seemed that Daly was right, but not exactly in the way he meant it. Other states also passed as Obama neared the total votes he needed to be nominated, and then New Mexico yielded to Illinois (Obama's home state), which then yielded to Hillary Clinton's home state of New York. Video screens showed Clinton entering the hall and joining the New York delegation. "In the spirit of unity and with the goal of victory," Clinton said, "let us declare right now that Barack Obama is our candidate."

It was a big, dramatic moment and the partisans ate it up as the band broke out "Love Train" and everyone danced and cheered. This was the business of politics in America, and it did have a certain dreamlike quality, a surreal veneer to such a serious realm. And at the end of these days, it was all about who could get into the best nighttime parties.

San Francisco Mayor Gavin Newsom threw one of the hippest parties of the week, a shameless salute to the "Obama Generation" by a politician who had enthusiastically backed Hillary Clinton. Even though he didn't get a speaking slot at the convention, Newsom was widely seen as a rising star in the party, far cooler than most elected officials, maybe even too cool for his own good.

Comedian Sarah Silverman did a funny bit to open the program at the Manifest Hope Gallery (which featured a variety of artworks featuring Obama), then introduced Newsom by saying, "I'm honored to introduce a great public servant and a man I would like to discipline sexually, Gavin Newsom."

Apparently Newsom liked it because he grabbed Silverman and started to grope and nuzzle into her like they were making out, then acted surprised to see the crowd there and took the microphone. It was a strange and uncomfortable moment for those who know about his past sex scandal and recent marriage to actress/heiress Jennifer Siebel, who watched the spectacle from the wings.

But it clearly shows that Newsom was his own biggest fan, someone who thinks he's adorable and can do no wrong, which is a dangerous mindset in politics. When his campaign for governor of California the following year went nowhere, I think only Newsom was surprised, although he did go on to be elected lieutenant governor in the 2010 election.

After letting go of Silverman, Newsom took the microphone and thanked the event's corporate sponsors, from PG&E (a horribly corrupting influence in San Francisco politics) to AT&T (facilitators of Bush Administration warrantless wiretapping). "Thanks to everyone who made this happen," Newsom said. "We appreciate their largesse."

Newsom urged attendees to aggressively campaign for Obama, telling them, "It is one thing to talk about hope, but it's another thing to manifest it."

I was already getting that impression. After supporting Obama's call for a new kind of politics all year, it was hard to see how this party and this political system was going to allow him to manifest it in the doses and with the substance that the country needed. But I still felt hope as we prepared to hear from The Man.

Man in the Middle

Barack Obama finally took center stage as the Democratic National Convention drew to an explosive close in a packed Mile High Stadium. Most on hand thought he gave a great speech and left smiling and enthused when it was over, but I and some other progressives had a few cringing moments that left us slightly unsettled — and previewed the disappointments that we would feel during the first year of his presidency.

While Obama and the Democrats made a clear and compelling case for how much better for the country they are than John McCain and the Republicans, there were also many points of concern for progressives and the alienated Left — not to mention the relatively apolitical citizens that were partying in Black Rock City at the time.

Obama played hard to the center of the political spectrum, talking about "safe" nuclear energy, tapping more natural gas reserves, and ending the Iraq War "responsibly." He stayed away from anything that might sound too liberal, while reaching out to Republicans, churchgoers, and conservatives with reassurances that the "change" he was pushing was more rhetorical than radical.

But he also made a statement that should — if we are to truly restore hope and democracy in this tattered country — shape American politics in the coming years: "All across America something is stirring. What the naysayers don't understand is this isn't about me — it's about you."

Well, if this is really about me and the people I spend time with — those of us in the streets protesting war and the two-party system, people at Burning Man creating art and community — then it appeared that electing Obama is just the beginning of the work we need to do. If we were going to trade guns for butter, or armories for art, it was going to come from the people, not a president promising to escalate the war in Afghanistan.

During one of the most high-profile points in the convention, halfway between the Gore and Obama speeches, a long line of military leaders (including one-time presidential candidate General Wesley Clark, who got the biggest cheers but didn't speak) showed up to support Obama's candidacy. They were followed by so-called average folk, heartland citizens — including two Republicans now backing Obama. One of the guys had a great line: "We need a president who puts Barney Smith before Smith Barney," said Barney Smith. "The heartland needs change, and with Barack

Obama we're going to get it."

Yet I'm a progressive whose big issues (from ending capital punishment and the war on drugs to transitioning from the Age of Oil to creating a socialized medical system and more justly distributing the nation's wealth) have been largely ignored by the Democratic Party. I understand that I wasn't Obama's target audience in trying to win this election, but I was hoping that Obama would begin to educate Americans as he led us in a more responsible direction. And that he would offer some reason for the burners in Black Rock City to begin to see value in involvement with the political system.

So I was a little disappointed, despite appreciating this heady moment. After all, this was certainly a historic occasion. Bernice King, whose father, the Reverend Martin Luther King Jr., gave his famous "I Have a Dream" speech 45 years to the day before Obama's acceptance speech, echoed her father by triumphantly announcing, "Tonight, freedom rings." She said the selection of Obama as the nominee was "decided not by the color of his skin, but by the content of his character. This is one of our nation's defining moments."

But there is still much work to do in convincing Obama to push a progressive vision once he's elected. "America needs more than just a great president to realize my father's dream," said Martin Luther King III, the second King child to speak the final night of the convention. Or as Congressman John Lewis, who was with King during that historic speech, said in his remarks, "Democracy is not a state, but a series of actions."

Yes, there is no end point at which democracy is attained — or when a new, more effective and inclusive culture is created. Both are processes that require lots of time and work. During this 5,000 mile, 10-day trip, starting and ending at Black Rock City in the Nevada desert with Denver and the convention in between, I was coming to see Obama as what I took to calling the Man in the Middle.

That creature is essential to both Burning Man and the Democratic National Convention, a figure of great significance — but also great insignificance. Ultimately, both events are about the movements that surround and define the man. It was up to us to participate in those movements in ways that inform and shape them.

And even then, despite my fervent hopes for both Obama and Burning Man, I was having doubts that either entity was capable of facilitating the kind of big fundamental changes that I felt the country desperately needed on so many fronts after being so badly damaged by eight years of President George W. Bush and the post 9/11 mania he encouraged.

The county had become so myopic, fearful, and divided, so utterly dysfunctional in its ability to deal with its problems in ways that didn't rob from future generations. I had lost so much faith in the modern political and economic systems, yet Obama and Burning Man seemed to be the antidotes, offering fresh perspectives and inspiring messages. Surely, they had the potential to help us correct our course, right?

Every year, my visit to Burning Man restored my faith in humanity and its infinite creativity and goodwill. It is such a beautiful and inspiring place, Black Rock City, shining out from the dark desert like a harbinger of human possibility. As I rode my silly, furry, whimsical burner bike away from Mile High Stadium, on a freeway closed down for security reasons, I thought about the playa and how anxious I was to get back.

Back to the Burn

Kid Beyond, Donnie Fowler, and I left Denver around 1:30 a.m. Friday, a few hours after Obama's speech and the parties that followed, driving through the night and listening first to media reports on Obama's speech, then to discussions about McCain's selection of Alaska Governor Sarah Palin as his running mate.

The Obama clips we listened to on the radio sounded forceful and resolute, directly answering in strong terms the main criticisms levied at him. Donnie said the Republicans made a very smart move by choosing a woman, but he was already getting the Democrats' talking points by cell phone, most of which hammered her inexperience, a tactic that could serve to negate that same criticism of Obama.

We arrived back on the playa at 5:30 p.m. Friday, and when a Burning Man Information Radio announcer said the official population count was 48,000 people, the largest number ever to date, I thought about what Larry Harvey had told me earlier that year: "That city is connecting to itself faster that anyone knows. And if they can do that, they can connect to the world. That's why for three years, I've done these sociopolitical themes, so they know they can apply it. Because if it's just a vacation, well, we've been on vacation long enough."

Yet when I toured the fully built city, I saw few signs that this political awakening was happening. There weren't even that many good manifestations of the American Dream theme, except for Tantalus, Bummer (a large wooden Hummer that burned on Saturday night), Altered State, an artsy version of the Capitol Dome by artist Kate Raudenbush, and Opulent Temple interrupting the Saturday night dance party to play some of Obama's acceptance speech.

Most of the people who attend Burning Man seem to have basically progressive values, although many have a strong libertarian bent, and some of them are involved in politics. But the event is their vacation. It's a big party, an escape from reality. It's not a movement, at least not yet, and it's not even about that Black Rock City effigy, the Man. But I could feel Burning Man's impact on the culture, feel it building toward… something.

But it certainly wasn't about the Man, whatever that symbolized to people. Hell, in 2008, many of my friends who are longtime burners left on Saturday before they burned the Man, something most veterans consider an anticlimax. After a long fun party day on Saturday, my first full day of Burning Man that year, Rosie and I slept through the burn, got up in the middle of the night, costumed up, and roamed the playa through dawn and into the next day.

So, ultimately, it isn't really about the Man in the Middle; it's about the community around it and how that community was being shaped by its involvement with Burning Man. And if the community around Obama wants to expand into a comfortable electoral majority — let alone a movement that can transform this troubled country — it was going to have to reach the citizens of Black Rock City and outsiders of all stripes, and convince them of the relevance of what happened in Denver and what's happening in Washington, DC.

Larry Harvey can't deliver burners to the Democratic Party, or even chide them toward any kind of political action. But the burners and the bloggers are out there, from Archedream for Humanity to the Big Tent, were ready to engage — if they can be made to want to navigate the roads between their worlds and the seemingly insular, ineffective, immovable, platitude-heavy world of mainstream politics.

"As hard as it will be, the change we need is coming," Obama said during his speech.

Maybe. But for those who envision a new kind of world, one marked by the cooperation, freedom, and creativity that are at the heart of this experimental city in the desert, there's a lot of work to be done. And that starts with individual efforts at outreach, like the task undertaken by the guy standing alone in the heat and dust, passing out flyers to those leaving Black Rock City as Burning Man ended on Monday.

"Nevada Needs You!!!" began the small flyer. "In 2004, Nevada was going Blue until the 90 percent Republican northern counties of Elko and Humboldt tilted the state. You fabulous Burners time-share in our state for one week per year. This year, when you go home please don't leave Nevada Progressives behind! ANY donation to our County Democratic Committee goes a long way; local media is cheap! Thanks!!!"

Change comes not from four days of political speeches or a weeklong party in an experimental city in the desert, but from the hard work of individuals with the vision, energy, and tribal support to help others see that vision. To realize a progressive agenda for this conservative country was going to take more than just dreaming.

The Party's Over

I returned from the desert with these grand political notions swirling in my head, but neither Barack Obama nor Larry Harvey had the answers that I was looking for or the perspective that I needed. The men in the middle of these movements didn't seem to really be leading them. At best, they were figureheads.

Sure, I wanted to believe in Obama's hope and change after a dismal eight years of Bush. And I wanted to believe that Larry could steer Burning Man toward the socio-political relevance that he was seeking. But I didn't believe that either of them were actually capable of leading the way, particularly given the disparate band of outsiders in their respective realms.

The people I knew who voted for Obama, and those who attended Burning Man, just weren't followers. They were leaders, millions of them, people who had been resisting the country's leaders for so long that they were probably incapable of following anyone anymore. And now, they didn't need to. This was their time to shape their worlds.

So that's who I turned to for my perspective and inspiration, my contemporaries, those once deemed the slackers of Generation X who had discovered something about the world and themselves out in the desert, something that shaped who they chose to be. I talked to Tom Price and Carmen Mauk, who worked different ends of the Burners Without Borders movement, and Rebecca Anders, my Flaming Lotus Girls mentor, who was moving on to bigger things within the larger Burning Man world.

"The opportunity for you to see yourself in this great creativity is the gift that everyone is offering to you," Carmen told me. "Burning Man, as an organization, is really becoming a curator of this community's activities, projects, successes, culture, and as an event production company. We are now in a position to be about to broadcast this and help people grow these things in a way that we never have before."

Burning Man is really more of a cauldron than a movement, a place where people learn about themselves and others. Here's how Tom put it: "I've said for years that if you go to Burning Man and pay attention, you will learn who and what you are. You will learn whether you're generous, whether you plan ahead, whether you're thoughtful, whether you're open-minded, whether you're selfish — you will learn exactly who you are because there's nowhere to hide in that big emptiness. All you have is who you are, for better or worse, and that kind of openness allows you to get real with people."

The burners who stick with it and are influenced by it are these people, the ones who find themselves on the playa and like what they see. It is the thousands of people having those kinds of simultaneous epiphanies that binds the culture together more than any art themes or statements of principles. People intuitively know they are creating a new kind of community on this blank canvas. And that's why Tom agreed with me that the 2004 presidential election helped trigger the Burning Man renaissance.

"I think the natural organic evolution happened to coincide with that. And also, a culture that was based primarily on survival for a long time, both a physical survival, a critical mass of people learning how to survive in the desert, once you've created that, then they can create the nuanced and rich and deep culture and the many permutations of it, the subcultures within the culture, that has happened within the last few years at Burning Man. And that needs to continue to grow and evolve or it becomes stuck, it become static, it implodes under its own weight. Since creativity is the engine that drives it, once it stops being creative, the motivation to participate becomes diminished and you get a city full of tourists coming to experience a thing that has already stopped happening," he said.

But that isn't what happened to Burning Man. Instead, the culture blossomed in ways that surprised even hardened cynics. Rebecca became reinspired by that creativity by 2009, losing her earlier cynicism as she watched the culture mature and extend its shoots in all directions.

"I think it's sort of understood as something that has potential paths to greater thought or wisdom or deep inspiration because crazy things happen out there and people come back from it changed and they go, 'Wow, I never considered this and that,'" Rebecca said. "It's part of people's cultural identification. It's a mark of pride for a lot of people that they went to Burning Man and got something out of it. And there's still a lot of misconception about Burning Man by mainstream culture."

Rather than the bacchanalian freakfest it was once purported to be, and how Rebecca remembers it from those early years, "Burning Man is becoming way more mainstream," she said, uttering a label that might make some burners cringe. "The fire is gone out of the belly of Burning Man. It is not the wild, untamed beast that it once was. It just isn't, and that's okay. That's the way it fucking goes," Rebecca said.

"But the overall cultural impact of even the most short-term, superficial, party kind of experience at Burning Man has some really, really potent effects, even if they're like low-level effects, in people's lives regarding their tolerance and their openness and their ability to accept something weird that's being done in the name of information or art or whatever," she said. "So I'm noticing a lot more of the lower level effects fanning out into society, and I'm finding that to be a really positive and productive thing."

Rebecca, Tom, and Carmen have seen it happen all over the world, from corners of San Francisco to the regional events around the country. Rebecca said it's gotten to the point where people don't even need to go to Burning Man anymore, particularly once it has infected them.

"They're opening up their minds and making metal shops in their garage and learning how to papier-mache and thinking up new weird things, without going too far out of their area, which is critical for this country. We need those people to stay home and be creative. Yeah, they can go away, but they gotta come back. The Midwest needs them. I'm from there, I know," Rebecca said.

Carmen and Tom both agree, saying that it isn't the party, lights, and music — or even the art — that had come to define Burning Man. It was its spirit, its ethos, that certain burner something.

"People are starting to say that's the celebration event, not who we are. People are starting to define themselves around these community events they're creating, and those are starting to become the culture of Burning Man," Carmen said. "Burning Man is starting to be more in its proper place, as an event."

But the culture that event spawned, in its multitude of forms, in pockets all over the world, orbiting around Black Rock City, that's what has motivated this trio to stay so involved with Burning Man.

"Even if it ends this year, the fact that it had a 22-year run as a counterculture is extraordinary. I can't think of anything else that comes anywhere close," Tom said in late 2008. "I think it is so durable because they have resisted attempts to force meaning on it."

The Burning Man culture had become quite durable, partly because of key burners that were ensuring the event and its artists had spaces where they could flourish.

Big Art Studios is Born

The story of Burning Man art has an arch that runs roughly from Baker Beach in San Francisco to the massive American Steel workspace in West Oakland, which was renamed Big Art Studios when longtime burner artists Karen Cusolito and Dan Das Mann signed the lease on the entire building on April 1, 2009.

The eight-foot wooden Man that Larry Harvey built and burned in 1986 presaged the oversized steel artworks that would follow in its wake over the coming decades, the tinkering of individual DIY hobbyists supplemented by ambitious teams of countercultural artists seeking something more than just an annual showcase for their work.

They wanted to make art full-time, collaborating with a huge community of creative strivers, and to transform their culture into something permanent and sustainable. And to do so, they founded gigantic workspaces in the East Bay Area, including The Shipyard, Xian, and NIMBY Warehouse.

But the biggest and most technologically advanced was American Steel, a relic of a bygone industrial era that was slated to be converted into a huge condominium complex when it was intercepted by a confluence of a sagging national economy and rising demand from Burning Man artists.

"Between 2004 and now, many of us have found a way to make a life of what we did in the counterculture that became Burning Man," Dan told me, emphasizing that it was the countercultural artists of the Bay Area that created Burning Man, not Larry Harvey or the organization he created. "We put Burning Man on. The LLC doesn't put it on. All they brought are a fence and some porta-potties."

Dan can be a little harsh when it comes to discussing the Borg, and he admits that his relationship with them has been strained at times. He gives John Law far more credit than Larry Harvey for sustaining the event and nurturing its DIY spirit in the early years.

"John did everything. Larry is no doer, he's a thinker," Dan said, a critique he extends to the whole organization that formed after John's departure in 1996. "The LLC was just the people who were around Larry to help him make it happen."

While there may be a kernel of truth to the criticism, Dan probably goes too far in denying credit to Larry and the LLC. If nothing else, Larry has long recognized that it's the community that builds Black Rock City and the job of the LLC is mostly to facilitate that process, provide a basic infrastructure, and run interference with the authorities.

But Dan was probably right when he said, "The counterculture of the Bay Area resulted in Burning Man, not the other way around."

"We made Burning Man because we needed it," Dan said, explaining that it was an outgrowth of what was already a formative component of the Bay Area counter-culture. "It was engrained in our psyches from a young age, in our very genetics."

Dan started making art for Burning Man in 1997, a labor of love that supplemented his work doing commercial artworks during the dot.com era. "Then I started to get into bigger and bigger projects, and then started to actually make money from them," Dan said.

He founded Headless Point Studios on Hunter's Point in 1997, and when it burned down in 2003, he went looking for a new workspace and found American Steel. It was like a dream come true for an artist as ambitious as Dan, a block-long, 250,000 square foot facility with a dozen separate bays with entrances large enough to drive semis through, the high-ceilings criss-crossed with 18 bridges cranes capable of lifting whatever multi-ton masterpieces that artists could dream up.

"Who has bridge cranes, 20,000 square feet, and 40-foot ceilings? It was just amazing," said Dan, who started dating and collaborating with Karen, a Flaming Lotus Girl at the time. "It's one of the largest artist workspaces in the world."

At American Steel, they learned to use the tools and facility as they built Passage, the evocative steel sculptures of a mother and daughter walking plaintively away from the Man, which debuted at Burning Man 2005. They rented one of the bays at American Steel and learned to do large scale pipe fitting from Vast Engineering, which occupied a neighboring bay, developing techniques for creating these 10-ton sculptures from steel cables, chains, and other recycled industrial materials.

"We didn't really get them right, but we got the thumbs up for trying," Dan said of Passage, steel sculptures of a scale that was new to the event, with a style they would hone and one that served as a template for later works, such as the figures that surrounded a massive wooden oil derrick in their 2007 piece Crude Awakening.

American Steel eventually came to be populated by these haunting, hulking figures that would reach down at you like the giant trying to steal Jack's ax, stand sentry, look up in reverence, or strike other evocative poses. And despite their size, they have received subtle alterations over the years.

"We've installed Passage three times and each time I've made revisions," Karen told me, referring to a run that included its placement at Pier 14 along the San Francisco waterfront in 2006, among the first Burning Man art installations to appear in the city where the event was born.

Along the way, Dan and Karen developed a strong reputation in the art world that they were helped to forge, as well as a large network of artists and other burners who wanted to work with them or chart their similar paths of creating large-scale artworks and the other festivals that were starting to solicit such pieces, such as Coachella, Bonnaroo, and Electric Daisyland.

By the time they were building Crude Awakening, the most ambitious project that Black Rock City LLC had ever funded, the footprint that Dan and Karen occupied in American Steel had grown from one bay to four. And still, they knew the demand was even greater within their community, so they decided to take a chance.

"This type of culture, we're always looking for more," Karen told me with a sly grin.

When they heard that the condominium project proposed for the American Steel site had fallen through, they talked to the owner of American Steel, who was open to the idea of leasing out the entire facility if their financials penciled out.

"Fortunately, we had been working with big projects for long enough that we had financials," said Dan, who worked with Karen to develop a 25-page proposal for leasing the entire facility and renting out space to artists and small commercial ventures.

"We're lucky the owner of the building let us just take over his property," Karen said, chuckling as she noted that they signed the lease on April Fool's Day. Since then, they have filled the facility with around 100 leases at a time, representing more than 400 artists using the space at once, by their estimation.

"American Steel is a product of Burning Man," Dan said, noting how the event and the culture it fed have empowered a growing number of people to pursue their artistic ambitions. "Burning Man is about finding a vision of ourselves that we want to share," Dan said.

Karen agreed that it's exciting to be at the epicenter of a world of Burning Man artists coming into their own and realizing their dreams. "It's happening, it's emerging, and it's pretty exciting," she said.

And for this intriguing Burning Man couple, it was a risk, but one worth taking.

"We wanted to create something of value so we have something," Dan said. "But if this didn't work, we were ruined for many, many years."

Who's Really in Charge?

There had been many challenges to the leadership of the event, to Black Rock City LLC, by current and former attendees who felt it was their event as much as the Borg's.

That tension had always been there, but it came fast and furious during the renaissance years, starting with the Borg2 rebellion in 2005, continuing the next year with John Law's lawsuit, and the next when Paul Addis torched the Man early, and again the next year when people heckled the American Dream theme and were upset with the Borg's role in sending Addis to prison.

But it wasn't just the outsiders who raised concerns. Even the true believers, many of whom drew paychecks from the Borg and helped do its bidding, decried a leadership structure that didn't seem to fit with the event's hyper-collaborative nature.

Tom Price publicly evangelized Burning Man culture more fervently than anyone I knew. When he married Burning Man spokesperson Andie Grace in October of 2008 — with Reverend Billy officiating, all the Borg brass in attendance, and colorful Indie Circus performers livening up the event — it was like a Burning Man royal wedding.

But later, Tom told me that the Burning Man culture blossomed almost in spite of its leadership. "Mitigating against that is the absolute train wreck that is the management of the Burning Man event itself. I don't think you could find a group of people that is less equipped and less likely to be running a multi-million-dollar corporation than the six people running Burning Man right now. And I think they'd tell you that themselves," said Tom, who had been increasingly involved with the Borg since founding Burners Without Borders. "The great dichotomy is the event itself is a countercultural institution that is run in a way that is very traditional and the result of that has been enormous dynamic tension from inside the community aimed at the organizers of the event."

If it can get its shit together, Tom said, Burning Man could be a big force for change. "But, having created these tens of thousands of newly empowered, self-actualized people, if it stumbles in that, the children will eat their parents just as readily as they will eat the dominant culture that they are raging against."

While Burning Man has its "10 Principles," Tom noted that those were really only guidelines that were developed 18 years into the event, and many burners aren't even familiar with them. The event was really too vast to have a common purpose: "There's the kids from Thunderdome, and Cuddletown, and the Japanese Tea Garden people, and on and on, and they're all there mashed up on top of each other, and they all think it's their place, and they're all right. Because the things that they share in common, which is a decision to express themselves and a decision to tolerate the expression of others, is very rare."

"Burning Man, I believe, happened organically as a response to the culture that we've created in this country over the last 40 years, that celebrated, even fetishized, consumption for its own sake. And people need an antidote to that. They needed a place where they could be decommodified. And now that capitalism is literally breaking at the foundations, there's this tremendous appetite for an alternative," Tom said during the Wall Street financial meltdown of late 2008.

Rebecca Anders saw that as well, noting how people continued to attend the event, expensive as it is, even as the worst economic downtown since the Great Depression kicked in. "I'd like to think that, as supposedly happened in the Depression era, that people coming to terms with real financial problems that are actually endemic in our society, maybe helps folks simplify their values and focus a little better on what's truly valuable to them and truly worthwhile. You're still spending retarded quantities of money making your crazy little art car and going out to the desert, but you're saying it's really important that I have my teeny weeny little triceratops car. This is really important that I make this crazy beautiful thing and show it to other people," Rebecca said.

Times of unrest are great opportunities for positive change, and Burning Man represented many of the values that the country needed most. Rebecca saw that as deliberate: "It has gotten more mainstream, but that's just a factor of it opening up and not being exclusive and so hidden and so underground. And that was an intentional move by the organization."

But it's probably closer to say that was an intentional move by the new generation of movers and doers that had filled in underneath the Borg — those who ran the regional events, the big art spaces, the volunteer networks — rather than the six people who were nominally in charge of Burning Man.

Consider Burners Without Borders, which by 2008, Carmen Mauk was running almost entirely as an autonomous organization yet under the auspices of the Burning Man business structure.

"You don't need a lot of people to run a grassroots organization, particularly if you're connecting people with other people," Carmen said, noting that BWB operates under the fiscal sponsorship of Black Rock Arts Foundation, but is essentially an autonomous organization. "Burning Man pays me to administer, facilitate, direct this entire program with no oversight. Larry Harvey has never asked me one question about Burners Without Borders."

That model is pretty standard within Black Rock City LLC, which stages the event, controls the brand, and encourages the creation of splinter organizations, from BRAF, BWB, and Black Rock Solar to the regional groups that operate all over the world, then basically lets them to do their thing.

"It's an autonomous thing that people are running and that's the real story about 2004 to now for me. It was sort of when the reins were given over to the people," Carmen told me. "Like the shamans who go to the desert, we are now ready to bring this wisdom back to our real world, everyday lives, and do something significant with it. What's that going to be? Well, it's going to look like a lot of different things and Burners Without Borders is just one way to catalyze and organize some of those efforts."

Facilitating Events

That can-do culture took many forms after the 2008 event, from the big and inspiring to the small and stupid, while Burners Without Borders continued to evolve. It responded to the massive earthquake in Haiti in early 2010 with supplies and relief workers, just as it had in Pisco, Peru two years earlier and to the Gulf Coast hurricanes two years before that.

"Burners Without Borders has become a beacon when something happens in the world and people want to help, in this community and beyond. Currently, with Haiti, we are a hub for communications with people who want to help," Carmen told me shortly after the earthquake in early 2010. "So I'm preparing people now to go and work with them and then also be looking to see what else is needed. How is that burner specialty going to find roots here?"

But Carmen was doing even more work facilitating small projects and helping proactively hatch burners' ideas, something she sees as the evolution of Burning Man, that turning outward to face the world after perfecting our little experiment in community-building.

"Most people when they come forward, they have an idea for what they want to do but they don't know how to execute it. My experience before I came to Burning Man was executing big projects on big problems in the world internationally. And we also learned (how to find creative solutions to big problems) from Katrina, and we're still learning in Peru, two years after that earthquake. So now we have a lot of connections that makes this natural ability this community has, to come forward and offer their skills, even more impactful," Carmen said.

Carmen was actually not particularly happy that the organization has been so closely associated with disaster, but she recognizes that is a good way to generate media exposure and get support. And that translated into Burners Without Borders having about $15,000 in donations in the bank when they broke camp in Pearlington, so Carmen put out a call for projects seeking small grants.

"I put very little parameters, but people came back with really amazing projects," Carmen told me in early 2010. "So last year we funded about 15 projects with only like $5,500, ranging from permaculture to helping kids get off huffing and off the street in Kenya. Four kids are now living in apartments and learning how to spin fire and then going into hotels and getting paid. Not even on the street, but dignified. Some woman just saved a lake for 500 bucks, to put in a graywater natural system where African women are using bad soap to wash their clothes and that soap is killing the fish, so they set up a system to make it stop. And I sent her that money in three days. There's no middle man, there's no bureaucracy, there's nothing stopping you from being able to do what you want to do. And almost every single person and has said, omigod, I can't believe how easy this has been."

The Kenya project was a great example of the new spirit. Burner Will Ruddick, a former Peace Corps volunteer, was living in Mombasa, Kenya and met some desperately poor streets kids living in a park where he would spin flaming poi. They were interested in Ruddick and his fire, so he saw an opportunity to help them escape a dangerous life that included huffing paint thinner to escape their problems.

So, with input from the Burning Man Fire Conclave, he used materials found in Kenya to create flaming poi for the kids to use, and with a couple thousand dollars in support from BWB, Ruddick turned them into the Motomoto Circus, a fire performance troupe that did paying gigs in hotels in the region. Carmen said that's a good example of how the Burning Man culture has changed and expanded.

"It's much more international. When those folks go back home, they are having the experience that people say they have when they go to Burning Man, that their life is changed, that they now know who they are and they're going to quit their jobs and do the person who are now rather than the job they thought they had to do for money," she said.

And that has in turn drawn people to the culture who weren't even familiar with Burning Man.

"What we saw in Peru is people came from all over the world, some of them having never heard of Burning Man. More people than burners supported our project in Peru and now they're burners. Fifty people then came to Burning Man the following year after they had volunteered and they thought they were just going to come stay for a week and then leave and continue on their travels. And like everyone who came to Katrina that was a burner, people ended up staying longer, if they could, than they intended," she said.

So the event is being fed by other aspects of what the Burning Man culture has come to represent: these counterculture figures — with their tattoos, piercings, artsy inclinations, and strange sense of recreation — doing good works in communities around the world. But Carmen prefers to see the situation in reverse, Burning Man finally realizing its potential as more than just a party.

"Now, people are seeing Burning Man as a celebration, but they feel compelled and accountable to this larger idea that we had to be doing something else other than putting on parties. And Burning Man has now seen that. It's changed in the regional coordinators contract that they sign, that there have to be civic projects now and that's what's expected. The events and the parties, yeah whatever, that's one way to gather people, but it's not what's expected," Carmen said. "Now it's shifted to: How is your community showing up and leading these principles and not just kind of copying what you thought you saw in the desert?"

Carmen, Rebecca, Tom, Chicken, and many other burner luminaries are relentless networkers, constantly expanding the community with key new connections. Carmen started working with Daniel Pinchbeck, a writer who does semi-monthly Evolver Spores workshops exploring life after money, a return to mysticism, and similar topics. He wrote a book on 2012 and the modern use of psychedelics, and he started to translate that into what he discovered at Burning Man.

"I'm working with them to make what we do even bigger and capture some of these folks — some who go to Burning Man and some who don't — who are saying we have all these ideas about changing consciousness and how we're going to change the world, but what are we going to do? A lot of people have all these ideas and they don't know how to land them," she said.

And her list goes on and on, from the burner who worked on the BWB project in Peru then went home and started European Disaster Volunteers — "It was basically because of BWB that he created this organization, that he felt like he could. You know, that Burning Man feeling, like I can do anything," Carmen said — to working with Kostume Kult, Figment, and other New York City burners to create a burner-certified business network called OK Culture.

"It's a label to verify how people are doing business," Carmen said, noting that she's actually gotten a bit of pushback on the idea from the Borg, which is wary of wading into anything that seems like a commercial venture. "Larry is scared to death of this."

It's understandable, particularly after the burner community backlash to some of the business partnerships that popped up around the Green Man theme. But many longtime burners were also looking for a way to sustain what they were doing, and that means developing some revenue sources for the members of this decommodified culture, because there are practical limits to volunteerism.

"It's an immature relationship that we have to commerce. Commodification is one thing, but commerce is another," Carmen said. "And as Burning Man is starting to put more businesses on the JRS (Jack Rabbit Speaks email blasts) and promote people who are doing work, anything from EL wire to whatever, it's starting to change."

In fact, that were many manifestations of the Burning Man culture that had made the jump to mainstream acceptance without losing track of where they came from.

Playa-born Mutaytor Keeps Rockin'

Mutaytor might be the ultimate Burning Man tribe, an eclectic group of Los Angeles-based performers who came together on the playa more than a decade ago, forming into a band that's like a traveling circus that evangelizes the burner ethos and culture everywhere they go, just by being who they are: sexy, scruffy, wild, warm, colorful denizens of the counterculture.

Mutaytor is perhaps the most popular and iconic musical act to emerge from Burning Man, a group whose spirited performances on and off the playa reflected and helped to shape and define the culture that birthed them. And if that's not enough cultural cred, many of the two dozen members work for Burning Man in various capacities, from building Black Rock City with the Department of Public Works to forming the backbone of event's regional network in Los Angeles.

My path has crossed Mutaytor's many times, from watching them play at my first Burning Man in 2001 to joining them on the burner-dominated Xingolati cruise ship in 2005 to later being invited in March 2010 to watch them record their fourth album, "Unconditional Love" in the sprawling Westerfeld House, a Victorian mansion on San Francisco's Alamo Square that is the legendary former home to such countercultural figures as Satanist Anton LaVey and members of the Manson family to noted '60s promoter Chet Helms' Family Dog Productions and the band Big Brother and the Holding Company.

The house is now owned by Jim Siegel, a longtime Haight Street head shop owner and housing preservationist who did a masterful restoration job, showing a striking attention to detail. Siegel owns the Distractions store on Haight Street, one of the few walk-in outlets for buying Burning Man tickets, and became a friend of the Mutaytor family in 2004.

Although the dancers and other women who perform with Mutaytor weren't at this recording — Siegel said they usually prance around the house topless and lend a debaucherous energy to Siegel's house — he still loves the energy that the band brings when it invades his house: "It reminds me of my hippie days living in communes."

Buck A.E. Down — a key band member, singing and playing guitar, as well as producing and arranging their songs — said the album and accompanying documentary film is Mutaytor trying to build on a career that began as basically a pickup group of musicians and performers on the playa.

"We're a total product of that environment," Buck said of Mutaytor's musicians, dancers, acrobats, fire spinners, aerialists, thespians, producers, culture mavens, and facilitators of the arts. "We've been underground for 10 years and have a voluminous body of work."

Mutaytor tapped the lingering rave and emerging Burning Man scenes with a mix of electronica-infused music and performance art to develop a distinct style and loyal fans. "So, between that and Burning Man, we developed just a ravenous following." With this built-in fan base of burners and ravers, Mutaytors was able to start getting gigs in the clubs of Hollywood, San Francisco, and other cities that had significant numbers of people who attended Burning Man.

"We became a very recognizable and tangible part of that culture," Buck said, noting that burners sought out Mutaytor to plug into the feeling of Black Rock City, if only for a night in their cities. "What we were able to do is provide that vibe."

Christine "Crunchy" Nash, Mutaytor's tour manager and self-described "den mother," said that Larry Harvey has been very encouraging and supportive of Mutaytor, urging them to essentially be musical ambassadors of the event and its culture. "That's one thing Larry said to us is I want to do this year round and that's what we're doing in LA," Crunchy said. "Most of the people in the band have been going to Burning Man for more than 10 years."

Buck added, "We're like the Jews, the wandering Jews," which totally cracked up the group, but I understood what he meant, particularly as he went on to explain how the burner tribes are scattered through the world, but they retain that essential cultural connection.

Particularly down in Los Angeles, where the Mutaytor crew regularly works and plays with other Burning Man camps, from the Cirque Berserk performers and carnies to longtime members of my own camp, Garage Mahal, Crunchy said their extended tribe really is a year-round, active community of burners.

"It really is like we are there in LA and we just pick up and move to the playa," she said.

Crunchy said they have family-like connections in San Francisco — to such businessman-burners as Jim Siegel and JD Petras, who both have sprawling homes where the band can stay — and in cities around the country that have big, established Burning Man tribes, from New York City to Portland, Oregon.

"It's the movers and shakers of the San Francisco community and others that have allowed us to survive as we've tried to make it," Crunchy said. "It has made traveling so much easier because we have places to stay at many places we play."

Buck said that was essential to their survival: "You take that kind of culture away from Burning Man and we would have broken up a long time ago, or we wouldn't have even formed." Just as Mutaytor is rooted on the playa, its members also wanted to root this album in a special place and immediately thought of the Westerfeld House.

"There are just places where stuff happens, just certain environments that are special places," Buck said, noting that Mutaytor is made up of musical professionals — from session players to sound guys at venues like the Roxie and for concert tours — who have three recording studios at their disposal among them, but they chose to do the recording here because it felt magical and personal to them.

"We had an epiphany on the road and decided we just had to record it here," Buck said, adding how well the decision has worked out acoustically. "Rather than just recording the band, we want to record the house. That's how we've been miking it up."

Each room on the group floor was filled with musical instruments and recording equipment, and Buck said excitedly that they have been resonating with this 150-year-old building: "We're getting some of the best tones."

Granddaddy of the Sound Camps

By 2008, Opulent Temple had been on the corner of Esplanade and 2 o'clock for four years, longer than any sound camp had held onto such a high-profile corner. But then again, most big sound camps only last a few years at Burning Man before they burn out and fade away, mostly because of the cost and difficulty of throwing the party.

Syd Gris didn't give up on dealing with that dynamic and in 2009, he made another run at Black Rock City LLC, trying to get them to allow sound camps to apply for art grants, and kick down some free tickets — something, anything. OT and other big camps, such as Sol System and Root Society, were spending $50,000 per year or more to stage the event's nightlife, and Syd felt like he had finally made some headway with the board.

But then Larry arrived back from a trip to Africa and nixed the deal. "Larry called me to say this is not happening, and it's not happening because I don't like it, and I don't like it because I think it complicates the process. So my read was it makes their life harder, so they don't want to deal with it," Syd said.

Had they recognized the importance of the sound camps, "There could be more diversity of nightlife options," he said in 2009. El Circo wouldn't have left the event, nor Lush, Illuminaughty, or The Deep End. Syd even considered pulling the plug on OT, but he just couldn't, not with the way they were still rocking it.

In 2008, the camp hosted legendary DJ Carl Cox, the latest new arrival to Burning Man among the world's top DJs. "I had heard about Burning Man many years ago, as Paul Oakenfold was talking about it and he was saying that it would be the best thing you would ever go to, as it was a real eye opener. That was 15 years ago, so I had known about it then and ever since then I have been trying to get myself there," Cox told me. "I have been to many festivals around the world as you can imagine, but my impression of this was just out of this world."

In fact, Cox was so affected that he named his next album Black Rock Desert, promoting it with Burning Man photos and references that caused a conflict with the Borg, which insisted that he make some changes to honor its copyrights, a dispute that Syd helped to mediate. Cox was truly taken with the event and seemed to quickly understand its ethos.

"The thing here is that you truly have to make the festival into whatever you want out of it. At a rock or pop or even techno festival, you would go there to see a band or DJ play, but at Burning Man, people go to meet other people with similar interests and let their hair down, which is refreshing," Cox said. "This festival is like nothing I have ever been to."

And after he left, Cox wanted to keep giving back to his fans and Opulent Temple, so he played for a small fraction of his usual fee at a huge fundraiser party for OT on Treasure Island — dubbed Massive Cox — in early 2009. The party featured a variety of Burning Man camps and art installations, including the Flaming Lotus Girls' Serpent Mother and Peter Hudson's Homouroboros.

The party was great and made a killing, about $28,000, clearing out all of OT's debts for the year and setting them up for the Burning Man to come. As Cox said, "The money has to come from somewhere. No one is going to give it to you, so if I can help out a bit, to make sure that the OT carries on…I will be there."

March was actually a big month for the Burning Man's party and performance tribes. A few weeks after Massive Cox, the Burning Man community stepped up again to help one of its own, performance artist Hollis Hawthorne, who was in a coma after a motorcycle accident in India. The event at Slim's nightclub in San Francisco turned out a wide range of talented acts and community-minded burners that raised a staggering amount of money for a one-night event to bring Hollis home to the Bay Area.

The Burning Man story itself also came to the stage in San Francisco that January as "A Burning Opera: How to Survive the Apocalypse," telling the event's story, covering many facets but focusing on the philosophical divide between Larry Harvey and John Law. After receiving critical acclaim for a limited engagement in a small theater, the crew held two fundraisers in March to stage another successful run in Teatro Zinzanni's cool theater space.

There was also the release of a well-received documentary film about the event, "Dust & Illusions" by Oliver Bonin (who was embedded with the Flaming Lotus Girls at the same time I was and beyond), which told the story of the event's early history largely through the lens of its Borg2 existential struggles. And on and on it went, the Burning Man culture's myriad manifestations stretching off in every direction.

Reverend Billy for Mayor

The more I tried to capture and define the Burning Man culture, the more vast and ever-expanding it seemed, impossible to nail down, even as I devoted all my vacation time and spare energies to it in 2009 as I worked on this book. I planned to attend Burning Flipside, Austin's regional event, and I made a trip to New York City to meet with key burners there.

Reverend Billy and his Church of Life After Shopping had evolved from a San Francisco theater troupe to street corner performance artists in New York City to a collective with special resonance on the anti-commercial Black Rock City to something like a real church that preached Burning Man values in cities around the world. And now, that evolution (a word that was also Burning Man's art theme in 2009) was taking another step.

When I visited Reverend Billy in New York City that spring, he had just launched his Green Party candidacy for mayor, taking on Mayor Michael Bloomberg — the latest burner to make a foray into mainstream politics, just as Chicken John and Alix Rosenthal had recently done in San Francisco. Within a couple minutes of meeting Billy in his SoHo campaign office, he broke into song, loudly singing a campaign jingle that he'd written to the tune of "New York, New York":

Start spreading the wealth, I'm hoping to stay
I came to live my life here, New York, New York
Those neighborhood shops, they call out my name
Don't need no supermall, in old New York
I want a city made of 500 neighborhoods
Where we pay decent rent, buy a home if we should
Those billionaire blues, they cannot compete
The greatness of this town, it's on my street
I made it here, ain't moving anywhere
It's up to us, New York, New York

Billy's message of resisting the hypercapitalism of Wall Street and billionaire Mayor Bloomberg had special resonance at the time, coming within months of the near-collapse of the banking system and the bursting of the housing bubble. Even the Wall Street Journal had just written an article about Billy's candidacy and said that his message of localism being good for the economy was right on.

"The bubble economy of Mike Bloomberg, which is Wall Street, tourism and real estate, the speculation on real estate, its relationship to the neighborhoods is like it's trying to invade a third world country. It's coming in with gentrification and rent hikes and chain stores, we call it the demon monoculture," Billy said, punching those final two words with a preacher's flair. "We seem to be getting a wonderful response. It's so clear that common sense is radical right now."

This was his first day of calling supporters for political donations, which he would do several times during our afternoon and evening together. It was still early in the campaign and Billy had only given a dozen or so speeches at that time, so he was still trying to find his way from performance art preacher to serious politician.

"We want people to make decisions about the big system, but they don't have a second system to go to because in the United States, we don't have a way to consider socialism, so we tend to make it is a psychologized, Puritanical decision: oh it's me, I'm spending too much. We can't talk about the system," Billy told me.

While Bloomberg was indeed a Wall Street baron, he was also a mayor who presided over a major leap forward in bicycle lanes and the creation of pedestrian spaces, as well as supporting the Burning Man regional festival Figment and other alternative arts endeavors. Billy's campaign was still figuring out its niche.

"We're still exploring right now how systemic to make our critique. It's a balance between Mike Bloomberg and the narrative of the extremely rich man who takes over the government, that's an Olympian narrative of consumerism. But he's smart enough to play the art card, and the bike card, and he keeps the iconoclasts happy so that you can't accuse him of being Lee Scott, the president of Wal-Mart. He's not a very sophisticated man. He has a very narrow life. But he's smart enough to know about imagery and hire marketing people to give him the very best advice."

Later, Billy shared with me an essay that he had just written to explain his altered version of the "New York, New York" song. It was a call for New York to adopt values and an ethos that was closer to Black Rock City's than this capitol of capital. In a way, it was a call to renew the American Dream, yet one that allowed people to pursue art and good works rather than just a house in the suburbs, which Billy considered a perversion of the American political bargain, that faith in opportunity and self-reliance.

"The city has welcomed and protected so many millions of us. We moved here believing in this faith. We believe the big green lady in the harbor. We took her at her word. She offers us freedom from want if we work hard, be bold, raise our standards, go for it — the old New York myth, belted by Broadway hookers," Billy wrote. "That promise is no longer kept. The faith has been broken. You can't live with a family here. You cannot do your art, with enough support to paint or dance or write."

Billy said Bloomberg and other corporate titans, like Donald Trump and George Steinbrenner, "the self-appointed high priests of the old God, have fundamentally changed the deal." Commodification has become king, he said, and that mindset must be replaced by something closer to the burner mentality, with a focus on the collective needs and the freedom to create art and culture in an organic way, unmediated by corporate interests, a quest in which cities must lead the way.

"You don't have New York anymore without rent you can pay and public transport you can use. End of story. If you don't have these two basic rights, then you have another city. Then it's not New York," Billy preached. "Those three stooges — Donald, George and Mike — they dream of stadiums, skyscrapers, and Olympics and they say that the great city must have no less. Actually, that's not New York at all. New York is a deal. It's a mark of faith, between an individual and a place, a family and a neighborhood, a young artist and a street."

Billy didn't end up winning his race, or even being much of a factor. But he was espousing a value set that had been incubating at Burning Man for a generation, one that was informing what Black Rock City was becoming. It wasn't going to save the world or have a big influence on American politics, but it was becoming a beacon of hope, a maturing city that offered itself up as an example of what could be.

Regionals Reinterpret Playa Life

Also while I was in New York City, I met with Dave Koren, better known as Not That Dave, Burning Man's regional contact there and a founder of Figment, the New York City arts festival on Governor's Island in New York that would end up helping to inspire Larry Harvey's choice of the 2010 Burning Man art theme, "Metropolis."

In New York, the creation of Figment was a true collaboration of Burning Man camps such as Smoochdome, Disorient, Kostume Kult, Image Node, and Asylum

Village, along with three New York-based arts collectives: SEAL (the Society for Experimental Art and Learning), Circle Arts, and Action Arts League.

The first event in 2007 had 60 art projects and drew 5,000 people rather than the expected 500. By the next year, they had 250 registered art pieces and 10,000 attendees over three days. "And it has worked really well," Not That Dave said.

"We really wanted to link the arts community in New York with Burning Man's sense of do-ocracy, volunteerism, decommodification; take a lot of Burning Man's principles and link it up with a creative resource that is already here that isn't Burning Man related," he said.

"What's the resistance to just calling it a Burning Man regional?" I asked.

"Sex, drugs, partying — that's the brand here. The brand of Burning Man is all-night raves, sex, and drugs. But Figment is a daytime-only event on an island with a lot of kids. And so those two worlds don't have much intersection," Dave said. "So, I'm a Burning Man regional contact for New York. There are five of us here. And I think that what makes Burning Man amazing is the art first. The art, to me, is like a Trojan Horse that lets everything around it happen. A lot of things that happen around Burning Man are really important, in terms of community, in terms of personal exploration, in terms of personal transformation — but the art is what allows that to happen. Without the art, it's just a rave in the desert."

Many people criticize Burning Man as a waste of resources and not a very sustainable urban model, as Dave seemed to do, but I've always thought that criticism was overblown. It actually uses far less resources and produces less waste than most cities of 50,000 people. But still, given all the energy and stuff that must be marshaled for that trip into the middle of nowhere, there were a growing number of people who, like Dave, embraced the move toward regional events or even a year-round institute, something Larry had recently started talking about.

"Burning Man starts to feel like a festival of consumption, with all the waste that goes into it. What if we took all that energy, and all those resources, and invested that locally? And what if a lot of people did that? What would that mean?" Not That Dave, who does marketing for a major architectural firm, asked. "I think Larry's vision for it is that Burning Man eventually becomes the retreat. That it's like something you go to once in your life, like going to Mecca [for Muslims]. You gotta go there once and you never need to go there again, but you can if you want to. I think that's interesting as an idea."

I had always covered Burning Man as a movement or culture rather than simply an event, so I was always interested in the exponential growth of the regional events, which Larry has been very excited about since our first interview back in 2004. There are more than 100 regional Burning Man events and formal networks over five continents.

So when I decided to finally attend one in 2009, I chose what I'd always heard was one of the biggest, best, and oldest: Burning Flipside in Austin, Texas. I had never been to Texas, a place whose politics fascinated and repulsed me. So I got some contacts there from Borg spokesperson Andie Grace, who was also excited about the role of the regionals.

Burning Man was important, but for those who were really affected by it, Andie said the key question was, "What are you doing to fill in the gaps in your own community?" She said it wasn't enough to simply have this annual experimental city, where culture is created. "That's the key thing to me, how it's repeatable in so many places," she said.

And in Austin, Texas, they've repeated the basic model of Burning Man in their own creative fashion. One of Flipside's main founders, Pat Wheaton, told me: "Flipside has evolved from an event thrown by a small group of friends with little management into an approximately $200,000 event with levels of management, community selected advisory boards, teams of leads, lawyers, etc. The leads appreciation party has more people than Flipside itself used to have. The one thing that has not changed about Flipside is that it is still entirely volunteer run — no one draws a salary from Burning Flipside."

He described the event's relationship to Burning Man as a good one, mutually supportive and respectful. "The relationship with Burning Man has not changed greatly throughout the years, they have always been very good to us in terms of helping us avoid mistakes that Burning Man made along the way. They have been much like a benevolent Godfather in a way," he said. "And in a personal way, the people that I have met, the art I have seen, the experiences I have witnessed and taken part in have been nothing short of stunning and life changing."

Burning Flipside

Burning Man regional contacts like Pat Wheaton in Austin and Not That Dave in New York City obviously played important roles in leading their local events, but I discovered the same thing in Texas that I was beginning to really understand about Burning Man: it is the attendees of the event that create its content and character far more than any of the official leaders, organizations, or doctrines.

Mark and Shiree Schade were the first couple of Spin Camp at Burning Flipside, a 10-year-old camp that included some San Franciscans I knew from working at the Box Shop with Opulent Temple and the Flaming Lotus Girls: Marty Combs and Kurt Bollacker, who are in a three-person romantic relationship with Rich Martin, OT's main builder.

"Over the last several years, a lot of the core people are the same," said Schade, a 49-year-old psychologist from Austin. "It's grown from a big party for a bunch of local freaks into a big event. Some people think it's gotten too big."

But rather than decrying the growth, Schade embraces it: "If it doesn't grow then it's just sort of a closed community." He felt the same way about Burning Man, which benefits from its scale and the tentacles that it has sent into communities around the world: "It's now just like a giant powwow of all the regional tribes."

In fact, when Schade looks into the future, he sees the regional events becoming stronger and more important to the larger community of burners. For now, though, Flipside is the premier regional event: "I don't know why it's thrived so much in central Texas except that we're all a little freaky."

Indeed, Austin's unofficial motto, found on T-shirts and bumper stickers all over town — "Keep Austin Weird" — is a testament to its countercultural values. The vibe at Flipside is remarkably similar to Burning Man, but maybe even more neighborly, a point of pride for Texans. As we spoke, some camp members asked Schade about whether they could give all the camp's pancake mix to neighboring Flip Jacks, a pancake-based theme camp that was running low on supplies. Of course they would, he said without hesitation.

"The heat and fewer clothes," was how Schade described Flipside's differences from the main event, and there was probably even more nudity at Flipside than Burning Man. The two events had even grown up in a similar fashion, with more structure required as they got bigger. But its growth is a testament to the appeal that the event holds for those with countercultural tendencies.

"The community of freaks has grown because we bring in new people and then they bring in new people," Schade said. In fact, some campmates sitting nearby were a testament to his point. Schade brought Bruce Weatherford to Flipside years ago, and he just loved it and brought his friend, Jack Hamm, the next year. And now they're all regulars.

"It's just amazing, this family," Hamm, a school administrator in nearby Dripping Springs, told me. "I look forward to this event every year. It is the best release."

"For me, this place has really made me a more creative person," Weatherford said.

As we talked, Shiree, Marty, and other camp members were sitting in the shade painting cool designs on their parasols, sewing sequins onto their clothes, and engaging in other artsy endeavors.

Marty first attended Flipside in 2003 and returned every year except 2008, which he missed for personal reasons. "I like the size of this event," Marty, who's been going to the playa since its early years, told me. "It's like Burning Man used to be."

He's been around this counterculture long enough to know that it wasn't formed by Burning Man, but it was shaped by it. "It was like a fire starter. It was already out there, but it was disjointed and separate," Marty said. "There's always been these niches, but it provided a focal point."

I liked his description of Burning Man: "It's like a counterculture conference where all the ideas are germinated." And when Marty said, "It's like a short course in how cities can form," something clicked for me. Yes, Burning Man was less like the sociopolitical movement that Larry Harvey and I had each tried to nudge it toward becoming, and more like a city, a disparate collection of people looking to create the hometown of their own design, one that nurtured their values.

Black Rock City is, after all, a city — perhaps one of the greatest cities in the world during the week that it exists, even if it's only the third largest in Nevada. Maybe this strange, temporal, super-concentrated Metropolis had something to offer to our understanding of the life of cities. Little did I know at the time, but Larry was thinking the same thing as he pondered the theme that he would announce in September.

Yet Marty was no longer so grandiose about Burning Man. In fact, he thought it has gotten too big, so much so that he had stopped going. "It started to be affected by the weight of its own size," Marty said. "It will still have succeeded if its spawns all these other new events."

As Rosie and I wandered Flipside, checking out the art and beating the heat with regular skinny dips in the dammed river, we stopped to chat up the guys from Electric Numbstastic, Keith Kettrey and Parker Williams, who have provided the massive sound system for Opulent Temple since 2006. "Syd was looking for a little more sound," Parker told me, noting that Rich approached them about the idea at Flipside in 2006. "This is our art. Other people have crazy costumes."

The pair live and work in Dallas, staging everything from concerts to corporate events to church revivals. "We used to do all the raves in Dallas from 1997 to 2001," Parker said. And Keith added, "Our sound system was in such demand that they wouldn't do their parties until they could set a schedule with us."

But that heyday ended with the federal Rave Act, which caused a crackdown in Dallas, with even DJs in coffee shops getting shut down. Both say they love Flipside, even more than Burning Man. "When you leave here, you just have a feeling of love and gift and sharing, and it's kinda hard when you reenter the world," Keith said.

That kind of pure joy is infectious when you see it. One of the highlights of my Flipside trip came on Saturday night, walking through Sound Town (a protected gulch with several sound camps) and stopping by Winners Circle to take in a beautiful, young, topless DJ just rocking out, filled with pure joy, playing and dancing to her favorite music for a five-hour set.

As I learned the next day, she was 30-year-old Melanie Marcee, aka DJ Whatamelon, who volunteers as the sound marshal of Flipside. She's married to Christian Ducayet, aka Cherubic, and they live in Austin. They approached Burning Man in a different order than many Flipizens, the name given to event attendees.

"The big burn is actually what got us interested in the regional," Whatamelon said, noting that they first attended Burning Man in 2003 and Flipside the next year. "It was like finding another planet you could party on."

Before that, they were into raves and other countercultural events, DJing for the last 10 years, trying their best to create a world they wanted out of what the larger culture offered and allowed. But going to Burning Man, she said, "made the whole 'taking it out and living it' thing real."

So, I had to ask, how did you summon five hours of such joyous abandon last night? "I don't play a track unless I love it. I don't know if everyone feels the music the way I do," she said, adding that Burning Man struck that same heart-string in her. "I saw for the first time something that awed and flabbergasted me enough that I wanted to know how they do that."

Fourth of Juplaya

There was one other blank that I felt needed filling in as I worked on the reporting for this book in 2009. And so we arrived at the Black Rock Desert on Friday afternoon for the Independence Day weekend known as Fourth of Juplaya, which is sort of an unorganized, unofficial counterbalance to Burning Man, and something that has been going on almost as long.

Actually, for some desert denizens who predate the word "burner" — and who sneer at the annual party that has overtaken a place they consider sacred — it's been going on even longer. People have been using the playa as a playground since long before the Bay Area freaks discovered it.

But the Fourth of Juplaya weekend does have a subtle Burning Man vibe to it (although it's probably more accurate to say Burning Man has a Black Rock Desert vibe to it), albeit with theme camps spread out over an area so vast that it makes Black Rock City seem like a dense refugee camp. And the playa is normally a lawless frontier, without any of the rules that Burning Man instituted after 1996. You can race across the desert as fast as you dare, shoot guns, blow things up, swim in the hot springs (which are closed during Burning Man), shoot fireworks at each other — whatever you want.

"Welcome to Burning Man 1995," Adrian Roberts — a San Francisco DJ/promoter with Bootie SF and the longtime editor of Piss Clear, Black Rock City's alternative newspaper — told me when I saw him and his DJ wife, Dee, entertaining a dancing crowd of a few hundred at their camp, Fandango, on Saturday night 2009.

Shortly thereafter, I ran into Polly Superstar with Kinky Salon in San Francisco, and some other party people that I also knew from The City. Earlier in the day, we randomly ran into San Francisco friends who camp at Burning Man with the Flaming Lotus Girls, Space Cowboys, Garage Mahal, and Opulent Temple. And this was beyond the people that we knew were going to be there, who gathered in the deep playa at Not the Camp You're Looking For, which included staffers with Burning Man's Department of Public Works (whose official-looking logo has become ubiquitous in San Francisco and Gerlach) and members of the Gigsville theme camp, along with a big bouncy castle and wet bar.

At the center of it all — which was about eight miles up the playa from the 12-mile entrance — was the couple that I had come to consider the closest thing to Burning Man royalty, Tom Price and Andie Grace, and their lovely one-year-old princess, Juniper Pearlington Grace.

Camping with them at Fourth of Juplaya were some key members of Burners Without Borders and Black Rock Solar: Richard (aka Big Stick) and Spoon, who live in a house in Reno that was a staging ground for Black Rock Solar.

In just a few days out there, I got a sense of the wild west feel that I hear about from the early years of Burning Man, when there was genuine danger. When our car barely escaped getting stuck in wet playa on our first night (Tom's earlier advice to slowly back up if that happens saved us), miles away from anywhere or anyone, I gained a new appreciation for the term "radical self-reliance."

You could drive your car at 60 miles per hour with the lights off — and you could hit a sand drift and crash. Or you could get lost in the sheer vastness of the open playa, which plays tricks on your mind and perception. But then you find Frog Pond, and float naked in a big irrigation ditch filled with warm spring water, completely at play with dozens of smiling strangers and friends.

It truly seemed like the frontier, this place that nurtured Burning Man after its exile from San Francisco. But the frontier has now been settled, transformed into a culturally rich city, Black Rock City.

Through my Sister's Gray Eyes

I went into my seventh Burning Man feeling a little jaded and over it, despite all the work that I'd been doing on this book — or perhaps because of it. Burning Man was consuming most of my waking thoughts as I wrestled with what it all means, with the big takeaway to tell you all.

Plus, how excited can anyone really be over an annual event, at least since we stopped believing in Santa Claus? The excitement just stops coming as naturally, the enthusiasm becoming something that needs to be deliberately summoned. Everything eventually becomes routine, even the edge, and I had been dealing with Burning Man way too much in 2009.

But then my only sister, Kim Williams, came to town a few days before we planned to drive to the playa together for her first burn. I saw the coming burn reflected in her wide eyes and that old twinge of anticipation began to form in my gut. I couldn't wait to drive onto the playa with her.

She was excited but nervous, not quite sure what to expect but open to the experience. I really hadn't been playing it up too much, preparing her yet trying to keep her free of expectations, the best way to do it. But she seemed to know that she was in for a life-changing experience and her spirit was infectious. Just six months after separating from her husband, unsure what the rest of life had to offer her, Kim was in the ideal position to get her head split open wide by Burning Man, letting it inform her understanding of the future's myriad possibilities.

San Francisco was buzzing with Burning Man preparations, which almost seemed connected to the heat wave that peaked on Friday night, August 28th, when the 80-degree temperature at 10 p.m. lent an aura of unreality to normally foggy San Francisco. We still had two days to prepare and our bags were already packed with costumes, so we pedaled our bikes around the city, just playing and partying and feeling more free together than we had since childhood, when we'd play with the neighborhood kids until long after dark on summer evenings.

If Burning Man really were a cult then I'd say the gods were with us, lining the planets up in our favor, pointing the way toward our destiny in an alternate universe. I cut work short so we could ride our bikes to the pre-parties for that day's monthly Critical Mass bike ride — another first for my sister, who hadn't ridden bikes much since she was young. The ride included hundreds of decorated bikes — fake fur, electroluminescent wire lighting, disco balls, and an endless array of other geegaws — that were clearly bound for the playa, their riders exchanging giddy grins and offering, "See you out there."

The ride wound its way into Golden Gate Park, where the sprawling Outside Lands concert festival was underway. Pearl Jam was headlining on the main stage later that night, but when a group of bicyclists stopped to smoke a joint across from one of the fenced concert stages, we realized that the walkway across the street afforded a perfect view of the stage and was directly in the soundscape. And the hugely popular and fun band Thievery Corporation — which would find added significance at the close of Burning Man that year, as I spent my final night dancing my ass off to the Thievery Corporation DJ, who was attending his first burn — was about to go on. That serendipity seemed like an unofficial start to Burning Man and we all danced and smiled, marveling at the good fortune that seemed so strangely normal in our little rock star world.

But Burning Man hadn't really begun, and our list of things to do was long. My new Mohawk needed to be dyed red, Kim and I were going to get manicure-pedicures (my nails red, hers gray, another choice that picked up psychic significance along the way), we had several random supplies on our lists, and we still needed to buy all of our food and water for the week. Of course, by then, the water sections of every grocery store in San Francisco were emptied of large containers, as were many of the stores along the road to Black Rock City, as we later discovered when we finally settled for gallon jugs rather than the 2.5-gallon size favored by most burners.

We peppered our preparations with periodic cocktail stops, and our conversations grew deeper and more significant, even as our mood lightened and the anticipation mounted. Kim was juggling dating a few guys at the time — two of them significant — and doing a pretty good job at maintaining her independence with them, even as they pushed for commitments and expressed concerns about what she'd do on the playa. Male jealousy can be a scary force of nature. I'd been encouraging her to remain free and was a little bothered by her suitors' forcefulness, as was she, and we seemed to really connect with the issue over sangrias and tapas on the night before we left.

"Don't let them force you to make decisions that are either black or white," I told her. "It's okay not to know what you want right now. You can embrace the gray."

"Yeah, embrace the gray," she said, smiling beautifully and seeming to be looking all the way to the Black Rock Desert 360 miles away.

"You know," I said, lighting up with inspiration. "That should be your playa name: Gray."

"Ooooohhh, yeah, Gray, I like it," she said. And her random choice of metallic gray nail polish earlier in the day suddenly seemed significant, a confirmation that we were onto something. She flashed me her nails and a conspiratorial grin. Kim was Gray, an identify she assumed in that moment, effortlessly identifying herself by the new moniker for the rest of the week.

We raised our glasses in a toast — Gray and Scribe were leaving for Burning Man the next day.

Exploding Very Slowly

We hit Gerlach around midnight, just as the gates opened on Burning Man 2009, with its Evolution theme. And from there, we were basically in line and content to spend the next few hours working our way toward our Garage Mahal camp, a trip that would take about 30 minutes mid-week.

And then, we were there, on the dusty playa, simply at play. Gray's apprehension just seemed to fall away with every interaction she had, a calm ease and warmth overtaking her. I could feel it. We're social people from a party family and it's easy to fall into social grooves, even in such an otherworldly place. My sister seemed to undergo a real personal transition, almost a rebirth, and it helped me see Black Rock City with fresh eyes.

Larry and I ran into each other one night early in the week at the Flaming Lotus Girls piece, Soma, serendipitously. We've always enjoyed talking to each other, perhaps because we had both wanted Burning Man to affect the world, but I also think it's because we're both just talkers, people who enjoy the art of conversation and like to weigh the weighty stuff.

We fell into conversation, like usual, talking about everything and nothing, just catching up really, until one of his people dragged him away to go to their next stop. I barely even remember what we discussed, only that it was warm, unusually so. There was an ease about him that I'd never really seen on the playa, an openness.

Our relationship was a little prickly after I publicly criticized his American Dream theme and the execution of his Green Man theme. And it was just nice to reconnect again so easily with this man at the event he spawned. He later told me that he had experienced and appreciated the sense of community this year more than any of the previous Burning Man events. He said it finally seemed like a real city.

Yes, it was like a city, a beautiful, chaotic city, filled with old friends and new perspectives, where trying challenges push our sense of our own endurance, only to morph into epic moments and the realization that we're all going to be okay. Better than okay — we're blossoming. And we're changing.

Artist Rebecca Anders, my fire arts mentor, broke away from the Flaming Lotus Girls for the first time and worked with Jessica Hobbs and a great crew to create Fishbug, a beautifully primordial creature that slowly respirated fire and its fabric body and shined its video thoughts onto its head, one of my favorite pieces that year.

"We were aiming to make a little monster, but on a scale that a human can relate to," Rebecca told me. "We wanted people to feel the presence of a creature, which is why I wanted to build up a series of subtle effects — the form, the breathing, the fluctuation of the light and the fire — we wanted all of these things to add up."

It was a real breakthrough for Rebecca, who had always had a great artistic eye and solid technical skills, but who relied on the Flaming Lotus Girls vast web of experts and an infrastructure that had become well-developed over a full decade.

"I realized a dream of like 12 years to do a piece of my design with my name on it," she said. "It was like a dream coming true, on one hand, and at the same time, I've never had less fun at the party."

That wasn't to say that she was working alone, because Rebecca had developed quite the network of her own. In addition to having sister FLG Jessica by her side, Rebecca worked closely with Don Cain and his Department of Spontaneous Combustion crew, which had built some innovative flaming tricycles. Fishbug renewed Rebecca's enthusiasm for Burning Man, which had not been as strong when I met her five years earlier as the Borg2 battle was on.

"I was focusing on myself and I was focusing on my experience there. And I think for my personal evolution, what's critical and has become really clear to me is what's important in my life is the work that I get done. That matters more than my perspective," Rebecca said. "It matters most that my work is relevant and potent to the people in my culture and beyond."

But the people in this culture had become like family to Rebecca and many long-time visitors to a city that had existed for more than two decades, a longevity that was shaping both the event and the people who attended. This was a city they loved, where they knew their neighbors, and had developed an identity.

"Some of those relationships are based on 20 years at Burning Man. That's a

20-year friendship. That's a big deal in someone's life," Rebecca said. "I've developed friendships with all kinds of folks of all different ages and all kinds of places, some of whom I probably would not have initiated a friendship with had we not had that in common or made friends out there, where you're much more open and less concerned about what you do for a living or what kind of car you drive or whatever."

It was something that I felt in my own world as I introduced my sister to people from our current camp, Garage Mahal; my past camps of Ku De Ta and Opulent Temple; and the people that I'd gotten to know in my reporting, many of whom I had come to consider friends. Garage Mahal threw a rockin' Tuesday afternoon dance party at our camp, with the brother-sister team of Gray and Scribe opening as the life-of-the-party bartenders, drawing fun energy toward us from all directions.

And the week just flowed that way: dancing on the Garage Mahal art car, pedaling our bikes through warm evenings to art pieces spread through the playa, doing the naked slip-n-slide at Duck Pond, handing out fresh breakfast sandwiches on Garage Mahal's McCrackin' dawn tour, making out with friends and strangers, communing with our campmates, dancing to DJ Dan at Opulent Temple, enjoying our morning Bloody Mary ritual with our friends in Agua Mala's section of Illumination Village as we lounged on their couch swing.

It was big moments and small: deep personal insights with my sister, dancing with random strangers, and vice versa. When my sister left on Friday because of responsibilities to her kids, we were each sad, but she already knew that she had just begun to really experience this place and be affected by it, and she made me promise that we would return, together, all week, the next year. And we did.

As the artworks on the playa have become more creative and evocative, and as the avenues for greater numbers of people to get involved with contributing to that progress expand, Rebecca said the Burning Man culture has been rippling across the larger culture.

"I have this idea that they are trying to explode very slowly and be something that spreads out and becomes many other things instead of this one thing. And I think that would be the healthy thing," she said.

On Sunday night for the Temple Burn, which is usually sort of melancholy for me, exhausted from a big week that was about to end, I found peace. I ran into Reverend Billy, Chicken, and Lightning in Maid Marian's cat car, caught up on the Borg gossip, watched a great burn, and rolled through the night into a glorious final dawn atop a massive spinning butterfly fluttering over fallopian tubes, as if birthed into newfound enthusiasm for the event, just what I needed. And then came the biggest gift of all, a serendipitous gift just as the moment I was looking for inspiration: Larry announced the 2010 art theme — "Metropolis: The Life of Cities" — which was precisely how I was coming to finally see Burning Man.

Many burners attend Fourth of Juplaya, an Independence Day on the Black Rock Desert. ~ Photo by Dave Le (Splat)

The central effigy changes every year at Burning Flipside, the regional Burning Man event outside Austin, Texas. ~ Photo by Alix Rosenthal

Fishbug by Rebecca Anders and Jessica Hobbs was their first solo project after the Flaming Lotus Girls. ~ Photo by Neil Girling

Artists Karen Cusolito and Dan Das Mann created the Bay Area's biggest burner workspace.
~ Photo by Scott Beale / Laughing Squid

Tantalus by Peter Hudson. ~ Photo by Pilar Woodman

Tantalus shows a man fruitlessly reaching for a golden apple, a commentary on the American Dream.
~ Photo by Steven T. Jones

Miles from San Francisco to BRC and the DNC.
~ Image by Ben Hopfer/San Francisco Bay Guardian

Packed for both events.

Floor of the convention hall in Denver.

I explored the connection between Burning Man's American Dream theme and the 2008 Democratic National
Convention in Denver for my newspaper, the San Francisco Bay Guardian. ~ Photos this page by Steven T. Jones

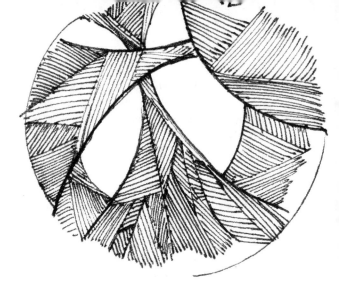

Part VI — Metropolis (2010-The Future)

Saturday, September 5, 2009

The Man is finally burning, but I'm feeling more of a sense of relief than excitement, although there's plenty of whooping and hollering from the dense crowd around me, stretching in all directions as far as I can see. For an event with "no spectators" as a central tenet, I've always found the burning of The Man — truly a spectator spectacle — to be the antithesis of Burning Man.

I arrived here almost an hour ago, riding my bike out to join our Garage Mahal art car, which created a fine base of operations, social hub, and dance party during the wait — and which now offers a nice vantage point for watching the burn. I'm surrounded by dozens of friends and thousands of fellow burners.

Yet I'm feeling restless and — dare I say it? — a little bored. Sure, the fireworks show that kicked off the burn was pretty cool, particularly when The Man started shooting sparks and rockets out of the ends of his raised arms. And I felt a warm rush of awe when a massive fireball erupted under the Man's feet, engulfing him and illuminating the crowds' wide eyes and grins.

The explosion reminded me of last year's Crude Awakening burn, when the massive oil derrick was ignited by the biggest fireball any of us had ever seen, but this one was on a smaller scale. The Man has been fully engulfed in bright flames since the explosion, burning evenly all over his body but showing few signs of toppling. His base isn't burning yet and neither is the thicket of large wooden spires poking in all directions below him, although there are now some red flares going down there, as if someone is trying to move things along.

"Whack," a solid spank on my ass makes me jump, and I turn to see Jack's devious grin. "Ow, you motherfucker, that hurt," I respond and his smile widens. "How's it going?" I ask and he just shrugs. It's good to see him, and it brightens my spirits that he followed through on his earlier pledge to try to find me at the burn so we can prowl the playa together tonight.

Jack and I are friends back in San Francisco, yet he's always been a big figure, sort of socially elusive, and we camp separately. He's with Agua Mala, a camp of urban planners and other professionals within Illumination Village, which I visited more mornings than not this week along with Lucky and Gray, seeking his Bloody Marys, an originally impromptu routine that had become part playa ritual, part inside joke. And then we had a big and unexpected adventure yesterday that bonded us a bit more.

"You on your bike?" I ask.

"Yeah, it's over there with the Agua Mala crew, sorta by the Rocketship."

"Cool, mine's here too. Are Claire and Gabe over there?" I ask and Jack nods, watching the Man burn. "Great, I'll go back there with you when you go to say hey."

We stand on the playa off to the edge of the Garage Mahal group, and Jack shows no sign of wanting to plunge deeper and say hello to others he knows, probably still wary of interacting with his ex-girlfriend who camps with us.

The burn is starting to get a bit more engrossing as all the wooden spires burn, looking like glowing latticework as the flames shine through the series of two-by-fours, and the crowd has grown a bit more solemn and reverent, although occasionally punctuated by the odd howl or shouted comment.

Friends stop by to chat with us then fade away to visit others or fill drinks or whatever. Damn, the Man is taking forever to fall, as usual. But just as I think that, he starts to wobble a little, and a palpable surge of energy sweeps through the crowd.

"He's going down," Jack says evenly.

"It's about time."

And then, the Man falls into the burning spires, knocking a few down but leaving others still jutting up into the air, like the wreckage of the World Trade Center, sparks and smoke billowing up into the air. The crowd rushes forward to dance around the fiery remains, and Jack gives me a flick of his head toward the Rocketship.

My bike is leaned up against the dark side of the Garage Mahauler, and I grab it, tell a few campmates that I'm rolling with Jack and will see them back at camp, where I need to fill my water and grab a few other supplies, and I join Jack to wade through the crowd toward his bike and peeps.

Neither one of us seem to have much energy or enthusiasm tonight, but it's been a big week, and I'm content to be a little even-keeled after the emotional rollercoaster of the last few days. Besides, Burn Night no longer holds the magic it did my first few years at Burning Man, when there was such debauchery in the air that it seemed anything could happen.

But there's still something unsettling about Black Rock City once the Man is gone, I remember as we pedal off across the open playa and into the neighborhoods on the 9 o'clock radial. Without the Man as compass, you lose your bearings and forget where you are, a feeling compounded by departing burners stealing the street signs that mark each intersection.

So we count the streets to find D, turn right, and head into my Garage Mahal camp to fill our water bottles and grab my fur coat to hedge against the cooling night air, making it a fairly quick stop. And from that point on, the night seems to pass quickly and relatively uneventfully for Burning Man's supposed climax.

We ride by our friends' Brass Tax camp, but they've already dismantled their massive Boombox, although the beats keep pumping and we dance for awhile and enjoy some conversation and laughs with friends. We hear Bassnectar is playing Root Society, so we head over, but the dome is packed solid so we don't stay long.

"The slide?" I suggest, gesturing out toward the deep playa, where The Wedge looms, a long, steep slide with figures shooting down its lit green turf, crashing in carnage at the bottom.

"Hell no, I still have rug burns from that thing," he replies.

So we automatically ride out toward the Temple, where its inner fire tornado seems to be going, drawn like moths to flame. And it just continues on like that: after spending some time up in the Temple, impressed by the swirling fire encased in glass and getting my flirt on with Polly, we ride over to lie under the fire ceiling, chatting up a pair of 30-something hotties there, who decide to join us as we head back to 10 o'clock for more dancing.

Jack and I each liven up as we dance and laugh with the girls, turning up the charm as high as we can muster, and after about an hour they say they need to be somewhere and we group hug goodbye. Perhaps the flirtation has sapped the last of our energy because our conversations grow less frequent, our dancing slowly replaced by just the bob of our heads.

Then, after hitting most of the sound camps along that radial — it might be 2, 3, 4, or even 5 in the morning, who knows? — Jack says he's done. I am too. We hug, slap backs, and head home in opposite directions.

Becoming a City

My next conversion with Larry Harvey was more typical than the leisurely one we had on the playa: rapidly rambling for more than an hour, impossible to end the conversation because it always seems like there's so much more ground to cover, even after all these years.

I learned a long time ago that it's hard to have a short conversation with Larry. That trait gave me a good story for the Guardian two weeks after the event ended, one that seemed like a perfect transition point from trying to save the world to just trying to perfect its little experiment in it:

Urban Man

Burning Man seeks a higher perennial profile as Black Rock City cultivates the metropolitan ideal.

Maybe Burning Man can't save the world, but its leaders and participants are increasingly focused on using the models and principles involved with building and dismantling Black Rock City in the Nevada desert every year to help renew and restore urbanism in the 21st century.

The arts festival and countercultural gathering that was born in San Francisco almost a quarter-century ago defied the doomsayers and became a perpetual institution, particularly here in the Bay Area, where it has become a year-round culture with its own unique social mores, language, fashion, calendar, ethos, and infrastructure.

Now, the SF-based corporation that stages the event, Black Rock City LLC, has set its sights on taking the next big steps by trying to create a year-round retreat and think tank on a spectacular property on the edge of the playa and by trying to move its headquarters into a high-profile property in downtown San Francisco — perhaps even the San Francisco Chronicle building.

Complementing those ambitions is the art theme that Burning Man honcho Larry Harvey recently announced for 2010 — "Metropolis: The Life of Cities" — which seeks to connect the event's experiments in community and sustainability with the new urbanism movements in places like San Francisco and New York City. Harvey told us the idea came to him earlier this year as he attended the Burning Man regional event called Figment and toured some of New York City's efforts to reclaim public spaces from automobiles.

"I found that inspiring," Harvey said of the recent changes to Times Square, marveling at the conversation circles people set up in the gathering spaces that used to be traffic lanes. "Here we have New York City creating a civic space that works like the city we create. It would be even better if they'd put up some interactive art."

In a video segment on the 2009 event by Time.com entitled "5 Things Cities Can Learn from Burning Man," Harvey spelled out some key urban living principles cultivated in Black Rock City: ban the automobile, encourage self-reliance, rethink commerce, foster virtue, and encourage art.

"It's become a better and better social environment," Harvey said of Black Rock City, the population of which peaked at about 43,000 this year, down slightly from last year. "People have come to respect its urban character, so we're ready for a discussion like this."

As part of the next year's theme, Harvey said he plans to invite urban planners and architects from around the world to come experience Black Rock City and share their ideas about encouraging vitality in cities, before and during the event. Cultivation of the vast interdisciplinary expertise that creates Burning Man each year is also why the organization is seeking to buy Fly Hot Springs on the edge of the Black Rock Desert.

"That's what the think tank is about: Let's get together and think about the world and use Burning Man as a lens for that," Harvey told me. "I think art should imitate life, but I'm not really happy until life imitates art."

Harvey is reluctant to talk much about his plans for the property until they can seal the deal — something the attorneys are now actively trying to hammer out — but he said the basic idea is to create "a laboratory for ideas."

To try to raise capital for the project, Burning Man bused 100 rich burners — including Ben Cohen of Ben & Jerry's Ice Cream and Laura Kimpton of the Kimpton Hotel chain— to a dinner at the site on August 27.

Meanwhile, back in San Francisco, where Black Rock City LLC was earlier this year forced to move from its longtime Third Street headquarters because of plans by UC Mission Bay to build a hospital on the site, Burning Man and city officials are collaborating on plans for a showcase space.

"While all this is going on, we have been talking to the city about moving downtown. They really want us there," Harvey said.

The organization came close to landing on a big space in the Tenderloin, but that fell through. Recently, Harvey and city officials even toured the San Francisco Chronicle building at the corner of Mission and Fifth streets, which Hearst Corporation has had on the real estate market for some time, exploring the possibility of it becoming the new Burning Man headquarters.

For that site and other high-profile spots around downtown, city planners and economic development officials are actively courting significant tenants that would bring interactive art and creative vitality to street life in the urban core. "Well, that's like a theme camp," Harvey said. "That's what we do."

In recent years, Black Rock LLC has expanded what it does through Black Rock Arts Foundation (which funds and facilitates public art off the playa), Burners Without Borders (which does good works from Hurricane Katrina cleanup to rebuilding after the earthquake in Pisco, Peru), Black Rock Solar (which uses volunteer labor to do affordable solar project for public entities), and other efforts.

But simultaneously creating a think tank, retreat, and high-profile headquarters — with all the money that would require — could reshape the institution and its relationship with San Francisco in big and unpredictable ways. Harvey describes it as entering a new era, one he says he is approaching carefully and with the intention of maximum community involvement in key decisions: "You want to build trust and enthusiasm as you go along."

Inspiring Urbanism

Gabriel Metcalf was just giddy when he heard about Burning Man's 2010 art theme: "Metropolis: The Life of Cities." It beautifully brought together two of his two passions. In addition to being a four-time attendee of the event at that point, he's the executive director of the San Francisco Planning and Urban Research Association, the city's premier urbanism think tank.

"I can't believe the Burning Man theme. It's just so awesome," he told me after the 2009 event, barely able to contain his glee. "Black Rock City is one of the great cities of the world."

That's high praise from someone whose days are devoted to studying urban life and its myriad challenges, and a testament to the fact that Black Rock City has successfully made the transition from frontier to city.

"I try to capture the zeitgeist with the themes," Larry told me. That particular sense of the times really settled in during his visit to New York City, which was experiencing its own urban renaissance at the time, converting traffic lanes into separated bikeways and open space, setting out tables and chairs and letting people create informal spaces to just be with one another.

"It looks like the playa," Larry told me. "I watched people creating conversational circles."

In discussing the urbanism ideals that led to the theme — using design to facilitate community, getting past automobile-based systems, transforming cities into the basic societal building block — Larry once again showed himself to be well-read in the works of influential thinkers: "Urban planners, ever since way back in the '70s, when Jane Jacobs wrote about the *Life and Death of American Cities*...have been waiting for years to do stuff like this."

Gabriel certainly had been, which is why Larry's theme was so exciting to him. "One thing I love about Burning Man taking on the question of urbanism is it's going to not just be about physical placement, how you lay out the blocks and streets, but about community in a larger sense," he said. "The exploration of different forms of community is what I think is so interesting and transformative for the people who go there."

Gabriel saw great potential in what Burning Man was trying to do next. He said that Larry "is trying to make it relevant and to speak to the big issue of the day.

Metropolis speaks to the biggest issue, human settlement, how we're going to live together. It's asking the big question."

Larry confirmed this to me and said that the burner community finally seemed ready for a discussion like that, particularly given the stubbornly sluggish economy in those years. "As people reduced their consumption, they seem more attracted to our values," Larry said. "They come for the art but stay for the community."

I think he's right. The art is the draw, the thing that really defines the event and is the focal point for the community. But most of us wouldn't keep going to that much trouble and expense, year after year, just to see the art. After all, the fire arts may have been cultivated by Burning Man, but by 2009, they also existed elsewhere, from Oakland to Governor's Island in New York to Amsterdam's Robodoc.

The Crucible's Fire Arts Festival in Oakland had it biggest year ever in 2009, with some truly mind-blowing new pieces and old standards, combined with the performance art and fashions derived from the Burning Man culture. And it was just 50 bucks and a quick trip from San Francisco.

But most of my friends and acquaintances who had been to Burning Man went back again in 2009, even those who had recently lost their jobs or were wrestling with other economic hardships. With the future looking uncertain, Black Rock City was still grounding, affirming, and exciting, a place where they still wanted to be.

"People are reassessing what they value, and apparently they value us," Larry said.

One indicator of that was the fact that even as the population dropped slightly, the number of theme camps applying for placement increased, a signal that the communities that form up around camps were still thriving even if independent or newbie burners weren't.

"We had so many theme camps they couldn't all get placed," Larry said. "People were putting more effort into it than ever. They're valuing their social connections to people."

Larry said he felt more social than ever that year. In previous years, First Camp (where Larry and other Burning Man employees and VIPs camp) used to be like "a command compound," Larry said. But this year, he said it felt more social and open to outsiders. "I probably had the best year I ever had. I felt like I was in a village for the first time," he said, a claim that rang true with my own interaction with him on the playa this year.

Not having attended Burning Man in the anarchic early years, Gabriel has always seen Black Rock City as a city. "In the absence of state-imposed authority and control, you take 50,000 anarchists and put them in the desert and they'll create order out of chaos." And the city they created, he said, is "like being a protagonist in a movie when you arrive in the big city. The Esplanade is one of the great main streets in the world."

Gabriel has also pondered its symbiotic relationship with the city where he lives and works. "Is Burning Man an expression of San Francisco, or has Burning Man reconceptualized San Francisco? I think Burning Man has had a big influence on San

Francisco, and at the same time, it is San Francisco's gift to the world."

But Larry said BRC had only recently been accepted as a city — with roads and rules and a distinctive urban culture — finally making it possible to use the event to discuss urbanism. "Four or five years ago, this would have been a hard sell. They still discussed whether they liked the streets and the rules we imposed," he said. "People have come to respect its urban character, so we're ready for a discussion like this."

Larry said his personal observation, and what he has heard from many others, is that "it's become a better and better social environment." And that's what finally led him to let go of his sociopolitical ambitions for Burning Man and just let it become what it was: a beautiful, inspirational city.

"I thought it was about the rest of the world for a long time. It's really about the world that we go back and live in," he told me, bringing some closure to our long-running conversation about exporting Burning Man's big ideas and ethos. "It's got to be about something that is in the world."

Assessing the Bottom Line

Larry's acceptance of earthly constraints didn't mean that he or those close to him stopped dreaming big, quite the contrary.

The Black Rock City LLC board members returned from Burning Man 2009 with ambitious plans for their evolution, combining the pursuit of a high-profile new head-quarters in San Francisco with the dream of buying Fly Ranch and Hot Springs on the playa and creating a year-round retreat and think tank on the site.

Larry and the other board members wouldn't say much publicly about how the Fly Ranch deal was going, but they were reaching out to all the rich burners and other potential partners they knew to try to put together a deal that sources told me was in the $10 million neighborhood. Among those they reached out to were Google founders Larry Page and Sergey Brin, who were both burners.

But there were two big problems: the Fly Ranch owners didn't want to sell, and Burning Man didn't have very much money. It's hard to say exactly how much cash the Borg had. Every year, the LLC released a financial report detailing its expenditures. "We voluntarily share more than any LLC enterprise of our size," Marian Goodell, director of business and communications, told me.

Those reports showed that the LLC had grown steadily from a $7.3 million organization in 2003 to a peak of $14.1 million in expenditures (including a $3.1 million payroll) in 2008, before scaling back to a $12.3 million operation in 2009, which Marian attributed to the lingering recession.

But these numbers don't really show how well the organization was doing financially — or whether it was capable of some big capital projects — because the LLC has never fully revealed its revenues. Only its expenditures were made public. And starting in 2007, it stopped providing any indication of its bottom line.

Before that, the financial chart that was released with each year's Afterburn Report was accompanied by a "financial report" that was a narrative of the finances written by Larry. But by 2010, that website link for 2007-2009 yielded the message, "This report is not yet complete, and is forthcoming. Thank you for your patience."

Actually, it wasn't forthcoming, and neither was a line at the bottom of the financial chart that gave some indication of the LLC's year-to-year financial situation. The last one from 2006 read, "Increase in year-end current assets (cash, pre-paid expenses): $855,000."

Marian was fairly dismissive of my inquiries about Borg finances, saying the financial reports were eliminated because they were a "pain to write and we found most people just read the chart," and explained away the steep expenditure growth in 2007-08 and sudden decline in 2009 as just business cycles.

But there was also something else that happened during those growth years: co-founder John Law's Paper Man lawsuit and the confidential settlement that made it go away. Could that be why the "independent contractors" expense went from $449,000 in 2006 to $1.6 million in 2007 and $1.3 million in 2008, before dropping back to $161,000 in 2009?

Marian wouldn't answer that question, but she did tell me, "The lawsuit and subsequent settlement and the need to be confidential reminded us there were some challenges in how we talk about the money and where it goes."

Nonetheless, it's easy to do some basic calculations and see that the Borg had some cash-on-hand in early 2010. The first three tiers of Burning Man tickets — 9,000 each at $210, $240, and $280 — were sold by the end of February, grossing the Borg $6.6 million. And with some of it, they added a couple more independent contractors.

Loring Sagan and Lou Vasquez, principals of the San Francisco design firm Build Inc., quietly began meeting with the Borg every Tuesday evening after Larry announced his Metropolis theme, helping them develop plans for a high-profile headquarters, year-round retreat, think tank, and other ideas.

By December of 2009, sources told me that it was becoming increasingly clear to everyone that the Fly Ranch deal wasn't going to happen yet, but that only increased their resolve to do what they could to bring Burning Man back into the communities where burners live the rest of the year.

"We've been working with the board in a number of efforts over these last five months," Sagan told me in February 2010. "We want to make what happens in the desert happen in the city."

That ambitious goal had become like a mantra to many longtime Burning Man leaders, from Larry and Crimson Rose to Tom and Carmen to those involved in all the offshoot organizations, from the regionals to Black Rock Arts Foundation to the myriad scattered burners that were trying to make it happen in ways big and small.

Addis Returns

Burning Man has always had its true believers and its haters, and sometimes they are even fused together, people frustrated that the event and its culture don't quite live up to their highest hopes. After 25 years, Burning Man offered ample targets for disappointment.

In early 2010, when Paul Addis returned to San Francisco from Nevada — where he served a two-year prison sentence for prematurely torching Burning Man's eponymous central effigy during a Monday night lunar eclipse at the event in 2007 — he fueled the criticism that old burner malcontents held about the event.

Perhaps most provocative was his charge that the Borg deliberately worked to send him to prison for two years by testifying at his sentencing hearing about how the early burn ruined the event and cost more than $30,000 to replace the Man, greatly exceeding the $5,000 threshold that elevated to a felony the destruction of property charge to which Addis pleaded guilty.

"They chose a low and despicable route. They didn't have to do this," Addis told me, sounding a frustration shared online by many of his supporters, some of whom had lobbied Burning Man to low-ball the damage. "Instead, they decided to deliberately take action they knew would send me to prison."

I was the first journalist to get an extended interview with Addis, who distrusted the media but needed some help promoting the one-man play that he began to develop while still in a prison work camp outside Las Vegas, "Dystopian Veneer," which opened April 30, 2010 at a small San Francisco theater, The Dark Room.

"It's a brand new life and I've got all this potential and I want to make the most out of it," said Addis, an intense guy who exhibited a wide range of emotions during our three-hour interview, from easy laughter to frustrations with what he sees as the lack of risk-taking in San Francisco to excitement over his future to flashes of real menace when discussing those who have done him wrong.

Addis is a lightning rod whose torching of the Man still elicited strong reactions from those who attend Burning Man. Some angrily condemn an act they see as destructive and dangerous, while others appreciate the ultimate symbolic assault on an event that they think had become too orderly and calcified. But what I found most interesting is how much Addis believed in the Burning Man experiment, even though he felt it had gotten away from its roots.

Addis first attended Burning Man in 1996, the last year in which anarchy and danger truly reigned, when a tragic death and serious injuries caused Burning Man organizers to impose a civic structure and rules, such as bans on firearms and high-speed driving, on future events.

Addis said he immediately became "a true believer," seeing Burning Man as both a revolutionary experiment in free expression and political empowerment, and as a "wild, risk-taking thing for pure visceral power." He came from what he called the "San

Francisco arts underground" and had a libertarian's love for guns, drugs, and explo-sives, but a progressive's opposition to war and consumer culture.

"When you go to Burning Man, everyone has that feeling at a certain point in time. It is the most incredible thing you've been at. You do see the possibilities laid out in front of you," Addis said.

Addis poured himself into the event, but became frustrated with the rules and restrictions after three years and stopped going to Burning Man, although he remained in its orbit and closely followed it. In fact, he even confesses an appreciation for the do-gooder offshoots of the event that sprouted in recent years, such as Black Rock Arts Foundation, Black Rock Solar, and Burners Without Borders.

"There are some people who go to Burning Man who have extraordinary ideas and they are extraordinary people. They embody the type of concern and substantial action that I found so wonderfully possible in those early years. And to those people, thank you for what you do. But they are a minority," said Addis, who shared co-founder John Law's anarchist attitude about what Burning Man was about.

When I wrote about Addis in the Bay Guardian and on its Politics website, dozens of people weighed in with reactions that were still quite visceral and raw, some con-demning him as a dangerous and delusional egomaniac, others using his fate to blast Burning Man as an uncaring corporation willing to send one of its own down the river.

But the Borg wouldn't be drawn into the debate. Marian wouldn't address the charge that by sending LLC board member Will Roger to the sentencing hearing with an expensive Man replacement price tag, they ensured Addis would be sent to prison. "It doesn't do us or him any good to open that wound again," Marian told me. "We're not going to discuss it."

But an internal memo written by Executive Project Manager Ray Allen shortly after the hearing — as well as private conversations I had with event leaders — argued that they were required to respond honestly to requests for information from pros-ecutors and to do otherwise would have required perjury on behalf of an adversary.

"Part of putting on the Burning Man event means maintaining good relations with Pershing County so that we can continue to have the Burning Man event on BLM land within that county. Good relations means cooperating with criminal prosecu-tions," Allen wrote to Burning Man employees.

Many of those employees remained profoundly offended by Addis and his act, mostly for the extra work it caused and the principle of such a selfish gesture. "The basic ethos out there is build your own stuff, burn your own stuff," said Andy Moore, aka Bruiser, an employee since 2001 who helps build the city. "How would you have felt if he went to your house and burned it down because he didn't like you?"

Bruiser and Addis each showed me real flashes of menace when speaking about each other: Bruiser when I made light of Addis's act during a conversation in 2008; Addis when I mentioned Bruiser had recovered his knife and dared him to come retrieve it. Yet Bruiser also agreed that two years is a long prison term for this: "It seems a bit over the top. After all, it was a structure made of wood that was meant to burn."

Neither Addis nor Bruiser were keen on the idea of letting the arsonist work off his penalty in service to Black Rock City. Both sides took the other's sleights too personally. The early burn may have been a strike at the Man — both Larry and the wooden one — but it was also an attack on everyone who attended Burning Man.

"Refusing to press charges for a felony arson that threatened human life would not bode well with the government and law enforcement agencies in Nevada that support our event. Nor would it bode well with the participants and staff who could have been seriously injured or killed by this crime," Allen wrote, later adding, "The Organization feels that the defendant's plea bargain is a fair and just outcome for all parties involved."

Addis told me that he was upset to see how Burning Man board members Marian Goodell and Michael Mikel made light of his early burn in Olivier Bonin's film about Burning Man, "Dust & Illusions," calling it hypocritical in light of the punishment they sought for him.

Yet Addis, for all his years away from Burning Man and for all his concern about what it had become, still considers his act a "successful operation" that he's proud of. "I didn't do this for me, I did this for everyone else," Addis said, once again sounding the heroic role of a reformer of something very important.

Because if Burning Man is worth the thousands of hours and dollars that its lovers spend on it each year, and the two years in prison that Addis spent to make his statement from the event's central podium, then it's likely something significant is happening here.

Designing the City

The Metropolis theme fit right into the renewed interest in urbanism that was percolating through San Francisco and other U.S. cities in 2010, so Larry Harvey was invited to speak at the San Francisco Planning and Urban Research Association's Urban Center on April 27th.

"We're the first Bohemian scene to turn itself into a city," Larry told a packed house that spilled into an adjacent room, explaining how the San Francisco counterculture transplanted itself onto the playa's flat expanse, an urban planner's dream, the chance to design a city from scratch.

At first, Burning Man was just a scene, without rules or a prescribed ethos. But as it grew and an ethos developed organically around the event, Larry said that some rules and structure became necessary, both to deal with the logistics of such a large event and to convey to newcomers what the culture was about in order to maintain and spread it.

"We didn't start out with gift-giving as dogma. It was just natural human behavior," Larry said.

Everyone brought something, more than they would need, so that they could share it with the group. Performing and making art was warmly encouraged and appreciated. There was great tolerance for even the freakiest lifestyles and forms of expression. People picked up after themselves.

And eventually, this lifestyle was enshrined as an overt ethos expected of attendees, conveyed to newbies on the Burning Man website as the "10 Principles": Radical Inclusion, Gifting, Decommodification, Radical Self-Reliance, Radical Self-Expression, Communal Effort, Civic Responsibility, Leaving No Trace, Participation, and Immediacy.

"We said to everyone that you can basically live by the ethos that guides Bohemians," Larry said. And that ethos then helped shaped the culture that formed up around the event. Or as Larry told the SPUR crowd, "The whole city is an engine for producing culture."

The evolution of Black Rock City's civic structure also transformed it into an experiment in urbanism. The need to navigate the growing city and provide emergency services as needed led to the creation of its semi-circular grid, with all the street radials emanating out from The Man, or what Larry referred to as the axis mundi, an ancient term referring to the center of the world, the point of creation from which all things flow.

It was also dangerous and impractical — not to mention a disruption of the otherworldly feel that is so central to Burning Man — to allow people to just drive around, so the use of automobiles was restricted to arrival and exodus, with the art cars (which had to be "radically altered" to get a permit to operate, and were restricted to 5 mph) becoming a de facto public transit service.

"We did what a lot of people said was unachievable: we got Americans out of their cars," Larry told the SPUR crowd.

Larry drew parallels between the city he helped create and the one he has long called home, noting that Black Rock City is five square miles, about the same size as downtown San Francisco. But only in the last few years has San Francisco begun to embrace the city it birthed.

The neighborhood that has been the most welcoming is Hayes Valley, where the neighborhood association there has discovered burner art and "they're curating their own neighborhood," starting with a David Best temple in 2007 and continuing to Dan Das Mann and Karen Cusolito's Ecstasy, which was placed in Hayes Green in the spring of 2010 with help from BRAF.

"Do you know how many warehouses in the Bay Area are filled with art like this?" Larry asked, motioning to a slide of Ecstasy he showed. "Why couldn't San Francisco become one great rotating gallery of art?"

That very notion had been a great source of frustration for many artists in the Burning Man world, a well-supported feeling that San Francisco hasn't really embraced the culture it helped spawn, like a parent embarrassed by her weird, freaky looking child.

"It will be an embarrassing chapter in the history of San Francisco culture, and a very ironic one, that one of the greatest cultural and artistic movements of our times came from here and was kicked out and regularly excluded from local life on the financial and civic level — regularly excluded by an Arts Commission with a chip on its shoulder so big that they can't see out from under its shadow. It's a sad and hilarious fact of life here," Rebecca said.

That began to change in San Francisco after 2005, when some pieces of art started to come home from the playa to civic placements in San Francisco, with help from BRAF's Leslie Pritchett. And Rebecca said it got a boost in the fall of 2006 when Alix Rosenthal ran for the Board of Supervisors as the first "burner candidate," celebrating the culture, being supported by it, and winning a solid 30 percent of the vote against an entrenched incumbent.

But the San Francisco establishment has a history of being hostile to — or at least slow to accept — its most vibrant countercultures, from the Beats in the '50s to the hippies in the '60s to the gay rights movement of the '70s. Rebecca said San Francisco's civic leaders treated Burning Man the same way, particularly the established arts community, which felt strangely inferior to Los Angeles and New York and compensated by focusing on big names in the traditional art world.

So even as the San Francisco-centered burner culture blossomed, the civic structure remained calcified. Similarly, the larger art world didn't embrace Burning Man culture in the same way that the worldwide electronic music community embraced the event as one of its premier showcases, as many of the world's most successful DJs discussed in earlier chapters.

For example, for all the Flaming Lotus Girls international acclaim, with invitations to major cultural events all over the world, and technology magazines and cultural publications writing glowing accounts of the group, Rebecca said they and other burner collectives have been basically ignored by the mainstream art magazines.

"The music at Burning Man, the performance of music at Burning Man, the dance party at Burning Man — which is integral to Burning Man — gives Burning Man a greater cultural status within the new music world than it has within the new art world. The same kind of large scale installation art for public consumption," she said. "Having made art at Burning Man, I believe has much lesser importance in the established art world than it does in the established music world, even if you're talking about the newest and freshest of both."

But at Burning Man, the installation artists are richly appreciated, enjoying a rock star status on the playa that outshines even the greatest DJs or musicians, to the point where Syd and other sound camp creators grumble about their second-class treatment. And Larry feels great pride in how the artist has been elevated within the Bohemian city he conceived.

By financially supporting art collectives and giving them a unique cultural space to display their work, Larry told me, "We took the best of the bourgeoisie and the best of Bohemia and put them together for the first time."

Larry disagreed with the criticism that Burning Man has subsumed the arts underground and stolen its energy. "I don't buy that. If anything, it's stimulated creative efforts. It's amplified them," he said. "We've created a market for art that didn't exist before."

Since then, festivals like Coachella and the Fire Arts Festival have adopted the model of fusing community gatherings with the massive artworks, creating even more opportunities for artists to create new works or display existing pieces.

"We're the cultural influence that created the model that people have adopted," Larry said, noting that the principles Burning Man embraced and projected "have proved to be terribly infectious."

The Next Act

On the night after his SPUR speech, I interviewed Larry in the rent-controlled apartment on Alamo Square where he's lived for almost 30 years. It was the last in a series of extended conversations that we've had over the last five years, and it seems serendipitous that my book deadline came just as Burning Man was transitioning into a new phase.

So I asked him how the story ends, my story, which he had already dubbed Burning Man's Second Act. "This phase ends when we complete the transition to a non-profit, and then a new story begins," he told me.

I had heard from several sources about the plans to put many Burning Man functions under the auspices of a nonprofit, but Larry told me that's the intention with the whole shebang, including the event itself, although the Burning Man trademarks and the office on Main Street in Gerlach would still probably remain with the LLC.

"All of it is framed in terms of the legacy down the line," he said.

Initially, he said the changeover would probably begin with the volunteerism at the event and through groups like Burners Without Borders, contributions to which are already made through the nonprofit Black Rock Arts Foundation. But placing everything into a nonprofit would help with governance (both getting more people involved and removing the stigma of the event being run by a closed "corporation") and funding.

"At some point, it needs a revenue stream besides the event," Larry said. Every year, Burning Man is basically a break-even venture, which has been problematic as the LLC has tried to buy a new headquarters building and event space. But Larry said that becoming a nonprofit would allow Burning Man to pursue foundation funding and give tax deductions to wealthy donors.

"The event, as far as the little engine that could, I don't think you can put another car on it," Larry said.

But The Burning Man Project, which Larry said the nonprofit will be called, could have more flexibility and ability to draw donors, as well as being more transparent and accountable to its community.

"It started with John Law's lawsuit," Larry said of pursuing the nonprofit. "That led us to assess the future in a new way."

Law sought a financial settlement and threatened to try to force control of the event into the public domain, where anyone could use Burning Man's logos and photos for whatever they wanted, including corporations. And it challenged Larry's control of the event in a way that caused turmoil between Michael Mikel and other board members.

"For awhile, it looked like the band was breaking up," Larry said.

But when Law sued them all, it united the board, pulling them together closer than they had been in years, an assessment that other board members confirmed. Talk in the larger community about governance and control — fueled by Law's lawsuit and then Addis' attack on The Man — led to board discussions about why they hadn't been a nonprofit all along, and how that made sense for the future.

"And that corresponded with the Great Recession," Larry added, noting how the event hit financial hard times and needed to significantly scale back its expenditures after the 2008 event, when the art grants peaked at $521,000 (including a six-figure contribution to the Crude Awakening project) along with other expenditures and the city's population.

Yet they needed to dig deep to pay off Law and deal publicly with the fallout from his accusations that the event was becoming essentially corporate-controlled. "The best thing that happened, in a sense, was John Law suing us," Larry said.

Plus, Larry said that after a quarter-century of Burning Man being centrally run by a handful of key players, it was just time to turn it over to the community.

"We all care immensely about the project without us. To tell you the truth, we always thought of ourselves last," Larry said of the LLC board members. "We have not put away vast sums of money for us. When it becomes a non-profit, everybody will see what we made. Not one partner is greedy."

But at the same time, they are thinking about retiring at some point, particularly Larry, 62, and Michael, 65, and they want to create a structure to protect their most loyal longtime employees. "We have an obligation to our employees to make sure they're secure in their positions."

For the last year, the LLC had channeled much of its time and energy into creating the think tank and private playa event space at Fly Ranch and a new headquarters in San Francisco. But Larry said the Fly Ranch deal was done for now because "the seller wanted too much money."

At the time, Larry was still hopeful about the new headquarters building they planned to buy at 50 Fell Street, a 25,000 square foot space large enough to hold events and to rent out space to other ventures within the large Burning Man world.

"If we have someplace where we could assemble people, we could do events constantly," Larry said. "We could do all kinds of things."

But that deal also fell apart a few weeks later, partly because of seismic issues with the building and partly because the Borg decided start putting its energies back into making the transition to non-profit status, an idea first conceived in 2008 that had gotten derailed by the Fly Ranch and headquarters pursuits.

"We're poised to do what we can to make that a priority," Marian said of the non-profit plans. "We've been discussing this thing for over two years."

There was a lot going on within the Borg, but it seemed to me as disorganized and wishful as ever, particularly as I plugged back into the large scale artwork communities that were incredibly ambitious, uncannily capable, and thriving in American Steel and other warehouse workshops around the Bay Area.

It was a community that was ready to accept the reins of control over Burning Man, reins they believe that they had been holding the whole time.

The Playa Provides Some Familiar Temple Builders

There's a saying at Burning Man: the playa provides. It's a riff on the spiritual belief — which cuts across many faiths — that things happen for a reason, that if you open yourself up to the universe without fear or expectation, you'll get what you need as you need it. And that's how the project that concludes this book came to me.

It was in March of 2010 and the rough draft was pretty much complete, right up until the last few chapters that you just read. A few months earlier, my publisher and I had decided to extend this book's narrative up through Burning Man 2010, partially because the Metropolis theme seemed like such a poignant illustration of where the event was headed, toward its realization of the urban ideal.

Already, the playa was providing, and it was about to provide again. But before I explain how, I should say a bit more about the temples of Black Rock City. Temples are the spiritual centers and gathering places for the communities that build them, standing as testaments to their faith.

In traditional culture, they are lasting monuments. At Burning Man, these complex and beautiful structures are destroyed at the end of the festival, turning toil to ash, testing our faith. But in this evolving culture, that faith is placed not in some unknowable deity, but in one another and the value of collective artistic collaboration, a faith that is strengthened and renewed every passing year.

"The Temple" — the simple name used by burners while it exists, regardless of its full name that year — is a relatively recent addition to Black Rock City. The original temple builder was artist David Best, who created Temple of the Mind in 2000 using scraps from a puzzle factory in Petaluma. Shortly before the event, a close friend of David's died and the temple was transformed into a memorial site, a concept that resonated with other burners, who gathered in growing numbers during the week and wrote messages to departed loved ones. At week's end, the community watched the temple burn, said their goodbyes, and released their pain.

The project caught the attention of Larry Harvey and the LLC, which began funding the temples and giving them special placement the following year — at midnight on the Man's axis — when David returned to build Temple of Tears with a crew that he had begun to assemble on the playa the previous year.

The Temple and its burning quickly became an important ritual at Burning Man, akin to the burning of The Man but with a very different feel. While the Saturday night Man burn is to many the bacchanalian climax to a big week, the Sunday night Temple burn is a more somber denouement, a time of reflection and remembrance.

David continued building his temples every year through 2004, when he passed the torch to architect and Temple crew member Mark Grieve (who I got to know and work with doing Hurricane Katrina cleanup with Burners Without Borders in 2005) and instead built his first temple back in the default world, which was placed in San Francisco's Hayes Green in 2005.

Best returned to build the Temples in 2007 and 2008, after which the Austin-based Community Art Makers built the Fire of Fires Temple in 2009, which included a spectacular fire tornado at its center, encased in thick glass during the event but unleashed to set the structure ablaze at the end.

In early 2010, David was still undecided about whether he wanted to build that year's Temple, so some members of the Borg and its Artery started quietly putting out feelers into the Burning Man art world to see who might be interested in taking on the project if David didn't.

Then, out of the blue, I got a telephone call from artist Jessica Hobbs, who had collaborated with sister Flaming Lotus Girl Rebecca Anders — my fire arts mentor — the previous year on Fishbug. She said the pair, along with PK Kimelman from the Space Cowboys, had been contracted by Burning Man to build the Temple. It struck me as a unique collaboration that drew from different Burning Man worlds, the artists and the ravers, the city finally coming together.

"Do you want to help us document the project?" she asked me. The stars seemed to align and the conclusion of this book started to write itself. Yes, I told her, yes, I wanted to chronicle this project in the same fashion that I had with the Flaming Lotus Girls back in 2005.

As I learned the fire arts from Rebecca and the FLGs in 2005, I would show up at the shop at least once a week. I did my interviews and took notes, then put my notebook away and put on my work gloves to help build Angel of the Apocalypse, a kind of experiential journalism that I believe gave me deeper insights into the creative process and how projects draw participants in.

And now, I was going to get the chance to do the same thing on the Temple, built by a new crew that included many Flaming Lotus Girls (the collective wasn't doing a Burning Man project for 2010) and guided by their same collaborative, feminine-centered ethos, which had earned the respect and admiration of Larry and almost everyone who had experienced their work.

"The Flaming Lotus Girls have such a solid reputation and you know it's going to be solid," Bettie June, Burning Man's associate director of art management, told me later when she revealed that she had lobbied Rebecca and Jess to take the project. "I'm the one who talked them into doing it."

Rebecca and PK had already been talking about collaborating on a large-scale art project that year or the next, and with his architectural training and desire to do something significant after more than a decade at Burning Man and having his life threatened by brain tumors, it seemed like kismet.

"It sounded absolutely ridiculous, so probably worth doing," PK said of his reaction when Rebecca proposed doing a massive wooden Temple on shortened timeline, which would require a call-out to the sound camp world that PK came from, Jess and Rebecca's fire arts community, and just about everyone one else they knew or whose expertise they could tap.

"We see the (building of the) Temple being offered to a slightly broader community, whether it's the Flaming Lotus Girls or the Space Cowboys or all these other groups that have never really been involved with the Temple," PK said.

But first, the three principles would need to settle on a design for the project, and they decided on something that initially seemed an incongruous choice for the art theme of "Metropolis: The Life of Cities." Then again, maybe that's why they dubbed it the Temple of Flux.

The Nature of Cities and Citizens

After moving beyond its grand sociopolitical ambitions, represented most starkly by Larry's "American Dream" theme in 2008, Black Rock City finally settled into its role as a Metropolis, a relatively mature urban culture scattered around the world that unites for one glorious week in the desert. Yet as it embraced its status as one of the greatest cities in the world, the Temple that this trio decided to build was a throwback to pre-civilization.

Previously, each of the annual Temples had been an architectural structure, buildings that often drew from the style of religious edifices from around the world.

"The Temple is always the most architectural item on the playa. It stands for the civic consciousness, if you will," PK told me. "They've always been amazing phenomenal things, but they've always had the architectural references, whether it's a Balinese temple or Russian orthodox. But this year, we knew the theme was going to be Metropolis, and it just seemed that the city was going to be the most urban it had ever been."

Intuitively and independently of one another, the trio was drawn in another direction. Rebecca was still thinking about the concept of seedpods, an idea the Flaming Lotus Girls considered in 2006 to follow up Angel of the Apocalypse, instead going with Serpent Mother, an idea proposed by Tasha Berg. PK said he wanted something like Superman's icy Fortress of Solitude.

"Even before we even discussed it together, we all gravitated toward the idea of natural formations, and the more we talked about it, the more it made sense. We wanted to relate Metropolis back to where we came from," Jess told me.

Ultimately, Temple of Flux wasn't really even a temple, but five massive wooden dunes that replicated land forms and created natural shelters from the elements, each named for notable ridges and canyons — Antelope, Bryce, Cayuga, Dumont, and El Dorado — the latter the biggest at about 40 feet tall. Together, they formed the kind of early gathering place that our city structures replaced.

"If the city was going to be architectural, then the Temple should stand in counterpoint to that and go back to where our collective enterprise began. Man originally sought shelter and dwelling in the land, in caves and in canyons, and it was only after existing in the cradle of the earth, literally, that man then started making and building structures that became more and more elaborate...and we relate to it in very much the same way we once related to the peaks and canyons," PK said.

Jess said the trio liked how the design would help people look at the modern world in a different way. "It gives us a richer discourse about how much we bring that need for nurturing land forms into our cities," she said. "Year after year, I run into people that are out there to look at the structure of cities and how they form, and this design is calling that out."

Yet PK also acknowledged early on that he wasn't sure how people would react to such a drastic reimagining of the Temple, a centerpiece that had become such an important part of the Burning Man experience for many participants, a place of reverence and spirituality, a church of sorts that always looked a bit like a church.

"We are intentionally tweaking that," PK said. "By changing that place and that space, we're challenging people about what that means."

There was also a deeper level to the design that marked this point in Burning Man's evolution. To the casual observer, Black Rock City could be seen as mimicking a very traditional patriarchal power structure, with everything emanating out from The Man, just as many cities are built with monuments to either civic or religious power at their centers.

"That's where the accusations of Burning Man being a cult comes from, because at the center is this icon. And I have to explain to people that that's not the culture of the event," PK said. "But I think that's where a lot of the misunderstanding with the larger culture comes from."

Yet the Flaming Lotus Girls and the other tribes that the project drew from operated on a very different paradigm, non-hierarchal models based on individual empowerment. So the Temple of Flux design ultimately reinforced that transition from a focus on the individual — be it an artist, an organization, or The Man — onto the community that has formed around it to create the city and its culture.

"Being an architect, I was very interested in working on a space that was non-centered, that didn't have a focal centerpoint that, knowing architectural history, has certain issues. Historically, the centerpoint is used as the place of authority, a point of reverence and authority, and that to me seems contrary to the collaboration that is Burning Man," PK said. "To have the Temple reaffirm that, spiritually, just seemed a bit much."

That's the story of Metropolis: The frontier, when Burning Man was all about rugged individuals doing whatever the fuck they wanted, was gone. It was replaced by a city, where free expression still reigns but our collective creations are more important than our individual desires.

Why else would thousands of us spend months, in grungy warehouses and on the open playa, collectively creating monuments to nothing more than the art of collective creation? To me, that seemed like the central question in understanding how Burning Man was shaping this new American counterculture, one I'd been trying to answer for years.

Early on, at the end of my 2005 immersion with the Flaming Lotus Girls, I felt that I was edging in on the answer when I wrote in my Guardian cover story, "People need a purpose, even San Franciscans leery of paths cut by nationalist, professional, or theological concerns. So we pursue projects — political, social, or artistic — sometimes just to see them done, so our time and passions have an outlet of our choosing, so we can be part of something bigger than ourselves."

I still think that's true, but it only partially answers a question that can elicit as many responses as there are people whose decision to participate animates the answer, ultimately numbering more than 200 voluntary builders of the Temple of Flux, an outpouring of support that itself said something about the purpose of Burning Man and the need that it filled in people's lives.

And as the Temple project progressed, my initial answer to the question seemed more and more true — but also more and more incomplete. Ultimately, the story of the Temple of Flux, and Burning Man as a whole, is about what people can accomplish when they work together, and what they learn and become along the way.

The Process Begins

From the beginning, it was clear that building the Temple of Flux was an ambitious and largely unprecedented project that would require a Herculean effort, for a couple reasons. First, the relatively late selection of the Temple leads and the scale and complexity of their project meant that it would take an aggressive schedule to get this thing built in just over four months.

Compounding that challenge was the fact that its art grant from the LLC was just $60,000, but the project's budget was about $165,000 (more than half of that just in the cost of the wood and other materials), requiring a huge fundraising effort to make up that difference. So this was truly an all-hands-on-deck affair that would require countless hours of work to build the project and to throw the dance parties and other fundraisers needed to support it.

"That's the story of why there are so many fundraisers because Burning Man is basically only paying for supplies," Rebecca told the group at the initial meeting of the project's 20 or so initial leaders and technical advisors, held in mid-May in PK's apartment in San Francisco's Mission District.

The project was broken down into teams devoted to design and structural engineering, fundraising, construction, a legal team, infrastructure and logistics, documentation, and the burn team, each headed by capable, experienced leaders (most of them women who had worked with the Flaming Lotus Girls) with the authority to make myriad decisions big and small along the way.

To facilitate fundraising and potentially help the project live beyond the coming fire that would reduce the Temple of Flux to ashes, they decided to form a nonprofit entity called the Flux Foundation. That way, financial donors could be offered a tax deduction and the human capital generated by the project would have a vehicle for moving forward into new projects.

It seemed like a good idea, and it was one that many project leaders still say is the legacy of the project that excites them most, but it also turned out to make an already complicated project even more difficult. The bureaucratic nightmare of forming a nonprofit on such a compressed timeline consumed more time and energy than the trio had anticipated, leading to an episode that nearly derailed the project just as it was headed for the playa.

But such potential pitfalls were hidden on the distant horizon during those hopeful, frantic early days of the project, when it moved forward on all fronts using the LLC's seed money and what seemed like a universal belief that this undertaking was as foolish as it was worth doing.

"Technically, we were funded on April 1, not a sheer coincidence," PK said at that first meeting shortly before everyone broke off into their subgroups, with almost half of the 20 people on hand diligently working out project details in their opened laptop computers, one of many indicators that these tech-savvy burners worked as smart as they did hard.

PK and his roommate Ben Anderson, who was also an architect, huddled over blueprints and small-scale models, discussing the technical designs of sail-like structures that would need to withstand 80 mph winds. Sarah Gill, Piper Hook, and others on the fundraising team honed details for a half-dozen events that were already in the works, from monthly events at burner-owned venues in San Francisco to the Joys and Panes of Metropolis, an auction of original artworks made on old window panes that were donated to the project, to a big name DJ-driven dance party called Pantheon at the club 1015. Jess, Rebecca, and a group of their FLG sisters penciled through artistic design details and what the construction process would look like. Another FLG, Mills, opted to work with Don Cain, who founded the art collective Department of Spontaneous Combustion, on how best to set the Temple of Flux on fire. And Olivier Bonin, producer and director of the Burning Man movie Dust & Illusions, filmed the proceedings and worked with other members of the documentation crew on how to capture this effort for posterity.

Already, with just this hand-picked group, even before the call for help had been put out to their communities, the project was taking shape, the pathway to a completed project starting to become visible. But, as Jess Hobbs would later tell me, it was the process to come that would really shape this project and its participants.

"A great art project that is open to the public," she said, "that process reinforces community."

The outlines of who that community would include began to form shortly after that meeting when the call went out, through the myriad e-mail lists and other networks that had formed and fed the exponential growth of Burning Man culture in the Bay Area, to come help create the Temple of Flux in West Oakland's American Steel workspace, also known as Big Art Studios.

Temple of Flux Builds a Home

The decision by the Temple of Flux to build the project at American Steel made sense from a logistical standpoint. It was the biggest shop in the region and maybe the only one that could handle all the project's supplies and volunteers. But it also seemed appropriate on another level.

The Temple of Flux was an unprecedented coming together of disparate Burning Man tribes, a new development in a community and culture that had been coming into their own over the previous few years. So too with American Steel, where Karen Cusolito and Dan Das Mann had finally realized their longtime goal of giving their community a solid, well-resourced, high-profile platform for their artistry.

"It's happening, it's emerging, and it's pretty exciting," Karen told me in early August of 2010 while sipping a Bloody Mary in the kitchen they had built in their Big

Art Studios bay. She had just finished overseeing the completion of that year's project, Infinitarium, a series of large plants made of steel that were on a truck bound for Black Rock City. "I'm here shepherding the art to completion while the first trucks start arriving out there," she said.

With that project, they demonstrated a new way of funding the culture's creativity, getting art grants from three different festivals — Burning Man, Outside Lands, and Electric Daisyland — which fully funded the work and actually allowed them to pay 20 artists to work on the project full-time, along with another 100 or so volunteers.

"It follows a model that allows artists to get paid for what they do," Dan said, noting how that was still such a rare thing, even with the exponential growth of the event. Besides himself and Karen, he mentioned just a few other artists — Michael Christian, Rosanna Scimeca, and Kate Raudenbush — who developed reputations through Burning Man that "are making our living as artists."

First came the creation of the culture around the catalyst that was Burning Man. And as that grew, matured, and found a longevity, "we then saw it as an opportunity to make it a lifestyle and a job," Dan said.

Part of that was because the outside world had discovered Burning Man art and artists. Starting in 2005, when San Francisco hosted Flock by Michael and Passage by Dan and Karen, their public exposure was elevated, which led to festivals such as Coachella wanting their work.

"It's been a transition time for us. We're coming of age, spreading our wings, and finding a way into society in a way we always hoped we would," Dan said. "It's about bringing our ideas into the mainstream and sharing them."

Karen gave credit for blazing that trail to Black Rock Arts Foundation and its first executive director. "Leslie Pritchett had an amazing vision and ability to bring it all together," she said, talking about Leslie's efforts to impress upon San Francisco civic leaders how the Burning Man art that was being stored in warehouses around the Bay Area could be easily placed in temporary installments with very little cost, thanks to BRAF fundraising and logistical support.

Leslie deflected that praise back onto the community. "A lot of people came together," she told me. "There was a lot of luck, in addition to good judgment."

Those types of projects strengthened the communities of burners in the cities where they lived and worked. And now, at American Steel, Karen and Dan were feeding that culture even more by providing a base of operations and the reputations of being able to accomplish what they set out to do.

"We have a crew with a real diverse skill set, so we can handle anything," Karen said, explaining how fast the local burner community seemed to be growing and maturing in recent years. "There are more DIY folks out there, so they create bigger networks. The culture is getting stronger, bigger, and more diversified."

She said the artist/do-it-yourself culture in the Bay Area and Burning Man feed off each other. "It's symbiotic. This DIY culture needs a place to try this stuff out and make connections," Karen said.

Those connections, which have now been made or reinforced year after year for a quarter-century, have become incredibly vast and diverse, stretching around the world and across disciplines.

For example, when the Flaming Lotus Girls want to supplement their fire arts project with pyrotechnics or LED lights efforts, or when welders who want to build the Gothic Raygun Rocketship need complex electronics, they know experts who can help them out. Or at the very least, someone who is a contact or two away, and given the burner culture, someone who is willing to create the time to work on a cool project.

"Burning Man is about finding a vision of ourselves that we want to share," Dan said.

Through popular mainstream events like the massive Sand by the Ton party held at American Steel in the summers of 2009 and 2010, the artists are able to share their culture with the masses. "We were able to show them a way of life that we've discovered," Dan said.

He made the comparison between Burning Man and religions, whose teachings and holy sites are accessible to the public in a way that Burning Man wasn't for a long time, isolated as it is. "Burners have a way of living in the American culture that is unique, a special way of living, like the Amish have a special way of living," Dan said.

And that, in turn, affects the group, both internally and in how it is perceived by outsiders. "What we're after as a group is the richness of our life experience, which is so much more important than money," Dan said.

I asked Dan what he thought motivated burners to devote so much time and energy to the culture, and he said it was the camaraderie and sense of shared purpose.

"There is an innate need to succeed in all of us," Dan said. "We all sign up for teams."

He said that desire to be on a team ranges from an ancient tribalism to the modern equivalents in sports and the team building that many corporations try to promote.

"The team we find ourselves in at Burning Man is part of that tribal tendency," Dan said. "The thing Burning Man does is it gets us to sign up."

Dan said watching Crude Awakening — his massive wooden oil derrick surrounded by worshipful steel figures — explode at the end of Burning Man 2007 was one of the greatest moments of his life, akin to the birth of a child.

And now, with the community and facilities that he can call on, it is within his power to create more moments like that, when something impossibly weird and cool that was born in his brain comes to fruition after months of toil.

"Every year, there's a moment when I say I can't believe I did that," Dan said. "Then I say I can't believe they let me do that. Then I say I can't believe everyone helped me do that. Then, I think, wow, what a life."

The Temple's Gravitational Pull

Given their experience with the Flaming Lotus Girls and working on other large-scale art projects for Burning Man, Rebecca and Jess weren't terribly surprised when lots of people from their community and beyond started showing up to work on Temple of Flux. It's the way many burners work, bringing their commitment and expertise to cool projects without having to be pressed very hard to do so. Taking that as a given, the lead artists just needed to create good systems for maximizing the impact of that brainpower, muscle, and time commitment.

"Big projects are really tough if I try to think about the whole thing all at once," Jess told me June 6 during the regular Monday evening meeting and work session at American Steel. So they had developed a system for breaking down the project into its component parts and goals.

Each meeting began with presentations by the people leading the various project functions, from "tool goddess" Cheryl Fralick to Catie Magee, who was like the project's den mother, making sure the myriad tasks were all moving forward and finding people to provide leadership on those that weren't.

"It's one thing we learned a lot from the Flaming Lotus Girls is the value of multiple leads," Rebecca said.

And it was no coincidence that most of those leads were women who had worked with the FLGs, as Cheryl — an FLG who followed Rebecca and Jess to the Fishbug project in 2009 — told me one evening. "We know each other well enough to background with each other, so things have gone real smooth."

In fact, PK was a little surprised at how smoothly things had gone. This was his first large-scale art project and he wasn't sure quite what to expect. He came from the sound camp world of the Space Cowboys, which he helped elevate into an organization capable of providing fundraising and even direct financial support to lots of Burning Man tribes, a bank of karma he thought he'd have to tap to build Temple of Flux.

"I was under the impression that I'd have to call in a lot of favors, but people have been coming out of the woodwork," PK told me, seeming genuinely touched and humbled by the experience. "I've been amazed by people's dedication and devotion. That doesn't necessarily happen in the real world."

Indeed, a steady in-flow of volunteers showed up, ranging from experienced builders and grizzled Burning Man veterans to first-time burners (and a few who weren't even attending the event) with no relevant skills but a desire to help in any way they can. Almost all of them said they were honored to simply be a part of the project and were willing to devote themselves to it.

Jonny Poynton, a British carpenter and psychedelic therapist who didn't really know anyone with the project but joined it after his own request to Burning Man for "a ridiculous amount of money" for a lighthouse project was rejected, quickly became an integral member of the team, and perhaps its most colorful.

"I'm super excited. So far, everyone has been really wonderful, a great group of people," Jonny told me at the June 7 meeting when we met. Even though it was one of the first work nights, he had already earned Rebecca's confidence by bringing a master carpenter's touch and tools to the project.

He had been going to Burning Man for 10 years with his son, Max, who was 25 years old at the time. They have each been involved with a variety of camps, together and separately, something that has drawn them closer together. "It's something that we've bonded over, to say the least," said Max, who also came to work hard on the Temple.

That kind of connecting through a shared purpose is important to Jonny, who quickly developed affectionate relationships with those on the project. He said it is the project, the shared vision, that unites people more than casual social connections. "For me, it's not about how people are interconnected, it's about what they want to do," Jonny said.

Rebecca had shared a similar notion with me a year earlier, shortly after finishing Fishbug, reflecting on how the mild cynicism that she felt toward Burning Man in 2005 had morphed into a stronger appreciation for the culture that has developed around the event.

"I think for my personal evolution, what's critical and become really clear to me is what's important in my life is the work that I get done. That matters more than my perspective. It matters most that my work is relevant and potent to the people in my culture and beyond," Rebecca said.

Cougar was another capable and colorful character drawn to the work and willing to put long hours into it, a builder who knew engineering and saw to the structure while Jonny focused on the details. On June 7, Ben, Cougar, and other structural team members huddled over design blueprints and talked about how to ensure these big sails remained anchored to the playa.

The anchors were going to be placed into the playa by Burning Man's Art Support Services. "Apparently, the big ones will hold 10 kips, and we're exceeding that," Ben told the group, later explaining to me that a "kip" is a kilopound, or 1,000 pounds of pressure.

Elizabeth Marley, who had just moved from Los Angeles and had some architectural training and interest, lurked around the edges looking for a chance to contribute — a void that Jonny would soon fill when he delegated to her a request from PK and Rebecca that he start designing some caves within the dunes.

"You need to make it as idiot-proof as possible," Cougar offered to the structural team, one of many little nuggets he offered that helped ride the line between the expertise needed to design the project and the many hands that would need to pass over it.

That's because this project was so labor intensive, requiring thousands of person-hours doing jobs that weren't terribly complicated once someone had been taught what to do. So ultimately, attracting people, keeping them engaged, and making sure they always had something to work on was at least as important and knowing how to build sturdy A-frames that could withstand 80 mph winds. And if there's anything that FLGs were good at, it was directing their minions.

From an early point, Catie Magee managed the project on both ends — with Burning Man brass as well as Temple volunteers — while the three principles finalized design details. She said Larry and the LLC knew how underfunded the project was and promised to make up for it with more free tickets than art projects usually get, as well as lots of early arrival passes, which attendees need to show up before Burning Man starts.

"From what we gather, we get as many as we need," Catie said at the June 6 meeting.

Even at that early stage, before the design was done and all the wood had been ordered, there were already many moving parts to a project that was sprawling out to the edges of their bay at American Steel.

A demonstration wall had been built to develop the look for the exterior cladding of the five dunes; there was a cutting station for creating the plywood strips for the cladding and a painting station for whitewashing them; 10 A-frames from Dumont — the smallest dune, the only one that would fit in the workspace — reached about 20 feet up and created a slow twist; scale models of the whole project were built and refined; and the whiteboard above the team's makeshift kitchen counter was filled with fundraiser dates and other project details.

"I'm amazed at what's happened in two weeks," PK said the next week, when he returned from a trip to plug into the project full-time. "It's like bowling — it's tough to get the ball rolling, but now it's flying down the lane."

Or as Rebecca told the group on June 14, "We're looking now like we might actually make it."

Learning from Dumont

The temple's medium was wood — cut up into strips, triangles, and trapezoids — reassembled to look like earth and rock ridges. But the lead artists were really working with people as much as plywood, over 200 by the time it was done, tapping their creativity and using their random inputs to create Temple of Flux.

Each six-inch-wide strip of plywood was white-washed with imperfect brush strokes by a 100 different hands and placed at deliberately random angles to one another, totally subject to their placers' whims and muses. Yet there was a method to this madness, honed with computer designs and pencils on paper along the way. Ultimately, people were taught the basics then told to do what felt right.

"It's important that it's not an artist's sketch," PK said, but a living work of art that would be tweaked and honed in American Steel's industrial bay and on the Black Rock Desert's wide open playa. And yet still they sketched, generating new designs along the way, an important exercise for figuring out how much materials to order and a helpful one to promoting an artistic vision.

To represent the varied texture of hillsides, the wood was brushed with white latex paint lightly enough for the grain to show through. The ridge faces would also be slashed with rising veins of solid rock, represented by wide plywood sections, surrounded by the layers of sediment and dirt that would be created using strips randomly thatched together at varying angles.

"The metaphor we're working for is the rock face with the various strata and how it changed over time," Rebecca said.

Dumont was their teacher. She was the smallest of the five dunes and the only one completely built in American Steel. Built and rebuilt, over and over, at least its faces. The artistry of creating a physical work came in modifying Dumont and letting its lessons inform how the other dunes would look.

"We're still learning things from it," Rebecca said in mid-June, working on one of the many shells that Dumont would don over the next month or so, cladding that was ripped off by a team directed by one of the lead trio then reapplied by another's team. "It has to be harmonious."

So as they learned from Dumont, studied photos of their dunes' namesakes, and thought more about their art, the leads would draw new lines on the small, three-dimensional cardboard model they created in the shop, refining the design.

"I'm trying to use geological rules to do this. It's all conceptual geology," Jess said one Saturday in late June as she drew on the model with a pencil, shop glasses on her head, earplugs hanging around her neck, wearing a Power Tool Drag Races T-shirt. Each of the trio and more than a dozen others were working on the project almost full-time, some between jobs at the time, other hustling freelance work to get by.

When she wasn't working on the Temple, Jess helped run All-Power Labs with her then-boyfriend, longtime Burning Man artist Jim Mason, along with doing freelance graphic design. "Work gets in the way," she rued that Saturday, in a shop slightly depleted by the fact that the United States soccer team was playing in the World Cup that morning.

Jess was veteran of Burning Man projects going all the way back to the '90s, when she dated Dr. Megavolt and participated in his Tesla coil shows and pursued her own art projects, later supplementing that experience by studying at the San Francisco Art Institute, earning her MFA in 2005. So she brought an artistic eye to the innate social skills that made her an unflappable connector of key people.

As the lead artists learned from Dumont, so did all the volunteers, even those who never got the chance to walk the planks that surrounded her and use the pneumatic staple and nail guns to cover her with cladding. Much of that cladding was assembled into thatches, more than 700 in all, born in a work station dubbed the thatchery and designed to swath all five dunes.

"This week, we're actually starting cladding school, which is really cool," Rebecca said at the June 28 meeting.

Two of the main teachers at cladding school were veteran burner and Flaming Lotus Girl Cathryn Blum, aka Catbird, and Brian Krawitz, who was jobless and decided to work full-time on the project as he prepared to attend his first Burning Man. Thatches were made by taking two pieces of wood dubbed "nailers," three and four feet long respectively, and placing five to nine painted wood slats across them in random overlapping patterns.

Bottom thatches, where the dunes would be more dense, got more wood pieces; the middle thatches fewer pieces; and the tapered tops of the dunes even fewer. "So it'll be really elegant, as elegant as plywood can be," Catbird said. There were six-inch wide wood slats, and trapezoids that could be used for the top two sections, but it was mostly the three-inch wide pieces.

There were some diagrams to follow, and a couple guidelines for how many pieces to use on each thatch, particularly in differentiating the top, middle, and bottom thatches, which were placed on separate pallets, labeled, and cinched down for shipping to the playa, where they would be the basic building blocks for the project's most visible aspect.

But the important thing was to make them random, to just use your judgment and decide what angles seemed interesting to you as you laid them out. "It's okay to have them freeform and not matching. In fact, that's better," Catbird said. But, Brian added, "It should have a flow."

And then, when you felt that flow and liked the form — thwack, thwack, thwack-thwack — you used the gun to fire 7/8-inch staples into the wood, adding 1.5-inch screws to spots where a couple slats overlapped the nailer to make it all strong, giving it a good shake at the end to ensure it was secure and not flapping.

The learning process would be repeated several times. Brian and Catbird taught me to make thatches one Monday, Jane and Jess taught me how to whitewash the boards on another, Cougar taught me to make frames on another, and Jonny taught me to create little niches on another. And later, I taught others what I had learned.

"The design is about horizontal learning," PK told the group, referring to how the knowledge gets spread, with one person teaching another, who then teaches another. Later, he told me, "We set up a structure where people can contribute without being artists."

Having taught all she could, Dumont was finally broken down in late summer, her frames and cladding prepared for transport to Burning Man.

"The big logistical issue is actually getting it there," PK said, a process that involved building frames in the shop that would hold on the playa but be easily broken down onto the five semi tractor-trailers that would convoy out there. But the artistic part, and the part that built skills and community, was in creating the project's building blocks.

"Now we have the puzzle pieces and it's about how we fit it together," Rebecca said, a statement that could have referred to either the stacks of thatches, the bundles of frame sections, or the individual groups of people that began to form into a cohesive whole that summer.

During a meeting at American Steel, PK said the architectural term for the way shapes are created that only fit together a few different ways is a "kit of parts," adding, "It's like building a puzzle without the box."

Built to Burn

While most of the Temple of Flux crew worked out of American Steel, the burn team led by Don Cain mostly toiled in his workspace and home in Emeryville known as the Department of Spontaneous Combustion, which is like a burner clubhouse complete with bar, rigging, classic video games, old art projects, and the equipment to make new ones.

Don grew up on military bases learning shop skills from his dad and did stints as a police officer — where he cross-trained with the fire department and developed a bit of pyromania — and in the Army, after which he lived in Humboldt and then came to the Bay Area to study art photography at San Francisco State University.

He attended his first Burning Man in 1999 "and my very first night there was epic." So he immersed himself in the culture, making massive taiko drums later used by the burner musical ensemble Mutaytor, creating liquid fuel fire cannons, and building massive fire-spewing tricycles.

"I've been doing the fire stuff for awhile and I have all my fingers and toes and I haven't set anyone on fire yet," Don told me in his shop. Plus, he had been dating Rebecca, working side-by-side with her on Fishbug, bringing his expertise to that project as well.

So he was the natural choice to lead the team that will "choreograph the burn" of the Temple, as Don put it, an experienced group that loves geeking out on the best ways to burn things. "We have a collection of very experienced people in the fire stuff," Don told me during the group's regular Thursday night meeting. "About 50 years of experience."

They ranged from Pistol Pete Blake, a longtime Bay Area firefighter who volunteers with the Emergency Services Department at Burning Man every year, to Rosa Anna and Mills, the "rookies of the year" from the Flaming Lotus Girls' Angel of the Apocalypse project in 2005, to Peter Youngmeister, who joined the FLGs after helping build Dance Dance Immolation (which was like the popular Dance Dance Revolution video game, except participants wore fireproof suits and got blasted with flames when they made a mistake) and even doing this stuff professionally for Phish concerts and other gigs, to Joe Dacanay, a professional photographer who worked with FLGs on Soma in 2009.

"I have always been a pyro," Joe told me as he tested a homemade fuse that he'd made by soaking rolled up newspapers in a blend of kerosene, white gas, and liquid soap. "Chemical science and art has always been my blend."

Also slowly burning on the sidewalk outside the Department of Spontaneous Combustion on that mid-summer evening was a pair of white takeout food containers filled with a pink goo, the first test of a mixture of sawdust, paraffin, and what Don called "Barney gack."

He explained that this strange substance, which he guessed was petroleum jelly and other similar substances, was what artist Matthew Barney had coated onto a series of objects during an exhibit at the San Francisco Museum of Modern Art earlier that year. And somehow, as that show ended, the Borg2 instigators Jim Mason and Chicken John had ended up with 13 55-gallon drums of the stuff, which sat at The Shipyard waiting for a purpose.

"We already know the paraffin and sawdust will burn. Now we're seeing if the Barney gack will burn because we have a lot of it," Rosa Anna said.

The burn team was as resourceful as it was crazy about fire, with the members tapping their wide networks of contacts to get the stuff they'd need, getting donations that included burlaps sacks from one source and barrels full of paraffin donated by Mill Valley Candle Works.

"Because of Don Cain's super sleuth-like abilities, we're actually under-budget right now," Rebecca said at the Temple's June 14 gathering. At another meeting a couple weeks later, "the immolator-in-chief," as Rebecca labeled Don, explained his elaborate burn plan and said, "We have a lot of things that nobody has seen before, that we've never seen before, that we're inventing."

The plan included 13 sawdust cannons, color effects in the blue-turquoise-purple range caused by the burning of chlorine and copper shavings, 110 gallons of various fuels, and a few hundred "pyro packs" mounted in the structure from the beginning that would be turned volatile on burn day.

"We have a definite battle plan as far as burn techniques and some of the colors we want," Don told me. "But we're still figuring out how to do the cascading fuel burn effect."

He was talking about the methanol waterfalls that would flow down the sides of the dunes at one point in the burn, set off by fuses that would dance up the sides. Yet such effects were hush-hush at that point. Considering how solemn the temple burn is, they might be a tad controversial, so as PK told the crew, "Nobody needs to know that there's going to be anything special."

The most basic goal was to create hundreds of "burn packs" made of paraffin, sawdust, burlap, and other burnable materials to "add a lot of calories in one spot, which is what we're after," Don said. The burn packs, stacks of kindling, and tubes of copper and chlorine shavings to create a blue-green color were to be placed strategically throughout the Temple as soon as the framing was done.

The idea is to break the structure down before the cladding burns away, so the A-frames aren't standing up the air. "I would like to get the structure to collapse relatively quickly," Don said. "Then we'll have a pile of fuel that will burn for awhile."

They also created 13 "sawdust cannons" using the finest, cleanest sawdust from the cutting of wood at American Steel, one of many creative reuses of the project's byproducts. Tubes of the sawdust, so fine they called it "wood flour," were placed over buried air compressors that would be silently fired off during the burn to create flammable plumes.

As Don told me in his typical understated way, "I've taken the opportunity to turn this burn into more than just setting a structure on fire."

Forming New Dimensions

So while the builders built and the burners burned, the fundraising crew organized regular events and online fundraising drives, another source of both stress and socializing with one another. Sarah Gill gathered and distributed dozens of old window frames that many of us painted into artwork auctioned off at the Joys and Panes of Metropolis party.

We all bonded even more strongly as we drank and danced together at Temple events in burner-owned clubs such as Shine and Triple Crown, but it's work to throw a party that makes money, work we were all doing on top of tasks that were more immediately related to building and burning the Temple of Flux.

"The events people are amazing, but definitely tapped out, so give them some love when you see them," Catie said at the July 12 meeting, with Sarah looking a little haggard to drive home the point. Catie said the online Kickstarter campaign had raised about $20,000, including a single $10,000 donation, which was making up for some fundraising events bringing in less than hoped for. "The fundraising is good, but we have to keep it going."

PK, whose DJ friends donated a lot of their services to the project's events, also advised people to be frugal with their use of materials and other project resources because "every dollar someone spends here is another dollar that someone else is raising."

Building dunes, raising money, and planning to burn through them both had always been the project's main plan. But along the way, Temple of Flux also picked up some new dimensions that would help define the project, elevate its collaborative nature, and personalize the involvement of dozens of its participants.

As soon as basic project designs were done in June, Dumont started taking on new features that hadn't been part of the original plans or discussions.

Benches were added along some of the dunes' curves, benches that later morphed into double- and triple-deckers. There was talk of maybe doing a cave or two, and then a prototype cave was built into Dumont, and plans evolved into adding a cave or two on every dune. Niches, built like small cubby holes, appeared on Dumont's walls, triggering a full work station to crank them out by the dozens to give visitors spots to place their mementoes.

As a finish carpenter, Jonny had been tasked with designing the benches and building their early prototypes, but the principals were still haggling amongst themselves about how many there should be and where they ought to be placed.

"We had our first disagreement yesterday," Rebecca told me in late June, saying it was over the benches and commenting on their decision-making process. "We've reiterated a few times that there has to be consensus."

So while he waited for his marching orders on the benches, Jonny — who lived just six blocks from American Steel and had decided to pour himself into the project, working almost every day — was asked by PK if wanted to take the lead on another project.

"He turns to me and says we've just come up with this idea of putting caves in, would you be interested in doing them?" Jonny said, accepting the assignment and talking to Rebecca about what she had in mind for them. They needed to be intimate, individualized spaces that carried through the natural feel of the overall dunes.

Jonny had been getting to know Elizabeth, who was in the process of moving from LA and similarly pouring herself into the project. They had talked architecture and design, and Jonny said that he was so impressed by her ideas and ethos that he delegated the cave project to her.

"I needed someone I could pass it off to," Jonny said, noting that she did the conceptual design and he helped with the execution. "So we did the first cave together."

While the first cave prototype was built into Dumont at the shop and the site of the seven caves and their approximate dimensions were decided upon, the exact design and feel of the caves, as well as who would work on them, was left for later, on the playa, with the opportunities for anyone who showed a strong interest to help create them.

"The designers of the project made this a truly collaborative project by having the caves be designed and built by a whole slew of different characters, so it was opened up and that soul was able to grow because they trusted all of us to make these amazing spaces, and every space was different," Elizabeth said.

The caves did become the soul of the project, as even Rebecca later told me. They were intimate, immediate, and artistic, yet they were buried inside the larger project, small spots that some Temple visitors barely noticed, while others spent hours visiting and communing within them.

"It was one of the most life-changing things I've ever done," Jonny said of the Temple work. "And the caves, especially to me, were one of the things that made the experience of doing this so profound."

Jess said that for many people, the Temple is an intimate spot to mourn or reflect. "We recognize that some people don't want to do that in the open," Jess said of the decision to create caves. Then she added another reason for privacy, with a sly grin: "Or to have sex."

Jess explained the system of benches and caves were designed around the movement of the sun. "Light is important," she said, adding that the decision was finally made to not do benches on the sheer faces of the largest peaks to maximize the effect. "It's a great feeling of being very small but still very connected."

As the project moved forward, the crew of volunteers grew all summer until it reached more then 200, and they felt an increasing sense of ownership of and connection to the project. That was a result of a design and a medium that allowed collaboration, and an ethos that encouraged it.

"A lot of us come from groups where we encourage empowerment and teaching," Jess told the group during one meeting in June. "If the opportunity is there, please take it [and teach skills to someone who needs them]."

But the process was always more important than the product, something that was conveyed regularly through the project. At the July 12 meeting and work night, Jess, Rebecca, and Catie said the need for progress shouldn't compromise the central mission of teaching and learning.

They told the temple crew that one woman working on the project complained that some of the more skilled men weren't taking the time to teach her, and they said that was simply unacceptable. Rebecca invoked the original Temple builder.

"David Best said, 'Never take a tool out of a woman's hand. It's insulting and not okay.' But I'd like to expand that and say never take a tool out of anyone's hand," Rebecca said. "Hopefully we can take on that sexism and some of the other isms in the world."

The admonishment, delicately delivered by women with serious artistic and construction abilities, was instantly accepted by everyone and never became a problem again.

"Take a moment to teach someone," Jess said. "It's not going to slow you down that much and we need more people with skills."

Push to the Playa

The skills that people brought to the Temple of Flux took many forms, as was beginning to be clear by the time late-July brought the final push to the playa, where the first teams were scheduled to begin arriving on August 13th.

"Today, we built the last structural frames," Rebecca said at the July 26th meeting, sparking a big cheer from the crowd. "So congratulations, everybody, we're going to do it."

Eva headed up the kitchen crew, which would be feeding and watering everyone on the Temple of Flux crew throughout the three-week build, and she encouraged people to sign up for kitchen shifts — and not to simply tell her to assign them to a shift. "I'll make you cook bacon naked if you ask me to just sign you up," Eva said in her typical saucy way.

After all, Eva said, she had enough to worry about with the 5,244 meals she had planned, the menus based on her research of the dietary customs of desert cultures so everyone would be getting proper nutrition in the extreme climate of the playa. "You want to provide your own snacks, your own alcohol, your own drugs, but everything else is covered," Eva said.

The excitement was palpable as everything was starting to take shape and seem real, the long summer transitioning into the longest stint on the playa that most of the participants had ever experienced, including me.

"We're beginning to think about how to assemble our teams," PK said, "so let us know your preference now."

During the final meeting at American Steel on August 9th, with two trucks already headed to the playa and two more being loaded, Jess and the rest of the core crew looked a little ragged. "I'm running on empty, but no worse than anyone else here," Jonny told me.

Jess seemed tired, but she wore an unflappable if nervous smile, briefly popping over to the shop as PK, Rebecca, and Catie packed for the foursome's departure the next day. "Everyone seems to be in good spirits," she told the group. "We have two trucks loaded and two more coming Thursday."

Yet there was a big unforeseen factor that added to their stress. Jess informed the group that the project, which was already falling short of its fundraising goals and was going to end up in debt, had its finances unexpectedly frozen by PayPal just went it needed them most.

Attaining nonprofit status for the Flux Foundation from backlogged government agencies took longer than planned, and even though the difference in the fees that PayPal charges nonprofits was miniscule and the Temple crew worked diligently to address the company's concerns, "PayPal has frozen our account, so a big chunk of the money we thought we had, we don't have," Jess told the group.

She and other project leads, including Catie and treasurer Colinne Hemrich, for weeks had been going back-and-forth with both PayPal people and the California Office of Charitable Trusts, which must approve the creation of nonprofits before the IRS can grant tax-exempt status, trying to get the situation resolved. It was moving forward, but the government agencies had their budgets slashed in recent years, so it would be months before they could give PayPal the final paperwork it was seeking.

"There was never a time when they said it was going to affect our ability to access our funds," Colinne told me. And then suddenly, with no warning, PayPal froze the funds.

"All that money is sitting there and we can't touch it," Jess told me, later adding, "They are going to make money off the interest from our money and we don't get it."

Computer problems at the Burning Man office were also complicating the distribution of about 200 early arrival passes that the crew needed to get on the playa and start building. While the tickets had finally come in a week earlier and were being distributed that night, the early arrival passes still weren't in and Jess would need to deal with them from the playa.

"It's okay, don't panic, it'll all work out," she told the group, but it sounded more like a mantra she was saying to herself.

As a journalist, I recognized the PayPal incident as a good story. So the next day, I wrote "PayPal freezes the finances of Burning Man's Temple crew" on the Bay Guardian's Politics blog, which went viral overnight as the community spread the word through Facebook and other social media networks, generating more than 100 comments critical of PayPal on my blog post and prompting other media coverage of the controversy.

Donations and offers of large bridge loans poured in to the Temple project and the community demanded answers from PayPal, which had presented itself as a convenient funding source for grassroots groups but which had turned into an increasingly controversial corporation after being purchased by eBay in 2002.

PayPal lists no phone numbers for customer service or media inquiries, so I had to use their online request form to get a response, which I never received on the day I wrote the item. But at the end of a long string of blog comments criticized PayPal, company spokesperson Anuj Nayar weighed in doing damage control and offering to help.

We spoke by phone shortly thereafter and he told me, "We have released the funds." He cited privacy laws and said he couldn't do much to explain why the group's funds were frozen or unfrozen, but he did say that he and others at PayPal go to Burning Man and are familiar with the significance of the Temple and sympathized with the crew's plight.

Catie told me that when a PayPal representative called, "they agreed to release our funds and said they were doing us a big favor." But the gesture didn't earn much goodwill in the Burning Man community, with many people dropping their PayPal accounts and joining Temple of Flux in signing up with WePay, a more community-based alternative.

"It would not have come out the way it did without your article sparking their public relations nightmare," Colinne told me. But to me, the incident seemed to illustrate the power and resourcefulness of this community, as well as the special significance that the Temple had come to play to those with even a passing familiarity with Burning Man.

Attorneys volunteered to put pressure on PayPal, people from the nonprofit world offered to help with the nonprofit paperwork, those with money offered to give it to the project for as long as it needed it (Catie told me the project received $8,000 in donations on the day the controversy broke), and those working on the project poured even more of their time and energy in to give the Temple of Flux a strong sendoff to the playa.

And true to their irreverent style, some fluxers found humor in the situation, printing buttons that read "Flux 1, PayPal 0," which they wore along with buttons such as "What the Flux?" and the project mantra "It's gonna be great."

Playa Life

After hearing stories from me and others of the inspiring work going on at American Steel, my new girlfriend Syda Day, my close friend Scott Borchardt, and his girlfriend Nicole Spear were drawn to volunteer. After several weeks of working at the shop, they all got hooked and decided to help build it on the playa.

When we arrived on August 21st — eight days after the first Temple crew members got there and nine days before Burning Man officially began — all five dunes had been framed and Dumont was done, fully cladded and complete with a cave and graceful arcing bench with Jonny seated in the middle, alone, drinking whiskey and gazing out across the wide open playa at a nearly full moon rising over a distant mountain ridge.

Syda — a petite, curvy, and strikingly beautiful Indian woman who Jonny had a barely contained crush on — and I sat on either side of him. We talked about the week, enjoying a calm and clear night that was a marked contrast to what he said were that day's fierce dust storms, which let up just as the Early Burn party was beginning, the first real social occasion of an industrious week for the handful of art crews on the playa.

The camp was comprised of some tents but mostly of trailers and RVs, including those dropped on the site and rented to crew members by Metric and Flash Hopkins, longtime burners who had gone native in Gerlach and turned into entrepreneurs, skirting the edges of the event's no-commerce credo.

Things seemed a little deserted, and when we ran into Ben in the kitchen area, he said with a slight slur that they had finally finished all the framing that day and everyone was celebrating, inviting us to join a group that was headed across the playa to soak in Trego Hot Springs. But it had been a long and unexpectedly late and difficult journey, so we opted out to just crash in the trailer that Syda had reserved for us from Metric.

"It was such a pivotal moment for us," PK later said of that night, when the basic structures were up and the fluxers created what they called a "playa chicken" out of a set of frames that had been built wrong, the temple drawings and scale models, and other early scraps, which were set on fire during the Early Burn ritual.

The next day, everyone seemed a little haggard from a big night and work was sporadic, which was good for me considering the widely proffered rule of thumb that it takes a good 24 hours to acclimate to this strange and harsh environment, so it was best to just take it easy, drink lots of water, and let your body adjust before doing too much.

Still, there's always work to do on the playa, even on a down day. You can't relax in the shade until you've built your shade structure, secured it against the wind, and added artistic touches to make it a home. And there's always someone who can use some help. Scott and Nicole had arrived earlier than us the previous night and inadvertently set up camp in what PK told them was a road, so we helped them strike and set up a new camp.

The camp's social hub was the kitchen area, with amenities ranging from a beautifully ornate wooden prep station that that had been custom made for the build back in American Steel to dozens of camp chairs arranged around couches and tables under a big shade space made by three of the typical 10-by-20-foot carports.

The day had a lazy vibe to it that we wouldn't experience again until the temple was done, with people lounging in the shaded hammocks, braiding each other's hair, working in notebooks to track the inventory of the supplies, or making car trips to soak in the waters of the nearby reservoir, Trego, or Frog Pond.

But by dinnertime and the meeting that followed, the crew was anxious to start making good progress again, calling for a big work night and spelling out a multitude of tasks that needed to be done that night, from shoveling the decomposed granite that would protect the playa from baking during the burn to getting cladding crews up in each of the three boom lifts and the scissor lift used to attach wood a few stories up from the ground, a half-dozen people in each crew including support workers on the ground wrangling supplies.

"We're trying to shoot for being done by Friday, which is like world record-setting," PK told the assembled group of about 30 people. But he said they needed to maintain a fast pace because "a day like yesterday would devastate the project," he said, referring to the wind storms that can arrive suddenly, last for hours, and stall progress.

As guidance for the cladding crews, PK expanded on the artistic vision he had imparted at American Steel that summer, when he urged people to feel the flow of cladding and listen to the wood, this time getting downright Zen. "The pieces will tell you the way more than the guidelines," PK said, conveying that shapes have an inherent nature, something they want to be, and "they will show you the way if you let them."

It was an infectious vision that he combined with a hard sell, asking for shows of hands of who wanted to do what. "C'mon, we're going to crank the music and get some stuff done," PK said, momentarily cutting through the almost overwhelming fatigue that was weighing down me and Syda and eliciting regular yawns.

We had been planning to get a good night of sleep and wake up fresh for a good first day of work, a plan that PK had complicated by getting me to raise my hand, volunteering to work. But as we left the meeting, Syda said I needed to take care of myself, take my 24 hours of rest. And I must have looked like hell because Catbird and even Jess agreed, sending me off to bed.

The next morning, it was clear that lots of work had been done, but both Rebecca and PK acknowledged it wasn't as much as they'd hoped, mostly because of a double-whammy of a late start and an unexpected visit by some friends of the family, including DPW crew members and Burning Man brass.

And some of the work that had been done would need to be undone, including the toppers and cladding that had been nailed and stapled to the top edge of Bryce facing the wrong direction, fanning toward neighboring Cayuga instead of out toward the open playa. So my first task, assigned by PK and Rebecca, was to climb up there with a hammer and pry bar and rip it all down.

Making art is an imperfect process.

Temple of Fluff

Heavy equipment has become essential to creating the large-scale art that has been popping up in Black Rock City in recent years, so Burning Man created an Art Support Services crew to operate a fleet of cranes, construction booms, scissor lifts, and other equipment that big projects need.

For months, the Temple of Flux crew had painstakingly created all the project's building blocks, carefully packaged and labeled back in San Francisco to smooth the build. "Then I get to pop in and help them make it art," Davis Galligan, aka The Stinky Pirate, told me as he prepared to take Louisa "Lou" Bukiet (a Flaming Lotus Girl in her early 20s) and a stack of thatches up in the boom lift on August 23rd to staple the cladding to the windward side of Cayuga, with Jess and her artistic eye spotting from the ground.

Davis has been helping to build Black Rock City every year since 1999 when he joined DPW, in recent years operating heavy equipment for a variety of notable artworks, such as Big Rig Jig and the Steam Punk Treehouse. He said the groups do all the prep work and then "I get to come in and be a star player."

He was one of several heavy equipment operators who became like de facto Temple crew members, including Eli Lyon, who had been working for Art Support Services head Richard Scott continuously since I met her as a wayward young burner doing hurricane cleanup work with Burners Without Borders on the Gulf Coast in 2006.

Jess had been around the scene long enough to have relationship with many of these hardcore DPW and old-school burner types, and their respect for her showed.

"I can't say enough about your daughter. She's really cool," Flash, a legendary burner from the beginning, effusively told Marilyn and Rich Hobbs at the build site, where they had come for their first Burning Man to see their daughter Jess in action.

But the Stinky Pirate, with a gruff look and two long strands of hair extending way down from the corners of his goatee, wasn't prone to such gushing.

"This camp is sweet and filthy," he offered as he bantered intimately with Lou and Jess, adding, "I'm just here to give Jess shit."

"Someone's gotta do that. I'm all high and mighty," Jess responded, wearing a pink sparkly cowboy hat, tool belt, Illumination Village tank top, and infectious smile.

As they talked and prepared to go up into the lift, a pair of birds flitted around as if dancing together, as they had been doing around the build site all morning, a strangely striking appearance on this normally lifeless stretch of desert.

"They're not the smartest birds," Davis observed.

"Maybe we're that good," Jess replied, "we're fooling the birds."

But as Davis and Lou finally boarded the lift and prepared to ascend, he did offer a contrary notion, referring to the time they've spent tearing off cladding that the artists didn't think was quite right. "My goal is no more redoes, whatever time we have to take for a do," Davis said, and Jess nodded her assent.

As she directed their placement of cladding thatches from the ground, Jess made no apologies for her perfectionism. "This is a project I designed with PK and Rebecca so I have a lot of passion to get it done and make sure it's right," Jess told me.

It was something Davis actually appreciated, even if it meant a bit more work for him. It was part of the Burning Man culture that initially drew him and has kept him in it for so long, that drive to create and elevate one's art. But even more important is the spirit that various groups bring to their work, something that he said was epitomized in the Temple of Flux crew.

"This is a killer group. It's probably the best crew I've gotten to work with," Davis told me, explaining that it was because of their attitude and organization. "Art is more than just building the art. It's about community and this group is really good at taking care of each other."

Lou put it even more simply: "Everyone really loves each other out here."

Taking care of each other was a core value with this group. Not only did the Temple team have a full kitchen crew serving three hot, yummy, and nutritious meals a day and massage therapists to work out sore muscles, it also had a team of "fluffers" who would bring the workers snacks, water, sunscreen, cold wet bandanas, sprays from scented water bottles, and other treats, sometimes topless or in sexy outfits, always with a smile and personal connection.

Margaret Monroe, one of the head fluffers and one of my campmates from Garage Mahal, instructed her team (including Syda) to always introduce themselves to workers they don't know and to touch them on the arms or back to make a physical connection and help them feel cared for and supported.

PK said he initially bristled at the high kitchen expense and other things that seemed extraneous to the cash-strapped project. "People are eating better here than they eat back at home," he said. But he came to realize the importance of good meals and attentive fluffers: "If you keep people happy, then it's fun, and if it's fun then it's not like work."

The Highest Priority

On the playa, a warm sense of camaraderie and common purpose propelled the Temple crew to make rapid progress on the project, working all day, every day, and most of every night. Given the uncertain weather conditions on the playa, they still felt time pressures and the need to crack the whip on the crew periodically, particularly guarding against letting the great social vibe turn into a party that steals the focus from the work at hand.

"Let this temple be your highest priority," Rebecca told the group on Tuesday night the 24th, asking for a show of hands on when people were committing to work on the project: that night, the next morning, during the heat of the next day. "Look at each other and know that you're making a commitment to yourselves and each other."

That sort of hard sell, while it was used several times during the week, often delivered with a certain practiced FLG charm by Jess and Rebecca, hardly seemed necessary most of the time. People really were there to work long hours on the project, and seemed to take great pride in it, even while taking care of themselves, connecting with fellow crew members, and reveling in the experience.

During the hottest part of the day, many of us also took car trips to the nearby reservoir about 40 minutes away, a beautiful place to cool down, replenish, and soak in some cool moisture. Even though it was publicly accessible and visible from the road, it was still so remote that I saw only fluxers on each of my three visits. It was like our own private getaway spot.

But by Wednesday the 25th, word arrived that windy, rainy weather was on the way that weekend, a worrisome prospect that got the group even more focused on finishing the project. "We need to ask everybody for a really big push," Rebecca told the group that night.

"Tonight, we need a massive worknight. It'll be our last big night," PK said, laying down a new rule for the night: "No partying in the camp."

"We are so close, so we need everyone to get out there and kick ass," Jess added. "We're going to finish this tonight and then we're going to have fun for the rest of the time."

The appeal worked on a crew that had reached its peak size of about 100 people or more, almost all of whom worked on that warm summer night, the calm before the storm, the final push. With that kind of positive spirit, with everyone finding some way to contribute — cladding, wrangling, fluffing, or making benches — it seemed like there was nothing that could stop the Temple of Flux.

But Stalker, a member of the Department of Spontaneous Combustion, looked concerned. I asked him what was wrong and he said there was a problem with the caves, and that the Burning Man brass were talking about sealing them up, concerned about the fire hazard during the week. It was personal blow to him and others.

"It's really hard working on something when you want to cry," big, gruff Stalker told me, noting that he had lost six friends and family members this year, including Randall Issac, a DSC member who died suddenly of cancer and to whom the crew dedicated the largest cave in the temple.

"It'll work out," Jess assured him. "It's going to be fine."

That was when I noticed PK and Rebecca touring the project with Burning Man fire safety director Dave X (who founded the Flaming Lotus Girls in 2000), who had brought a delegation that included Bettie June from the Artery, lawyer Lightning Clearwater, Tomas McCabe from Black Rock Arts Foundation, and fire marshal Joseph P. So I pulled out my notebook and followed.

"The thing we're concerned about is closed spaces, ingress and egress," said Dave X who had assembled the group to participate in any decisions that needed to be made. "It's something that I wanted to get a lot of people in on."

Word of the impasse spread quickly among the most active camp members, weighing heavily on some. "The thought that those caves might not have existed, having been built, was the most upsetting thought to me during the project," Jonny told me later.

Eventually, the visiting group agreed that the risk was manageable if the Temple Guardians who work volunteer shifts monitoring the project during the week watch out for certain things. "Their mantra needs to be no smoking, no fire," Dave said, raising the possibility of setting occupancy limits on the caves, which the group ultimately decided wasn't necessary.

Joseph also said the caves needed to be named and a protocol developed for evacuation in case of accidental fire — or the emergence of another Paul Addis, someone who might torch the project on purpose. "The important thing is that whoever is calling in can use the terminology we use in our dispatch center," Joseph said.

The fire arts were largely developed in the Bay Area by burners, who have an expertise and understanding that exceeds most civil authorities. That was something I learned back in 2005 at the Fire Arts Festival, when the Oakland Fire Department signed off on the Flaming Lotus Girls' project, but then Dave X came around with his flammable gas detector and told them the fittings needs to be tightened.

And now, even though the Temple crew included friends with whom he had deep connections, Dave X warned them, "You guys are in the yellow zone here where you're taking precautions." Joseph agreed, but then said, "You guys are family."

And it was handled like a family, talking it through as a group but knowing that mom and dad — or in this case, Dave X — would have the final say, with the kids resenting that paradigm.

"Professionally, I know there wasn't an occupancy issue," PK told me afterward, noting that the rooms were too small and two doors aren't needed for nine people or less. "We pretty much planned for all the things they said."

So they agreed to implement the edict and from that point on, the path to completion was clear, with a huge crew working until the wee hours of the morning and finishing all the major work, leaving mostly fine-tuning to do as the winds began to pick up the next day, growing to zero-visibility dust storms by the evening when Syda and I headed to Reno to write a cover story on the project for the Bay Guardian.

When Scott and Nicole arrived in Reno the next night — a loving, playful couple whose strong life energies still shined through obvious fatigue — they said weather conditions on the playa had turned nasty, fraying the nerves of some on a crew that needed to put the final touches on the project, break camp at the site, and set up new camps for the main event.

Once the project was done, the crew scattered off into a dozen or more camps, with the biggest contingents staying in the venerable Illumination Village or the nearby Temple Town, a new camp of fluxers who shared a property with the project's storage containers and other equipment.

A few of us camped with my new camp of Shadyvil, a couple with my old camp Garage Mahal, some went to the camp that created the super cool Purgatory Cruiser and Neuroweapon art cars, PK camped with the Space Cowboys (which did their annual Friday night Hoe-Down dance party at the Temple of Flux, of course), and Jonny camped with a group of hot French single mothers (of course) and their Lord of the Flies brood, which we dubbed the French MILF camp.

But the Temple of Flux was finished with time to spare before the event began on August 30, a first in the history of Temples, on which burners are accustomed to still seeing work done during the first few days of the event. And that accomplishment came despite a particularly nasty storm rolling in and the handful of crew members who just couldn't let it go — particularly the cave men and women, who continued tinkering and toiling until they were made to stop.

Story of the Stalactite Cave

Something happened in the caves of the Temple of Flux. Actually, lots of things happened: Jonny and Elizabeth fell in love, Ben proposed to his girlfriend, Chris said goodbye to his dead brother, the Department of Spontaneous Combustion mourned a fallen member, Scott and Nicole placed niches honoring their families, Gal conveyed his vision of spiritual duality, Dylan went a little crazy, and thousands more visitors had experiences ranging from the mystical to the mundane, more stories than this book could possibly tell.

But there was a common thread to this multitude of individual experiences. The caves were developed organically, almost as an afterthought to the main project, brought to life by individual Temple crew members who gained as much from the experience as they gave, creating seven of the most intimate spaces in Black Rock City, each containing layer upon layer of meaning and symbolism.

Each cave has many stories, created by fluxxers and visitors who blessed them with their words, their hands, or the ashes of lost loved ones. But this is the story of the Stalactite Cave, and its inaccessible sister, the Stalagmite Cave. They are also known as Mignon.

Artistically, it was what Rebecca called the soul of the project, and which PK said conveyed "the beauty in the unsafe, the dangerous and unstable. It also speaks directly to flux: continuous growth, change, and transition."

It was like a cave within a cave, the first one beautifully finished down to the smallest detail, wooden stalactites hanging sharp and icicle-like from the ceiling, sparkling in the mind's eye even they were made of plywood in a couple weeks and not liquid minerals dripping for generations. Altars pocked the walls, filled with mementos and slashes of color. The whole space was big enough for only about a half-dozen close friends.

And on the far wall were three holes through which visitors could see another cave, that one inaccessible, unfinished, and sort of scary-looking, with jagged stalag-mites jutting up from the ground, dusty rays of sunshine shooting through by day, eerily backlit at night. Literally, it was like peering through a hole at the inside of the temple; figuratively, it was like peeking into purgatory.

"The inspiration was to create a secret space that was disconnected from the outside," said Gal Ohr Karmi, an earnest 39-year-old Israeli who came to Burning Man just to work on the Temple, as he had the previous year's Temple, seeking out crews he didn't know because of the spiritual connection he felt to the notion of a sacred space amid the crazy party side of Burning Man. "I wanted to give them a peek inside the temple and I wanted it to look very pure and untouched, like nobody had ever been there before."

By then, Elizabeth had built two caves that were beautiful, welcoming spaces once visitors noodled their way inside them, and she initially resisted Gal's idea. "I was challenging him, saying why do you want to have a room that's closed off? It would be awesome if people could go in there. And he said, no, I want there to be that kind of juxtaposition, I want there to be those opposites, where there's something you have to contemplate but you can't reach it. It's like life and death, because there's also this space that you are able to occupy, and feel around in. It's that positive and negative," she said. "Peeking into the underworld, that was a term he mentioned."

As she and others embraced the idea, they added to it and helped make it their own, even helping Gal let go and be shaped by the materials and the environment, a vision that Jonny had imparted to Elizabeth. "If you think you can build this how you have it in your head, forget it. That's a waste of time. What you have to do is work with the wood and let it create itself and what it wants to be," Jonny, the experienced carpenter, told Elizabeth in that first cave in Dumont, as they connected with the space and one another. "We weren't in love when we built it, but we fell in love building it."

Elizabeth's intention for Burning Man that year was already to free herself from a past love, the ruts she created in relating to the world, and her own self-conception, to open up to what was next, a process facilitated by her work on the Temple of Flux. She was a soft-spoken, gentle woman, yet with a quiet confidence and ability to wield power tools that contributed to her beauty.

"I realized I was thinking about it way too much," Elizabeth said of how she approached that first cave. "So by the time I worked on the stalactite cave, my third cave, I was coaching Gal not to think about it too much. It isn't until we were working in the tight spaces of the cave that we learned how to work together…I did achieve reconciliation with how I work with people, which is what I was striving to do."

The other main builder of the stalactite cave and someone who benefited powerfully from that lesson was Dylan Bergeson, a 26-year-old artist from Portland, Oregon who was invited to helped build Temple of Flux by his cousin, Jess Hobbs.

"When she invited me to come down and help out, I expected to just hammer nails and move stuff around. But I got really obsessed with [the Stalactite/Stalagmite Cave] and there was a lot of synchronicity in it for me," said Dylan, a spindly kid with intense eyes but a warm demeanor. "I ended up staying in the cave for days and nights on end, with a pee bottle. I kind of went nuts there for awhile."

As he tinkered with the cave, Dylan contemplated the myth of Inanna, the Sumerian goddess of love and war who descends into the underworld, is stripped of her clothes and her power, and hanged on a hook as a corpse for three days and nights before being revived. This version of the classic resurrection myth resonated with some of Dylan's performance art projects that involve suspending himself on hooks pierced through his skin.

"A lot of things fell into place for me to do my first chest suspension in the Temple," Dylan said, something he did on Burn Night before a crowd of about 30 fluxers. "It was like a prayer. It was really about trying to shed a lot of ego attachment and be a vessel for creativity."

It was the culmination of a rough week in which Dylan first had to learn to work collaboratively with Gal, Elizabeth, and the other crew members, which he did, bonding strongly with them by the end. Then he had a hard time accepting that the Temple no longer belonged to people who had become like family to him.

"It was hard to let go of the Temple," said Dylan, who sported a scraggly beard by the time he emerged from the cave. He was initially saddened to see people write on the Temple — a feeling many on the crew shared — or chat about small stuff in his cave. "Living on site and having the space to ourselves and putting so much into it — it was really, really hard to turn it over."

Likewise, Gal said he had a difficult time accepting other people making their marks on his vision, even fluxers. For example, Mignon Heck was a friend of Ben and PK's, a young woman who committed suicide that year. In was at her memorial service that Jonny first met Ben and PK and learned about plans for the Temple of Flux.

So to help honor Mignon and his new friends, Jonny created a large stencil to paint the word "MIGNON" on the outside of the stalactite cave, also painting it in reverse on the inside to emphasize the theme of the mirrored worlds that he felt the cave conveyed. The cave became a magnet for fluxers who helped personalize it.

People can bond quickly at Burning Man, particularly on a big art project, and that's what happened between my friends, Scott and Nicole, and Chris Culpo, a Burning Man veteran and builder who had long been friends with Syda, and at her urging, he joined the early build of the Temple on the playa.

Chris's brother had committed suicide earlier in the year, and Chris brought his ashes with him. "I always hoped he would come out to the desert and he never did, so there was a little of that," Chris said. "I almost put my thing on the outside, my little tribute to John, on the wall I built. I figured… the wall's part of me, John's a part of me. I even went as far as mounting a niche in that wall, and thinking this is where I'm going to stick him, his shrine."

Scott and Nicole had each made beautifully artistic niches back in San Francisco — Nicole to honor her recently deceased grandmother, Scott as a tribute to his parents in the Midwest, who were struggling with his mother's life-threatening illness. "I wanted to put them in a special spot," Scott said. "I wanted it in a cave for the reflection, the personal time, away from everything."

Nicole had been drawn to the stalactite cave, and spent a day in there working on it with Dylan, "filling in the sides, talking about how to angle the window so the light would bounce in and reflect into the cave." Working there, tapping into her creativity, her connection to the cave deepened and they decided to put their niches in there.

"I discovered you guys were building things in the cave, and I had a connection to you guys, and that sealed the deal on that particular cave, my bond to you guys," said Chris, who created an evocative altar to hold his brother's ashes, as we all chatted after Burning Man. "It was very much a feeling of it being our cave," Scott added, "and we went to visit it everyday."

"Seven or eight times after it was completed, we went to visit, just to see how it would change, because people would write all over it and add things," Nicole said. "I went in one day and noticed all this ash at the bottom shelf of my niche. At first, I thought it was playa dust, then I saw that it was human ash. And someone had taken their fingers and made this wave pattern in the bottom of my niche. I felt honored that someone liked my niche enough to put someone's ashes on it and make a little design."

Dylan and Gal eventually did let go of their cave, and they found the experience of doing so, of releasing the intense attachment they had developed, to be cathartic. Dylan said it was closely connected to his personal quest to let go of his ego. In fact, by the end, Dylan came to see the visitors to the temple infusing it with a sacred energy that even the most committed builders couldn't do themselves.

"It took hundreds of us pouring ourselves into that space to make the temple happen and make it special," Dylan said, "but it took the thousands of people who visited it and connected with it to make it sacred."

It was a sentiment that Gal, who was older and more settled than Dylan, also voiced separately, talking about how he felt when he saw so many people wanting to place their most personally important items into the space he created: "I was really honored and felt humbled by that. It was telling us that we achieved our goal with the space and made it a sacred space."

Sifting Through the Ashes

The Temple of Flux was a success by any measure, widely praised for its evocative artistry, its intimate accessibility, and a kind of seething spirituality that was enhanced throughout the week as it was covered with people's messages, stories, marks, images, and remembrances.

"It really works with the surroundings like nothing that has ever happened before," Jess told me as we sized up the completed temple and the way its gradual peaks played against the open playa and the distant mountain ridges.

"I don't even know how we did this," PK marveled as he sized up the completed Temple of Flux. "But it happened, and it happened naturally."

By the end of this project, even before it burned, some crew members were already starting to feel a strange sense of loss as they reflected the huge part of their lives they had devoted to this project, looking forward and wondering what would fill that void.

"It's an emotional rollercoaster," Catie told me, visibly filled with emotion, after returning to the playa from a few days back in San Francisco, visiting with her boyfriend and bringing back another load of plywood back to finish off the project. "Two days off playa, I decompressed just enough to know what I'm doing out here."

And what she and others were doing was devoting their lives to an epic act of creation. The accomplishment was particularly poignant for PK, who suffered a seizure at Burning Man in 2001, leaving the playa with Rebecca and ending up getting a golf ball sized brain tumor removed, the first of two craniotomies that left him partially paralyzed on his left side. Eventually, the brain tumors may claim even more.

"I should have been dead by now if you look at the averages. I should have been dead a long time ago. So you learn to appreciate life in a slightly new way," PK told me as the project was just getting underway. "The minute you give up the lust for life is the minute your life is over."

PK learned similar lessons from his illness and from this project, in both cases humbled by the outpouring of support from his tribe, most of which had formed around Burning Man projects. From his main crew of the Space Cowboys to his newly adopted Flaming Lotus Girls sisters to dozens of randoms who just showed up to form the Temple of Flux family, the network of people PK could call on grew exponentially that summer.

"Most importantly, you learn to appreciate the community, the people around you and your support system," PK said, later adding, "I've been amazed by people's dedication and devotion. That doesn't necessarily happen in the real world."

Considering it was his first big project of this nature, I asked him on the playa what surprised him most about how it all came together. "The structure went up a lot faster than I thought and the vibe is far more positive than I imagined. We're having our own little event here," PK told me. "It's a very diverse group of people in their personalities and backgrounds, but it's amazing how it's become just one cohesive group without any factions....It's a large group, but it's largely collaborative."

Even experienced Burning Man artists Jess and Rebecca had the same observation. "We wouldn't have the Temple at this point if we didn't have this kind of energy here," Jess told me late in the week, a gratitude that Temple participants and even those not with the project reflected right back at the three leads.

"I'm just proud there are two women, whose art has been in our community for a long time, building up a pretty amazing team to collaborate on this," the Borg's Marian Goodell told me on the playa. "It's helped propel them into a place where they could show their leadership and capabilities."

In turn, Rebecca and Jess praise PK and his commitment to the project, and he reflects it right back at them, and their little love fest circulates back to the whole crew. By the end, everyone was feeling downright mushy about everyone else. "You'd think that all these people knew each other, but they don't," PK said. "And there's been no dramas."

Why is that? Well, part of it was the nature of the work. "It's just the project," PK said, noting that it enabled flexibility, imprecision, and ownership. "People own separate parts of the project. We were able to just give people a cave and they own that cave."

And that sense of ownership had a profound effect on people, as my friends who worked in the caves all conveyed in uniquely moving ways during our conversations. When the relentlessly positive Nicole squeezed her long, lovely limbs into that cave, she learned something about herself and her capacity for creativity.

"I remember being in the cave and working with Dylan, and I remember asking him, how are we putting these boards together, like this or like that," Nicole recalled. "And he said why don't you just do what you feel, just be creative and go for it. And I was like, really? I can do that, really? And it took me a second to detach from that — tell me how you want me to do it — to just roll with it. We gotta cover the walls. It was a great feeling. I don't think society promotes that. You will plug in and do it this way. But this project was about going for it, being creative, making it work, and this is the vision."

When you combine that kind of creativity with the commitment that so many people make to this and other projects at Burning Man — often giving months of their lives to the process — people are transformed, and the possibilities of life in general get thrown wide open.

"During the Temple burn, I leaned over to Scott and said, 'Our handprints are all over that thing.' I mean, we started working on it in mid-June, and I took a second to imagine if my handprints showed up on everything I touched, on every piece of wood. I would have loved to see what that looked like," Nicole said. "I didn't do as much as some people, but I contributed everything I could for this period of my life and it was wonderful."

Jonny was an experienced carpenter and 10-year Burning Man veteran, but he spoke reverently and evangelically about his experience with Temple of Flux.

"It was a totally new experience for me, and I just decided that I was going to commit to this. I liked Rebecca, and I lived six blocks from (American Steel), so I thought I could actually come every night, fuck it, get rid of my social life," Jonny said. "I had been to Burning Man too many times as a spectator, and I'd never really done anything. And I'm kind of an all or nothing person, and this was big."

After it was done, Jonny had put in hundreds of hours of work, developed a whole new network of close friends, fallen in love with a new girlfriend, and developed a more expansive view of what Burning Man was really about and how it was affecting the counterculture.

"It was one of the most life-changing things I've ever done," Jonny said. "It made me realize that community work is incredibly powerful when it's well done. It made me realize anything is possible. In the most ridiculous circumstances, you can create absolutely stunning beauty with scraps of wood."

PK agreed that it is the communal, creative, non-hierarchal, empowering nature of making art and building a marvelous city every year, Black Rock City, that is shaping those who attend Burning Man.

"That's how it affects the counterculture. It's the collective, collaborative model," PK said. "If everyone does what they do best, we all benefit. If you look out for other people, you yourself end up benefiting."

That spirit stayed with the fluxers long after the Temple burned and they returned from the desert. Everyone pitched in to unload the trucks, deal with the remnants, and move out of the project's bay in American Steel. Big art projects can be

stressful, and after spending so much time together for months on end, the participants often need a break from each other.

But Rebecca observed that's not what happened with the Temple of Flux. Instead, she said that she had been amazed at how much love and appreciation everyone expressed for the project and each other after their return, and how much they still wanted to spend time together.

"It's the capacity that has been built in people and the skills they've discovered," Catie said of this project's real value. "Even in West Oakland, people were having profound experiences. At the shop, I tell people it's like being in love."

Catie, Jess, Rebecca, PK, and others said they were most excited by the possibilities of what would become of that love after the temple was reduced to ash, and they all placed their hopes in the Flux Foundation. "The thing I'm most proud of is not just the project, but the Flux Foundation project," PK said, later adding, "It might be the end of your book, but it's just the beginning for us."

That warm vibe was on brilliant display on the evening of September 17th when the crew gathered on Ocean Beach to burn the last of the Temple's leftover wood scraps in one of the steel flower fire pits that Rebecca had built back in 2007 in a collaboration with Burners Without Borders.

People who were strangers to one another just six months earlier cuddled together in the fire's warm glow, sharing food, drink, stories, and, yes, love. As close as any family, probably even closer than most, with a deliberate bond forged by the process of building a temple for some weird experimental city in the desert.

"Look at this, it's amazing, we all still want to hang out together," Rebecca told me with a giggle, smiling at all the illuminated faces around the fire, in animated conversations, laughing, passing bottles or smokes, intimately leaning into one another. "Just look at what we've created."

Sunday, September 5, 2010

The pre-dawn sky gets steadily brighter as we lean on the middle dune, Cayuga, facing east, waiting for a day to end and another to begin. The Temple of Flux is surrounded by hundreds of people like me, gathered in small groups and large, some people just alone, waiting, watching, becoming more clear to one another with each passing minute of lightening sky.

Dawn is a special time in Black Rock City, and the Temple just seems like the place that many people want to be at that glorious moment when the sun rises on another precious day in this fantastic, condemned city. This year maybe more than most. These five massive dunes are the closest things we have to large land forms, and people seem drawn to natural contours at times like this.

The top of the ridgeline is glowing orange now with the approaching sun, but I know from experience that we still have 10 or 15 more minutes until we see it. There is such anticipation in the air, an eagerness strangely mixed with calm serenity, like waiting for an approaching lover's kiss.

I can never be sure where most people's minds go as they await the dawn, but a sense of nostalgia usually sneaks into mine at some point, and this morning is no different. I remember my first dawn with Opulent Temple in 2004, watching it from the dusty dance floor with dozens of new friends in shiny, furry costumes, smiling, grooving, and posing for group pictures. Who knew that crazy little camp would have such staying power? They blew it up again this year, even after ceding the Esplanade corner to a new sound camp, helping establish Burning Man as the world's premier art and music festival.

Moments flood my mind, and I linger on a few of them. I involuntarily smile at the memory of that magical sunrise back in 2007, the end of burn night, when Cat and I were rolling around on the ground together, buried in our full length fur coats, cuddling, kissing, conversing, and feeling our bliss in that furry little bubble for what seemed like an eternity. And when we finally peeked out of our sanctuary to acknowledge a city bathed in the warm light of a fresh dawn, at the very moment we opened ourselves up to the world and in the very center of our field of vision, the basket of a huge hot air balloon touched the earth just a few yards in front of us, as if blessing our moment from above, its occupants smiling at the canoodling couple that was smiling at them.

And I flash to the next year, same post-burn sunrise, when Rosie and I napped through the Man's incineration and got up in the middle of the night — 2, 3, 4 in the morning, whoever knows out here? — donned our costumes and headed out to find some fun. Wandering across the playa as the dark sky started to show signs of lightening, we ran into our DJ friends Smoove and Patricio, lugging along a steel box of records, headed over to play a set in the Root Society's dome, telling us to tag along.

Once we arrived, the crowd was small but beautiful. Durand was swinging on the scaffolding like a monkey and big Jack was with a new girl, a British knockout in a turquoise bobbed wig, Claire, who would become our good friend over the next couple years. And we all smiled, theirs more weary than ours but still brilliant, as we danced and played and shared and rocked out until moments before dawn, when we stepped outside the dome to watch, arm in arm, the full panoramic sunrise.

Just like we're about to see now, as the sky brightens more and more, coming to greet us in just a few minutes.

More recent memories come to mind, like spending time this summer on San Francisco's Baker Beach, where Burning Man was born and where the communal nudists and burners who congregate daily on the north end still carry on its spirit. And I think back to just a couple days ago, sitting on the mobile Front Porch with my new love, Syda, and our friends Tish and Robin. It was the same porch that my daughter Cicely and I sat on earlier that summer at Makers Faire in the Bay Area, one of many events that has welcomed burners and their art back into the default world.

But here, on the playa, is where weird little country shack front porches from the '30s, unconnected to anyone's home, tugged along by a stripped down tractor and trailing a wooden outhouse with a crescent moon on its door, just make more sense. And so there we sat, snuggled together, waiting for the dawn, until we just couldn't sit still any longer — the anticipation of a new day too great — so we got up to move our bodies and as we stepped off the porch, the fiddle and banjo from a bluegrass ballad came wafting out of the tinny speakers.

"Rock me mama like a wagon wheel, rock me mama any way you feel. Heeeeeeyyyyyy, mama rock me. Rock me mama, like the wind and the rain, rock me mama like a southbound train. Heeeeeeyyyyyy, mama rock me," the crooner sang as the golden sliver of sun peaked out of the horizon, and we smiled and danced and happily accepted the slices of watermelon that a grinning stranger in a curly mustache handed to us.

But now, there is only this dawn, the last one that will ever shine on the Temple of Flux, which will burn tonight. In fact, the crew will gather here in just a few hours for a portrait and a day's worth of preparations, filling it with the fuel and fuses that will destroy our creation.

My head and heart swirl with emotions as the horizon turns a fierce orange, the sun about to burst through onto a reverent crowd. Am I sad that this project, this year, and even this book's long narrative are coming to an end? Am I happy to have come out the other side, richer for persevering through often trying experiences?

"The story of the Temple of Flux and Burning Man is about what people can accomplish when they work together, and what they learn and become along the way," I wrote nine days ago as the final line of my introduction in the Guardian article, "Burners in Flux," and the final phrase rings in my ears as fresh sunlight washes over my face.

What have we become, me and this big, vibrant culture that I've been chronicling? And as I wait for the bright new sun to answer my question, the people around me embrace each other and me, some whooping it up, some praying, some drinking wine from bottles being passed around, some just watching the sun rise slowly higher on a brand new day.

And I realize that my question isn't quite right. If Burning Man teaches us anything, it's that life is a process and not a destination. So the question is not what we've become, or how this strange event has shaped its participants. The question is what we're becoming, how we are being shaped, how we're choosing to focus our lives within a country that isn't meeting our deepest needs and desires.

The Temple of Flux will burn tonight and then Black Rock City 2010 will fade to a memory, their only lasting impact being what they imparted onto their builders. And then next year, and the year after that, Burning Man will build itself and destroy itself again, shaping tens of thousands more people.

Right now, the Temple of Flux is still here, bathed in a beautiful sunrise. And by dawn tomorrow, it will be gone, an ending but also a beginning.

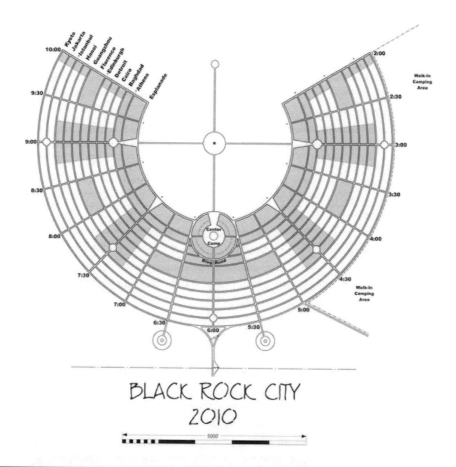

BLACK ROCK CITY
2010

The Man stands at the very center of Black Rock City, and its concentric streets get re-named each year. ~ Designed by Rod Garrett & used with permission from Black Rock City LLC

The Temple of Flux by Rebecca Anders, Jessica Hobbs, and PK Kimelman incorporated natural landforms into the Metropolis. ~ Photo by John Curley

Bliss Dance by Marco Cochrane stood 40 feet tall near the Temple of Flux. ~ Photo by Luke Szczepanski

For the 2010 Metropolis theme, The Man stood atop a tower and emanated the sounds from cities around the world. ~ Photo by Luke Szczepanski

Rebecca Anders has led some of Burning Man's most ambitious and evocative art projects in recent years. ~ Photo by Pilar Woodman

PK Kimelman came from the Space Cowboys to help lead the Temple of Flux project. ~ Photo by Pilar Woodman

Artist Jessica Hobbs was a resourceful and positive leader during the Temple of Flux build. ~ Photo by John Curley

Scott Borchardt, Nicole Spear, and Chris Culpo added deeply personal touches to the Temple of Flux. ~ Photo by Steven T. Jones

Gal Or Karmi (left) and Dylan Bergeson came from different places to build the Stalactite/Stalagmite Caves. ~ Photo by Sarah Miller

Temple of Flux replicated the shelter people once sought in caves, canyons, and behind ridges. ~ Photo by Luke Szczepanski

On September 5, 2010, the Temple of Flux was burned to the ground by its creators in a beautifully choreographed blaze.

Author Steven T. Jones.
~ Photo by Julio Duffoo

About the Author

Steven T. Jones, aka Scribe, is a native Californian who has worked full-time for newspapers in that state for 20 years. Before becoming City Editor of the *San Francisco Bay Guardian*, he worked for *Sacramento News & Review, New Times* in San Luis Obispo, *Coast Weekly* in Monterey, *Santa Maria Times, Auburn Journal,* and *Lassen County Times*. Steve has won numerous writing and reporting awards along the way, including a Maggie and awards from the California Newspaper Publishers Association, Society of Professional Journalists, National Newspaper Association, and Association of Alternative Newsweeklies (he also serves on AAN's Editorial Committee). He lives in San Francisco's Mission District, doesn't own a car, and can often be seen riding the furry, red, custom-welded bicycle that he created for Burning Man.

To read some of his past work or get updates on the series of burner-style parties that we plan to throw in connection with this book, visit www.steventjones.com.

Acknowledgments

This book and Burning Man are what they are because of all the people who have given their creativity, time, money, blood, and sweat to building Black Rock City and its component camps and projects every year. They/we have restored my faith in human beings, over and over again, and I thank them all.

On a more personal level, let me express my deep appreciation to those who supported me and this project: my daughters, Breanna and Cicely, who indulged my weird hobbies and hairstyles and always made me feel loved; Tim Redmond, the best editor I've ever had, and everyone at the San Francisco Bay Guardian, the conscience of San Francisco; Brad "Santosh" Olsen, for giving my stories a book to call home; Rosie, for encouraging me to cover our culture and write this book; Scott Borchardt, a good friend, inspiring burner, and master designer; Syda Day, for her loving support during a difficult period and for teaching me that writing needn't be a lonely pursuit; Tim Daw, for the timely pints and unconditional friendship; photographers Pilar Woodman, John Curley, Julio Duffoo, and Camera Girl, who tell beautiful stories without words; Brian Doherty, Dave Eggers, Ethan Watters, Mark Morford, Eric Meyers, Dara Colwell, Ted Weinstein, Jeremy Sugerman, Jess Bruder, and the other writers and readers who helped this book at critical stages; Gray, Kim, and all of my sisters, for letting their heads explode and helping put mine back together; Cat, for the adventurous inspiration; Lucky, for the inspiring adventures; Mom and Jim, for their love and support during my ridiculously long and low-paid journalism career; my Dad, for his early planting of The Great American Novel seed, and Jo for taking care of him; Adam and Gina Grandi, Dash, Blue, Smoove, Patricio, Dutch, Cosmic, Tamo, Darin, Tami, Chris, Nicole, Julian, Patrick, Jonny, Max, Gary, Jill, Donnie, Heather, Ted, Leah, Mary, Jim, Ashleigh, Catbird, Sarah, Tish, Gabriel, Claire, Brandee, and Deep for being my people; Jason, Brian, Dave, and other naysayers who kept me honest; and my adopted families in Garage Mahal, Opulent Temple, Flaming Lotus Girls, Ku De Ta, Temple of Flux, Shadyvil, and the other tribes that have embraced me and taught me so much.

I also want to say a special thank you to everyone from the Burning Man world, whose efforts and input formed the backbone of this book. In particular: Larry Harvey, for being generous with his time and insights about an event he has so carefully nurtured; Syd Gris, for bringing me into his world of sound and being a comrade; Tom Price, for beckoning me to the Gulf Coast and sharing his vision for the future of this culture;

Chicken John, for the exquisitely timed art spark and narrating what followed; John Law, for finally opening up to me about the early years; Jim Mason, for taking things seriously; Jess Hobbs, for keeping things light; Rebecca Anders, Pouneh Mortazavi, and Charlie Gadeken for introducing me to the fire arts; Bassnectar, Lee Coombs, Marvin Beaver, Scumfrog, and all the outstanding DJs who opened up to me and who bounce the scene; Joegh Bullock, for the cool parties and the great stories about cool parties; Marian Goodell, Andie Grace, Harley Dubois, and Will Chase for speaking for this culture and helping me cover it; Lightning and Thunder, the LLC's legal team, for their help and for not suing me; Paul Addis, for sharing his story; Carmen Mauk, for doing; Rich Martin, Captain Ken, Phil Spitler, Dave X, Hotmetal, and others who taught me skills; Jess Hobbs, Catie Magee, and PK Kimelman, for inviting me into the Temple and keeping me from losing my way; Jack, for the Bloodies and Whatnot; Monica, Simon, Greg, and Snook, for La Contessa and telling me her story; Dan and Karen, for the space they've created; Metric, Flash, and Shooter (RIP), for the Gerlach perspective; Jennesa, Darrow, and Vaughn, for my first burn; Ullie, Chris, Scott, Nicole, Gray, and Geo, for my last one; for you, you know who you are, who did that one thing that one time that I'll never forget; and for all of you that I did forget, or just forgot to remember here. Thanks. I love you all.

List of Contributors

Jake Balakoohi is a San Francisco-based photographer and graphic designer. Balakoohi Design + Photo can be accessed at www.balakoohi.com.

Scott Beale has covered Burning Man from the beginning with photography, writing, and hosting cool websites through the company he founded, Laughing Squid. Check out www.laughingsquid.com, www.scottbeale.org, and www.flickr.com/photos/laughingsquid.

Scott Borchardt designed every aspect of this book, doing illustrations, page design, typography, and art direction. He also designed the website of the author: www.steventjones.com. Professionally, he is an accomplished UX/UI designer whose work is at www.scottborchardt.com; personally, he's a longtime burner with a unique flair for the creative.

John Curley's long photography career in the Bay Area ranged from doing photojournalism for the San Francisco Chronicle to shooting weddings to doing contract photography for Black Rock City LLC. Check out his work at www.johncurleyphotography.com.

Julio Duffoo is an art, journalism, advertising, and wedding photographer from San Francisco whose work can be found at www.duffoophotography.com.

Kevin Evans is a Bay Area-based illustrator whose work is as www.kevinevans.com.

Neil Girling, aka Mr. Nightshade, is a photographer who has shot Burning Man subcultures and the Bay Area arts underground for more than a decade. Check his work at www.theblight.net.

Flint Hahn calls himself an Information Designer. Check out his work at www.xmasons.com.

KK Pandaya, also known at the Enemy Combatant, photographed Burners Without Borders on the Gulf Coast and other burner offshoots. His Flickr stream is at www.flickr.com/photos/conspicuous.

Gabe Kirchheimer is a New York City photographer and journalist is one of Burning Man's most prolific shooters, displaying his work at www.gabekphoto.com.

Dave Le, aka Splat, is a visual designer and photographer from Oakland whose work can be found at www.davelecreative.com.

Brendan Jones in a San Franciscan who worked on the Temple of Flux, sometimes wearing a short kilt.

Yasmin Mawaz-Khan makes fire, sculptures, and photographs with the Flaming Lotus Girls. Check out www.flaminglotus.com/category/photographer/yasmin-mawaz-khan.

Marcy Mendelson is an 11-year burner who works with wildlife conservationists to save the endangered cheetah. See her work at MendelsonImages.com, Cheetah-Watch.com, @MendelsonImages and Flickr.com/MMendelson.

Sarah Miller worked on Temple of Flux and displays her photos and artwork at www.sarahmillerdesign.com.

Caroline "Mills" Miller is a photographer and fire artist who worked on projects ranging from the Flaming Lotus Girls' Angel of the Apocalypse to the Temple of Flux. Her work can be found at www.firehussy.com and www.flaminglotusgirls.com.

Brad Olsen is a longtime burner, author, and illustrator who owns CCC Publishing. Find him at www.cccpublishing.com and www.bradolsen.com.

Mark Rahmani is a Bay Area photographer has extensively covered Burning Man, nightlife, and the electronic dance music culture for many years. Rahmani and photographer Gina Grandi post their work at MV Galleries, www.mvgals.net.

Alix Rosenthal in an attorney, amateur photographer, and member of the Black Rock Arts Foundation's Board of Directors.

Tami Rowan is a San Francisco-based world traveler who camps with Garage Mahal at Burning Man.

Karl Seifert's first visit to Black Rock City was in 1996. He has been photographing arts & culture throughout the US ever since. Please visit www.KarlsPortfolio.com.

Luke Szczepanski is a Canadian photographer also known as luke.me.up. His Flickr stream is at www.flickr.com/photos/lukemeup.

Waldemar is a photographer whose work can be found at www.naturalturn.fotki.com.

Gary Wilson is a photographer whose work can be found at www.mindfullight.com.

Pilar Woodman has extensively photographed the Burning Man culture, on the playa and back in the Bay Area. See her work at www.pilarwoodmanphotography.com.

Index

NX510.N48 J66 2011